Ideas about Illness

An Intellectual and Political
History of Medical Sociology

Uta Gerhardt

NEW YORK UNIVERSITY PRESS
Washington Square, New York

First published 1989

Published by
NEW YORK UNIVERSITY PRESS in the U.S.A.
Washington Square
New York, NY 10003

Printed in Hong Kong

Library of Congress Cataloging-in-Publication Data
Gerhardt, Uta, 1938–
  Ideas about illness.

  Bibliography: p.
  Includes index.
  1. Social medicine–History. I. Title. [DNLM:
1. Sociology, Medical–history. W 322 G368]
  RA418.G44   1989   306′46   88–34512
  ISBN 0–8147–3025–6
  ISBN 0–8147–3026–4 (pbk.)

Contents

Preface

This book on the history of ideas of medical sociology has itself a history of attempt, abandonment, and eventual breakthrough. It first took shape in my mind in the mid-1970s. I felt that my students at London University's (Bedford College) Social Research Unit's MSc. course, 'Sociology as Applied to Medicine', would benefit from an overview of sociology's conceptualisation of illness. After this had led to a couple of lectures, and then the plan of a short book, I began to realise that this was a major undertaking. In 1977, I submitted a synopsis to Macmillan (through Michael Mann who accepted the book for the series he edited, *New Studies in Sociology*). In 1980, after I had taken up a professorship in my native Germany, Dr Mann and I realised that the book was becoming much too long for the series. Since I felt this to be unavoidable, I eventually decided to abandon the manuscript (half regretfully, half relieved). In 1984, a new general editor at Macmillan asked me whether I could revive the project, offering some freedom as regards the scope of the book. Again, Dr Mann gave me wholehearted encouragement. Eventually the book was finished with valuable help from the libraries at the British Museum, the London School of Economics and Harvard University, and with invaluable help from colleagues and friends willing to discuss my ideas with both fervour and rigour.

Above all, I wish to thank Nicky Hart for reading large parts of the manuscript and advising me in unselfish painstaking detail on both content and style. Over the years, among those colleagues and friends commenting on chapters or ideas have been David Armstrong, Susan Bell, Cathy Charmaz, Eliot Freidson, James Greenley, Joan McCord, Hans-Peter Müller, Cathy Riessman, Günther Roth, Hans-Georg Soeffner, Anselm Strauss and Michael Wadsworth, to name but a few. Of course, the book's mistakes and shortcomings are my own. But many of its interpretations would not have become crystallised without my discussion partners' patience and resourcefulness. Also, the typing by Jutta Kreiling and Doris Turner of various versions of various chapters is gratefully acknowledged.

Last but not least, without the unfailing affection of my daughter, Agnes, I would have been in danger of becoming too obsessed with my work. Her love and friendship were strong enough to make me feel that it is all worthwhile.

UTA GERHARDT

Introduction: The Origin of Medical Sociology

Max Weber identified the essence of sociology as social action represented by types of legitimate authority. In this he ignored the mundane fact that physical or mental health is necessary if actors are to take part in subjective reciprocal meaning formation. Equally, he does not discuss the fact that the claim to authority or loyalty in asymmetrical relationships might be conditional upon the physical or mental health of the powerful.

In Emile Durkheim's *Suicide* (1897/1952), no mention is made of psychiatric categories when rates are attributed to the pathological state of society as a whole. In the social limbo between the abandonment of mechanical solidarity and the stunted emergence of organic solidarity, Durkheim regarded as improper terrain for sociology a view which relates the ills of present-day society to the physical or mental state of its members.

It might have sounded absurd had Marx made provision in the analysis of class struggle for the representatives of capital and labour to be mentally or physically fit. Of course, doctors in Marx's time were not what they are today. But in no way would Marx have identified the wrongs of capitalist society with the power which doctors acted out over their patients. Their right (or nerve) to define or refuse treatment was no topic for the critique of political economics.

For Herbert Spencer, the evolution from tribal to modern society was never connected with variations of the physical or mental make-up of the individual members of society. Rather, medical metaphors were used to explain the workings of society as a whole, and the 'sociological division of labour' seemed but an extension of the 'physiological division of labour' as is demonstrated by the following (rather lengthy) quote from *The Principles of Sociology*:

> we see the parts of the alimentary canal performing their functions one after another. There come in succession mastication, insalivation, deglutition, trituration, chymification, chylification, and eventually

xi

absorption by the lacteals. And here indeed it is curious to remark a unique case in which two sets of sociological division of labour of the serial kind, are joined to this physiological series of divisions of labour. We have first the ploughing, harrowing, sowing, reaping, carting, threshing, hauling to market, transfer to corn factor's stores, removal thence to be ground, and final carriage of the flour to the bakers; where, also, certain serial processes are gone through in making loaves . . . or . . . biscuits . . . Finally, in one who eats the loaves or the biscuits, there occurs the physiological series of division of labour. So that from the ploughing to the absorption of nutriment, three series of divisions of labour become, in a sense, parts of a united series. (Spencer, 1876, pp. 661–2).

This example of body–society folklore epitomises how remote in nineteenth century sociology was the idea that a person's normal organic or mental functioning was not to be taken for granted. Equally remote was the idea that medicine or medical practice might be seen as a social institution with integrative functions for society.

While Spencer and, to a certain extent, Durkheim used a structural analogy between society and physiology to explain the functioning of the social order, other authors referred to the body or mind to explain individuation in society. For instance, from the vast array of social formations taken from the documented history of Western civilisation, Simmel failed to draw upon health or medical practice as a subject of sociological enquiry. This is despite the fact that several of the *exkurse*[1] appearing in Simmel's *Sociology* (1908) focused upon issues of bodily conduct. For example, a rudimentary sociology of the senses was outlined, with special reference to the distinctive cultural meaning of olfactory versus visual stimuli.

Similarly, Norbert Elias' *Process of Civilisation* (first published in 1939) focused upon the social meaning and stylisation of body parts and processes (such as, for example, eating, burping, farting or defecating, and the rules of politely treating someone thus engaged temporarily as a non-person). But Elias failed to extend the topic to include failures of bodily (or mental) functioning. Thus he abstained from analysing the norms of deference and demeanour which signify and regulate the conduct of the able-bodied and the sane. Rather, Elias concentrated on the rules and regulations which define proper conduct, say, in the presence of ladies, or of superiors, between the sexes or between persons of different social ranking, and so on. Not even for the late nineteenth and early twentieth centuries, the most contemporary periods of his investigations, would Elias identify the explicitly hygienic nature of the then fashionable accounts or justifications of such centuries-old rules as that one should not eat from the same plate, let alone spoon, as another person. By confining himself to the published literature on etiquette and leaving out everyday-language sources justifying the etiquette rules, Elias paints a picture of the *upstairs-downstairs* world of yesteryear in which no trace of health or illness appears to enter the realms of dominant mores or norms.

Thus classical sociological thought attributed little significance to the physical or mental state of the person, while problems of social organisation and structure were prominent. Health was a sociological *non-issue* while sociology rigorously sought to define a terrain all its own. Perhaps health was seen as an aspect of the everyday world while sociology located itself in the world of science and higher learning; or sociology may have taken health for granted because Victorian standards of decency held that 'personal' health issues did not deserve the ominous limelight of public attention, let alone the dubious focus of sociological theorising. Especially in cases where health failed, it was to be shamefully confined to the private quarters of the afflicted person's home and family or neighbourhood. In all, a pervasive distinction prevailed between 'profane' life worlds incorporating matters of physical and mental health, and the 'sacred' world of academic achievement. It made it unlikely that sociology (which placed itself in the latter) would recognise the unreality of assuming a healthy physical and mental state as characterising human beings in general. Sociology's interest in the rationalisation of the world meant that the irrational – particularly if it equalled the unhealthy – remained beyond the postulated image of mankind.

What about Marx and Engels? Were they not concerned with illness and premature death in capitalist society? Sickness was exposed by them as one of the plights suffered by the exploited and disenfranchised masses whose fate depended on the state of the labour market. As Marx and Engels pointed out, sickness and subsequent death were perpetual risks implied in the insecure status of the labouring classes. Since physical strength and fitness determined the quality of one's labour power sold as a commodity on the labour market, each worker's, as well as each worker's family's, life chances depended on the state of the worker's health. Physical strength, however, was not seen as individual prowess but rather in relation to environmental conditions. Engels made it clear that it was the unhealthy aspects of work, area of residence, housing and life style which accounted for the low life expectation of workers and their families. This was in accordance with the then most up-to-date theories of medicine which related *miasma* (unclean emissions, such as smell or dirt, caused by lack of ventilation, lack of sanitation, etc.) to the incidence of illness (and possibly death), while the procurement of clean air through ventilation as well as of clear water and clean streets through sanitation were taken to promote and secure good health. Therefore, when published in 1847, Engels' *Condition of the Working-Class in England* provided a medically satisfactory explanation of the higher incidence of sickness in working-class communities by referring to issues of poor housing and nutrition:

> That the dwellings of the workers in the worst portions of the cities, together with the other conditions of life of this class, engender numerous diseases, is attested on all sides . . . That the bad air of London, and especially of the working-people's districts, is in the highest degree favourable to the development of consumption, the hectic appearance of great numbers of persons sufficiently indicates . . . Typhus, that universally diffused affliction, is attributed by the official report on the sanitary conditions directly to the bad state of the dwellings in the matters of ventilation, drainage, and cleanliness . . . When one . . . thinks how crowded their dwellings are, how every nook and corner swarms with human beings, how sick and well sleep in the same room, in the same bed, the only wonder is that a contagious disease like this does not spread yet further . . . Another category of diseases arises directly from the food rather than the dwellings of the workers. The food of the labourer, indigestible enough in itself, is utterly unfit for young children, and he has neither means nor time to get his children more suitable food. Moreover, the custom of giving children spirits, even opium, is very general; and these two influences, with the rest of the conditions of life prejudicial to bodily development, give rise to the most diverse affections of the digestive organs, leaving life-long traces on them. (Engels, 1953, pp. 131–4)

Engels cited evidence from chemistry to reinforce the idea that the bio-mechanics of illness are triggered by environmental hazards. He related lack of oxygen and surplus carbon monoxide to 'physical lassitude and low vitality' which, according to eighteenth-century medical theory,[2] accounts for the exhaustion of vital energy:

> Two and a half million pairs of lungs, two hundred and fifty thousand fires, crowded upon an area three to four miles square, consume an enormous amount of oxygen, which is replaced with difficulty, because the methods of building cities in itself impedes ventilation. The carbonic acid gas, engendered by respiration and fire, remains in the streets by reason of its specific gravity, and the chief air current passes over the roofs of the city. The lungs of the inhabitants fail to receive the

due supply of oxygen, and the consequence is mental and physical lassitude and low vitality. (Engels, 1953, p. 129)

However, for Engels as for Marx, ill health and premature death (albeit suffered by individuals) were indicators of the capitalist society *sui generis*. Their analysis focused on the wrongs inflicted by class society upon the working class as a whole rather than its individual members. Their aim was to arouse concern or compassion in the bourgeoisie and class spirit in the proletariat. Health issues could be used to instigate revolutionary action in the hope of superseding capitalist society, but were not an essential part of the latter's conceptual analysis. The reproduction of healthy labour power was not conceptualised as an element of social theory but as a matter of living conditions to be overcome by revolutionary action. In essence, neither Marx nor Engels was interested in the question of whether the physical or mental state of an individual was sufficient to enable him or her to fulfil the duties of a normal person.

This topic was first raised in the 1930s. It followed the somewhat earlier recognition that medicine and medical practice were appropriate objects of sociological enquiry. Only after the Second World War did the view gain momentum that physical and particularly mental health are important for the social fabric.

The earliest citation of the illness issue was as a metaphor to illustrate the workings of the social system. Lawrence J. Henderson, MD, who held a chair of biological chemistry at both Harvard College and Harvard Medical School, brought together between 1932 and 1934 several eminent scholars from such diverse fields as English literature, history, economics and sociology to discuss the social systems perspective proposed by Vilfredo Pareto's *General Sociology*. The crucial idea was the mutual dependence of components of society. In his lecture on the topic of physician and patient as a social system (1935b), Henderson argued that since medicine is applied science, thereby distinct from the natural sciences where cause–effect relationships prevail, it is based on mutual dependence between physician and patient in anticipation of acted-out or repressed expression of sentiments from both sides shaping the relationship. A further major idea extracted from Pareto's sociology related to the working of society as a whole rather than its components. Social systems were depicted in equilibrium, a state of mutual dependence between their constituent elements. If disequilibrium should occur, return to the state of equilibrium would promptly ensue. Henderson compared social equilibrium with physiological equilibrium, relating the former by analogy to the self-healing power of the living organism, and describing the latter through a *vis medicatrix naturae* which ensures recovery of the diseased organism even if no outside help should be available. Thus Henderson maintained that physiological equilibrium is logically identical with social equilibrium, and the latter may be understood by using examples illustrating the former (Henderson, 1935a, p. 46 *et passim*; Heyl, 1968, p. 326).

These ideas drawn from Pareto were later used by Parsons whose intellectual debt to Henderson is acknowledged in the preface of his *Social System* (1951a). But Parsons developed two further lines of thought during the 1930s which were to shape the sociological analysis of medical practice. First, he correctly claimed that his was a more physiological model of systems than Henderson's (who, after all, was a physiologist). Parsons' conception of equilibrium incorporates the idea of *homeostasis* derived from Walter B. Cannon's *The Wisdom of the Body* (1932). In this classic study, Cannon maintains that homeostasis is the hidden principle of life itself. The vast range of circumstances and stimuli which impinge upon the body are self-regulating. Body temperature, blood sugar and fluid contents of tissues remain remarkably constant and tend to return to their normal levels should temporary imbalances occur. Parsons used this idea but developed it into a four-phase balancing mechanism. In other words, Parsons derived from this physiological finding the idea of a social-control mechanism rectifying deviance through institutional and/or professional help.

The second issue where Parsons went beyond Henderson concerned the sociological analysis of the professions. His conceptual framework (outlined in 1939) identified medical practice not as an example of a social system but, rather, as one among four major professions representing partially non-economic but rational solutions of ongoing social problems: namely, medicine, technology, law and teaching (1939, p. 48).

Partly as an outcome of Henderson's staff seminar, by the end of the 1930s one major topic of medical sociology had surfaced in the academic interchanges between physiology and sociology at Harvard University. The analysis of medicine and medical practice as part of society's institutional and professional structure had yielded insights which would bring the analysis of medical care into the realm of sociological theory. The second major topic – namely, illness as deviance – had not yet taken shape. This would happen in the following decade of worldwide war and mass murder in Nazi concentration camps.

The connection between the political issues of the day and the medical perspective occasionally surfaced in the early 1940s, but it was not until the end of the Second World War – after knowledge of the holocaust had become widespread – that the question arose: can any member of a society be acknowledged as normal and sane if the society, simply by functioning, seems to rely on members who are far from normal and sane? In other words, deviancy and normality became foci of sociological attention because their boundaries had become blurred following recent historical events. Research in political psychology focusing on cognitive roots of Nazism showed that what had hitherto been regarded as utterly deviant (i.e., succumbing to Fascism or any anti-democratic regime) could be regarded as potentially normal. Millions of Americans were found to have attitudes congruent with latent Fascism. On the other hand, research into the mental make-up of Germans during and immediately after the Nazi period belaboured the point that the roots of the Fascist mind lay deeply entrenched in the institutions history and particular culture of the German nation. What did it mean if morally repugnant deviant acts became normal; if an entire society could be found guilty of gruesome crimes against humanity? In this situation the sociological endeavour was to re-establish the analytical boundaries between deviancy and normality. This laid the foundations of medical sociology as we know it.

Through this debate the notion of illness and its social control was formulated as part and parcel of sociological theory. In the very same year, 1951, Parsons' *Social System* and Edwin Lemert's *Social Pathology* were both published, each destined to become the cornerstone of one of the two main approaches in medical sociology.

As early as 1942, in an article on the sociology of modern anti-Semitism, Parsons pointed out (if indirectly) that this was a psychiatric topic. Elaborately in a later article on mass aggression in the modern world (1947b), Parsons drew attention to unconscious aggressions propelling the anti-Semite to hate (if only in the muffled form of latent aggression). This would produce acquiescence with crimes against despised groups, by self-appointed 'revengers' (Gestapo) prosecuting publicly acclaimed scapegoats. Parsons hinted at psychiatry at the end of his article on anti-Semitism when he dealt with the question of what was to be done: that is, looking at what he elsewhere called 'The Problem of Controlled Institutional Change' (1945). In 1942, he wrote:

> The situation may be compared to that of a psychiatrist in treating a patient. The psychiatrist resorts neither to admonishment to 'be reasonable' nor to coercive measures, for he knows that this will do no good. What he does is to study the case from every angle; what he endeavors

is to understand the sources of the trouble. It is only then that he may find an effective cure for his patient . . . Similarly, anti-Semitism can be dealt with effectively only by fully apprehending all the problems involved in it. In other words, a rational policy towards anti-Semitism cannot consist in suppressing and punishing its expressions, but only in some analogous way in an attempt to control its deeper causes. Mere indignant repression of an evil is the treatment of symptoms, not of the disease. (1942a, pp. 121–2)

This passage is of tremendous interest. It conjectures that anti-Semitism resembles a psychiatric disease two years prior to the 'Psychiatric Symposium on Anti-Semitism' which was held in San Francisco in 1944. This conference was the first forum for the ideas ventured by the group of researchers whose investigation into the psychological foundations of Fascism appeared in 1950 under the title of *The Authoritarian Personality*. All four major contributors to the research endeavour were present at the conference, plus such eminent scholars as Max Horkheimer who, in 1939, formulated the view that anti-Semitism was the epitome of the potentially Fascist and exploitative character of capitalist society in general.[3] Various participants stressed the view that anti-Semitism was a psychiatric symptom not of the individual but of society. The issue was one of mass psychopathology which called for collective forms of overcoming 'anti-Semitism as an irrational mass phenomenon' (Simmel, 1946, p. 33). In the preface to the conference proceedings, psychoanalyst Ernst Simmel argued along lines remarkably similar to Parsons four years previously:

Anti-Semitism is irrational and since it dethrones reason as the regulating power in human interrelationships, it is bound to have a disintegrating effect on community life . . . We proceed on the assumption that anti-Semitism must be a manifestation of a pathological mental process and that this process, under present economic and political conditions, leads to a decomposition of society and to the destruction of the anti-Semites themselves. Since it is obvious that the anti-Semitic concept of the Jew is clouded by a complex of persecution, anti-Semitism requires investigation by the psychiatrist. General descriptive psychiatry, however, cannot clarify the problem. For this, the dynamic psychology of psychoanalysis must be employed. (1946, p. xix)

Accordingly, Freud's ideas on mass psychology were invoked, and controlled institutional change (or, to a certain extent, drastic political action bordering upon the revolutionary if necessary) was advocated. It promised to fulfil what Freud had expected from psychotherapy: namely, to convert some of the (collective unconscious) id into ego, and thus to submit the (societal) irrational partly to the control of rationality. These ideas were also in the background of the extensive empirical study investigating the attitude syndrome of *Authoritarian Personality* (Adorno *et al.*, 1950). The latter was defined as a conglomerate of anti-Semitism, ethnocentrism, political-economic conservatism and latent Fascism, which were to depict a person's attitudinal propensity to vote and/or act in a way that conformed with any Fascist government or social environment.

One of the mechanisms characterising the person with an authoritarian personality structure was suggested as 'projection onto the body' of fears and anxieties. This showed a particular 'concern with physical symptoms' bordering upon 'hysterical conversions', especially in women. As proof of the significance for an authoritarian character structure of, for instance, putting emphasis on physical prowess or appearance, a number of interview excerpts were quoted:

> F 71: Wouldn't like to be a nurse or M.D. – admires anyone who does, but 'I hate hospitals . . . I've been in so many; two mastoid operations and heart murmur. I have a great fear of doctors' offices. My heart has been giving me trouble so I go to the doctors for check-ups but haven't really been sick. Now I'm full of energy but they think it's nervous energy. I tire easily. I had scarlet fever when I was 10.'
>
> M 45: 'Always sick, always going to the doctor.' (What was wrong with you?) 'Well, I don't think they ever knew.' (Adorno *et al.*, 1950, pp. 459–60)

The striking issue about these statements growing out of the attempt to determine the structural relevance of anti-Semitism for modern society is that they focused upon topics, and used wordings, that were to become part and parcel of medical sociology which emerged during the ensuing years. The emphasis on psychoanalytic terminology describing the person's motivation to deviance is but one of the common characteristics of this literature as well as Parsons' ideas on aggressiveness and anti-Semitism. The same emphasis extends into early Parsonian medical sociology, and it reveals how strongly the latter was embedded in the explanations of Nazism focusing upon social prejudice as a disease. To a considerable degree, these ideas shaped the views on deviance outlined in Chapter 10 of *The Social System*.

By contrast, the second major starting-point of medical sociology, Lemert's *Social Pathology*, drew upon a considerably different background of ideas which had been circulating in American sociology since the early twentieth century. This second brand of theorising, if more indirectly, also raised the problem of how to explain political deviance sociologically; not just Nazism but any extremist view. Once again society rather than the individual was to be invoked as the agent of crime as well as its punishment (and the recurrence of crime through some agents of its institutional punishment), and as the origin of illness as well as its treatment (and the aggravation of illness through some forms of its institutional treatment). The main issues of this debate were discussed in a succession of six books (all bearing the same title of *Social Pathology*) published over a period of less than three decades (Queen and Mann, 1925; Mangold, 1932, with a second edition in 1934; Gillin, 1933, with a second edition in 1939, and a third in 1946; Queen and Gruener, 1940; Brown, 1942; Lemert, 1951). Lemert perceived the line of thought as explicitly anti-Freudian supporting this with a statement by the psychoanalyst Otto Rank as a protagonist of a 'new ' non-psychological view of the deviant personality. Lemert stressed that he wished to endorse:

> Rank's main criticism of the Freudian psychoanalysis . . . that it creates a sense of guilt over aggressive acts. By seeking to reeducate the client to 'adjust to' or 'accept' reality the Freudians deny the obviously aggressive, emergent, and creative nature of human society. From this point of view Freudianism is a disguised variety of ancient Hebrew conservatism. (1951, p. 14)[4]

This view may contain a tinge of the anti-Semitism the overcoming of which had been the aim of the research on the authoritarian personality, and which had inspired the debates on controlled institutional change aimed at converting Nazi Germany into a future democratic nation. Lemert attempted a 'systematic theory of sociopathic behavior' which explicitly endorsed aggressiveness as not necessarily anti-social, and he chose to explain social facts through non-psychological processes producing rationality together with irrationality in society.

This endeavour was based on American sociology's concern since the early twentieth century with social problems and social science's capacity to mastermind social change which could act as a remedy for the ills of social disorganisation. Medical metaphors were widely used to characterise society's disintegration, and M. E. Richter's book on *Social Diagnosis* (1917)[5] is said to have been influential. It in turn inspired the various monographs entitled *Social Pathology* (1925–51). The ideological side of these views was put in perspective by C. Wright Mills, who pointed out that they lacked a theoretically viable notion of social structure (1943). Moreover physical sickness as well as mental disease were but two of a catalogue of some 20 topics of individual or 'domestic-relationship' pathology comprising, for instance, blindness and deafness, drug addiction, alcoholism, suicide, divorce, illegitimacy, prostitution and old age. The general idea was that cultural relativism had come to prevail in American society, due to a breakdown of the social organisation (social order) in the wake of urbanisation and industrialisation, leaving individuals, groups and social classes deprived of the moral guidance which should have helped to avoid deviance. The optimistic general tone of this literature, and its liberal use of the medical metaphor, resulted from an optimistic persuasion, strengthened by the era of the New Deal, that social policy and the welfare state, together with an active community spirit, could solve the problems of modern society. The following statement from Frank's 'Society as the Patient' illustrates this:

> Instead of thinking in terms of multiplicity of so-called social problems, each demanding special attention and a different remedy, we can view all of them as different symptoms of the same disease . . . If, for example, we could regard crime, mental disorders, family disorganization, juvenile delinquency, prostitution and sex offences, and much that now passes as the result of pathological processes (e.g., gastric ulcers) as evidence, not of individual wickedness, incompetence, perversity, or pathology, but as human reactions to cultural disintegration, a forward step would be taken. (Frank, 1936, p. 336)

The sociological theory embedded in the literature on social pathology amounted to scarce references to C. H. Cooley (1902, 1909, 1918). His widely cited view that socialisation, the influences of groups upon the individual's attitudes and beliefs, was the key to understanding deviant social actions became generally adopted. Lemert relied heavily on the list of social problems dealt with in the previous books on *Social Pathology*: each of these had set out to unite the various forms of deviance under a common explanatory perspective. He added to the scope of solutions offered by the literature only a seemingly minor idea. Realising that Cooley's theoretical conjecture of 'looking-glass self' was but the forerunner of George Herbert Mead's idea that significant others, and symbolic meaning, shaped the structure of selves in interaction, he based his interpretation of the origin and prospects of deviance on Mead's idea of symbolic mediation.

It seems ironic that the pragmatism which pervaded much of American social science for a good half-century should have been all too readily discarded in the wake of the Second World War.

Today Lemert's book, which draws heavily on the then well-established perspective of social pathology, is regarded as an original work beyond its genuinely novel contribution. This only documents how much the Second World War acted as a watershed of ideas which shaped the sociological endeavour. This may be no coincidence; rather, it may represent a historically logical achievement that the two books which 'started' medical sociology were but reformulations of topics entrenched in the two main lines of thought prevailing immediately after the Second World War. While Lemert's *Social Pathology* was embedded in the long-standing tradition of pragmatism in American social thought, Parsons' *Social System* introduced novel elements of psychoanalytic thinking which had only recently become respectable in social science. The latter had proved their usefulness through explaining as deviance not only drug addiction and juvenile delinquency, but also mass murder and the asquiescence to it.

During the 1950s, medical sociology made rapid progress. At the end of the decade, it had already become a section of the American Sociological Association. Like most other subspecialties which developed after the Second World War, sociology analysing the structure *in* or *of* medicine (Straus, 1957) spread from the US to various European and non-European countries where, in turn, prospering sections of national Sociological Associations developed. For instance, the Medical Sociology Group of the British Sociological Association held its first annual conference at York in 1964; in Germany, it was only in 1972 that the section of the Deutsche Gesellschaft für Soziologie was established, but in the same year the German Society for Medical Sociology was founded and its membership is now one-fifth of that of the German Sociological Association. Today, medical sociology represents a respected field of knowledge in most countries outside the Eastern bloc. The European Society of Medical Sociology was founded in 1983 while the International Sociological Association established its Research Committee 15 in 1966 (named 'Medical Sociology' but known since 1986 as the 'Sociology of Health').

In spite of successfully becoming a part of the sociological endeavour, and being incorporated into medical education in many countries, medical sociology has found itself unable to achieve the unity of analytical perspective which is thought to be an indispensable prerequisite if acknowledgment is to be won from the medical profession. Medical sociology often regrets not presenting a cohesive picture. It mirrors the diversity of theoretical approaches which has characterised sociology since its inception in the nineteenth century. This may not be a disadvantage, however.

If social science is to be different from natural science in taking account of the fact that its subject area concerns human beings who more or less consciously engage in social action, rather than *nature morte* where general laws invariably apply, medical sociology might as well be proud that it lacks the unity of perspective which many of its protagonists seem to want.

However, it is also true that little comparative work has been done so far which would make explicit the different theoretical views in medical sociology. It is far from clear how they relate to the main approaches of the 'mother discipline' in general.[6] Since most authors are content with propagating one view which is more or less adequately derived from one of the major theoretical perspectives or 'grand theories', often a degree of *eclecticism* is reached in their definition and use of concepts that may sometimes be unsatisfactory. In order to counteract this, a comprehensive overview seems to be needed of the history and main ideas of medical sociology, and how they relate to *mainstream* sociology.

The development of medical sociology can be separated into four phases each introducing aetiology, therapy and organisation of medical care under one of the major sociological paradigms. The earliest conceptualisation – which received widespread acclaim and, in fact, became the only acknowledged approach in the 1950s – was that of Parsons, supplemented by other structural functionalist views. Soon after publishing the *Social System* Parsons, together with Renée Fox, published on the topic of family, therapy and illness (1952). Fox also contributed to research at Columbia University focusing on the *Student Physician* and how students learn to practise medicine (Merton *et al.*, 1957). During the early 1950s, Parsons continued to illustrate his general theoretical points using medicine and, in particular, sickness as examples (Parsons, Shils and Bales, 1953). After this time, he wrote on special aspects of the health-and-illness topic, and in 1964 included some of this work in a collection of essays, introducing the organic as a fourth system beside the cultural, social and the psychological. However, by that time medical sociology had not only become a fast-growing subspecialty but was also rife with conflict regarding the question of whether structural functionalism was the right approach. The heyday of systems theory was long over, and it has never been restored to the hegemonic role which it played in the 1950s. Indeed, so widespread became the tendency to 'overcome' and 'supersede' Parsons, and structural functionalism in general, that not only were later contributions to medical sociology by Parsons hardly noticed, but even those colleagues who today follow him are often unaware of the heritage.

Structural functionalism was eventually toppled by Goffman's introduction in 1959/61 of a situational-analysis approach. This owed little to systems theory but everything, albeit unconsciously, to Georg Simmel. Without giving credit, it also relied heavily on Lemert's recognition of the relationship between symbolic meaning construction, stigmatisation and deviance. During the decade, authors like Howard Becker, Everett Hughes and Anselm Strauss had begun to develop a view upon drug addiction and other 'classic' forms of deviance which was indebted to G. H. Mead's ideas on the links between mind, self and society. In fact these authors, together with Julius Roth, Fred Davis, and Rue Bucher (except Hughes who was a professor) belonged to a cohort of graduate students at Chicago University where G. H. Mead's interactionist perspective had been kept alive after his death in 1931. Despite this ongoing work it was only the political thrust of Goffman's compassionate account on the plight of prison inmates and patients in mental hospitals which caused the breakthrough of 'symbolic interactionism' at the start of the 1960s. Already Dahrendorf's acid comparison (1958a) between the Utopia hidden behind Parsons' *Social System* and Aldous Huxley's *Brave New World* (1932) had prepared the ground for abandoning structural functionalism as the one and only acclaimed theoretical perspective. At this strategic point, Goffman's books turned the tables. The 1960s emerged as an era of 'labelling theory' in general and medical sociology in particular. From then, the debate continues whether and to what extent medicine represents a political endeavour. The definition of what constitutes illness or health is itself said to be far from politically neutral.

As noted above, Parsons' views in Chapter 10 of the *Social System* owe much to the intellectual shock of Nazism. It became disconcertingly clear that what constituted health, as a collective if not an individual mental state, seemed largely determined by social definitions of normality. Among others, Parsons made attempts to neutralise the threat of political definitions of normality in the early 1950s. In pointing out that the sociologically relevant aspect of health or illness would always be connected with mental aberrations, mass neurosis could be acknowledged and seemingly demystified. Furthermore, by identifying the 'power' of the doctor as professional expertise, which precluded exploitation and domination, Parsons offered the assurance that dangerous political aspects of medicine were contained within the norms and values of society. If this quenched the debate during the 1950s, the topic came back with a vengeance in the early 1960s. The self-righteousness of structural functionalism was rightly questioned and effectively shaken. Becker, in particular, reasserted the view that deviance was all but political, retrospectively claiming Lemert as the chief witness for his argument. In *Outsiders* (1963), a collecton of earlier essays which now became widely read,he maintained that Lemert's thesis had been political all along. In essence, Becker identified the political implications of Lemert's thesis on the cultural relativity of standards of health and normality, implications Lemert had failed to recognise.

As the debate on the '*NeoChicagoans*' (Matza, 1969) continued unabated throughout the 1960s, a third theoretical approach emerged within sociology. For a period, phenomenology epitomised the source of radical or maverick views. Medical topics stood at the cradle of ethnomethodology even before Harold Garfinkel in 1967 phrased the book title which gave the name to the approach. When and how a suicide verdict is reached, what happens when a patient gets away with self-induced change of gender in spite of medical supervision monitoring that no artificial hormones are involved, how mental illness is a collective achievement of mutual behavioural practices between patient and professional in treatment institutions, were but a few topics of interest which preceded the publication of (and were included in) Garfinkel's *Studies in Ethnomethodology* (1967a). But in spite of the havoc created by the rise to short-lived fame of this seemingly untenable and allegedly all-pervasive theoretical approach, it never managed in medical sociology to receive as widespread an acclaim as other analytical perspectives. Nevertheless, ethnomethodology (including Cicourel's splinter *Cognitive Sociology*) has continued to make valuable contributions to medical sociology. Some of its most useful ideas regarding medical practice were possibly elaborated in England and Germany in the early 1970s. Recently, its focus has shifted to language structures in multiple treatment settings where promising links with sociolinguistics have developed.

The fourth and last addition to the theoretical scope of medical sociology originated partly in the ranks of the Marxists. In 1968, as students in the US, France and Germany plunged into what was prematurely considered as a revolution, medical sociologists began to realise that injustice and inequality were legitimate topics for academic enquiry. Two main directions emerged: on the one hand, medicine was identified as an institution of social control proliferating in modern society such that there was an increasing tendency to 'medicalise' whole areas of everyday life. This view, angrily stated by authors like Zola and McKinlay just after 1970, was loosely connected to the general belief that poverty and deprivation are an outcome of power and prejudice. In the middle

1970s, Illich's rabid criticism of 'medical nemesis' (1975a) owed much to this perspective (at least in how and by whom it was received), elaborating the view that through its very growth and improvement as a technical endeavour, modern medicine created iatrogenic disease and even death to a hitherto unthinkable extent. In its more recent form, this argument holds in equally radical fashion that diagnostic categories, and even the notion of illness, were but repercussions of repressive life circumstances in various periods of history including the present. The issue is debated whether the views collected, for instance, in Wright and Treacher's *The Problem of Medical Knowledge* (1982) represent relativism. The incorporation of Foucault's work into medical sociology might denote an offshoot of symbolic interactionism, or a genuinely new view on the social roots of medicine.

The second line of argument focuses on the individual's experience of illness. It aims at proving through research that the social origin of mental as well as physical illness is loss produced by life circumstances. In this, a mildly radical tendency is combined with the view that self-help might serve the patient equally as well as professional help. The view has sprung up since the early 1970s that discrepancies between person and environment influence health negatively. This has drawn into sociology the stress model which originates in a strictly medical framework.

In this, the *political* aspect of the health–illness division and of medical endeavours again occupies the forefront of interest. The political motive derives from disadvantage and deprivation in modern mass society making for increased premature mortality rates of the lowest-income strata. The general theory relating to this is one of social conflict.

These four paradigms – namely, Parsons' key perspective within *structural functionalism, symbolic interactionism* merging with so-called labelling theory, ethnomethodology as the core perspective within *phenomenological* sociology, and the self-styled Marxist view which has been supplemented by a non-Marxist model to represent a *conflict-theory approach* – have become the cornerstones of the theoretical foundations of medical sociology. The latest of these approaches was introduced in the 1970s. Since then, no further paradigm has been outlined which claims thoroughly to reform the theoretical foundations of medical sociology. Although recently Foucault's work has been used with this aim, it refines the conflict paradigm's idea of power and knowledge rather than representing a new approach in its own right. During the last ten years, all paradigms continued to be used, if only in the guise of widespread concepts (such as, for instance, sick role or stigma) seemingly with no origin in general theory. It seems appropriate to look back and take stock of where we stand. What are the current as well as the permanent problems regarding the conceptualisation of illness as part of sociology?

In the four parts that follow a systematic format has been adopted. The presentation of each of the four paradigms will comprise four steps of reconstruction.

1. A general outline of each theory's notion of illness will be presented. This includes a short account of what each paradigm considers as political in the definition of illness. Mostly, this relates to the issue of cultural relativity, on the one hand, and economic connotations of health which determine one's work strength and, hence, earning capacity in modern industrial society on the other. The basic theoretical argument usually also contains a justification of why sociology finds in medical issues a legitimate topic, though its own reasoning is non-medical.

2. Illness must be elaborated to incorporate some notion of causality. Conceptualisations of the origin and aetiology of disease, illness or sickness are a major part of the sociological effort in medicine. Of particular interest in this book is how these conceptualisations use the perspectives from wider frames of sociological theory, namely, structural functionalism, interactionism, phenomenology and conflict theory (Marxism). Each paradigm makes an independent endeavour to understand illness, and to make plausible how the aetiology may be understood as a social process rather than, or supplementary to, a medical one.

3. This leads to the issue of treatment. Aetiology and treatment appear as two consecutive phases, the former explaining emergence, the latter dealing with management and recovery. It is interesting that the analysis of treatment needs to follow the same principle as that of aetiology such that the two form phases of a process. It is a matter of definition, however, whether the social element of the treatment side of illness would be perceived as predominantly one of institutional care or, rather, one of individual experience. Both views, to be sure, have their counterparts in conceptualisations of aetiology.

4. These accounts only fall into place if the book succeeds in making clear the illness explanations' theoretical viability. For instance, what is it that is structural functionalist about Parsons' ideas on illness? Are they an example of 'true' systems theory, particularly in view of the fact that psychoanalysis plays a major

part in Parsons' medical sociology (i.e., the sociology of deviance) while at least not openly shaping his general sociology?
Do the sometimes odd explanations of labelling theory hold
water under the broader auspices of 'symbolic interactionism'
as grounded in G. H. Mead's work? Do the concepts used to
conduct research under an ethnomethodological (including
conversational-analysis and 'cognitive sociology') point of view,
fit into the lines of the 'classic' argument drawn out in the late
1960s? And does, for instance, Goldthorpe's criticism that its
epistemological position is untenable (1973) undo the credulity
of the phenomenological approach in general? Last but not
least, would conflict theory in medical sociology, whether or
not an offshoot of modern Marxism, necessarily come to endorse critical views on society? Is there a clear linkage between
the more health-concerned writings on the welfare services and
the more economic writings such as, for instance, O'Connor's
The Fiscal Crisis of the State (1973), or would there be a gap
between medical sociology and its more materialistic counterparts? Therefore the final part of each chapter will draw a line
between each viewpoint outlining the social side of illness and
medicine, and the general idea of what *social action* is meant to
be; that is, how the latter squares with illness and the doctor's
task as well as the generalised *notion of society*. In this, to be
sure, the stance of each of the four paradigms on the idea of
'sick society' matters. It is here that the problem of anti-
Semitism helps to highlight the conjectures regarding the general nature of the social order.

As it happens, nearly all theoretical paradigms when used in
empirical research seem to be broken down into various specific
views. These often appear so diverse that it seems hardly feasible
to piece them together into a comprehensive picture of each
original theoretical perspective. The theoretical paradigms of
structural functionalism and symbolic interactionism divide into
two more or less independent models which nevertheless maintain
a certain degree of unity. The conflict-theory paradigm may be
separated into two or three different models. But since no attempt
has been made so far to draw these writings together under their
explanatory perspective, two models will be outlined, the second
one a conglomerate of approaches which could be subdivided into
Marxist and non-Marxist. Phenomenology only presents one
model so far, but a second one is emerging. In essence, it is
through research that the viability of a theoretical endeavour must
prove itself, which also affects the number and scope of explanat-

ory models contained in a theoretical paradigm. It is here that progress takes place in the development of medical sociology.

I hope that the reader will bear with me exploring the meanders of arguments and counter-arguments. Medical sociology, in my view, is more than a casual offshoot of social science in the age of proliferation of subdisciplines. I am confident that this book provides enough evidence for the reader to feel able to corroborate or refute the claim that medical sociology is to be considered the legitimate offspring, if not a vital part, of what has come to be named *general sociology*.

Part I
The Structural-Functionalist Paradigm: Illness as Social Role and Motivated Deviance

Talcott Parsons' theory of social systems

Introduction: the structural-functional pledge

Building upon ideas from physiology and biology[7] which introduced a systems notion of the functioning of the organism, Parsons' highly stylised description of the workings of *the* social system plunged sociological theory into a era of analytical abstraction. The book offered a comprehensive view on a wide variety of processes under the auspices of a single all-pervasive analytical perspective (referring to itself as an action frame of reference). It came to dominate theorising as well as research in sociology for more than a decade. Curiously enough, medical practice as a setting of complementary institutionalised roles is the only field where experience and observation enter into this otherwise taxonomical endeavour. Classifications and definitions which characterise this major opus only come to life in Chapter 10 which deals with 'The Social Structure and Dynamic Process of Modern Medical Practice'.

The second tradition on which Parsons relies in his medical sociology is that of structural functionalism in anthropology in the 1920s and 1930s. Malinowski (1922, 1926), Radcliffe-Brown (1935) and Linton (1936) analyse societal structures as well as their component elements in terms of homeostatic self-sufficiency of cultures.

Rejecting a simplistic physiologist interpretation of illness, in the wake of his friend and mentor's (the physiologist Henderson's) conceptualisation of the doctor–patient relationship as a social system (1935b), Parsons adopts the idea that illness is related to role structures. At the same time, his reinterpretation of

1

his mentor Malinowski's structural-functionalist anthropology produces the view that role conformity makes for social-system integration and maintenance.

He does not, however, content himself with repeating what the two scholars thought out. Generalising Henderson's view that doctors and patients engage in an institutionalised set of complementary roles forming a social system in miniature, Parsons conceives of society in general as a concatenated system of systems of social action. Thus, medicine appears as but an example depicting a general principle of institutionalised structure. With regard to understanding the doctor's work, Parsons adds to Henderson's extension of physiology into non-physiological realms the view that health rather than illness is the primary concern of the sociologist who adopts a social-system perspective. This shift of emphasis from illness to health as the basic analytical focus is due to the search for functional prerequisites, that is, presuppositions for structure formation within social systems regarding both thinking and doing. Developing further the ideas of Malinowski, Parsons builds on the teachings of anthropology that organic or social phenomena, as units of organisms or cultures, may be analysed in terms of their contribution to the maintenance of a structure. The degree of formalism shared by this analytical focus with the anthropological viewpoint becomes apparent when A. R. Radcliffe-Brown's classification of the 'concept of function in social science' is remembered:

> The continuity of the social structure, like that of organic structure, is not destroyed by changes in the units. The continuity of social structure is maintained by the process of social life, which consists of the activities and interactions of the individual human beings and of the organised groups into which they are united. The social life of the community is here defined as the *functioning* of the social structure. The *function* of any recurrent activity, such as the punishment of a crime, or a funeral ceremony, is the part it plays in the social life as a whole and therefore the contribution it makes to the maintenance of the structural continuity. The concept of function as here defined thus involves the notion of a *structure* consisting of a *set of relations* amongst *unit entities*, the *continuity* of the structure being maintained by a *life-process* made up of the *activities* of the constituent units. (Radcliffe-Brown, 1935/52, p. 180).

Superseding this view, Parsons stipulates that what matters is not only what the contribution is of each element to the survival of the whole but, rather, what its significance is in terms of four distinctive functions which are fulfilled if a social system is to maintain itself. In fact, his attempt at a non-causal explanation of phenomena and developments of social life adopts a structural-functionalist line of argument by depicting a set of structural as well as functional *categories*. They represent the baseline of sociological thinking about society both as structure and process (Gerhardt, 1971, pp. 47–63).

The four functional categories, taken together, are related to the perpetuation of social systems as such. They distinguish between four exigencies of system continuity under the heuristic caveat that in no other way is sociology able to conceptualise society in general. This then helps to answer the Hobbesian problem of how the social order is possible. The four functional categories – namely, adaptation, goal attainment, integration and pattern maintenance ('latency') – are the principle scheme of differentiation in society (making for the subsystems of economy, polity, 'societal community' (1966, p. 29), and a sphere of cultural learning). These four also determine what functional significance is to be accrued to any particular action system. At the same time, read in *reverse* order, these functional categories define the stages of how any element of society comes to be of use – that is, conform with normative expectations – from a societal point of view; in other words learning as well as therapy and correction follow the patterning of the reversed function scheme of social systems.

Connected with these functional categories is a set of what Parsons intends as structural categories. These characterise the action orientation or normative element in each part of a social structure. By 'choosing' one alternative among five pairs of normative baseline qualities organised in dichotomies ('pattern variables'), structural units acquire characteristics which make them comparable with any other element of any other society, be it historical or contemporary, primitive or modern. On the other hand, groupings of pattern variables into types of social structure are far from arbitrary. Four basic patterns along the achievement-ascription/universalism-particularism lines constitute the taxonomy meant to apply to any social system, large or minuscule in extension or duration (Parsons, 1951a, p. 180ff.). This is clearly compatible with Weber's view that modern occidental capitalism is the outcome of a development towards rationalisation (see also Parsons, 1966). The rationale is that the achievement–universalism formation of society offers most scope for rational action and individual freedom of choice (Weber, 1922/68).

In this picture, medicine represents but a paradigmatic pattern of an institutionalised universalism-achievement structure. However, it is not its confessed *raison d'être* – namely, illness –, but its acrimonious counterpart – that is, health – which plays the decisive role concerning the level of generalised thinking about social systems.

Chapter 1
Parsons' Notion of Illness

In the 1960s, Parsons recollects how he came to the field of medical sociology 30 years earlier. He insists that he was always predominantly interested in how modern capitalism works, and he claims that he focused on the medical profession precisely for this reason. He writes:

> It is perhaps not irrelevant to remark, that at the time I became interested (in the middle 1930's), the principal link between medicine and the social sciences was by way of 'medical economics', not medical sociology. The focus of this was the immense project of study of the costs of medical care, which was a rather typical foundation supported economic study in its attempt to bridge considerations of academic economics and of public policy. In the latter connection its report set off a storm in the relations between its proponents and the American Medical Association, being stigmatized by the latter's Journal as socialistic, though by present standards it was very mildly so, if indeed at all . . . It gradually became clear to me that the principal theorists of capitalism, notably Marx and those in his tradition, tended to characterize the whole of modern industrial society in terms of this conception and to treat the business firm as *the* typical unit of its organization, beyond the family. In doing so they tended to ignore the existence of another major component of the social structure of the same society precisely at the relevant occupational level; namely, the professions, a category of members of which explicitly repudiated the allegation that orientation primarily in terms of economic self-interest was legitimate for them, or that empirically it characterized the typical orientation of the incumbent of a professional role. Moreover, from the point of view of the theorists of capitalism, it seemed paradoxical that the professions should have been growing in importance in the same society in which private business enterprise had prospered, while at the same time they belonged mainly to the private sector; they were not, as elements of government, a 'socialistic' element. (Parsons, 1964, pp. 325–7)

While his original intention may have been to prove that he (as a member of the background research staff of the Wilbur Committee) was wrongly accused by the American Medical Association

(AMA) of socialist leanings, Parsons (as early as 1939, and as late as 1978) postulates from a systematic sociological viewpoint that: there is an intricate link between the nature of capitalism and the non-business character of the (medical) profession. This, in turn, suggests a special role for health. Health is related to what most modern sociologists and, in fact, sociology since its inception in the nineteenth century analyses as progress; that ours is or should be a society where achievement matters more than ascription, and universalism has overcome particularism as the main principle of value orientation. In this achievement–universalism culture merit is defined by talent plus hard work on the basis of equal opportunity for everyone regardless of status of origin. Moreover, power ideally accrues to those who through success in education and/or occupation prove to be the most apt to wield it (preferably in elected office on a rotating basis). Thus the hard core of the idea of democracy against the background of capitalist economy is merciless competition in the academic and economic marketplaces. It is there that the most capable are selected who qualify for higher prestige and power, and the rank and file are separated out. For rational reasons they have to renounce the blessings of meritocratic society. It is self-evident that, in this world of competition and excellence, the individual must be fit: that is, as fit as other (if not fitter). In his latest as well as in his earliest writings on medical sociology after the Second World War, Parsons stresses the idea that health represents one basic condition for participation in an equal-opportunity society. In other words, health is a *gatekeeper*, guaranteeing equality for all who strive for status and spoils in modern society.

At the end of his life, in 1978, when he saw 'the human condition' epitomising an ever-precarious balance between forces of gratification and constraint, Parsons introduced a new term for health: *teleonymy*. He claimed to borrow it from the biologist Ernst Mayr. He wrote: 'Teleonymy may be defined as the capacity of the organism, or its propensity, to undertake successful goal-oriented courses of behavior' (Parsons, 1978a, p. 68). Some years earlier, in 1970, the idea was voiced in more traditional terms: 'Health is vital, because the capacity of the human individual to achieve is ultimately the most crucial social resource' (Parsons, 1970a, p. 281). Again, 12 years earlier the same perspective prevailed, but was phrased more from society's point of view:

> Equally important is the provision of the society with units which have the capacity for valued achievement . . . It is in this connection that the relevance of . . . health appears . . . The possibility of achievement is the function of opportunity . . . But on a 'deeper' and in a sense more

generalized level, this achievement is dependent . . . on health. (Parsons, 1958/64a, p. 279)

The systems-related perspective eventually comes out most clearly in the 1951 version of the idea. There, Parsons makes it plain that a functional prerequisite of system formation in any society and a precondition of continuity of a social structure is that individuals who are society's members have to be positively motivated. This means that psychological (and physical) health ought to be the same for all participating in society: that is, equal proficiency and prowess are to be conditions which guarantee, on the one hand, that there is true, if only hypothetically equal, opportunity for all at the outset of societal competition. On the other hand, such equal opportunity ensures that members of society feel that they get what they desire (i.e., that their wishes and needs, more or less, are indeed fulfilled by what their society offers them). Thus health is a basic condition of democracy and justice insofar as it suggests equality. Parsons wrote:

> The problem of health is intimately involved in the functional prerequisites of the social system . . . Certainly by almost any definition health is included in the functional needs of the individual member of the society so that from the point of view of functioning of the social system, too low a general level of health, too high an incidence of illness, is dysfunctional. (Parsons, 1951a, p. 430)

It is only in juxtaposition to health thus formally defined – that is, defined as the capacity to fulfil roles which make up society (which, in turn, is understood as social system) – that, on the conceptual level, illness enters the picture. In 1951, Parsons maintained that 'too high an incidence of illness is dysfunctional' (i.e., dysfunctional to the maintenance of the social system in its status quo).

In 1970, the same formalism prevails:

> The problem of illness has been a critical one in Western civilization generally, in its more modern phase, because of the extent to which these societies have been oriented to the values of active achievement in instrumental contexts, to the mastery of the physical environment, and to the development of effective social organization itself. (Parsons, 1970a, p. 281)

When, in 1978, Parsons introduced the term 'teleonymy', illness was defined as its breakdown. But the idea was not the simplistic image of reversing health. Over the whole period of writings on medical sociology, Parsons followed a second line of argument which then merged with that of control of environment. Pre-war physiology, elaborated by L. J. Henderson and W. C. Cannon, emphasised that illness constitutes *deviance* from systems equilibration. The *vis medicatrix naturae* which Henderson and Cannon invoked was to justify a self-healing potential of the body in case of, for instance, a fever. Parsons gave the term a much more comprehensive meaning and saw in the 'healing power of nature . . . a property of living systems . . . by virtue of which such systems have a capacity to cope, often without outside intervention' (Parsons, 1978a, p. 67). It follows that where nature's forces fail, it is nurture which forms a 'second line of defense' (Parsons, 1958/64a, p. 259). Then the *vis medicatrix* of medical therapy takes over to mend the person's 'teleonomic capacity'. In this vein, the medical effort temporarily replaces, in order to more or less durably restore, the *vis medicatrix naturae*. In a sense, the latter constitutes the 'rock bottom' – to use a Parsonian term – of mankind's ability to realise the indispensable minimum of pleasure within any, even the most repressive, role systems.

The dual nature of illness

Mankind is not simply a living organism, insists Parsons, but a 'social animal' who is 'participant in cultural systems and patterns of meaning of what is sometimes called "the human condition"' (Parsons, 1978a, p. 67). Therefore role and task capacity involve both somatic functioning and social action. Breakdown disrupts a person's normality on either level: 'Health and illness, as human phenomena, [are] both organic and sociocultural' (Parsons, 1978a, p. 81).

Sociology is concerned more with the latter than the former. Its specific subject area is society analysed as a social system constituted by roles. This directs the sociologist's interest towards what are the conditions of satisfactory fulfilment of role expectations. Accordingly, aspects of health jeopardising role reciprocity become important themes of sociological enquiry. *Mental* illness is the most disruptive kind of deviance because it is apt to create emotional disturbance together with reality distortion. These prevent people in social roles from correctly perceiving others' interactional messages and adequately responding to behavioural and attitudinal expectations.

> Since it is at the level of role structure that the principal direct interpenetration of social systems and personalities come to focus, it is as an

incapacity to meet the expectations of social roles, that mental illness becomes a problem in social relationships and that criteria of its presence or absence should be formulated. (Parsons, 1958/64a, p. 258)

The continuum between somatic and mental aspects of any illness involves two sides of breakdown. On the one hand, there is physiological breakdown where illness and medicine are concerned with task performance and non-motivational conditions of role fulfilment and, on the other hand, there is psychological breakdown. The latter is of particular interest to the sociologist analysing how the social system functions. Society's members must find reasonable pleasure in the pursuit of economic and other achievement in society if they are to conform to normative expectations. Since their need dispositions must be satisfied through social action, disruption of this (i.e., the mental side of breakdown of role performance) is a major concern for the sociologist. Sociology's interest justifies itself, according to Parsons, through the fact that 'a larger component of the phenomena of mental illness presumably operates through motivation' (Parsons, 1958/64a, p. 281). In essence, the issue is to understand how the ' "motivational" economy of the social system' works (Parsons, 1951b, p. 452), with special reference to medical practice.

Two ideas strengthen the connection between medical practice as agent of social conformity (competition) and social control, on the one hand, and the individual's happiness and satisfaction realised through social action, on the other. The first is that society's 'motivational economy' derives from, and safeguards, role compliance which in turn ensures society's normative integration. The other is that behaviour is motivated causally as well as orientationally which means that it is based on need dispositions and meaning structures. These two ideas unite to determine the aspect of motivatedness in the social-action side of illness. Parsons and Fox write:

Illness, in so far as it is motivated, is a form of deviant behavior, and, as such, may be subjected to a standard sociological analysis of deviance. Compared with other types of non-conformist behavior, sickness characteristically entails passive withdrawal from normal activities and responsibilities. As such, it should be distinguished from active rebellion against the normal social expectations, and from the types of deviance characterized by compulsive conformity. For it is an escape from the pressures of ordinary life. (Parsons and Fox, 1952b, p. 32).

However, the motivation of illness is far from conscious. The duality represented by health and illness 'as human phenomena, . . . both organic and sociocultural' (Parsons, 1978a, p. 81) thus

contains two further dualities. Conscious attitudes and unconscious motives blend together to form the 'continuum between the
most completely "mental" of mental illnesses, through the various
ranges of psychosomatic phenomena to the category of completely
"somatic"' (Parsons, 1964, p. 331). Furthermore, motivated factors exist side by side with non-motivated ones (Parsons, 1975, p.
260).

The distinction between the mental and somatic components of
illness, with special focus on its mental (i.e., motivational) side
serves to establish the analysis of medical practice as a proper part
of general sociology. The idea is to provide a *sociological rationale
for the doctor's work*. To show that medicine is more than a
business means that the doctor–patient relationship appears as
roles whose interrelationship restores society's basic precondition
of functioning, namely, generalised role capacity. Parsons wanted
to explain this as a mechanism of society's self-regulation and also
to explain why such regenerative work is effective. Using ideas
from Freud's psychoanalysis, innovative in the treatment of mental illness during the 1930s and 1940s, he recognised psychotherapy
as the model of medical work as such.

Relativism as a political answer

In this connection, the political side of Parsons' notion of illness
must be pointed out. It is contained in his concern with the
psychiatric and his focus on the normal. Basically he equates
health with normality, and illness with deviance. The argument is
that the substantive issues defined as deviant are relative in any
society to its notion of health. This involves a relativist view of the
socially defined quality of normality since the normal is but what
figures as psychiatrically (or physically) healthy. From this vantage
point, the idea is rejected that societies develop neurotic (or
criminal, for that matter) overall states determining 'sick' normative definitions of normality.

The normal, to be sure, is understood as a *formal* quality of
roles: that is, one expressing itself through expectations of others.
Matters of content are not necessarily implied; normality is not
judged from a 'value rational' point of view. With regard to mental
health, this means that a morally defined *cut-off point* of decency
and decorum is not suggested which determines that a person
could be 'deemed sick' while 'acting healthy'. Rather, as long as a
person functions as an esteemed or efficient role partner the label
of normality would apply. The *non-specificity* of what constitutes

normality, independent of moral standards, relates health to actual political standards of functioning of a society. From a 'value rational' point of view, to be sure, this does not rule out the potential immorality of achievement-orientation in a society. The sociologist (or doctor) in a given social setting can only diagnose deviance if the norms or values of that society are violated. Normality and health as *formal* properties of social life are mirrored in the contents of the surrounding 'normative climate': 'Since being a normally satisfactory member of social groups is always one aspect of health, mental or physical, the therapeutic process must always have as one dimension the restoration of capacity to play social roles in a normal way' (Parsons, 1951b, p. 453). Parsons introduces relativity not only as a property of social life defined by standards of performance; he also sees a development towards increasing salience of relativity in the history of modern society. The degree to which 'purely mental' as opposed to 'purely somatic' aspects of health prevail in a society are seen as related to, and in this way relative to, the historically unique character of a culture or social structure. The idea is that the more 'mental' a prevailing concept of health is in a society or epoch, the more conspicuous is 'the prominence of the factors of relativity as a function of culture and social structure' (Parsons, 1958/64a, p. 258). This, in turn, is linked to the amount and speed of social change.

This concept of relativity has two implications. One is that relativity signifies social progress. The distinction between health and illness is fluent such that, for example, what constitutes health in one society may represent illness in another, and also what constitutes crime or sin (as forms of deviance) in one society may represent illness in another: 'The crucial point is the variability of the boundaries between health and illness and hence illness and other forms of deviance, from society to society and within the same society over time' (Parsons, 1960/64a, p. 112). Homosexuality may be a case in point. While it is (was) denounced as sin in some societies, and prosecuted as a criminal offence in others, modern Western standards today tend to incorporate it into the realms of health after having recognised it for some decades as illness bordering on the psychiatric. The shifting of type of deviance under which certain behaviours become classified (and acted upon) depends on the values characterising society as a system. These determine what classificatory categories are deemed adequate and what 'pattern variables' are used to 'understand' certain behaviours. German Fascism prosecuted homosexuality as a criminal offence not only by punishing it through the courts but also by confinement to concentration camps. From Parsons' vantage point, this would appear as 'less modern' than Western democracies where an illness definition prevails. The criminality categorisation is superseded in democratic countries by achievement orientation incorporating more and more types of deviance under an illness label. This, to be sure, invokes medical rather than atavistic corrective types of treatment.

The other implication of the concept of relativity is that deviance appears in the eye of the beholder, so to speak. As long as it is through the reaction of others and their application of sanctions or gratifications that a role performance is judged to be normal or not, any behaviour, in principle, might be found acceptable. The criticism has been raised against Parsons that 'social objectivity is reduced to a formalized system of subjective utterances, expectations, and impulses' (Maus, 1962, p. 156). If this criticism holds, an element of arbitrary stipulation through received reaction becomes visible in Parsons' definition of normality. The sociologist must then accept that any role relationship forms a legitimate part of a social structure which produces reciprocally satisfactory interchange. As long as no criteria are introduced which differentiate between acceptable and non-acceptable normal role obligations, implicit acquiescence to possibly morally reprehensive political regimes looms large in sociology's attempt at 'value-free description'. As long as no firm stance enables sociologists to denounce or reject some approvedly normal ways of behaviour in some societies, certain topics may confront medical sociologists with the dilemma that they are unable to avoid politically dubious or morally ambiguous relativism. A case in point is mental illness in societies with Communist regimes. Medical sociology, it seems, finds it difficult to criticise the use of mental illness labels there, from a social-system point of view. If deviance is what is so regarded in a society, there seems to be justification to the 'punishment' of political dissent through confinement to a mental hospital.

The issue of relativity contains one answer to the political debate of the immediate post-1945 period. It was discussed then how Fascist societies function and how sociologists ought to deal with them in their analyses. One possible stance is that of relativity. The relatedness to the social system as a whole of normative orientation in any role relationship implies that to be different may mean to be deviant. This invokes the view that social control is morally neutral. The sociologist who analyses how a society functions must accept its type of prevailing social control, a formal mechanism, irrespective of how the society chooses to deal with its non-conformers. This might lead to the attitude that a Fascist society is just one example of how a social system works. It may be clad with the seemingly value-free concepts offered by social-systems taxonomy.

That boundaries are fluid between health and illness, crime and illness, and so on, makes it difficult for the sociologist to denounce Fascist versions of societal integration. Parsons' concepts mirror his incapacity to make moralist statements. If his is a subjectivist view it is essential to find out whether he suggests that a line ought to be drawn and where. Weber's demand that science and politics be separated in sociological thought can partially justify why Parsons refrains from openly taking a moral viewpoint. It is true that a subjectivist perspective, even if clad in an 'action frame of reference', cannot solve the problem of how repulsive and repressive acts can be denied implicit approval by being analysed as examples of social action. Standards are needed by which sociologists find certain actions inadmissible irrespective of whether or not the frightened majority of the terrorised population in a Fascist country joins them in deeming such actions 'sick'.

However, Parsons is not just concerned with a subjectivist perspective. Most critics charge him with leaving out the standpoint of the individual (and promoting an 'oversocialised' conception); but this must be revised in the light of his illness theory. The baseline of his health–illness thinking is that health and illness are but *individual* states of the mind and body. The statement that 'we wish to stress that we regard health as a state of the human individual, not of collectivities' (Parsons, 1978a, p. 67) emphasises in his last book again his option from the late 1940s and early 1950s that a formalist and relativist notion of health serves the sociological purpose better than a substantive moralist position. This avoids reifications such as 'sickness of society' but produces the potential political acquiescence engendered by relativism.

Whether or not to favour a moralist stance would have produced a different set of conceptual dilemmas is, of course, an open question. At least Parsons' relativist formalism enables him to avoid the dangers of reification of 'society as an actor' which can lie behind denouncing whole groups or races as 'sick'. The latter, as Parsons knew well, can be used to justify 'treatment' given to them of an utterly cruel kind. (It may be remembered in this context that the Nazis used the euphemistic term of 'special treatment' for murder in concentration camps.) However, as has been said, some implicit dangers are also invoked by the relativist conceptual option. Weaving social fabric from individual actors' orientations within a formalist analytical framework seems to offer only partical protection from acquiescence with the political use of sickness categories. In particular, it seems not to exclude sociologists remaining speechless when Communist regimes extend the illness label to become a political device for prosecuting dissidents or disenfranchised minorities.

Two models of illness

On the basis of this general political line, Parsons proceeds to analyse health, and its counterpart illness, as crucial dimensions of modern society. The central idea is that illness is related to achievement. It becomes clearer, and splits into two aspects, when the nature of this link is discussed in detail. He explicitly introduces the distinction between the negative and the positive side of achievement-relatedness in his *Social System*: 'One may say that it is in a certain sense a "negatively achieved" role, through failure to "keep well", though, of course, positive motivations also operate, which by that very token must be motivations to deviance' (1951a, p. 438). Most secondary literature acknowledges only some part of this conception. Parsons himself felt awkward about commenting on the unsatisfactory reception of his work in medical sociology when he was asked to do so. The secondary literature, to an overwhelming degree, omits the crucial two-model structure of his thought. In most writings on Parsons, illness is noted for its character of deviance while its care and cure are perceived in terms of the sick role as a device of social control aiming at redressing the balance towards health or normality. In fact, on the basis of this insufficient understanding of Parsons' views, most endorsements as well as criticisms of his ideas discuss the question of whether his theory is (un)able to analyse chronic illness and explain actual patient experiences during sickness incumbency and so on in theoretically unsatisfactory terms (Mechanic, 1959; Twaddle, 1969; Freidson, 1970a; Segall, 1976).

   At the session given in his honour and devoted to his work at the 1974 World Congress of Sociology in Toronto, Parsons hinted at the possibility that most secondary literature was based on simplifications of his ideas. If only politely arguing against his admirers' assurance that his view of the sick role as deviance has been a major step forward in the sociological understanding of illness, Parsons tried to make the point that there were, in fact, two models. In a cautious but nevertheless unambiguous statement, he stressed the fact that for him deviance and sick role are two *different* aspects of the problem. The sick role, he said, was related to the concept of capacity; furthermore, there was 'the *other* most important issue', namely, deviance linked to 'the concept of "motivatedness" of illness' (Parsons, 1975, p. 256; my emphasis). At the same session, Gallagher ventured a hypothesis suggesting a somewhat different distinction between two models, but was the only one to propose that there was more than one conception. (The paper was honoured with a prize after publication.) He drew the distinction between an adaptation–maladaption model, which he suggested retaining, and a deviancy model based on psychodynamic thinking which he proposed to discard. This is the only acknowledgment in the secondary literature that there is more than one explanatory scheme in Parsons' writings (with the exception of Gerhardt, 1979a). However, Gallagher overlooks how important for Parsons are the concepts of 'secondary gain' in sickness incumbency and 'unconscious psychotherapy' in medical practice. Therefore reducing Parsons' ideas to the truncated scope of the adaptation model which seems to be solely perceived by most secondary literature does not seem a viable solution.

The *incapacity* model concentrates on the negative-achievement aspect of illness. It offers a view on aetiology which focuses on the gradual erosion of a person's role capacity and explains the breakdown of role capacity in terms of failure to keep well, to use Parsons' own words. Since it is in role capacity that the person fails, it is through a role (namely, the sick role) that the person recovers; the sick role is perceived as some kind of niche in the social system where the incapicitated may withdraw while attempting to mend their fences, with the help of the medical profession.

The *deviancy* model is concerned with the positive-achievement aspect in this: that is, its motivational forces. It is here that psychoanalysis plays a major part supplying the main ideas. If only slightly altered to serve a *tabula rasa* rather than an instinct-drive image of the (un)socialised person, psychodynamic views are behind the concept of the unconsciously motivated aetiology of illness. They also inspire the idea of 'unconscious psychotherapy' incorporated in medical treatment.

The two models, the incapacity model and the deviancy model, seem different enough to be presented as separate. The dividing line between the concatenated negative and positive sides of achievement in illness may, however, be a matter of debate. In fact, a previous view presented in 1979 differs, to a certain extent, from that of this book.

Chapter 2
The Capacity Model

If illness, as an achievement, is analysed from the perspective of the doctor's work, its imputed nature is negative in two ways. First, it represents the state of the organism or personality whose overcoming (treatment, cure) is what matters to society as a functioning system. Second, the agent of this is the medical profession, a non-business group in an otherwise business-oriented society. Thus illness as well as its treatment upset the equilibrium of exchange relationships in society and follow other than the usual domination–exploitation lines of the business world.

The focus on illness is from the vantage point of the sick role. It forms a system with the doctor's role, both being characterised by the same pattern variables. Both are geared towards recovery of the patients (i.e., their return to well-being) which includes the return to normal non-sick performance. Accordingly, illness is 'failure to "keep well"' (Parsons, 1951a, p. 438). This failure, denoting the aetiology of illness (under the capacity model) takes place in three stages: first, that of everyday functioning of the person in his or her roles amounting to certain frustrations or lack of gratification but no undue deterioration of the usual role conformity; second, that of 'vicious circles' which eat away at the individual's coping ability, causing deterioration of his or her interpersonal relationships due to others' negative reactions to the individual's worsening fulfilment of their expectations; third, a state of withdrawal of coping capacity equalling 'hoarding' rather than 'expending' necessary energy towards role performance.

It is crucial that the latter, the failure to fulfil one's roles, is defined as involuntary withdrawal rather than voluntary action. This makes the sick role – as institutional counterpart of the doctor's role – a 'niche' in which the individual may recover rather than undergo enforced renormalisation with punitive overtones. With regard to how a person's interpersonally acceptable role conformity is re-established, the medical profession offers less repressive forms of sanctioning deviance than the three other

16

institutions serving this purpose: namely, justice, religion and, to a certain extent, social work (Parsons, 1958/64a, pp. 266–9). The doctor's role, characterised by universalism, achievement, functional specificity, affective neutrality and collectivity orientation, is organised along the same attitudinal–orientational alternatives ('pattern variables') as the sick role.

The three stages of aetiology

The normality stage

Coping and capacity.   All social action is seen as exchange. The relentless obligation to conform to others' role expectations is a continuous validation of symbolic meanings through interpersonal exchange. The importance for Parsons' political standpoint of the economic world view where exchange is what holds society together has been pointed out by Mitchell. He stipulates that Parsons' 'actor is constantly faced in the polity – especially so in democracies – with uncertainty' (Mitchell, 1967, p. 92). However, one might look beyond the economic analogy to identify Parsons' emphasis on exchange with his homage to the work of Weber who, in turn, owed much to Simmel (1890, 1908). Simmel's most influential contribution to sociological theory was the conceptualisation of social phenomena in terms of reciprocity (*Wechselwirkung*). Uncertainty, in Simmel's terms, is a constant challenge in social interchange because one's opponent or partner may never be known so well that one can adapt one's actions perfectly to his or her needs. Social forms such as authority, or regularities of group affiliation, ease the burden for the individual by partially stereotyping expected responses.

Parsons follows this tradition to a considerable extent although there are conspicuous deviations from Simmel's and Weber's thoughts. The most interesting one, in the present context, is that he includes personality and organism in his analysis which are explicitly excluded by both earlier theories. He gives a psychological basis to economic metaphors with which he interprets reciprocity in social life. His postulate is that purpose-oriented (means –end rational) behaviour representing meaning in social action is due to actors' generalised capacity to engage in such activity.

Uncertainty, a constant challenge to social functioning, calls for strategies and resources to master it. What could serve this better than a human *need* for rational action? Parsons stipulates a basic orientation termed 'capacity of an organism, or its propensity, to undertake successful goal-oriented courses of behavior' (1978a, p. 68). It not only enables the individual to be 'a member of structured social systems, and a participant in cultural systems and patterns of meaning' (1978a, p. 67), but it also structures our personality organisation.

This 'teleonomic' capacity has clear-cut economic connotations. For once, 'in sociological terms, the essential component of labor may be said to be "motivational commitment to role performance"' (Parsons, 1960/64a, p. 122). The link between achievement capacity and rational capitalism in the modern occidental world becomes apparent in a passage where the salience of illness for society is explained:

> The problem of illness has been a critical one in the Western civilization generally, in its more modern phase, because of the extent to which these societies have been orientated to values of active achievement in instrumental contexts, to the mastery of the physical environment, and to the development of effective social organization itself. Health is vital, because the capacity of the human individual to achieve is ultimately the most crucial social resource. Illness is, to the sociologist, essentially a disturbance of this capacity to perform in socially valued tasks and roles. (Parsons, 1970a, p. 281)

This capacity for purposive meaningful action is defined as a *limited resource*. Achievement capacity, while being 'an "energy" category' (Parsons, 1960/64a, p. 122), may abound in insufficient or inflationary quantities; that is, it may undergo shortages or suffer oversupply. The equilibrium idea of 'motivational economy' (Parsons, 1951b, p. 452) implies that the output of purposeful instrumental action depends on the pool of 'teleonomic' capacity which the individual has at his or her disposal. This, then, raises the question of what the conditions are under which the ' "pool" of available energy' (Parsons, 1960/64a, p. 122) becomes insufficient. What allows for 'generalized disturbance of the capacity of the individual for normally expected task or role performance' (Parsons, 1958/64a, p. 274)? Levels of disturbance, or sufficient flow, of achievement capacity (illness and health) may vary, and sex, age and level of education, among other things, are factors involved in this. Value commitments remain secondary or are relatively unimportant for the variation of expected levels of task performance, Parsons assures us.

The concept of strain.   The economic analogy includes the idea of *cost*, together with that of gain or gratification. Cost or expenditure in the course of reciprocal action may exceed the investment of resources or the scope of capacities which the individual may feel able or willing to use. It is here that illness abides, and 'medicine has, seen in this light, been a "second line of defense" of the somatic welfare of the individual, tending to step in where the difficulties exceeded the capacities of the family to cope with them' (Parsons, 1964, p. 315). Yet somatic illness is but one outcome of a situation of strain: that is, a discrepancy between available capacity and necessary coping. Although it is true, Parsons assures us, that 'a state of illness may result from some failure to cope with the exigencies of the physical environment, as in the case of invasion by agents of bacterial infection . . . [or] may arise from malorganization of the relations of organic and action level subsystems of the more general human condition or from internal pathological processes such as a malignant tumor' (1978a, pp. 69/70), this is obviously only half the story. As he himself and many others have argued over the last decades, even the much-quoted *common cold* (Meyer and Haggerty, 1962) is selective regarding who does and who does not become infected. This points in the direction of environmental conditions as well as hereditary dispositions defining the likelihood of breakdown of host resistance (Cassel, 1976). The decisive concept, therefore, is susceptibility.

Strain indicating a condition increasing the likelihood of illness incumbency is described in two ways: namely, focusing on the interchange between seduction and rejection, and emphasising a stress–adaptation cycle. 'Pathogenic strains' in 'a person's relationship to others', says Parsons (1951b, pp. 453–4), may come about in a particular process. Individuals fulfilling their need to be emotionally wanted irrespective of their role behaviour may try to 'seduce' others. They would particularly 'seduce' the more powerful members of their group who could grant extra favours or bestow more than the due amount of gratification or honour. However, a necessity of 'upholding the value patterns which are constitutive of the group' limits the 'seducibility of the other', particularly those who are 'members of responsibility for enforcement of norms'. This calls for eventual '"legalistic" enforcement of them' which, in turn, is invariably experienced as withdrawal of support, or rejection. By way of 'reactions to strain', this, in turn, is coped with through 'anxieties, production of phantasies, hostile impulses, and the resort to special mechanisms of defense'.

The second way in which Parsons describes strain is borrowed from Selye (1946, 1956). His idea was that internal or external noxious stimuli (cold, heat, hemorrhage, etc.) are responded to by a three-stage process of reactions to stressors. If strain exhausts an organism's coping capacities, maladaptation results on a physiological level representing illness ('General Adaptation Syndrome' or GAS, 'Local Adaptation Syndrome' or LAS). Parsons (e.g.,

1960/64a, pp. 122/3) extends Selye's notion from the organic to the psychological and even social levels. He identifies conflict as well as prejudice ('ideological selection and distortion') as indicators of ongoing strain impinging on an individual's or collectivity's coping resources. Illness, in this vein, is the state of the organism or person brought about by overuse of limited capacities. Organic lesion or personality disorganisation is a foreseeable, if unintended, consequence of this. Behind illness is a person's attempt on a physiological or action level to stretch his or her prowess or potential beyond the point of reasonable means.

'Vicious circles' and the exhaustion of exchange

Since strain is ubiquitous, special mechanisms explain why and how it leads to illness. Parsons and Fox (1952b, pp. 33–5) envisage in detail how every role in the family involves strain which could motivate its incumbents to forgo their obligations and withdraw into an ill status. The same may be said about occupational work in factories or offices. In the military or prisons, illness affords alleviation of some of the most dangerous and dreaded circumstances of life (Waitzkin, 1971)[8]. Most people, however, do not follow this option most of the time. This, on the other hand, indicates the strength of their wish to be regarded by others as sane or normal. At the same time, it signifies the strength of the mechanisms which counteract the ubiquitous tendency to fall ill (or 'play sick').

It is not altogether clear under what conditions strains are neutralised in cycles of coping, and when they are not. There is some evidence that a breakdown of coping supposedly happens more easily to individuals with a comparatively low endowment of the generalised coping capacity (Parsons, 1958/64a, p. 259; 1978a, p. 72). Vicious circles, to be sure, are the outcome of continuous strain producing a deterioration of person–environment fit; in this context (mental) illness is perceived as maladaptation:

> It is when the mechanisms involved in . . . adjustive processes break down ('adjustive' as between personalities involved in social interaction with each other) that mental illness becomes a possibility, that is, it constitutes one way in which the individual can react to the 'strains' imposed upon him in the course of social process'. (1958/64a, p. 259)

Elsewhere, Parsons clarifies how the downward spiral of person–environment fit develops:

> If the strain is not adequately coped with in such ways as to reduce anxiety to manageable levels, the result will, we believe, be the generating of ambivalent motivational structures . . . Attitudes toward others thereby acquire the special property of compulsiveness . . . The presence of such compulsive motivation inevitably distorts the attitudes of an individual in his social relationships . . . In general it may be suggested that most pathological motivation arises out of vicious circles of deepening ambivalence. (1951b, p. 454)

However, this does not occur as an automatic deterioration of health to a point of no return, nor does it occur in continuous fashion. Rather, Parsons envisages layers of system organisation, ranging from culture to organism, and, accordingly,

> thresholds beyond which 'strain' . . . will lead to a breakthrough of control and the setting up of a pathological process involving some kind of 'vicious circle'. Any complex living system of course has many different mechanisms of control at many levels, so a state of being 'out of control' at one level very generally activates 'defenses' at the next higher levels, which in turn of course may or may not be successful in the particular case. (1960/64a, pp. 123/4)

The idea of thresholds and layers of control refers to the idea of hierarchy of systems. It relates to that of disorganisation followed by withdrawal, or return to less advanced systems of behavioural development and self-control. It is at this point of his argument that Parsons introduces the notion of 'exchange media'.

The analogy to economic thinking contains the idea that interpersonal relationships function as structured exchanges of cost and gain (expenditure and reward, sanction and gratification) on a supply–demand basis. Parsons likens the capacity for rational meaningful action to the economic medium of money. In this, 'health might be treated as a symbolic circulating medium regulating human action and other life processes' (1978a, p. 80). Using this analogy, the 'breakdown' of barriers of behavioural control becomes envisaged as a loss or reduction of accessible quantity (or quality?) of the interchange medium *motivational commitment to role performance* (1960/64a, p. 122). In this, 'the flow of pleasure-reward, in relation to various somatic functions, can be conceived as diminished or blocked' (1960/64a, p. 121).

The state of illness

Illness – insofar as its capacity side is concerned – is conceived as negative achievement. This means failure to adequately fulfil interpersonal commitments and, in due course, failure to receive the support and esteem required from others. Through this, the person loses emotional rapport with others. Systematically, Parsons locates illness neither with the cognitive nor evaluative side of social life (it does not denote either intellectual or moral failure). But he places it on the emotional or, to use his own term, cathectic side of the person–environment fit. He assures us that 'allowances' (i.e., others' alleviating what they expect from the sick) are grounded in the fact 'not only . . . that [the sick] may have physical disabilities, but that they are in various ways "emotionally" disturbed' (Parsons, 1951b, pp. 458/9).

Illness as such is characterised by three negative achievements: *passivity* (in a predominantly active society), *helplessness* (in a society where independence is in high regard), and *emotional disturbance* (in a world of means–end rationality where emotionally neutral relationships prevail in politics and the economy : See 1951a, p. 439ff.).

The impact of such 'failure to "keep well"' is pervasive. Parsons integrates body and soul, organism and personality into the four-fold hierarchy with social structure and culture. The idea is that a continuum exists between somatic and mental illness, signifying a gliding scale between illness from predominantly organic lesions to illness causing predominantly psychiatric disturbances (while most diseases are both to a varying degree). In this is incorporated the idea of an *isomorphy between physiology, psychology and society*. It is based on a hierarchy of systems ranging from low-level physiology to complex mechanisms of social exchange and control. He writes: 'Thus, from the bottom up, we have enzymes and coenzymes, hormones, such neurological mechanisms as pleasure, and probably cognition, at the psychological levels "affect", and at socio-cultural levels, language, money, and power' (1960/64a, p. 126). The idea 'that here is complete continuity in the sense of hierarchy of control and of other factors, between the cultural, social, psychological, and organic levels' (1960/64a, p. 126) brings to the open that a disturbance of cathexis is basically a deficiency on an endocrinological or neurological level with repercussions on all higher-order levels. Parsons thus assumes that the loss of *self-control* which illness entails is due to a disturbance of neural mechanisms or enzyme cycles regulating one's perception of pleasure such that all four levels are potentially affected. It is at this point of his argument that the experiments conducted by James Olds on self-regulation of pleasure stimulation fit into Parsons' view. Olds found that rats left to incite their pleasure system themselves through electrodes implanted in their brains were

capable of administering to themselves a nearly constant experience of 'lust'. Parsons cites this to prove the overlap between
culture and nature (1960/64a: 117).

The economic metaphor emphasises the *energy to achieve* introduced as exchange medium. The 'psycho-physiological borderline'
allows easy transfer of energy and makes for virtual system inter-
dependence. Parsons cites the similarity between money and 'teleonomic capacity' (1978a, p. 71) to clarify that the latter operates
on both sides of this 'borderline'. The energy-exchange medium
concept clarifies that 'emotional disturbance', which is a negative
achievement, is also a *loss*, if only a temporary one in the sense of
Keynes' notion of voluntary unemployment. What is lost is capacity to be in control of one's surrounding world, and thus are
lost esteem and gratifications received from others in return for
useful services (i.e., as rewards for fulfilling their expectations).

At this point the difference between becoming a criminal and
becoming sick matters. The particular characteristics of the
emotional disturbance (and/or physical disability) denoting illness
is that it develops *beyond* the reach of rational decision. Parsons
states that in a situation of temptation to commit a crime one is
expected to arouse internalised moral restrictions and abstain from
forbidden acts, while on the verge of bacterial infection one may
not be expected to refrain from falling ill (1978a, p. 70). Whether
or not this contradicts Parsons' other postulate, that illness is
unconsciously motivated, may be discussed later. In any case, he
wishes to preclude confusion between voluntary and involuntary
action-aspects of illness. It is wrong, he says, to mistake its component of helplessness to mean powerlessness. In the World Health
Organization's (WHO) definition of health, he states, conditions
which are within the individuals' control are unduly confounded
with those beyond the scope of purposeful action. For this reason,
the WHO should have thought twice before equating exposure to
the risk of illness with powerlessness: 'They are quite different
aspects of the human predicament' (1978a, p. 71).

Therapy and the doctor–patient interaction

Aetiology in the incapacity model means gradual loss – through
'vicious circles' of stress and ineffective coping – of one's capacity
to conform with others' expectations (followed by loss of their
support and esteem). The turning-point, where stress-coping cycles become 'vicious', is not quite clear. The incapacity model's
notion of treatment focuses on an unspecific societal locus or niche

where the sick may recover from their weakness under the supervision of a helpful and concerned environment. By envisaging the sick role as 'semi-legitimate channel of withdrawal' (Parsons and Fox, 1952b, p. 34), it is made clear that the theme is not medical treatment as such. Instead, Parsons analyses its function for the continuity of society, a community of non-sick members.

Therapy's task is to relieve suffering. But those sociologists analysing it are little concerned with the suffering individual involved. They wish to understand how normative constraints on the practitioner ensure that the patient is neither exploited nor harmed. They also analyse how the normative constraints on the patient ensure that the doctor encounters favourable conditions for his or her responsible job. Since aetiology implies loss of capacity for control and rational action which protects the individual from becoming a victim of force and exploitation, therapy must take place under conditions which guarantee that a lack of this capacity would not lead to being taken advantage of or mishandled. By emphasising the value of technical competence and scientific knowledge for modern medical practice, Parsons shows how a system of orientational checks and balances effectively curtails temptations of one-sided power use and excludes opportunities for unscrupulous victimisation.

Medical treatment is understood in terms of 'the' situation where it takes place, and 'the' rules governing doctor–patient interaction. In particular, the capacity model focuses on three issues:

(a) identification of treatment and sick-role incumbency, based on that of sickness and sick status;
(b) the idea that doctor and patient act within a system of reciprocal symmetrical, albeit hierarchical, role relations;
(c) that chronic and acute illness follow but two courses of the same pattern.

Identification of treatment and sick-role incumbency

From the perspective of the social system as a whole, not much notice is taken of specific diagnosis and therapy administered to individual patients. What matters is that treatment gives access to a status of reduced social responsibilities open to all undergoing medical therapy. The main sociological point is that sick-role incumbency lowers the standards of excellence defining the range of performance in most roles.

In a way, the sick role may be compared to a 'master status' since it potentially offsets all other membership statuses, depending on the degree of incapacity. To be sure, sick-role incumbency 'in the type case' (Parsons, 1951a, p. 438) is meant to be temporary. That is, this quasi-generalised status negating most other statuses allows but for transient incumbency. It is conditional upon two instances. First, symptoms of sickness are to trigger off a visit to the doctor who, second, is to certify the incapacity after a diagnosis which is followed by treatment. The latter, in turn, makes the patient return to the state of previous role capacity.

Parsons devises a cycle of insulation and reintegration which may represent the treatment counterpart of the aetiological cycle of stress and diminishing coping:

> The first of these is the insulation of the sick person from certain types of mutual influence with those who are not sick, and from association with each other. The essential reason for this insulation being important in the present context is not the need of the sick person for special 'care' so much as it is that, motivationally as well as bacteriologically, illness may well be 'contagious' . . . By defining the sick person as in need of help and tending to bring him into relation to therapeutic agencies, the role of illness tends to place him in a position of dependency on persons who are not sick. The structural alignment, hence, is of each sick person with certain categories of nonsick, not of groups of sick persons with each other. (1958/64a, pp. 275–7, emphasis omitted)

That the ill status is the *same* irrespective of the widely differing range of diagnoses and courses of treatment distinguishes the social from the medical aspect of illness. Critics who castigate Parsons for undue identification of sociological and medical perspectives (e.g., Gold, 1977) frequently overlook this point. Unlike Parsons, they prove unable to propose a notion of the genuinely *societal* in sickness while leaving intact the medical view that diagnosis matters. Parsons is wrongly criticised about adopting a medical view because his idea of a *wholesale* status of sickness is misjudged. Most secondary literature does not see that he *abstracts* from the empirical variation of experienced diseases and stipulates the sick role as a *unitary social form* (Mechanic, 1959; Kasl and Cobb, 1966; Freidson, 1970a; Segall, 1976) while occasionally its generalised nature has been acknowledged (Arluke, Kennedy and Kessler, 1979; Gerhardt, 1979a, 1987). Were sickness not such a generalised-cum-transient status, there would be no good reason for Parsons failing to place emphasis on such obvious empirical differences as, for instance, treatment in general practice and hospital care, or courses of treatment, say, for diabetes as opposed to pneumonia.

The doctor–patient system

While the literature abounds with quotes enumerating Parsons' four characteristics of the sick role (which may be regarded as the only widely recognised part of his medical sociology), it is hardly noticed that the sick role is envisaged as but a complementary counterpart of the practitioner's role, and both are introduced as concatenated elements of the social system of medical practice.

To be sure, Parsons frequently describes only the two rights–two obligations structure of the *sick* role (1951a, p. 436ff.; 1951b, p. 455ff.; 1978a, pp. 76–7). Regarding the *physician*'s role, he fails to describe in matching clarity and detail the corresponding structure of exemptions and obligations. However, it is evident that the physician's role, governed by the same value orientations (defined through 'pattern variables'), is envisaged as being complementary to the sick role.

The two *rights* on the patient's side are exemptions: first, from the normal being rewarded for fulfilment and punished for non-fulfilment of one's duties in the family, at work, and so on, and, second, exemption from the blame of being held responsible for one's failures or incapacity. Instead, the ill have a right to receive, at least to a certain degree or for a certain time, a 'regular' income and others' 'regular' support (esteem) without 'earning' or 'deserving' them. They may plead irresponsibility for their present state without being sanctioned like anybody normally would who proves unfit to take responsibility for his or her own actions (or failures to act). The two *duties*, on the other hand, safeguard the conditional nature of the two rights' being granted. First, the obligation to get well ensures that those who enter the sick role pledge themselves to leave it speedily, not at their own discretion but at that of their significant non-ill environment. It is the latter who dictate the conditions of sick-role incumbency. This dependency on others' definition is enhanced by the second obligation. To seek competent help from a physician and follow that advice (i.e., participate in the treatment to the best of one's ability), urges the patient to relinquish his or her adult rights to master and manipulate others (until, in turn, their being reappropriated through relinquishing their ill status).

For the sake of symmetry, the two rights–two duties structure of the physician's role ought to be delineated with similar clarity. Since Parsons does not explicitly describe the practitioner's role in terms of role expectations, the relevant evidence has been pieced together, mainly from his Chapter 10.

Complementing the patient's *duty* to seek competent help is the doctor's obligation to be solely guided by the welfare of the patient

(1951a, pp. 438, 477). Similarly, the counterpart of the patient's obligation to get well is that the doctor must apply the highest possible standards of technical competence and scientific knowledge (1951a, p. 437ff.). The two duties which are proposed for the doctor's role are those to serve only the patient's welfare, and to ensure that this is done with utmost professional competence.

It is more difficult to determine the two *rights* of the doctor. If they are to be symmetrical to those of the ill they also mean exemptions. Parsons' extended argument on the physician's need to injure a patient's body and to gain access to confidential information on a patient's private life indicates a right as well as an exemption. The right which is granted to the physician is to 'enter' every sphere of a person's body or life story, and the exemption is from being sanctioned by the patient or others for intruding into forbidden territory. One of the doctor's rights *qua* role is his or her 'free' access to highly guarded taboo spheres; Parsons clarifies: 'Some of these may not otherwise be accessible to others in any ordinary situation, others only in the context of specifically intimate and personal relationships' (1951a, p. 453).

The other doctors' right is possibly that to exclusiveness of trust and contact. Parsons epitomises the special non-business nature of the doctor–patient relationship by pointing out how odd it would be if a car buyer were to approach 'the Chevrolet dealer only through the Ford dealer' (1951a, p. 439). The behaviour expected from the patient, however, complements expectations defining the doctor's role. Doctors expect patients to entrust them exclusively with their treatment and, in turn, if a 'second opinion' is sought, doctors are expected to cooperate rather than compete with colleagues. Parsons describes in detail what is the counterpart of the doctor's right to exclusive care: namely, that the patient is not supposed to 'shop around'. The right of the physician is expressed in exemptions. Exclusiveness of care relieves doctors from the threat and worry that they might lose the patient through unpleasant or painful therapy. Being exempted from 'third-party control' of other physicians or a concerned lay public may also mean that not every step of an ongoing treatment is judged, and colleagues or clients do not interfere with what they might consider unnecessary surgery or medication. In fact, exemption from being taken to justice for violating others' bodily (or personal) integrity is the necessary counterpart of the doctor's right to administer controlled '"injury" of the body' (1951a, p. 452). The rules of normal reciprocity are thus stifled, if only in a carefully monitored way, under the auspices of an ongoing diagnostic or therapeutic relationship.

Under a social-anthropology perspective, one might add that

this 'reciprocity moratorium' concerns some of the most vigorous spheres of self-preservation, namely, that of revenge or else punishment as retaliation for injury. Generally, what is at stake is the principle 'an eye for an eye, a tooth for a tooth' in the face of bodily harm (which nowadays would be enforced by criminal courts). If doctors were not protected in their role performance by this exemption, they would be utterly incapable of applying the most effective and competent therapy under the best technical and scientific standards.

This symmetrical two rights–two duties structure of the practitioner parallel to the sick role is related to their identical 'pattern variable' normative orientations. *Universalism* in the sick role means that it is generalised rather than personalised criteria which determine how ill one is, while universalism in the doctor's role relates to the generalised rather than personalised standards of professional competence (as realised through technical procedures). *Achievement orientation* in the sick role ensures that, in Parsons' words, 'it is a contingent role into which anyone, regardless of his status in other respects, may come. It is, furthermore, in the type case temporary' (1951a, p. 438). Achievement orientation in the doctor's role refers to the fact that through intensity of training high standards of excellence are achieved, and the position of physician is not acquired by inheritance, for example. *Affective neutrality* in the patient role relates to the fact that getting well is to be tackled as general problem, says Parsons (1951a, p. 438), rather than one connected with the emotional value of specific people. (Whether or not this contradicts his ideas of emotional needs promoting transference in therapy may be left to later discussion.) Affective neutrality in the doctor's role is the necessary corollary of the fact that medical practice is applied science. He writes: 'The physician is expected to treat an objective problem in objective, scientifically justifiable terms. For example whether he likes or dislikes the particular patient as a person is supposed to be irrelevant, as indeed it is to most purely objective problems of how to handle a particular disease' (1951a, p. 435).

Functional specificity in the sick role is the same as that in the doctor's role since all goings-on are strictly confined to health matters. For the doctor, this includes the necessity of high technical competence. Last, both the sick role and the physician's role follow a *collectivity orientation*. For the former, it ensures that getting well is seen as accomplishing a common task in cooperation with the doctor. For the latter, above all it means a ban on the profit motive for all diagnostic and therapeutic considerations.

In empirical research, the view on the patient or sick role has often been tested and frequently found unsatisfactory for the wrong reasons (Kassebaum and Baumann, 1965; Gordon, 1966; Levine and Kozloff, 1978). Many researchers are unaware of the societal form or normative nature of the Parsonian concept (Gerhardt, 1987). However, one study investigates the doctor's role and explicitly tests Parsons' view (Mayntz, 1970). It hypothesises that the specific quality of *impersonality* varies with the doctor's specialisation. Reducing alter to 'an instance of a general category' (Mayntz, 1970, p. 429) is assumed to be endemic in the doctor's role which is clad in affective neutrality, functional specificity, and an absence of inhibitions about asking intimate questions, touching intimate parts, and so on. It is assumed to be less common with generalists than with specialists among a snowball sample of 100 West Berlin physicians. Significantly more generalists experienced or admitted to feelings of dislike for their patients than did specialists, and more specialists expected their patients to want to be treated 'with cool objectivity' (1970, p. 440). The system aspect of checks and balances emphasised by Parsons for the doctor–patient relationship is recognised as a field for medical ethics in Mayntz's concluding statement:

> On the behavioral level (where it ultimately counts) the composite norm of universalised concern, or more specifically the norm of helping and the high respect for human life as a value in itself, can effectively prevent potentially negative consequences of impersonality. Impersonality is not harmful in itself and may in fact even facilitate effective performance. As long as impersonality remains instrumental to the achievement of such positive goals as saving lives, improving health, and easing pain, there is not much to be feared, because these goals implicitly put a restriction on the means that may be used to reach them. It is only where this fabric wears thin that an impersonal attitude, dissociated from a restraining normative framework, can become a threat. (Mayntz, 1970, pp. 445–6)

In his recollections of how he became a medical sociologist, Parsons (1964) stresses the importance of Chapter 10 and therefore the doctor–patient relationship as the epitome of social systems. This 'minimal relevant collectivity' (1964, p. 338) consisting of but two roles nevertheless demonstrates the principles of 'disinterestedness and rationality' (1964, p. 329) which he claims to have emphasised in his first major opus, *The Structure of Social Action* (1937), as the key to what he terms the Hobbesian problem. The age-old question of how the social order was possible, he explains, had been newly answered through reference not to the direct or indirect effects of contracts alone. But the non-contractual aspects of the contract – that is, normative orientations based on integration between personality, society and culture (as systems of action orientation) – were shown to play a strong part in establishing and upholding the social order. In the doctor–patient system, their 'common commitment to the goal of therapy' uniting practitioner and sick role prevails despite the fact that 'this common value commitment does not prescribe identical courses of action' (Parsons, 1964, p. 338). The key idea of systems theory thus emerges that orientational sameness can be combined with action-pattern differentiation.

The very neatness of this intriguing solution leaves Parsons in a conceptual dilemma. When his mentor L. J. Henderson first introduced the idea that doctor and patient enact a social system (1935b), he wanted to promote a science of social relations equalling the progress of modern technology (Henderson 1970). Parsons' doctor's obligation to follow highest possible standards of technical and scientific competence appears hardly compatible with Henderson's sceptical proviso: 'that the personal relations seem to have become less important, if not absolutely, at least relatively to the new and powerful technology of medical practice. This condition . . . might perhaps be modified if it were possible to apply to practice a science of human relations' (1935b, p. 819).

While Henderson claims that it is 'the interaction of the sentiments of the individuals making up a social system' (1935b, p. 820) which the new medical science is to analyse, Parsons appears to abandon the idea of sentiments. In his *Social System*, a short reference to sentiments in a particularly 'dry' wording (1951a, p. 41, especially footnote 10)[9] is all that is left from Henderson's proposition. Sentiments now mean value attitudes which, in turn, mark the personality aspect of voluntary (internalised) role conformity. Henderson's implicit criticism of modern doctors' technological leanings seems forgotten. However, Parsons adds the uneasy insight that technology and science, although forming vital ingredients of modern medical practice, are bound to interfere with the university-trained doctor's obligation to put the welfare of the patient above all other goals. In an article entitled 'Research with Human Subjects and the "Professional Complex", first published in the late 1960s, he argues that the problem of an increasing 'professional complex' is not confined to modern medicine. Rather, research-orientation emanating from progress of modern science enters into many types of traditional client–practitioner encounters. This suggests a contradiction between the doctor's obligation to use the best possible knowledge from science and technology, on the one hand, and the therapeutic ethic deriving from the ancient 'art of medicine', on the other hand. He writes:

> Medicine has lost many of its previous prerogatives to science as it bears on health and will lose more . . . Just as a large part of 'medical' physiology was taken over by natural science, so scientific jurisdiction over much of the earlier 'art of medicine' is beginning to be taken over by social science. (Parsons, 1970a, p. 288)

However, the social science which is so badly needed has not yet caught on as source of viable practice knowledge. The sameness-cum-difference characterising the doctor–patient relationship which, in turn, makes it a model of social systems is but an analytical abstraction. On an empirical level, *imbalance* prevails between an overdeveloped natural science component and an underdeveloped social science component. Unlike many medical sociologists, however, Parsons refrains from blaming the medical profession for the apparent contradiction between the scientific and the humane.

The distinction between the *analytical* level where he depicts the idealised social system, on the one hand, and *empirical* level of historical-political developments and beliefs on the other, saves Parsons from confining himself to taxonomical model-building (where most of his critics locate him). Nor does he content himself (like some of his critics) with 'diagnosing' undue authority of doctors while blaming them for the discrepancy between natural and social science in modern medical practice. He conjectures that the doctor–patient relationship is, at the same time, reciprocal and hierarchical.

The reciprocity idea is based on the economic exchange metaphor as between producer and consumer. While the doctor is not only a producer of care but also a consumer of the patient's willingness to be treated (and, eventually in some systems, also of the resulting fee which the patient pays), the patient emerges as a producer of the health service by the very token of consuming it. Parsons writes about the patient: 'The case of his being treated "purely" as an object, rather than as a partner, however "junior", becomes a limiting case, the point where his contribution is zero. Short of this he is not, for instance, just a "consumer" but to some degree a "producer" of health service' (1964, p. 338). To be sure, this is compatible with a basically *unequal* relationship within the doctor–patient dyad. The doctor's technical and scientific expertise is more effective in treating severe incapacities than the patient's practical and lay knowledge, and the doctor also has available hospital and other medical means unavailable to the patient alone; not to use these would seem utterly foolish. Therefore, Parsons opposes the recent trend to define the doctor–patient relationship as 'fiduciary' following the general tendency towards democratisation in modern society. He sees the implicit albeit indispensable, asymmetry of the treatment situation endangered. Fiduciary relationships presupposing equals who take care of and share knowledge and resources with each other, may be all right even for educational settings; but bridging the obvious gap of competence and information (1951a, p. 441) through deliberate non-use of sophisticated knowledge by the doctor cannot be the adequate answer to the question of patient participation in therapy. He explains:

> This fiduciary responsibility . . . should be regarded as shared by sick persons . . . I fail, however, to see how it is at all possible to eliminate the element of inequality. To go too far in attempting to do so would surely jeopardize the therapeutic benefits of the vast accumulation of medical knowledge and competence which our culture has painfully built up over a very long period. (1975, pp. 267, 272)

The question of chronic illness

Although Mechanic's (1959) impression that Parsons' sick-role concept is unable to incorporate chronic illness is based on a misconception, its message is still widely taken for granted (Freidson, 1970a; N. Hart, 1986a). Even Gallagher (1976), who acknowledges the two-paradigm structure of Parsons' thought and corrects various errors of the secondary literature, feels that without suitable amendments Parsons' idea only applies to acute illness.

Parsons himself, in careful appreciation of Gallagher's views, points out that no contradiction between acute and chronic conditions needs to be perceived. If it is taken into account that the sick-role perspective focuses upon the process of re-establishing 'the capacity of the sick person to function, as the saying has been, "normally"' (1975, p. 259), the relative nature of the meaning of normality becomes the solution to the apparently overrated problem of chronic illness. He writes:

> There are many conditions which are, in any given state of the art of medicine, incurable. For them the goal of complete recovery becomes impractical. However, recovery is the obverse of the process of deterio-

ration of health, that is, a level of capacities, and in many of these chronic situations tendencies to such deterioration can be held in check by the proper medically prescribed measures based on sound diagnostic knowledge. (1975, p. 259)

Parsons cites his own mild diabetes as an example. Under suitable medication it obviously did not prevent him from continuing his professional pursuits with little infringement upon what one could consider a normal life of an academic. At the bottom of the conceptual issue, then, is the question of how permeable the boundary is between the acute and the chronic from a sociological point of view. Parsons himself clearly opts for relativism in this matter, and he stresses 'the relativity of "capacity", the maintenance of which is focussed in our meanings of health. The central question is, then, capacity for what?' (1960c, p. 166).

It is here that the distinction between physical prowess and intellectual prudence matters. Parsons imagines a sliding scale of different kinds of capacity required over the course of one's life cycle. In order to fulfil what, at each age and stage, are relevant normal expectations, the young may function more on a physical level, while the old may engage more in intellectual activity. This balance between capacity and incapacity makes rights and obligations themselves relative, and the sick role loses some of its rigour. The chronically ill are not well but strive towards as much approximation to residual normality as they can muster. Parsons emphasises that the healthy and the ill alike share the positive evaluation of health and the negative image of illness. It is the key to the doctor–patient interaction's importance as a social system, and he clarifies: 'This sharing involves a commitment to the attempt to recover a state of health or in the case of chronic illnesses or threats of illness to accept regimens of management that will minimize the current impairment of teleonomic capacity and future risks' (1978a, p. 76).

Chapter 3
The Deviancy Model

The incapacity notion of illness depicts 'failure to keep well' as a negative achievement. What is the positive achievement on which the counterpart notion focuses? This leads to the further question: what is the nature of deviance? Is deviance a positive goal achieved through particular types of nonconforming action which may either be learned through socialisation, or derive from residual non-socialised needs? Or is deviance an unanticipated consequence of normal purposive action such that economic or academic achievement, so to speak, produces as its *faux frais* a positive-achievement incentive to deviate? The idea of 'motivatedness' of illness suggests that the positive achievement involved is not one borrowed from other actions, and therefore it is not conditional upon failures of positive achievement elsewhere.

Much secondary literature, while crediting Parsons with 'the' deviance concept of illness, overlooks the fact that, in his dualist proposition, it is the 'other' important issue (namely, that linked with 'the "psychic" factor': 1951b, p. 459). For instance, Freidson (1966, 1970a) appears to overlook the duality while suggesting that the idea of the (deviant) sick role should be adapted to the patient's actual experiences. He justifies his suggestion with the allegedly anti-Parsonian proposition that the health–illness continuum is relative to a society's beliefs and values. The following comment on the above criticism emphasises that Parsons' crucial idea regarding deviance is misunderstood even by most authors who claim to use it:

> Parsons's capacity–deviance duality is reduced to a truncated capacity model under the misplaced label of illness as deviance . . . While the relationship between Parsons' theory of illness and psychoanalytic theory is nearly forgotten and Parsons has been effectively reduced to having introduced the sick rôle concept, the psychodynamic hypothesis about unconscious motivation leading to illness and accidents has been revived in writings which understand themselves as alternative to a Parsonian approach. (Gerhardt, 1979a, pp. 239–40)

34

The basic distinction is that 'health and illness are conceived, as human phenomena, to be both organic and socio-cultural' (Parsons, 1978a, p. 81). As outlined in the previous chapter, the locus of the socio-cultural – with health as a special case of purposive behaviour – is the person or personality system. Parsons adopts the capacity perspective in order to make clear what the specific deviance side of positive achievement is. He writes: 'In sum, . . . the relevance of the category deviance from the point of view of the sick role itself should be confined to the impact of motivated components in, on the one hand, etiology and therapy, and, on the other hand, maintenance of . . . illness' (Parsons, 1975, p. 260).

Indeed, 'that there [is] a component of motivatedness in almost all of illness' (1964, p. 331) brings up the question of specific diagnoses. Parsons answers it by referring to a 'complete continuum between the most completely "mental" of mental illnesses . . . through the various ranges of psychosomatic phenomena to the category of completely "somatic"' (1964, p. 331). The motivational component varies since 'a larger component of mental illness presumably operates through motivation' (Parsons, 1958/64a, p. 281). Chapter 10 clearly endorses psychosomatic medicine:

> To take the simplest kind of case, differential exposure, to injuries or to infection, is certainly motivated, and the role of unconscious wishes to be injured or to fall ill in such cases has been clearly demonstrated. Then there is the whole range of 'psycho-somatic illness' . . . Finally, there is the field of 'mental disease' . . . At one time most medical opinion inclined to the 'reduction' of *all* illness to a physiological and biological level in both the sense that etiology was always to be found on that level, and that only through such channels was effective therapy possible. This is certainly not the predominant medical view today. If it ever becomes possible to remove the hyphen from the term 'psycho-somatic' and subsume all of 'medical science' under a single conceptual scheme, it can be regarded as certain that it will not be the conceptual scheme of the biological science of the late nineteenth and early twentieth centuries. (Parsons, 1951a, pp. 430–1)

The message is that psychotherapy defines the very fabric of medical practice. Parsons' interests in Sigmund Freud's work first arose in the 1930s after he had completed *The Structure of Social Action*. In fact, in the introduction to the second edition of the book in 1949, he regrets its agnostic attitude towards psychological ideas. Henderson's view on the doctor–patient relationship as social system contains no reference to Freud or psychology. It is said to have been Elton Mayo (who loosely also belonged to the

Harvard Pareto circle) who pointed out to Parsons the importance of reading Freud (Schwanenberg, 1970, p. 195). In the following years (decade?) Parsons allegedly underwent psychoanalysis himself and may even have qualified as an analyst without ever practising (Schwanenberg, 1970, p. 195). In an autobiographical account on his intellectual development written in 1959, Parsons claims that he first encountered psychosomatic medicine in the 1930s when he conducted interviews for an empirical study with physicians at Harvard Medical School. A few years later (1964), in his recollection of how he became a medical sociologist, he explains that it was the problem of the *controllability* of illness which made him take into account Freud's writings. He contends: 'With respect to the ["conditional"] components, medical practice utilizes a complex technology, whereas with respect to the [motivated component], it involves processes of *social control, i.e.* acting upon the "intentions" of patients, as Freud above others has taught us, at unconscious levels' (1964, p. 335). The 'science of human relations', which both Henderson and Parsons hope to entrust with counteracting technology in modern medical practice, is (at least for Parsons) meant to derive from Freudian psychoanalysis. Although the latter enters Parsonian thinking only in what a critic calls 'suitably amended' notions (Dawe, 1970, p. 209), it is noteworthy that the sociological idea of illness in its – little recognised – 'positive achievement' side (expressed in the deviance model) embraces a psychodynamic view.

The aetiological process envisaged along these lines emulates the development of neurosis. A normality stage is described, merging the reality principle and the pleasure principle in what may be seen as a precarious equilibrium between control and pleasure. The process of falling ill includes the breakdown of superego functions and a breakthrough of ordinarily repressed id forces (dependency needs). The state of illness equals regression to the emotional state of early childhood.

The therapeutic process follows the reverse pattern of reestablishing control. A four-stage process redresses the balance between what we want and what we must by gradually increasing the instrumental, and decreasing the expressive input into the therapeutic relationship. The analogy with psychoanalysis is hard to overlook. Since illness is seen as 'the' most prominent type of deviance in modern industrial society, psychotherapy, the deliberately communicative therapeutic effort to restore sanity (normality), is the sociologically most viable form of 'controlled change' counteracting deviance.

The three stages of aetiology

The normality stage

Control and pleasure. The tripartite composition of any act (namely, the combination of cognitive, cathectic and evaluative endeavours) lets Parsons propose a 'suitable amendment' to Freud. He suggests that the internalisation of cultural controls involves also cognitive and emotional sides of the personality, not only moral or evaluative standards, as Urie Bronfenbrenner explains: 'First, Parsons criticises Freud for failing to recognise that identification results in the internalization not only of moral standards (the superego) but also the cognitive and expressive features of the parent and through him of the culture as a whole' (1961, pp. 199–200). Accordingly, Parsons perceives the influence of society upon a child's developing self as much more pervasive – and less tied to the anachronistic heritage of archaic 'primordial horde' imagery – than Freud saw himself able to outline in his own writings on society and culture. 'Yet we may wonder what is lost in altering Freud's idea of introjection . . . to that of straight internalization', remarks D. Atkinson (1971), attempting to present a radical alternative to Parsonian orthodoxy's focusing on societal consensus.

What Freud lacked, in Parsons' view, is 'a systematic analysis of the structure of social relationships in which the process of socialization takes place' (Parsons, 1955a, p. 104). That is to say, Parsons wishes to amend Freud's views regarding the childhood roots of adult sociability. He advocates separating the *Gesellschaft* (social system) from the *Gemeinschaft* (family) social bonds (Tönnies, 1887) in order to overcome Freud's alleged inner-psychological standpoint where family and society are merely the outside world to a 'psychic apparatus'. The criticism focuses on the fate of emotional forces:

> The second problem of Freud's theory concerns the relation of cathexis or affect to the superego. In a sense, this is the obverse of its relation to cognition. The question here is perhaps analogous to that of the transmission of light in physics: how can the object's cathectic significance be mediated in the absence of direct biological contact? Indeed, embarrassment over this problem may be one source of the stressing of sexuality in Freudian theory, since sexuality generally involves such direct contact. (1952/64, p. 24)

Cathexis or affect, of course, are related to pleasure. What, then, is pleasure? Enno Schwanenberg, whose account of Parsons' action theory is based on personal discussions during an extensive visit to Harvard in the 1960s as well as on thorough study of the literature, sums up the idea of 'pleasure mechanism' as follows:

> Pleasure is the preferred example of a generalised media which serves hierarchical control. Pleasure is a symbolic medium which is not tied to specific organs or specific objects of gratification but – referring to Olds' psycho-physiological investigations of the reward center in the brain of rats – is a central organ-neutral general mechanism which makes available to the personality the energy and capacities of the organism and, at the same time, controls the activities of the organism for the purpose of maintaining a functioning psychological system. Since the organisation of personality predominantly consists of learned cultural patterns, the pleasure mechanism exerts normative controls over the organism. Affect is an analogous control mechanism between social systems and personality. (1970, p. 172)[10]

This notion of 'pleasure mechanism' refers to normal adults' exchange of labour and discipline for esteem and power. Role compliance avails them of the support and authority bestowed on conforming members through society's reward system. The pleasure incorporated in the 'pleasure mechanism', however, is not the unlimited need fulfilment associated with Freud's pleasure principle: rather, the pleasure mechanism's pleasure side is intimately related to the opposite force, control. In other words, one's efforts of 'pulling oneself together' are what eventually leads to pleasure. But this still concerns a socially viable form of what Freud called *libido*. Parsons understands it as 'exchange media'; he writes:

> It is interesting that Freud in talking about the libido often spoke of an 'economic' aspect. Though, so far as I know, he was completely innocent of any knowledge of technical economics, I think there was a fundamental correctness in this usage, because of the analogy . . . that pleasure is to the 'economy' of behavioural energy as money is to that of societal economic 'production'. (1960/64a, p. 117)

It is on this basis that Parsons rejects Freud's distinction between the pleasure principle and the reality principle (1958/64b, p. 89). He claims (in one of his autobiographical accounts) that the question of economic motivation, self-interest versus collectivity interest, was triggered by his interest in psychology in the 1930s (1959, p. 9). It will be hypothesised here that in the middle 1930s – although his first acquaintance with psychology concerned psychoanalysis – it was not Freud's work with which he first became familiar but that of an emigré from Vienna, Franz Alexander, who came to Harvard while being connected with the Chicago Institute of Psychoanalysis. Alexander conducted a research project on criminality in the Boston area (Alexander and Healy, 1935). His book, *The Medical Value of Psychoanalysis*, published in England as well as the USA in 1932, undertakes to explain Freudian theory to an English-speaking audience. As an introduction to the influx not only of the ideas of psychoanalysis into the Anglo-Saxon world but also of the analysts themselves, who had to flee from their native Germany and Austria, this book tries to make Freud's teachings particularly appealing and non-controversial. In particular, Freud's primordial-horde theory of culture, mass-psychology interpretation of anti-Semitism and repetition–compulsion hypothesis of neurosis are completely left out of the picture. Alexander delineates a theory of psychosomatic illness identifying psychological forces with those of the central nervous system. He focuses on the cortex as the apex of health and illness: 'The connection of the cortex with the visceral organs through the sympathetic and para-sympathetic system is sufficiently well known and this connection implies that essentially every physiological process, in whatever part of the body it takes place, can potentially be influenced by psychological factors' (Alexander, 1932, pp. 175–6).

This idea of psychological power lodged in the brain over the organs is emulated in Parsons' idea of hierarchy between personality system and organism. It ties in with reciprocally related control and pleasure characterising the fourfold hierarchy of systems. Asked by Schwanenberg what a short definition of control could be, Parsons 'explained that it meant the integration, from a higher-system level, of the variability within a lower system' (Schwanenberg, 1970, p. 154). In other words, control is synonymous with forces which guarantee *order*. On a psychological level, this may involve repression of forces, organic or otherwise low level, which disturb the picture of order. Alexander's account of psychoanalytic thinking again seems to convey the same idea:

> One part of the personality accepts the code of education and becomes a representative of demand of society and this part Freud called the superego . . . The existence of the superego explains how in every form of civilization there is a self-regulating or self-restrictive force in the individual which is indispensable for the social order . . . Repression, in contrast to conscious rejection, is a process of inhibition which arises on a deeper level of personality . . . and saves the conscious personality from becoming aware of a painful conflict . . . This unconscious censoring function we ascribe to the superego. Repression, in contrast to conscious rejection, is a process of inhibition which arises on a deeper level of personality . . . and saves the conscious personality from

becoming aware of a painful conflict . . . This unconscious censoring function we ascribe to the super-ego. Repression is consequently based on a kind of unconscious censorship which reacts automatically to unacceptable tendencies . . . We have to assume that it operates schematically, is incapable of subtle differentiation and reacts uniformly to certain emotional factors in spite of their actual and sometimes important differences. (Alexander, 1932, pp. 92, 101–3)

Such clear-cut delineation of the principle of repression should not be mistaken as what Freud, in fact, originally devised. His was a more ambivalent notion of the superego, as the following passage from 'The Ego and the Id' documents: 'The derivation of the super-ego from the first object-cathexes of the id . . . brings it into relation with the phylogenetic acquisitions of the id and makes it a reincarnation of former ego-structures which have left their precipitates behind in the id' (Freud, 1922/61, p. 48).

The dual meaning of motivation.   In his criticism of Freud, Parsons emphasises that pleasure has a dual nature. On the one hand, the 'pleasure system' is the principal link between personality emanating from membership in society and culture, and biochemical and physiological processes of the organism. It thus constitutes the principle of interactional gratification of acceptable need dispositions, and repression of non-acceptable needs. Because the 'pleasure principle is itself a mechanism of control – a way of imposing order on still lower-level processes and "needs" of the living system' (Parsons, 1960/64a, p. 125), it incorporates social constraints. This pleasure is built into what Parsons calls need dispositions: that is, socialised motives to achieve legitimate permitted ends acceptable, mandatory or typical for the adult actor (Parsons, Shils and Olds, 1951/62).

On the other hand, motivation also is the undifferentiated force driving the individuals towards fulfilment without too much regard to their social environment. The latter state of motivation characterises 'pre-social' or, rather, 'more generalised motivational structures [which] are laid down in early childhood' (1960/64a, p. 103). Referring to Freud's assumptions with a terminological caveat, Parsons admits that they are sexual. He writes:

In a *genetic* sense, . . . the system in which the erotic component is central remains at the 'root' of [the actor's] whole personality system. It is this circumstance which underlies the element of truth in Freud's conception of the "sexual" – I prefer to say erotic – basis of all the neuroses. (1960/64b, pp. 303–4)

The process by which the former type of motivation (namely, that characterised by need-dispositions) develops from the latter type (namely, that characterised by more or less sexual or erotic unsocialised needs or even drives or instincts) is what Parsons calls the 'socialization process'. Its aim is to replace the undifferentiated motivational needs of sexual and/or erotic impulses (Parsons omits Freud's reference to destructive forces, however) by the refined differentiated need dispositions of the adult. They make an individual's behaviour acceptable to a well functioning environment in, as Parsons prefers to say, an industrial society. It ought to be remembered, in a Freudian frame of reference, that if unsocialised is replaced by socialised motivation, the former is not destroyed but confined to the unconscious where motivational forces represent the id. The process of motivational channelling and segregation of ego and id takes place in *families* in all known cultures. This universal circumstance, according to Parsons as well as Alexander, is crucial for understanding the origin as well as the cure of illness.

The crisis of cathexis

Collapse of control and realisation of unconscious motivtion. The function of the superego is two-fold: it selects norms from the environmental scene and incorporates them in the person's action repertoire; the fulfilment of these norms means gratification or absence of punishment from others. It further selects people and things ('objects') from environmental settings and incorporates them in the person's attachment repertoire; emotional ties with these 'objects' produce gratification of need dispositions. Parsons calls this the 'cathectic mode of orientation': 'Cathexis, the attachment to objects which are gratifying and rejection of those which are noxious, lies at the root of the selective nature of action' (Parsons *et al.*, 1951/62, p. 5). Sickness, as a generalised motivational deficit, is likened to deliberate though unconscious withdrawal of cathexis through a breakdown of superego functioning. In an analogy to economic thinking,[11] Parsons emphasises how similar it is to Keynes' idea of voluntary unemployment. There workers are unable or unwilling to spend their energy on work, and it is not that they are pushed out of the labour market against their will. Parsons clarifies:

> It is very suggestive that libido or some such concept may be a category analogous to labour commitment; it is energy originating in the organism which is suitable and available for motivating action-commitments

in social roles . . . This is to say there may be general states of 'withdrawal of cathexis' which are closely analogous to the famous Keynesian 'voluntary unemployment'. (1960/64a, pp. 122–3)

In this context, the discrepancy between obligations and gratifications may be resolved in two ways: first, by reducing one's role performance (which, however, may lower one's experienced gratification due to increasing negative sanctions received); second, by opening the floodgates giving access to repressed sources of gratification experienced in early childhood such that pleasure-principle forces of the id come to govern overt adult behaviour. The latter, one may notice, resembles Freud's idea of the genesis of neurosis; the former, perhaps, comes close to Freud's interpretation of melancholia.[12] In illness, Parsons sees both possibilities combined. 'So far as it is motivated . . ., it is an escape from the pressures of ordinary life', making for 'strategic expression of deviance' (Parsons and Fox, 1952b, p. 32), for two reasons:

First, because our culture enforces an unusually high level of activity, independence and responsibility on the average individual; and, second, because it connects so closely with the residua of childhood dependency (which, we may suggest, are more intensive in our society than in many others, because of the peculiar structure of our urban family. (Parsons and Fox, 1952b, p. 32)

In Parsons' article on the illness side of the American way of life, the scope of reasons for such 'strategic expression of deviance' is broadened. He suggests that the 'general upgrading to higher levels of responsibility' (1958/64a, p. 281) is due to the general conditions of the modern world, that is 'the development of industrialization, urbanism, high technology, mass communication and many other features of society'. In other words, behind the mechanism of falling ill supposedly lies the notorious change from *Gemeinschaft* to *Gesellschaft* (Tönnies, 1887), accompanying the change from agrarian to industrial society. According to Durkheim, because the transformation from mechanical to organic solidarity fails to take place in modern society, crisis ensues (with egoist and anomic suicide seen as symptoms of this crisis: See Durkheim 1895, 1897). Parsons, in the same vein, sees the modern individual's lack of capacity to fulfil his or her all-time high responsibilities as an unanticipated consequence of the development of modern society. The urban nuclear family (unlike the extended family of yesteryear) and the industrial workplace (unlike the traditional artisan's workshop) are unable to provide sufficient nurture and attachment opportunities to render one's normal role functioning universally gratifying and worthwhile. Illness as a widespread contemporary social phenomenon therefore suggests a crisis of cathexis.

The mechanism of breakdown of superego controls, and subsequent breakthrough of formerly repressed tendencies towards more or less unlimited pleasure, is regarded by Schwanenberg as surfacing of *anti-control*. He contends:

> The case of anti-control is presented to the theory of action by psychotherapeutic empirical issues where system processes on the lower psychological level – where conditionality is represented more strongly – are drawn into a pathological vicious circle and break through the normal controls, which are issued and realised by the higher system. What then becomes dominant are motivational elements of the lower system which independently assert their own 'regressive' order. (Schwanenberg, 1970, p. 155)[13]

It is not clear from Parsons' few remarks in what way the crisis of cathexis impinges upon the individual. Either strain creates an excessive demand for compliant behaviour which the individual cannot fulfil without exhausting his or her capacity to tolerate insufficient gratification, or certain persons whom one might call neurotics have weaker internalised controls (and/or stronger emotional drives) which, in turn, make them more likely to suffer a breakthrough of repressed dependency needs.

The first of these explanations refers to the capacity model's use of the stress metaphor and may also be found in the more modern life-event approach.[14] The latter explanation refers to personality syndromes which single out certain 'accident-prone' or 'illness-prone' people. 'Such people', explains Parsons, 'may unnecessarily expose themselves to the risk of such accidents. Probably somewhat similar considerations apply to such fields as infections, and, indeed, to the degenerative diseases like cancer' (1975, p. 260). Such propensity to fall ill, in psychoanalytic terms, is typical for neurotic types of personality which, in turn, derive from childhood trauma. Parsons writes: 'Because the internalization of the nuclear family is the foundation of personality structure, I suggest that *all mental* pathology roots in disturbances of the relationship structure of the nuclear family as impinging on the child' (1958/64a, p. 264). At the bottom of such personality disturbance is the 'need for love' as the apex of one's 'relational needs' (1958/64b, p. 82). That is to say, the unconscious motivation to fall ill is stronger in those persons who, because of trauma or deprivation in childhood, have developed relatively weak superego controls. This makes them less able to repress their pre- or anti-social needs and thus more prone to 'catch' an infection or fall victim to a non-infectious disease.

How, we may ask, does this work? The exact mechanism would remain mysterious if it were not supplied by Alexander's simplified version of Freud's teachings. Alexander insists that although psychic energy is centralised in the brain (cortex), it can find its outlet in the body's organs and functions through a mechanism of selective endowment with tension management. He credits Freud with his conjecture:

> Freud, and more especially his follower, Ferenczi, drew the bold conclusion, again on detailed observation, that practically all parts and functions of the body can be used to express emotion. The use of the striated muscles of the face and extremities is only one special case in which an idea or an emotion influences the function of the organs. Theoretically, however, all organs can be used to express emotions or to release psychic tensions. The anatomical and physiological basis of these innervations is well established. Through the peripheral and vegetative nervous system all portions of the body are directly or indirectly connected with the cortex. Psychogenic disturbances of the stomach or heart are no more mystical than the stimulation of the lachrymal sac by melancholy thoughts. (Alexander, 1932, pp. 67–8)

The 'wish to fall ill': endowment or contingency?   One problem shows a loose end of Parsons' thought. The incidence of treated illness is known to be considerably higher for women although death rates are higher for men of nearly all age brackets. Parsons makes no claim that the organ neurosis theorem which he adopts from Alexander (1932) – cited from the *Fundamentals of Psychoanalysis* and *Psychosomatic Medicine* published in 1949 and 1950 – applies to the sexes differently. At the same time, the strain hypothesis is presented in a male and a female version. The 'regressive motivational structure in the psychological sense' stemming from 'the residues of the pre-oedipal mother-child relationship, that phase of which Freud spoke as involving the "first true object attachment"' (1958/64a, pp. 285–6) has different intensity, if not different meaning, for men and women. Parsons repeatedly focuses on the 'American dilemma' which is more marked for the male sex and therefore should make adult adaptation to role expectations far more difficult for men than for women. The latter, at least, may retain their gender identification with the mother (and her expressive role), while the man has to completely overcome and change into the opposite sex-role identification from that of early childhood. Parsons and his co-authors state in the

Working Papers: 'Put a little differently, the boy must proceed farther and more radically on the path away from expressive primacy toward instrumental primacy. He is, therefore, subject to greater strain' (Parsons, Shils and Bales, 1953, pp. 98–9).

Why, we may ask, does this not predetermine men to become more rather than less ill? If the motivation to deviance originates in repressed dependency needs surfacing during a breakdown of behavioural controls after a spiral of 'vicious circles', would not men be worse off in any case? Either they must have more repressed dependency needs (this would be because of their heavier burden of self-discipline under the auspices of the 'American dilemma' which forces them to repress their dependency much more strongly), or they experience more strains because their obligation to fulfil primarily instrumental expectations leaves them more precariously craving for nurture from others. Within Parsons' approach, it appears, the contradiction cannot be solved by taking into account what he said. On an analytical level he must postulate what on an empirical level cannot be validated: namely, that men tend to experience more illness than women. This leaves open whether men's 'wish to fall ill' is markedly stronger than that of women. If the answer is 'Yes', a crucial piece in Parsons' argument ought to be why they then fall ill less often. If the answer is 'No', one would have to look for a different set of explanations. One should, however, acknowledge that Parsons, if unsuccessfully, attempts to reconcile Mowrer's idea of the 'American dilemma' (1950) with Freud's idea of the vicissitudes of the male and female Oedipus complex.

Within Parsons' own lines of thought, one hypothesis seemingly resolves the contradiction. Despite their obvious privilege, women experience typical educational circumstances which may explain their higher sickness rate. Let us follow this hypothesis briefly with a quote from *The Social System*: 'We know that dependence on the mother is particularly intense in the American kinship system, and we also know that emancipation from that dependence is particularly important for the adult in an achievement-oriented individualistic society. Too abrupt and drastic a transition might involve intolerable strain with neurotic consequences' (Parsons, 1951a, p. 241).

The question becomes whether women suffer 'too abrupt and drastic a transition' between early and later stages of emotional development. A time when women are subject to setbacks as compared with men is the end of puberty and beginning of what Freud (and occasionally Parsons, too) calls the genital phase: at this point, male students are likely to get ahead of their female co-students in academic and other areas of achievement. Women, at least in modern American society, drift into conflict between desire and capacity for instrumental achievement at school and at work, on the one hand, and the sex-role based expressive wish to have and raise a family, on the other (Parsons, 1942d). But would this late transition from latency to adulthood hold enough danger of being 'too abrupt and drastic' for the average woman to end up with a predilection for neurosis in her personality? Since no other plausible hypothesis seems to be raised in Parsons' work which could account for women's higher incidence of illness, we are left to accept that this is what he proposes. It is not difficult to realise that this 'explanation' is far from convincing. Parsons himself endorses Freud's emphasis on early childhood as crucial period of the genesis of neurosis. The end of latency, however, can hardly be taken for early childhood. So would women have precursors of what happens at the verge of their adulthood in their early childhood experiences? If this is so, then it might be difficult to argue at the same time that little boys bear more of the brunt of what Parsons – supposedly following O. H. Mowrer (Bronfenbrenner, 1961) – calls the 'American dilemma'.

The state of illness

If illness is the fulfilment of positive achievement motivation, what is achieved? This achievement, undoing adult identifications, produces regression to an early-childhood stage of love dependency.

To complement his theory of conversion of undifferentiated primary needs into differentiated secondary need dispositions, Parsons introduces a generalised need-disposition for conformity (Parsons, Shils and Olds, 1951/62, p. 144). It represents the actor's willingness to realise his need-dispositions rather than his needs. As its counterpart, Parsons introduces an *alienative* need-disposition making for a generalised component of any specialised motivation *not* to do what one is told. The two generalised need-dispositions are seen as parts of a basically ambivalent generalised attitude to societal expectations. Projected on to the dichotomy of passivity versus activity, they yield a fourfold classification of types of deviance (1951a, p. 257). Among them, the passivity-alienation cell labelled 'withdrawal' represents illness. With an added dimension of 'focus on social object' as distinct from 'focus on norms', the withdrawal box splits into the two alternatives 'compulsive independence' and 'evasion' (1951a, p. 259). Parsons writes about the actor: 'If . . . he is passively inclined, his tendency will be, not aggressively to force a "showdown" but avoid exposure to uncongenial expectations on alter's part, to be *compulsively indepen-dent*, in the extreme case to break the relationship altogether by withdrawing from it' (1951a, pp. 259–60).

This amounts to saying that 'the American pattern of illness is focussed on the problem of capacity for achievement by the individual person' (1958/64a, p. 286), namely, it is so disposed by *negating* it. Such negation is achieved through a state of combined passivity, irresponsibility, dependency and helplessness. Illness thus becomes a *mental* state of withdrawal from cathexis bordering on what has often been described as melancholia, or – to use the modern term although it carries a slightly different meaning – *depression*. From this vantage point, it may be interesting to note that Parsons' mentor, Alexander, in his post-1945 re-writing of *Medical Value of Psychoanalysis*, namely, his now classic writings on psychosomatic medicine, made 'organ neurosis' the apex of an often-quoted '*holy seven*' of supposedly *psychosomatic* illnesses such as rheumatoid arthritis, asthma, ulcerative colitis and others (1949, 1950).

Two Freudian or, in a broad sense, psychoanalytic concepts fit into this framework. Parsons makes extensive use of the assumption that patients extract *secondary gain* from being ill (having their needs for irresponsibility, passivity and so on fulfilled). He also ventures the idea that from an impulse to share their secondary gain of negated achievement with anyone in their environment, patients would be tempted to *seduce* others, even their physicians, into their amenable state (1951a, p. 460; 1958/64a, p. 288; 1964, p. 335).

There are two striking aspects of this conceptualisation. Only the presumably pleasant 'achievement' of withdrawal, refusal to cooperate, lack of feelings of responsibility and so on is mentioned. The unpleasant or threatening aspects of suffering pain, being humiliated by not being able to walk, talk or use the toilet are not taken into account. The individual is visualised as one who, more through the force of social controls than through the free will of a rational being, wants to remain active and successful in an achieving society. The underlying *image of man* is much more one of the person 'walking on the vulcano of his unconscious personality' (Alexander, 1932, p. 81) than Parsons himself seems to openly endorse. Should he not have taken more seriously his own reservation against Freud where he criticised him for underestimating the importance of sublimation (Parsons, 1960/64a, p. 103)?

The second astonishing omission in Parsons' conceptualisation is the following: he fails to see the danger of impoverishment and deprivation in illness in modern (especially American) society.

While realising how pleasant – albeit temporary – exemption from work (everyday roles) is for the well, he fails to notice the threat of hardships for those finding themselves unable to retain their income. It seems to have escaped his gaze that the individual wishes to remain respectable, and that patients may suffer loss of reputation associated with passivity and withdrawal from responsibility.

Therapy and the treatment process

Since aetiology is an 'achievement' of deviance (negating, of course, the goals as well as the means of 'normal' achievement), therapy is geared towards re-establishing a normal non-alienative achievement orientation. Since the person is a member of a society which is held together by constraint and conformity, and the breakdown of superego controls lets loose the repressed craving for dependency, therapy aims at (or resembles) resocialisation of the person into fully-fledged adult status. After having been temporarily reduced to a childlike existence of carefree passivity, the individual is now cajoled into active participation in his or her own being re-funnelled into society's rat race.

Parsons' view of therapy is heavily influenced by the self-image psychotheraphy has held since its early days. Since the turn of the century, psychoanalysis has claimed to be a medical specialty avoiding the shortcomings of traditional specialised medicine. Three issues characterise this standpoint:

(a) the idea that therapy is a form of social control, an example of the four-stage socialisation process;
(b) identification of psychotherapy with medical practice such that the 'art of medicine' figures as 'unconscious psychotherapy';
(c) a basic contradiction between the concepts of individual and society leading to the 'Hobbesian problem of order' receiving a Hobbesian solution.

Identification of therapy and social control

The four functional categories, it may be remembered, are to explain the differentiated nature of social structure's existence. Through the fourfold division of labour between its subunits' contributions to its perpetuation as a whole, any system's *raison d'être* is meant to be explained. While one of Parsons' mentors, the

British anthropologist A. R. Radcliffe-Brown, defined the function of an element of a structure through its contribution to the structure's continuity (1935/52), Parsons separates four functional imperatives corresponding to four basic survival problems of social entities. These four problems are goal attainment, adaptation, integration, and pattern maintenance (this last, also called latency, safeguards the continuity of the structure over time through tradition and education). The all-pervasive nature of the functional categories for Parsons' notion of society has often been commented on: for instance, the economist Chandler Morse writes:

> The four functional imperatives, or problems, operate at both a micro-analytic and a macro-analytic level in the Parsonian model. At the micro-level they purport to specify the phases through which *individual actors* in a small action system and the action system as a whole must progress during an action cycle. At the macro-level the imperatives provide a means of (a) allocating roles analytically among four functional sub-systems of any given system, and of (b) sorting out the input–output flows among these sub-systems. (1961, p. 116)

Whereas in *The Social System* the four imperatives play a lesser role than in some of the later works (e.g., *Economy and Society*), the fourfold classification appears prominently for the first time *in reverse order* in the *Working Papers on the Theory of Action* (Parsons, Shils and Bales, 1953). Mechanisms of social control, however, are already explained as following what is later named the L-I-G-A scheme in an article on the doctor–patient relationship published in 1951, and one by Parsons and Fox on medical practice and the urban family (1952b). The four stages of permissiveness, support, denial of reciprocity and conditional rewarding and sanctioning which, from the *Working Papers* onwards come to be identified as the phases of social control, are explained as the four stages of the therapeutic process.

Parsons describes the four phases, in actual fact, only for the doctor's attitude, but it takes little to extract from his wording the experience of the *patient*:

> In the first place, there must be *permissiveness*: allowing, even encouraging the patient to express deviant ideas, wishes, and fantasies . . . The second . . . is . . . *support*: a more holistic kind of acceptance . . . This . . . consists in valuing the sick actor . . . as a bona fide member . . . It becomes doubly necessary that the permissive-supportive aspects of the therapeutic process should not stand alone . . . The therapist must frustrate desires by refusing the looked-for reciprocation . . . Concomitantly or increasingly the therapist *introduces conditional*

rewards . . . for the patient's good work in the therapeutic situation . . . Ideally speaking, the patient gradually gives up his deviant orientation and comes to embrace maturity in its stead. (Parsons and Fox, 1952b, pp. 40–1)

Seen from another angle, therapy for the patient means a learning experience which functions as social control:

Incapacitated and emotionally disturbed; relieved of the weighty responsibilities of the well world; removed in large part from the custodianship of his family and other significant actors who would be likely to reinforce or exacerbate his psychosomatic withdrawal – the ill individual comes to live for a while in a medical-dominated sphere. Here, he is granted nurture and sustenance; but never so much as to balance out the heavy impress of deprivation, subordination and loneliness to which he is also subject. These are the penalties which give impetus to the patient's desire to re-achieve wellness: the challenges to which he responds (ideally-speaking) by re-embracing the world of health. (Parsons and Fox, 1952b, p. 43)

From the *doctor*'s point of view, the sequence of four stages of the therapeutic process also outlines permissiveness, support, selective rewarding and reinforcement. A manipulative undertone may be heard in the following:

The permissive and supportive treatment of the sick person, by giving him what he wants, undercuts the alienative component of the motivational structure of his illness. He finds it much more difficult to feel alienated toward social objects who treat him with kindness and consideration than he would otherwise be disposed to feel . . . At the same time the element of dependency, through 'transference', is the basis of a strong attachment to therapeutic personnel, which can then be used as a basis of leverage to motivate the therapeutic 'work' which eventually should result in overcoming the dependency itself . . . Building on this, then, the active work of therapy, adapting to the fundamental conditions of the biological and psychological states of the patient, can take hold and operate to propel toward recovery (Parsons, 1958/64a, pp. 287–8).

The idea of reciprocal four-stage social control is stressed in all publications after *The Social System* focusing on medical practice as a topic, or as an example for system processes (1951b, p. 457ff.; Parsons, Shils and Bales 1953, p. 242, etc.; see also Gallagher, 1976, p. 208). It is still present in Parsons' last work on the health–illness issue. In his paper discussing the teleonymy proposition (1978a), he gives the following description: permissiveness of the physician presupposes that he acts under the affective-neutrality pattern; his support attitude resembles the 'parental concern for the welfare of young children who have not yet attained the capacities for autonomous performance in many areas'; denial of reciprocity 'takes the form of refusing to respond to various kinds of overtures that patients make towards the therapist, for example, defining the therapist . . . as love object or as target of inappropriate hostility and aggression'; and manipulation of rewards means 'to reinforce the patient's own attainment of insight into his condition and the motivational background manifested in such insight' (1978a, pp. 77–8).

When we ask why therapy and socialisation are similar, to answer that they both are processes of social control would be tautological. The reason is that both lead out of early childhood, with illness representing a state of regression to the stage of love-dependency nurture. Indeed, this is the second of the three stages of pre-latency childhood development following the Freudian triad of oral, anal and Oedipal phases. Renamed oral dependency (pleasure dependence), love dependency (love attachment) and Oedipal phase, they are characterised by identification with the mother as source of well-being (oral dependency), sex role identification as different from (or same as) but dependent on nurturant mother (love dependency), and internalisation of sex-generation divisions (Oedipal phase) (Parsons 1955a, pp. 35–131). Regression occurs: to the love-dependency stage where sex identification is embedded in the dependency-attachment relationship to an at once powerful and caring mother. This means that the family-relationship pattern of that childhood phase comes to dominate again the adult patient's expectations. It is this *isomorphy* between the patient's childlike wishes and the doctor's functioning as proxy parent which lies behind the identification of therapy and social control.

If in childhood socialisation the 'main structure of the personality is built up through . . . social interaction [and] develops through the internalisation of social objects and of the normative patterns governing the child's interaction' (1960/64b, p. 300), resocialisation in therapy must achieve just this.

The 'social system constituted by therapist and patient' is to recreate the social system constituted by mother and small child in order to recreate the development then achieved. The congruence of therapeutic and socialisation processes is possible because of structural congruence between the parent–child and doctor-patient dyads. Parsons writes:

For the patient to 'project' his internalized conceptions of earlier significant objects onto the therapist – and in this context, for the therapist's communications to have significant effect on the relevant aspects of the personality structure of the patient involved in his illness – it seems to be necessary to assume that these aspects of structure are congruent with current, though specialized, social relationships and, what is the second set of assumptions, that the relationships in the patient's life history in fact genetically derive from social or object-relations of the past. (1960/64a, pp. 114–15)

This re-enactment of early family ties in doctor–patient interaction, in fact, provides the 'leverage' – to use Parsons' own word (1952b, p. 40; 1958/64a, p. 288) – for the physician to achieve a cure for the illness. The psychoanalytic term which Parsons adopts to explain this is 'transference'.

'Unconscious psychotherapy'

Psychoanalysis in its therapeutic approach, according to Freud, is a 'technique' based on a 'pact' between the analyst and the patient's weakened ego (which, by the way, stands against a hostile alliance between the id *and* the superego). Freud contends, in his *Outline of Psychoanalysis*:

> The sick ego promises us the most complete candour – promises, that is, to put at our disposal all the material which its self-perception yields it; we assure the patient of the strictest discretion and place at his service our experience in interpreting material that has been influenced by the unconscious . . . This pact constitutes the analytic situation. (Freud, 1940/1964, p. 173)

There, however, begin rather than end the difficulties, as Freud is quick to assure us. One reason is, amongst others, that resistance against setting free unconscious repressed memories causes anxieties which act as a barrier against the progress of the cure. At the same time, transference interferes with the cure for which it also is a *sine qua non*. Freud goes on to write:

> This transference is *ambivalent*: it comprises positive (affectionate) as well as negative (hostile) attitudes toward the analyst, who as a rule is put in the place of one or other of the patient's parents, his father or mother. So long as it is positive it serves us admirably . . . The aim of pleasing the analyst and of winning his applause and love . . . becomes the true motive force of the patient's collaboration . . . Another advantage of transference . . . is that in it the patient produces before us with plastic clarity an important part of his life-story, of which he would otherwise have probably given us only an unsufficient account. And

now for the other side of the situation. Since the transference repro-
duces the patient's relation with his parents . . ., it almost inevitably
happens that one day his positive attitude towards the analyst changes
over into the negative, hostile one . . . The danger of these states of
transference evidently lies in the patient's misunderstanding their nature and taking them for fresh real experiences instead of reflections of
the past . . . It is the analyst's task constantly to tear the patient out of
his menacing illusion and to show him again and again that what he
takes to be new real life is a reflection of the past . . . Careful handling
of the transference on these lines is as a rule richly rewarded . . . The
method by which we strengthen the weakened ego has as a starting-
point an extending of its self-knowledge. (Freud, 1940/64: pp. 174–7)

Freud's main aim of psychotherapy, no doubt, is to strengthen
the ego in order to enable it to play a more prominent part in its
relationship with the superego as well as the id, on one side, and –
to use Freud's own term – the outside world, on the other.
Parsons' idea, however, is that it is mainly the superego which
needs strengthening against the id while the ego to a much larger
extent than Freud supposedly thought is conceived as structured
by and dependent upon the society-based superego.

For *Freud*, with regard to the unconscious, what matters is to
undo fixations of libido to object cathexes of early childhood which
have lingered into adulthood. Since repressed experiences, fanta-
sies and anxieties block the personality's development into a
mature 'psychical apparatus', the emotional and the object
cathexes of retarded drive representations have to be separated
through psychoanalysis. Only then can they be united either with
another object or emotion to which they *really* belong, or joined
together in a more enlightened way. In the process, the patient's
resistance against giving up his repressions is to be overcome. That
is, his countercathexis guarding the dangerous memories and
keeping them repressed must be weakened or bypassed by the
sensitive physician's channelling of transference, in particular
careful avoidance of countertransference.

For *Parsons*, however, the process is not so complicated. He
believes that the affective-neutrality rule automatically helps
physicians to avoid countertransference. This, in turn, allows them
to use transference in a way beneficial for the patient. The dangers
of getting lost in the jungle of unconscious motives which Freud so
vividly pictures during his whole career do not appear threatening
to Parsons. On the contrary, he assumes all medical practice has at
all times carried an element of psychotherapy. He goes so far as to
suggest that psychotherapy only brings into psychiatry characteristic aspects of medicine as such rather than having discovered
something original and precarious (1964, p. 331).

The element of 'unconscious psychotherapy' which Parsons locates in medical practice cannot, it seems, be directly traced in Freud's writings. Parsons himself argues that such aspects of therapy are the necessary counterpart of the unconscious-motivation nature of all illness insofar as it carries a psychiatric component:

> It is highly probable that, whether or not the physician knows it or wishes it, in practicing medicine skillfully he is always exerting a psychotherapeutic effect on his patients. Furthermore, there is every reason to believe that, even though the cases are not explicitly 'mental' cases, this is necessary. This is, first, because a "psychic factor" is present in a very large proportion of ostensibly somatic cases and, secondly, apart from any psychic factor in the etiology, because illness is always to some degree a situation of strain to the patient, and mechanisms for coping with his reactions to that strain are hence necessary, if the strain is not to have psychopathological consequences. (1951b, p. 459)

Parsons, no doubt, sees no reason to prove through detailed analysis of the psychotherapeutic endeavour as compared with medical practice why he sees himself justified in using the label 'unconscious psychotherapy'. At various points of *The Social System* he briefly mentions a few similarities between medical practice and psychotherapy. But one ought to note that the view of medical practice with which he compares psychotherapy in order to find the similarities is already an interpreted one. He enters into this comparison from the standpoint delineated by, for instance, Alexander (1932). What seemingly is a description of medical practice is thus already informed by the psychoanalytic perspective. The structuralist (pattern variable) and functionalist (social-control) scheme delineating the societal role of the doctor's work are, at most, only semi-independent from the psychotherapist's self-image. Three similarities between the structural-functional and the psychoanalytic view are obvious, and are explained below.

1. An element of *protection of the doctor against the patient* such that the latter may not successfully seduce the former into joint realisation of deviant motivation (and, presumably, jointly 'enjoying' the ill status). Parsons simply states that 'the same features of the physician's role, which are so important as protection of the physician himself, are also crucially important conditions of successful psychotherapy' (Parsons, 1951a, p. 461).
2. A similarity between the *kind of social control* realised by

psychotherapy as compared with that realised by medical practice in general and even with other types of deviance control. Since 'the mechanism of control of psychotherapy is one of a much larger class of such mechanisms' (1951a, p. 478), 'use of psychotherapy as an example is for purposes of convenience only' (1951a, p. 325).

3. A certain *share of psychological motivation* in the origin of any illness, irrespective of how 'mental' it is. This means that psychotherapy is part of medical practice in general because it *is* the procedure with which the unconscious *wish to fall ill* is to be treated. The 'general conclusion . . . [is] that a very important part of non- and pre-psychiatric medical practice is in fact "unconscious psychotherapy"' (1951a, p. 462). It suggests that where sociologists acknowledge unconscious motives to deviance, they may also have to acknowledge a potentially unconscious process of therapeutic help.

This leaves the question of what constitutes the 'art of medicine'. Parsons highlights a latent conflict between doctor and patient, on the one hand, by stressing the former's protection from the latter as an example of social control and, on the other hand, by recognising therapy as repression of inadmissible motivation to illness. Whatever this entails, it is not bound to be known by those who enact it. He clarifies:

> Psychotherapy to the militantly anti-psychiatric organic physician is like theory to the militantly anti-theoretical empirical scientist. In both cases he practices it whether he knows it or wants to or not. He may indeed do it very effectively just as one can use a language well without even knowing it has a grammatical structure. This has sometimes been called the 'art of medicine'. (Parsons, 1951a, p. 462 including footnote 16)

If Parsons argues, then, that 'therapy is beyond the range of direct ego function capacities but requires some kind of management of id functions' (1978a, p. 70), does he include the doctor in this idea of management of id involvement? Is unconscious therapy to be understood as interchange between the ids of *both* actors which has to be controlled? Does the 'art of medicine' consist in a doctor's taking into account not only what he *knows* about the patient's predicament but also what he feels, guesses, fears? To be sure, a grammatical structure consists of rules; in due course, this would mean that the doctor supposedly follows a more or less consistent body of rules even when he thinks he follows only hunches and his common sense. It would also mean, it appears, that by following his feelings and common sense in how to treat the patient, he follows what the sociologist might reveal as a consistent body of norms not hitherto clearly delineated. This would amount to saying that it is the sociologist who is needed to understand what the doctor does when he talks and (with the pattern-variable caveats) relates to a patient. It seems likely that Parsons here argues for the taking into account of *sentiments* which, it may be remembered, his mentor Henderson considered as the solution of modern medicine's problems.

If this were so, it means that Parsons identifies sentiments in the Pareto sense of classical sociological writing with emotions and cathexis in the Freudian sense. Although, taking the everyday meaning of the two words, sentiment and emotion may be identified with each other, closer analysis of the two terms within their original conceptual frameworks may reveal that they are not to be equated.

In any case, that emotion and its counterpart, communication, represent the personal side of illness and treatment is a standard argument in modern medical psychology. For instance, Shapiro (1960) argues that medical practice was a *placebo* during the entire history before modern natural science. Balint (1957) maintains that doctors *qua* role acquire an 'apostolic function' in the eyes of their patients as well as in their own view. It may tempt them into *moulding* their patients according to their expectations. Behind this is the idea that the placebo of 'unconscious psychotherapy' has always been a part of the 'art of medicine', especially when acquiring an 'apostolic function'. On the other hand, these ideas are used to denounce achievements of modern clinical medicine. 'Militantly anti-psychiatric organic physicians', to use Parsons' term, are charged with overlooking the social–psychological side of a patient's illness if they unduly focus on organic lesions.[15]

The undercurrent of presumptive deviance

While often being criticised for overestimating conformity and consensus (e.g., by Dahrendorf's notorious comparison with Huxley's terrifying Utopia), Parsons may not have taken consensus and conformity for granted. Schwanenberg works out three concatenated systems of control calling them, with a Parsonian term, 'lines of defence'. They safeguard society's functioning against tendencies to undermine it. The first is the 'hierarchy of systems' extending from organism to culture, where control means organisation of the system below next into orderly patterns of procedure. The second is the 'equilibrium system' which functions through learning and (re-)socialisation; it guarantees that a maximum number of conforming members are active at any time in a society. The third is the 'system of generalized media', in particular money, which facilitates communication but also represents control through 'conditional' deprivation (Schwanenberg, 1970, pp. 169–74).

If it is so necessary for Parsons to assert that order in society works, and that control is organised in three defence lines, it may not be far-fetched to suspect that he believes the ordinary society member's willingness to conform is not to be trusted. Three reasons may be given which suggest that Parsons envisages a basic dichotomy between the individual and society.

1. When doctors are said to need protection against the patient's tendency to seduce them into deviance, on the one hand, and when the patient is said to need to be treated tolerantly in order to find it difficult to refuse to give up the irresponsible state of illness, on the other hand, the relationship between doctor and patient appears to be one of covert *conflict* rather than consensus.
2. The generalised need-disposition for conformity which is behind norm conformity, based on specific need-dispositions, is a product of social learning. It derives from social expectations and constraints which have become internalised, and it structures goals which the individual sets for herself or himself. However, the counterpart of the generalised need-disposition for conformity, considering its *ambivalent* nature, is a generalised need-disposition for deviance. Although Parsons makes it plain that every actor has it – and hence may fall ill or become deviant in other ways – no satisfactory explanation is provided as to where it comes from. It certainly does not seem to be learned in the same way as its counterpart. The thought of parents teaching their children how *not* to fulfil society's norms seems to be beyond Parsons' ideas. It is only labelling theory, especially where it attempts to understand criminality in poverty-striken or lower-class milieux, which explains deviance through a combination of opportunity structures and learning experiences. But, alas, the latter explicitly rejects the view that deviance has motivational roots.
3. While 'vicious circles' clearly involve conflict with others, and of a deepening nature, it remains dubious whether this conflict emanates from the conformity with norms or whether an underlying current of conflict-prone deviancy motivation looms large in social interaction. The following amazingly detailed

description of a vicious circle leaves open this crucial question. Parsons writes in the deviancy chapter of *The Social System*:

> For example, alter, instead of recognizing the merit of a piece of work ego has done, may have shown marked disapproval, which ego felt was in contravention of the value-pattern with respect to competent achievement shared by both. Ego reacted to this with resentment which, however, he repressed and became compulsively anxious to secure alter's approval. This compulsive element in ego's motivation makes him excessively 'demanding' in his relation to alter. He both wants to be approved, to conform, and his need for approval is more difficult to satisfy because of his anxiety that alter may not give it. This in turn has an effect on alter. Whatever his original motivation to withhold the approval ego expected, ego has now put him in a position where it is more difficult than it was before for him to fulfill ego's expectations; the same level of approval which would have sufficed before is no longer sufficient. Unless a mechanism of social control is operating, then, the tendency will be to drive alter to approve even less, rather than more as ego hopes. (1951a, pp. 255–6)

It is evident that such a relationship is far from consensual although it still remains within the confines of conformity. Where, then, does the element of conflict come from which keeps the alter from giving the ego due approval, in the first place, and keeps ego from rectifying the deteriorating situation by laying open his resentment to alter?

The solution is that Parsons conceives of a dichotomy between the conformity-prone society which partly acts through internalised constraints, and remunerates its well members with power and prestige, on the one hand, and the basically anti-social anti-control individual who harbours deviancy motivation, on the other hand. The latter may at any time break the crust of superego controls whenever they are weakened by acrimonious vicious circles of ego–alter conflict. The main point made by Parsons in this context is that illness is always a product of deviant motivation; its presence documents beyond doubt that an individual is/was unable to control deviant motives. The very instance of falling ill thus bears witness to the 'wish to fall ill'. For anyone in the person's environment this then justifies exerting pressure on the sick to succumb to the demands of the well. This is used as 'leverage' to make the patient comply with whatever treatment is given by a doctor.

As a corollary, the demonstration of an unconscious motivation in illness implies the responsibility, if only unconsciously, of the afflicted for the disease. This suggests the question of guilt, and a verdict of 'blaming the victim' is not unlikely against Parsons. Indeed, this point was raised by the labelling approach. That Parsons for nearly three decades chose to completely disregard the writings of Lemert, Becker and their *'neoChicagoan'* followers only makes one suspicious about whether they held a convincing argument against him. By accusing him of not siding with society's 'underdog', they meant to argue that his conjecture of unconscious motivation made the patient automatically a victim of societal-control institutions.

Chapter 4
Structural-Functionalist Systems Theory and the Two Models of Illness

Illness – as social role and as motivated deviance – is categorised in two models, both belonging to the structural-functionalist systems theory which Parsons presents. Their common ground needs to be clarified. It is true that the voluntarism adopted by Parsons in his early writings and mostly abandoned with and after *The Social System* (Scott, 1963) is not what is present in one and absent in the other model? The 'unconscious wish' conceptualisation of illness might be understood as a return to his early voluntaristic thinking in the guise of his psychoanalytic leanings. But there is not enough evidence in the texts to substantiate this point.

How the structural-functionalist pledge comes to bear needs to be reconsidered in the light of the two models' addressing of the problem that sickness is not a matter of society (although its treatment is) but one of the individual's non-compliance with norms and values of responsible self-control. The two perspectives contribute to general sociological theory. Medical sociology after the Second World War addressed the political issue of the day: the question of whether a 'normal-but-sick' actor is sociologically conceivable. The emphasis placed on psychiatry as the main focus of such sociological interest makes one question what the place of psychiatry is and should be for sociology's analysis of sickness.

The two models revisited

Before the more general discussion, the relationship of the two models ought to be clarified. In pulling them together, it is argued that the capacity model elucidates the sociological interest in health whereas the deviancy model clarifies illness. Since, however, the issues are intertwined, so are the models representing them.

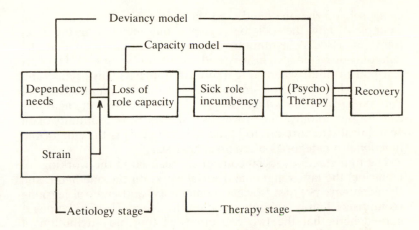

Figure 4.1 *Process diagram of Parsons' two-model idea of illness*

The breakdown of normality is first envisaged as withdrawal of the libido-like capacity to play roles. It suggests reactivation of this capacity through physician-role/sickness-role medical practice. At the same time, the deviancy model envisages the breakthrough of normally repressed dependency needs into active realisation (through passivity, as it were). It suggests the repression of these anti-social tendencies in a socialisation-like process of therapeutic interaction. The relationship between these two models is depicted in the diagram (Figure 4.1) adapted from Gerhardt (1979a). The flow of events is as follows: Dependency needs, which normally are neutralised by superego controls, under strain break loose and lead to loss of role capacity. This necessitates sick-role incumbency. This, due to insulating as well as reintegrative aspects, leads to re-establishing superego controls. These reinstate role capacity and once more instigate abandoning dependency needs in the interest of remaining a respected citizen in the eyes of one's significant others. The spoils of normality (that is, class, status and power) are thus conditional upon the willingness and, to a certain extent, ability to give up the intermittent indulgence in passivity and irresponsibility. Social equality necessitates reacquiring the full burden of self-control for modern self-propelled 'economic man'.

Within the dual conceptualisation of illness, the capacity model formulates the structural side whereas the deviancy model epitomises the functional side. The pattern-variable description of mirror-like similarity in orientational forms between the physician's role on the one hand, and the sick role on the other, is an example of how the sociologist goes about deciphering the 'anatomy' of a social institution. (It may be remembered that the 'anatomy of systems' in history and society was what L. J. Henderson had in mind when he gathered economists, historians, and others in his discussion group focusing on the ramifications of Pareto's *General Sociology*; see Heyl, 1968.) However, anatomy calls for physiology if the processes making for the continuity of an anatomical structure are to be understood. This is the side of the functionalist categories of systems analysis.

The four stages of social control are realised in the workings of medicine, the law, religion and social work, on the one hand, and the economy, politics, 'societal community' and cultural learning (comprising family, school, etc.), on the other. (It may be disregarded here that the two collections of fourfold attribution of institutions to the four functions seems not to end up with an uncontroversial four-cell matrix.)

As for medicine, where the therapeutic process follows the four-stage pattern, it is unclear which of the functions it represents. For the social system as a whole, it might be the adaptation, the integration or the latency function; all three cases may be argued. The capacity aspect (which lets Parsons very nearly agree with Gallagher's option for an adaptation, and against his own deviancy paradigm) points in the direction of economic activity characterising the adaptation function. The process aspect in therapeutic work re-establishing conformity through an experience (similar to learning) of social control points in the direction of the latency function. Third, since the very fabric of society's cohesion is jeopardised by illness, and since 'societal community' presupposes the health of its members, to place medicine with the integration function could also make sense.

In any event both the structural model based on the capacity notion and the functional model based on the deviancy notion draw upon different intellectual traditions. The former uses mainly thoughts taken up from Henderson, Cannon and other physiologists stressing the idea of homeostasis. The latter looks to psychoanalysis for guidance, especially psychosomatic medicine, and proposes a psychodynamic view. Both have in common that their point of reference is the *social order*: that is, one basic topic is the maintenance and perpetuation of the social structure through the processes which guarantee its existence. The other topic is how society's structural continuity is realised through the individuals who, in the last instance, make up its constituent members.

The main point, in both paradigms, is how medical practice works. The *capacity* notion sets out to show that medical practice is the 'eye of the typhoon' admidst the micro–macro whirls of social systems. The headline of Chapter 10, 'Social Structure and Dynamic Process: The Case of Modern Medical Practice' makes it clear that what Parsons envisaged in the 1930s still holds for his thinking in the 1950s. *The structure of social action*, he argued then, was normative orientations internalised by the actors which made up the motivational substratum of the social order. It is not only economic thinking (which sees every behaviour as an off-shoot of the profit motive) that governs social life: – this was the topic of his article 'Motivation of Economic Activities' (1940) and also of the essay on 'The Professions and Social Structure' (1939) which hails the *non*-business nature of medical norms and ethics. Again, in Chapter 10, he belabours the point that it is non-economic (or at least non-profit) orientations which characterise medical practice and may explain its particular normative–pattern set-up (with the two roles of physician and ill neatly symmetrical in pattern-variable terms). In the introduction he clarifies that he here wishes to apply what he has outlined in abstract terms throughout his book:

> It will perhaps help the reader to appreciate the empirical relevance of the abstract analysis we have developed if, in addition to the illustrative material which has been introduced bearing on many particular points, we attempt to bring together many if not most of the threads of the foregoing discussion in a more extensive analysis of some strategic features of an important sub-system of modern Western society. For this purpose we have chosen modern medical practice. (1951a, p. 428)

From the vantage point of how the social system works, and how it may be understood as a frame of reference explaining the exchange nature of social action, Parsons thus comes to endorse medical practice. Because it functions to treat and mostly cure illness, it provides the relevant angle from which to elucidate his abstract analytical perspective empirically. That the sick are re-turned to the ranks of the healthy, therefore, constitutes the point of departure for sociological analysis.

In similar fashion, albeit using different terms, the *deviancy* approach conceptualises the same problem. The deviancy para-digm is interested in how the pre- and possibly non-social motiva-tion surfacing during illness incumbency is tackled by the 'pre- and non-psychiatric' use of psychotherapy in medical practice. Since illness constitutes the typically modern (American) scourge among anti-social tendencies, if only following the increase of demands upon psychiatric (and physical) health in modern (American) economic life, medical practice must be the most important institution of social control. It safeguards economic success (as well as possibilities of reintegration after economic failure) by re-establishing conformity and sanity where they may have disappeared. If needs for dependency, passivity and irresponsibility have surfaced, if the crust of superego controls has been crushed or bypassed by primary motivation, medical practice through the therapeutic process re-establishes order.

Such primacy of therapy makes illness merely its other side. Within the structural framework, it is the breakdown of capacity which medicine repairs; within the functional, the breakthrough of uncontrolled forces. This view is different from what, for instance, the labelling perspective envisages. While it concentrates on how the afflicted become ill (and how evaluative judgments are involved in the predicament), Parsons focuses on how the institution functions which makes the unwell into newly healthy members of society.

In this vein, what matters about illness for Parsons is *how society treats it*; that is, how therapy as a social system goes about eliminating or curtailing it. What matters is the *social order*. Illness becomes a disturbing factor dysfunctional for the upkeep of order in society, lodged within the individuals' psychology. To be sure, illness in a psychological sense is of marginal interest to the sociologist; but as an issue of non-functioning in social roles it is at the same time of the utmost importance. The capacity for purposeful rational action belongs among the most general conditions of any system formation (therefore it is included among the functional prerequisites). Health, as Parsons phrases it, is the 'rock bottom' of the triad opportunity/education/health which safeguards the democratic-achievement structure of modern industrial society in the USA (1958/64a, p. 279). The issue, then, is that the social order works on the basis of powerful homeostatic mechanisms, and medical practice is meant to constitute one, if not 'the' most important one.

The contribution to general sociological theory

Critics such as Wrong (1961) castigate Parsons for embracing an over-socialised conception of humans. Likewise, D. Atkinson (1971) finds too much emphasis placed on the mechanisms of consensus, and too little on conflict. Even *within* a functionalist framework, as Coser's (1956) most insightful essay shows, a view on conflict as a source of consensus can be taken. This exacerbates Parsons' failure to perceive conflict as other than dysfunctional, and a source of structural disturbance. Offe (1976), one of the more recent critical voices, echoes the earlier reservations.[16]

It may contribute a new argument to this ongoing debate if a point is outlined here which justifies Parsons' views. In the introduction of this book, it was argued that the emergence of medical sociology after the Second World War in the USA and elsewhere was due to a new awareness in sociology of a mundane theoretical problem. Through the gruesome details surfacing in post-war media coverage of Gestapo terror in Nazi Germany and the mass murder in concentration camps, a hitherto taken-for-granted presupposition of theories of the social world became questionable. Although during the War conferences were held and books published analysing the Nazi regime with astonishing comprehensiveness, it may have been only after the battlefields were a thing of the past that the more theoretical problems emerged as urgent. That not everyone, for the sake of sociological theory, is normal and sane according to the laws of reason and logic, suitably amended by emotion, was to enter sociological thought and to become a more or less persistent topic.

It seems that Parsons perceived conflict as emanating from the repressed anti-social tendencies of the individual and therefore related to the health and illness issue. In this indirect way Parsons recognised that Fascism was a topic which sociology could not avoid. To be sure, he places the health and capacity issue at the very base of any system, no matter how micro or macro; health for him meant a reciprocity of social exchange which an anti-Semite certainly would refuse or undermine with Jews. Failure to respect reciprocity standards is viewed as illness. In his book on Parsons' political standpoint, Mitchell (1967) makes it clear that for Parsons democracy is equated with reciprocal interchange in systems; in this context, the use of economic metaphors is to highlight the exchange nature of social intercourse. In fact Homans (1961), who as a young student also belonged to Henderson's Pareto circle, epitomises this exchange view on society in his book *Elementary Forms of Social Behaviour* and Blau (1964) makes it the central piece of structural sociology. For Parsons, the political message is that liberal values are to be realised in a meticulous give-and-take which makes the individual repress selfish needs, and realise publicly approved common-good standards instead. The opposite – namely, compulsive obedience or uninhibited indulgence to sadist instincts – was perceived in the typical Nazi by most literature on Fascist Germany in the immediate post-war period. E. Simmel (1946) analyses anti-Semitism as mass psychopathology using psychoanalytic terminology. Schaffner (1948) in *Fatherland* analyses the German authoritarian family structure as a prere-quisite of the German nation's capacity to commit mass murder during the Nazi period. Schaffner's approach is related to Hork-heimer's (1936) application of psychoanalytic imagery to the analysis of the German traditional family's authority structure in relation to the then current Fascist regime.

Parsons defines health as the capacity for role conformity in reciprocal exchange, and illness as the breakdown of such capacity due to a breakthrough of primary motivation on a psychiatric scale. Would it not do his conceptualisations of consensus more justice if this background of his work was taken into account? Reviving his interest in medical practice from the 1930s, merging it with the topics of general sociology, he paid tribute to the then modern debate on prejudice and 'latent Fascism' using the insights on the intricacies of social systems which he had discussed with his late mentor and friend, Henderson. In this vein, he implicitly gives credit to his considerations in the Second World War period on how to interpret and overcome anti-Semitism (1942a) and how to bring about controlled social change in Germany (1945) which indeed were at that time political tasks of the immediate future.

Basically, the distinction between self-orientation and collective orientation is at the heart of the problem. Parsons' aim, according to Mitchell's carefully researched documentation, is to point out against alleged Marxist views that collectivity orientation matters more that self-orientation. That is, instincts and *homo homini lupus* ('man being man's wolfe', Thomas Hobbes' famous principle of unregulated society) albeit constrained by the forces of eco-nomic self-interest, are not the primary influences which hold society together. In this respect, D. Atkinson (1971) may be right in point out that Parsons did no more than underlay Weber's notion of motivation with a Freudian formula (although one might be reminded that Weber's notion of motivation is non-motivational, and that Freud is adopted in a truncated version). Nevertheless, Parsons addresses the issue raised by Durkheim that ours is a society of crisis where the necessary development towards organic solidarity is blocked by a crisis of the collective spirit. It may be tragic that he attempted to incorporate this idea of crisis of modern society into his systems theory through discussing the health–illness issue. In this he relied on immediate post-war gener-alisations of political psychology which, with hindsight, may appear partial and far-fetched.

The matter cannot be dealt with here in the required depth. Adorno, one of the protagonists of the Frankfurt School until the

1960s, was one of the authors of the study on the authoritarian personality which, in the immediate post-1945 period, diagnosed latent Fascism in the US. In an article published in 1951, *Psychologie and Soziologie*, translated into English in 1967/68, he criticises Parsons sharply for lack of concern with psychodynamic issues, and also class conflict in contemporary society. He even accuses Parsons of overlooking the pro-Fascist side of community integration which, at the time, was a harsh judgment. It meant that implicitly Parsons' theory acquiesces with the sides of social consensus facilitating mass murder. This criticism was taken seriously by most German sociologists including Habermas (1963/71) despite the fact that Parsons in his early article on anti-Semitism made it clear that he was concerned with what this meant for sociological analysis.

It may be said, however, that like many others in the post-war period, he overlooked the *organised bureaucratic* nature of German Fascism. Neumann (1942/66) maintains that the 'too-much-order' rather than the 'too-much-instinct' side of German Fascism is politically viable. This conjecture plays little role in sociological theory; neither in Parsons' nor in Adorno's. Parsons thus joins the *zeitgeist* of the 1940s when he analyses the psychopathology side of deviance.

The place of psychiatry

Anti-Semitism (or racism, for that matter) is sociologically not deemed illness-like. Reasons are not discussed explicitly, but may be the following: illness sociologically becomes relevant if the ill people enter the sick role (being urged to do so by their environment concerned that they seek competent help). If this is so, anti-Semitism in a Fascist society, or racism in our society, do not qualify for the label. If an institutionalised sick role is to 'match' deviance so that it may be illness, the absence of sick-role entitlement (or enforcement) makes an aberration an other-than-illness phenomenon.

Second, sociological interest in illness focuses on psychiatric disturbance. But for Parsons anti-Semitism is essentially non-psychiatric although he uses the psychiatric metaphor to suggest that the anti-Semite may need some kind of *treatment*. In general, 'latent Fascism' or the propensity to prejudice may be present in different societies to a similar degree while the relative value placed on psychiatric health varies. Parsons surmises that 'with respect to the scope given to mental illness, the British case is intermediate between the American and the Soviet'. He offers as explanation: 'I suggest that this has to do with the very strong British emphasis on the importance of self-control in social relations' (1958/64a, p. 290). Regarding the Soviet low tolerance for malingering (in constrast with an imputedly high British tendency), Parsons' knowledge base depends on Field's observations extended into a book (1957), and one R. A. Bauer's *The New Man of Soviet Psychology*. The conclusions drawn, however, are far-reaching. Soviet society's dominant deviance is not illness but 'compulsive acquiescence in status-expectations', analogous to Robert K. Merton's 'ritualism' (1949).[17] Parsons ventures that there the eventual opportunity for the unwell rather to freely enjoy being taken care of 'suggests primacy of oral components rather than mother-child love-attachment' (1958/64a, pp. 289–90).

No mention is made of the psychiatric illness label's use as punishment for political dissenters. Why is such medical practice in non-liberal societies not a topic for an action-theory of social systems? The only answer seems to be that Parsons identifies the sociological approach with the psychiatric endeavour, and this makes him unable to criticise psychiatric practice from a sociological point of view. But why does medical sociology wishing to go beyond physiology and anatomy feel compelled to endorse psychiatry as its natural ally? Parsons argues that since sociology is understood as a science of action systems it cannot account for the origin of deviance which, however, is omnipresent. This makes it necessary that the motivation which is beyond value-orientation becomes incorporated into the sociological analysis as the topic of another science, psychology. The situation equals what G. Simmel (1908, pp. 35–41) describes as sociology's *second a priori*: while individuals have to be thought of as incorporated into and determined by the social circles to which they belong, it is equally necessary to realise that individuality always, at the same time, means something beyond social participation. Parsons identifies this 'trans-social' element as psychological. By this decision he backs up by psychoanalytic understanding including that of the unconscious the idea that the social sphere represents freedom of choice. Since the actor, by definition, does not realise his or her unconscious motives, he or she can be freed from responsibility for falling ill while being prone to unconscious wishes propelling the actor towards illness or accidents.

By adopting many of Alexander's arguments, explicitly advocating their relevance in the opening passage of Chapter 10, Parsons identifies the medical–sociological endeavour with that of psychosomatic medicine. Psychosomatic medicine, however, claims to be based on classic Freudian thought, although a number of simplifications and deviations are hard to overlook. For instance, Freud diligently traces ambivalence in conscious and unconscious drive representations and identifies vestiges of collective unconscious in society and culture, supposedly preserving the memory of murdering the primordial father and joining the brother-horde afterwards. Psychosomatic medicine, discarding most of Freud's *phylogenetic* hypotheses, ends up with a theory that illnesses such as asthma, heart disease, ulcerative colitis and stomach or duodenal ulcers document the hysterical or neurotic nature of most diseases.

Can the hypothesis be substantiated that the stresses and strains to which the individual is exposed in the modern economy in fact produce psychiatric lesions? What if this is not so? Then the organic lesions presented by patients to doctors might have to be taken for what is treated by most doctors: non-psychiatric organic malfunctioning which possibly necessitates a drug regimen or surgical treatment.

Parsons sides with psychosomatic medicine without examining the case of whether there is a *non*-psychiatric alternative to the idea that the industrial and urban environment has an impact upon health. To be sure, one side of the argument which Parsons did *not* pursue has been presented by the pathologist, Virchow, who in 1848 examined the causes of the typhoid epidemic in Upper Silesia in the local poor population's general living conditions (Taylor and Rieger, 1984). In a sense, Virchow maintains, politics is medicine writ large; in this he is playing upon the famous saying by the Prussian military strategist, Carl von Clausewitz (1832), that war is but an extension of politics using other means.

Similarly, the medical historian Sigerist, having arrived in the US from his native Germany to avoid political persecution in the early 1930s, had his book *Introduction to Medical Knowledge* (1931) translated into English under the title *Man and Medicine* (1932). Sigerist argued that medicine was about to become a social science because, in the modern world, it had a social goal. The latter was defined, on the one hand, as safeguarding the prevention of disease by taking an active role on the shop floor, in schools, communities, and so on; on the other hand, medicine also aimed to reintegrate the ill or disabled person into the labour market. Sigerist claimed:

> that the physical restoration of a patient cannot be the final goal of a physician's actions. No task may be considered completed before the patient has been rehabilitated, reintegrated into society as a useful

member. A highly specialized and technical society such as ours has jobs for every degree of intelligence and physical capacity. Even the most disabled individuals, blind men, people who have lost extremities, and other invalids, can perform socially useful and therefore necessary work that deserves to be fully remunerated . . . Thus the scope of medicine has indeed broadened considerably, and nobody will deny that the physician is playing an increasingly important part in society. (1946/60, pp. 71–2)

This definition of a social goal of medicine enabled Sigerist to look at modern Soviet, European and American societies to compare the actual state of their medical care systems with what he perceived as medicine's ultimately unavoidable 'socialist' nature. That is, he stipulated that eventually medicine could not but accept the goal that it had to extend its range of care beyond cure into prevention and rehabilitation. The negative example of a racist 'blood and soil mystique' of highly unsocialist leanings in his native Germany (see Sigerist, 1936/60) spurred on his zest to contribute to the highly recommended adoption of sociology by medicine (not, however, the reverse).

The other non-psychiatric option of a medical sociology staying close to, but separate from, medicine has also been presented by Sigerist in the 1932 (1931) above-mentioned book, as well as in an article first published in 1929 in the Annals of the Leipzig University Institute of the History of Medicine (of which he was director).[18]

There Sigerist argues – comparing modern beliefs with those of the Kubu aborigines, Semitic cultures, antique Greek/Roman world, Middle Ages and modern society – that *the place of the ill* in society has always been, to a certain extent, divorced from the specific illness which was diagnosed in a particular patient. According to whether illness is understood as due to witchcraft, sin, physical inferiority, God's grace, or the hardships of an urban-industrial life, each culture has its own way of bestowing hostility or pity, exclusion or care upon the unwell among its members. The crucial influence explaining the difference, to a certain extent, is religion, but also the spiritual value of beauty of the body as opposed to beauty of the soul, so to speak. Sigerist sums up his observations on the modern situation by seeing a:

position of preference which the sick person occupies. To be sure, sickness isolates always in all cases, for the life of the sick runs a different course from the life of the healthy. But this isolation does not remove the sick from human companionship, but rather brings it closer . . . The sick occupy the center of the family whose life is devoted to them first . . . Even the poorest, most forsaken person, who has no one in the world close to him, finds himself through the simple fact of illness placed in a friendly, familiar relation to at least one person, the doctor, who is sent to him by the community. *Disease dispensates*. It relieves us of many obligations to society . . . Disease relieves us of the duty of working . . . In society today where work is an unquestioned essential for living, in which supply and demand govern the work conditions, the position of the sick would appear to be particularly hopeless. It is not so, for in nearly all European countries the sick man is financed by sick insurance . . . The state forces those who are economically weak to put aside part of their pay in the days of health for days of disease. In this way the workman wins the right to help and care. He can not work but he is still paid with money which he himself has earned. He is not thrown back upon the charity of society and is not a beggar accepting alms. The favorable position which he occupies when he is ill is to a large extent of his own making. The fact that a healthy workman who makes little use of insurance would place his salary deduction at the disposal of the weaker member is a nice expression of human solidarity. (1932, pp. 84–5)

It is not because Sigerist talks about European countries where illness, accident and old-age insurance had become state-guaranteed funds in the years between 1883 and the 1930s while Parsons talks mostly about the US where no such insurance existed until 1965, that Parsons' standpoint embraces the first half of Sigerist's thought but disregards or discards the second half. The reason may lie beyond any negative feeling concerning health insurance in the modern welfare state which Parsons seems not to have had anyway. In fact, he obviously welcomed the New Deal which eventually influenced some aspects of the American health care system, giving rise at least to some welfare-related medical services. The research into medical cost which, as Parsons deplores, earned the label *pro-Communist* by the AMA (1964, pp. 325–6) may have addressed the same matter as Sigerist. Parsons may have been aware that the economic metaphors with which he describes illness issues are not the only way in which health and its failure are related to economic circumstances. However, throughout his writings on medical sociology he avoids the topic of finance and economics, largely structuring the social side of health care in modern societies. He even neglects the individuals' experiences with economic aspects of the system. Recent studies have stressed how important the political and economic organisation aspects of health care delivery are (e.g., Andersen, Lion and Anderson, 1976; Anderson, 1972, 1985).

Part II
The Interactionist Paradigm: Illness as Professional Construction

Labelling approach, anti-psychiatry and 'grounded theory'

Introduction: the anti-Parsonian impetus

Lemert's *Social Pathology* sets out to 'solve the problem how social and personal disorganization are related to each other' (1951, p. 13). In this, it draws together two well-entrenched traditions.

The five previous books published under the same title between 1925 and 1942 (with a total of eight editions until 1946) established a catalogue of topics defining the scope of social pathology adopted by Lemert. Drug addiction, blindness and deafness, mental disorder, prostitution and homosexuality, delinquency and crime, to name but a few, are among the list of social problems which Lemert's book replicates. In terms of social theory behind this, unfavourable environmental conditions stemming from social disorganization in modern urban society are said to make for a person's misfortune, malice or vice. Accordingly, sociology becomes an ally of the welfare state, actively improving the moralities linking deviant populations with mainstream American society. In this, resocialisation is said to be more effective than punishment.

However, the solution of social problems cannot rely on the (re)integration of deviants into society alone. John Gillin points out in his revised *Social Pathology* published in 1939 that the crucial change is one of social institutions. 'Reconstruction of the individual' (1939, p. 620) is to take place through 'social reconstruction' (1939, p. 622), he suggests. His conclusive statement is clad in a rhetorical question:

Is it not clear that to correct socially pathological conditions it is necessary to readjust the attitude of the individual to his fellows and to

73

the institutions so that they harmonize with each other in meeting the needs of the individuals? As we have seen, the difficulties seem to grow out of the fact that one set of institutions . . . change, while there is a lag in adjusting the others in accordance with the changes . . . Society's methods of social control, adequate under former conditions, fail because the individual experiences emotional disturbances in trying to adjust himself to a changed system of relationships. They are secondarily pathological in the sense that the pattern of conduct in one set of relationships in which an individual is involved are not harmoniously adjusted to the pattern required in another set of relationships involving the participation of the same individual. (1939, p. 619).

The second tradition on which Lemert builds his views of social pathology is the pragmatism and *social behaviorism* practised at the University of Chicago since before the turn of the century. The Sociology Department under Robert E. Park, Louis Wirth and others during the 1920s and 1930s produces a vivid picture of the mostly darker sides of urban life (Bulmer, 1984). The 'naturalistic' approach of participant observation is carried over in the 1930s and 1940s to a next generation of researchers through one of Park's students, Hughes. Hardly related to 'Chicago sociology' (Downes and Rock, 1982, p. 73) at the time, G. H. Mead's philosophical lectures on *Mind, Self, and Society from the Standpoint of a Social Behaviorist* are published posthumously in a volume edited by Charles W. Morris in 1934. They gain momentum for sociology, for instance, by such attempts as Lindesmith and Strauss' *Social Psychology* (1949), which draws heavily on Meadian views. Sociological and philosophical branches of what we nowadays see as unified perspective of interactionism (or 'symbolic interactionism') seem not to have taken much notice of each other until the 1950s. Lemert's *Social Pathology*, while using a 'life-history approach' (see the book's Appendix), draws on the ideas of both sides without giving them explicit credit. He makes some critical remarks on C. H. Cooley's view of social disorganisation (Cooley, 1918; Lemert, 1951, p. 9ff.), and G. H. Mead is cited solely through his article on punitive justice (1918) which has little to do with what Blumer, in 1969, claims to have termed 'symbolic interactionism' in 1937 (Blumer, 1969a, p. 1). However, Lemert adopts Cooley's idea of 'looking-glass self' as well as Mead's idea of the reflexive character of symbolic reality. He bases on them his 'narrow' theory of deviance: 'From a narrower sociological viewpoint the deviations are not significant until they are organized subjectively and transformed into active roles and become the social criteria for assigning status. The deviant individuals must react symbolically to their own behavior aberrations and fix them in their sociopsychological patterns' (1951, p. 75).

Lemert unites the social-pathology (social-disorganisation) interest in social problems, on the one hand, with the sociological as well as philosophical theories developed at Chicago on the other. The book, however, was hardly noticed for its novel viewpoint until some 15 or more years after its publication. The combination of social-problem analysis and a 'symbolic-reaction' or 'societal-reaction' perspective remained practically unknown for over a decade. When the perspective became acknowledged, it was not credited to Lemert's book. It was long after Becker's, Goffman's and Strauss' interactionist writings had gained public attention in the early 1960s that Lemert's book retrospectively surfaced as probably the most comprehensive presentation of what eventually became the 'labelling approach' to social deviance. Lemert's work is only rarely recognised in its role as a forerunner. While he himself – a graduate of Ohio State University (1939) – pleaded 'allegiance to symbolic interactionism' (1972, p. X), he has not become accepted into the ranks of its acknowledged protagonists. For instance, no article of his is included in Becker *et al.*'s 1968 volume of papers presented to the foremost mentor of 'Chicago sociology' of the 1950s and 1960s, Hughes; nor does Matza's (1969) reconstruction of the labelling perspective sufficiently acknowledge Lemert's impact on the 'neoChicagoan' approach (eventually, Lemert himself identifies neither with labelling theory, nor with G. H. Mead's approach, see Lemert 1974, 1976).

The '*breakthrough*' of the 'societal-reaction' perspective, somewhat over a decade after Lemert's book, was *not* due to the fact that this new perspective was now being presented. Rather, the approach became 'suddenly' widespread after having remained unconspicuous for years. Downes and Rock (1982) reported that even Becker felt unable, at the time, to explain to himself why his 1963 '*Outsiders*' (containing mostly previously published material) should meet with overwhelming acclaim. Perhaps the rise of interactionism as explanatory paradigm in illness reconstruction in the early 1960s has to do with two developments. One is the loss of credibility suffered by Parsons' theory since the late 1950s. The other is the claim for a *more humanistic* sociology related to the emerging political scene of the 1960s.

In 1958, Dahrendorf's acid criticism suggested a brave-new-world likeness of Parsons' idea of social system. In 1961, Wrong charged Parsons with normative determinism making for a puppet-like image of man. That symbolic interactionism would regard itself as the solution to the problems of conceptual narrow-mindedness discovered in Parsons' work was highlighted by Blumer's retrospective account written at the end of the 1960s:

> Compressing the process of social interaction into a special form . . . is an outstanding vice in social science, both past and present. We see it exemplified in the quaint notion that social interaction is a process of developing 'complimentary expectations' – a notion given wide currency by Talcott Parsons and serving as the basis of his scheme of human society as a harmoniously disposed social system. (Blumer, 1969a, p. 53).

The first anti-Parsonian leanings showed in Becker's article about socialisation into marijuana use for pleasure (1953). It 'calls into question theories which ascribe behavior to antecedent predispositions' (1953, p. 235). The *anti-psychological* impetus was carried further when Blumer (1955) denounced the usefulness of the concept of attitude to understanding behaviour. Instead, he endorsed a notion where behaviour emanates from interchange between person and environment. Blumer made it clear that this 'looking-glass' impact of the social environment upon a person's identity had a *constructive* side to it. That is, motives were considered socially constructed (i.e., emerging from interaction between self and others). This view was directed against Parsons inasmuch as Parsons derived social behaviour from (conformist or deviant) need dispositions. It was this view which Becker denounced as 'sociological' when he put his own idea of the societal-reaction or social-definition nature of deviance against such sociology.

> The sociological view defines deviance as the infraction of some agreed-upon rule. It then goes on to ask who breaks rules, and to search for the factors in their personalities and life situations that might account for the infractions. This assumes that those who have broken a rule constitute a homogenous category, because they have committed the same deviant act. Such an assumption seems to me to ignore the central fact about deviance: it is created by society . . . From this point of view, deviance is *not* a quality of the act the person commits, but rather a consequence of the application by others of rules and sanctions to an 'offender'. The deviant is one to whom that label has successfully been applied; deviant is behavior that people so label. (Becker, 1963, pp. 8–9)

Thus Becker's often-quoted passage in which he introduces the idea of labelling may be read as a rebuke to Parsons' unconsciousness hypothesis of illness (deviance) motivation. Against it, Becker holds that 'social groups create deviance by making the rules whose infraction constitutes deviance' (1963, p. 9). The idea is one of external causation. This means that the symbolic *con-struction* by social agents or agencies making for the interpersonal reality of an illness (deviance) is more important than conscious or unconscious needs. The idea of social construction becomes the vantage point from which interactionism perceives sickness. At the end of the decade, Freidson's *Profession of Medicine* (1970a) clarifies that social construction of illness denotes power relation-ships between doctor and patient which reveal *professional domi-nance* (Freidson, 1970a, b). He tries to support his standpoint with a criticism of Parsons:

> Unlike Parsons, I do not argue merely that medicine has the power to legitimize one's acting sick by conceding that he is really sick. My argument goes further than that. I argue here that by virtue of being the authority on what illness 'really' is, medicine creates the social possibili-ties for acting sick. In this sense, medicine's monopoly includes the right to create illness as an official social role. (1970a, pp. 205–6; emphasis omitted)

There is no consensus whether and to what extent social con-struction equals one-sided self-interested creation. At the one extreme, anti-psychiatry argues that illness does not exist except through the labelling of the sick by their doctors. Anti-psychiatry emerging out of a medical setting in England (Scotland) adopts a Sartrean world view (Laing and Cooper, 1964). It haunts psy-chiatry with accusations of wrongdoing, supposedly contained in the very essence of its professional expertise (Sedgwick, 1982a, b). In the US, Szasz becomes a cult figure of criticism against psy-chiatry. He argues that since the image of mental illness is a medical fabrication ('myth'), madness is but an outcome of arbi-trary professional label construction ('manufacture') (Szasz, 1960, 1961, 1970a).

At the other extreme of the spectrum is the view that social construction merely means mutual involvement of various actors in medical settings. Strauss (1959) ventures that social identity formation consists of putting forward self-images (masks) which meet with significant others' projections (mirrors). This interactive notion of social construction is carried over to the medical scene where it is held against the allegedly Parsonian framework that norms determine behaviour. Strauss *et al.* (1963) aim at the short-comings of the then systems-theory based analysis of hospitals as formal organisations when they write:

> Students of formal organisations tend to underplay the processes of internal change as well as overestimate the more stable features of organizations – including its rules and its hierarchical statuses . . . The

bases of concerted action (social order) . . . have led us to emphasize
the importance of negotiation – the processes of give-and-take, of
diplomacy, of bargaining – which characterizes organizational life.
(Strauss *et al.*, 1963, p. 148)

The idea is that social construction is a *process* of fluid permanent reconstitution of social arenas. In this, rejecting Parsons' idea
that the sick role and the doctor's role form a stable social system
seems to pervade every aspect of the analysis:

Rules and prescribed procedures cannot be either extensive or intensive
enough to cover the fluid and ambiguous character of hospital work.
Nor can such formality prevail in the conditions of ideological ferment
and experimentation that characterize professional work . . . New
agreements must continually be worked out, and old agreements fade
away. Negotiation is not 'organized' in the sense that it lays down
permanent expectations. Rather, expectations are perpetually negotiated as new situations arise. The bases for working together are
continually reconstituted through negotiation. (Strauss *et al.*, 1964a,
pp. 373–4)

The other issue raised critically against Parsons is an anti-
psychological stance on motivation. Strauss *et al.* furnish a perspective focusing on *work*. Rules are understood to be 'worked at'
through negotiation, and Parsons' recourse on psychological forces is reinterpreted to mean 'psychological work' (Strauss *et al.*,
1982a, p. 258). This notion is deemed too crude to account for the
various types and nuances of sentimental identification with a task
or situation, and the term 'sentimental work' is introduced (consisting of 'composure work', 'biographical work', etc.) to account
for the social construction of consensus between a nurse (doctor)
and a patient. What Parsons tries to explain by taking refuge to
psychology – namely, the interchange between doctor and patient
in a medical context – is here credited to the mutual construction
of trust through 'sentimental work'. It is the latter which helps
towards (re-)establishing the patient's physical and psychological
well-being. In this, Strauss *et al.* argue more against the Parsonian
argument as reproduced by its critics than against Parsons' original
ideas. The simplistic view which Parsons supposedly provides is
rejected in a statement such as the following: 'Far too simple is the
conception that patients are relatively passive recipients of procedures done on or for them by rational, technical experts' (Fagerhaugh and Strauss, 1977, p. iv).
Parsons' standpoint, often distorted or exaggerated, becomes
the epitome of what the sociologist of the 1960s wishes to avoid.

But, at the same time, Parson's health–illness analysis is often adopted, even by unrelenting critics. For instance, his predilection for *mental* illness as supposedly the most sociological aspect of the illness spectrum is retained throughout most of the interactionism literature. Moreover, the idea that illness constitutes a social *role* is maintained, even in apparent opposition to Parsons, by such advocates of professional labelling as Scheff and Freidson. Furthermore, societal-reaction theory retains the functionalist view that the sick role serves the purpose of enhancing mechanisms safeguarding the healthy majority's conformity with work and family norms (keeping them from 'opting out' into illness). Erikson, in a mistakenly critical attitude towards structural functionalism, holds that for the societal-reaction stance, 'deviance cannot be dismissed simply as behavior which *disrupts* stability in society, but may itself be, in controlled quantities, an important condition for *preserving* stability' (1962/64, p. 15).

Even the systems notion is introduced by Scheff, whose *Being Mentally Ill* is among the most systematic applications of the idea of labelling in medical sociology. Clarifying that his intention is to spell out 'the basic assumptions for a social systems model of mental illness' (1966a, p. 24), he proceeds to outline the latter's main features. One is that this systems model is to be presented from the standpoint of the *patient*, not the medical profession. Thus, this anti-medical systems model legitimises itself by partisanship. It claims that 'the problems it clarifies are apt to be those that are most obscure when viewed from the psychiatric or medical point of view' (Scheff, 1966a, p. 25). To be sure, ten years later any *truly sociological* stance in medical sociology is identified with an anti-Parsonian view (Gold, 1977).

Throughout the last 25 years, Parsons' preoccupation with psychoanalysis has not been taken to mark his identification with patients' needs (although this is what already propelled Henderson's plea for the importance of sentiments). Instead, medical sociology has cultivated the prejudice that interactionism is patient-centred while structural functionalism is not.

The upsurge of symbolic interactionism in the 1960s may not owe everything to the downfall of Parsonianism. Rather, both may be due to a change in the *image of mankind* at the turn of the 1960s. The explicit or implicit anti-Parsonian thrust in labelling theory, anti-psychiatry and 'grounded theory' may not be sufficient cause to warrant their newly acquired credibility. It could be argued that the leading perspective in sociology changes independently of the critical injunctions against Parsons which are the landmarks of the change. Erving Goffman's second publication of

The Presentation of Self in Everyday Life (1959) – soon followed by *Asylums* (1961) and *Stigma* (1963) – became an unsuspected sociological bestseller because it was taken to give individual experience more credit than does systems theory. To be sure, Dahrendorf's criticism of Parsons ridiculed the lack of concern for individuality. The focus of the nation, in the US, turned to personal freedom and the rights of the disenfranchised at this time. In the early 1960s, the Civil Liberties Movement scored its first victories, and *The Other America* (Harrison, 1962/71) was discovered. Under the auspices of the newly acquired political visibility of the poor and other outsiders. Homans in his Presidential Address to the 1964 American Sociological Association Convention pleaded for *Bringing Men Back In*.

Becker, in his Presidential Address to the 1967 conference of the Society for the Study of Social Problems (SSSP), answered his rhetorical question *Whose Side Are We On?* by urging sociologists to take the side of the 'underdog'.

The argument set out here is that around the turn of the 1950s and in the beginning of the 1960s there was a shift of general outlook. Sociological theory, up until then, focused primarily on how society functions as a whole. This macro-perspective, so to speak, was replaced by a micro-perspective. The question now became whether individual needs for self-fulfilment and self-realisation were sufficiently met. There were strong political overtones in this change of perspective. It replaced structural functionalism by 'symbolic interactionism' as the leading paradigm in medical sociology.

The self-professed most important accomplishment of the new perspective was that it sacrificed the notion of individual pathology. Instead, it stressed the right of every citizen to a life style of his or her own. Goffman, for instance, was praised for *not* distinguishing between the normal and the pathological in conceptualising deviance: 'Even in dealing with the most bizarre human conduct, Goffman questioned the capacity to impute pathology. In so doing, he forwarded, more than the functionalists, an idea antithetical to pathology – diversity' (Matza, 1969, p. 65)

However, all this may not be as cut and dried as Matza attempted to make out. For instance, despite the claim that societal-reaction theory's view of pathology (i.e., its emphasising diversity) equalled that of G. H. Mead, it seems that this claim cannot be easily justified through Mead's writings. At least, one would have to assume a shift in Mead's standpoint during the last 15 years of his life if he were to be a credible source for the diversity hypothesis. In his 1918 article, G. H. Mead identified crime as the eruption of socially 'unmodified instincts' from underneath a surface of modified social responses. He diagnosed that 'through a breakdown of the organization of the social act there is enacted a crime of passion, the direct outcome of self-assertion' (1918, p. 580). On first sight, this view has more in common with Parsons' idea of unconscious unsocialised needs which surface in illness than with interactionism's view that motivation is the sequel of behaviour and identification.

Thus it is here left an open question whether 'symbolic interactionism' rightly or wrongly claimed that its idea of social construction of illness was derived from Mead's work. At the end of Part II, after the two interactionist models have been presented in detail, the question will be addressed again whether Mead's ideas are at variance with those of Parsons in this matter.

Chapter 5
The Interactionist Notion of Illness

Rejecting psychodynamic interpretations, focusing on structural environmental forces determining the origin and course of illness and treatment, the *labelling theorists* and *anti-psychiatrists* adopt a nominalist perspective. What matters is not the symptom which the individual develops but, rather, that it is perceived and categorised by the environment. The crucial action is that of agencies of social control. Thus, contends Kitsuse, 'it is the responses of the conventional and conforming members of the society who identify and interpret behavior as deviant which sociologically transform persons into deviants' (1964, p. 97). Correspondingly, Lemert (1951) maintains that the sociological question 'is not what causes human beings to develop such symptoms as hallucinations and delusions but, instead, what it is about their behavior which leads the community to reject them, and otherwise treat them as irresponsibles, i.e. as insane' (1951, pp. 387–8). In other words, the individual's situation – including that of illness – is conceptualised as a function of *environmental processes of normative evaluation*. The 'societal reaction' forms the core. Since deviance is 'a property conferred upon [the] forms [of behaviour] by the audiences which directly or indirectly witness them' (Erikson, 1962/64, p. 11), the crucial criteria of differentiation between health and illness, or normality and deviance, is whether or not a conspicuous ritual or a piecemeal process of 'societal reaction' is conferred upon the individual.

The *'grounded theory'* approach acknowledges that the 'societal reaction' is open to a certain scope of negotiation. This constitutes links with the social order understood as 'negotiative order'. It means that normative evaluation ensuring a person's status and identity is conceptualised as fluid adaptation to a situation rather than standardised application of fixed rules.

The notion that illness is a product of environmental normative categorisation validated in situational interaction is based on two premises. First, illness as biological fact is distinguished from illness as social reality. Second, the scope of what may be socially defined as illness or abnormality is, in principle, unlimited; that is, there is an intrinsic relativism in this notion inviting the view that the scope of illness in society is a *political* question.

The dual nature of illness

That 'a biology of illness is complementary to a sociology of illness' (Dingwall, 1976, p. 25) has its roots in what is defined as illness's dual nature. A *physiological* reality makes for disease as a pathological entity (Becker, 1963, p. 5). Its criteria is intercultural stability such that 'a case of pneumonia or syphilis is pretty much the same in New York or New Caledonia' (Scheff, 1975a, p. 7). This concept of disease is 'confined to conditions in which physical lesions have been found' (M. Roth, 1976, p. 321). Psychiatric disorder does not fall under the biological hypothesis but is proof that the social side of illness is independently valid. This social realm is one of *role incompetence*:

> Physical handicaps . . . tend to be transcultural in the sense that they are found all over the world. However, the *extent* to which the handicaps physically limit the playing of social roles is culturally variable . . . Biological variations which do not impede bodily functions become a basis for deviation only through interaction with cultural definitions and social perceptions. (Lemert, 1951, p. 29)

This distinction between a preculturally stable pathophysiological substratum, and a culturally variable significance of symptoms in terms of role incumbency, gives rise to the interactionists' *opposition against the medical model*. The 'medical model', it is suggested, fails to take account of the cultural variations of illness categorisation and incidence, respectively. Instead, it ideologically establishes disease as a seemingly culture-free 'entity within the individual' (Grusky and Pollner, 1981, p. v). This is seen to hold, in particular, for mental illness since 'most of the "symptoms" of mental illness . . . [are] far from being culture-free' (Scheff, 1975a, p. 7; see also Lemert, 1951, p. 387). But it is also held against the medical profession that it believes that illness abides in the terms of natural science. The latter is denounced as professional ideology, and Freidson proposes 'to analyse illness as a form of social deviance which is *thought* to have a biophysical cause and to require biophysical treatment' (1970a, p. 212).

The opposition against the 'medical model' reveals itself as criticism against the medical profession, in particular its practice.

Insofar as illness (the culturally variable product of deviancy labelling) is identified as mental rather than physiological, the assumption of a two-tier nature of illness results.

The opposition against the 'medical model' enters *grounded theory* in a weaker version. Here, the doctor's actions are frequently disregarded, or mentioned only as one among many sources of medical help. In this vein, the nursing staff's and patients' outlook and practices are made the primary focus of *Social Organization of Medical Work* (Strauss *et al.*, 1985). In a way, doctors as well as patients come to be seen as applying variations of humane and concerned care ideally rendered by a well-trained nursing staff. Even attempts at managing chronic illness at home are described as if patients and their families emulate the good care provided by an idealised nursing staff (Strauss and Glaser, 1975).

The political message of relativism

Methodologically, symbolic interactionism proposes a mixture of anti-positivism and positivism introduced under the label of 'naturalism'. 'Naturalism' has a positivist component in that it strives to be amoral and non-evaluational, 'having obvious statistical implications and derivations' (Lemert, 1951, p. 23). That is, it focuses on 'changes over time as are basic and common to the members of a social category' (Goffman, 1959/61, p. 127), thereby neglecting individual differences. At the same time, the intention is anti-positivist. It is to produce concepts which are 'sensitizing rather than operational' (Schur, 1971, p. 27; see also Blumer, 1954/69, p. 147; Scheff, 1974, p. 445). They are to inspire research which is not questionnaire-based and refrains from using statistical data analysis. The latter is rejected as objectivist, and it is equated with natural science in the 'medical model'. In contrast, social science studies human beings as 'real', that is, in their usual habitats. The idea is to get beyond operational terms in empirical research in sociology (Bierstedt, 1959; see also Rock, 1979, Ch. 6). Blumer explains: 'One has to get inside of the defining process of the actor in order to understand his action' (1969a/, p. 16).

In its anti-positivist component, 'naturalism' claims that researcher and reality can match in a way that is free from perspectivist conceptual world views. 'Its only commitment', claims Matza, 'is fidelity to the phenomenon under consideration' (1969, p. 8; see also Schatzmann and Strauss, 1973). However, it is exactly this denial of the gulf between concept and phenomenon, and the unabashed identification of perception with reality, which invites value judgments back into the picture. The message is one of 'real life' as opposed to scientific classification. Freidson states: 'While disease may be "there", it is what we, as social beings, think and do about it that determines the content of our lives . . . Illness as such may be biological disease, but the idea of illness is not' (1970a, p. 209).

This focus upon 'real life' entails a *relativist* standpoint. What is identified as illness is what given societies define and treat as such. 'What . . . do people who have been labeled deviant have in common?' asks Becker, and he responds: 'At the least, they share the label and the experience of being labeled' (1963, pp. 9–10). Therefore 'the same behavior may be an infraction of the rules at one time and not at another' (1963, p. 14). Medicine emerges as 'a moral ·enterprise like law or religion seeking to uncover and control things that it considers undesirable' (Freidson, 1970a, p. 208).

The relativist standpoint makes the definition of illness tautological: illness is what medicine defines as such, and medicine defines as illness what befits its function as social-control agency. The medical profession, understood as a self-propelled power-conscious body, is seen to use diagnostic and therapeutic decisions solely on the basis of unchecked clinical expertise. Parsons contends that a physician may, at times, inflict 'injury' (Parsons 1951a: 452) on patients, or violate their right to secrecy and intimacy. These actions, Parsons explains, are justified under the special role relationship into which doctor and patient enter. No such provisos are tolerated by the interactionists. To reveal the intrinsic power basis of the *professional construction* of illness means to visualise the doctor's actions as if they were non-professional behaviour. In this way, they acquire the features of violations of the patient's intimacy and integrity. Thomas Szasz derives from the alleged similarity between a doctor's and everybody else's actions the rationale for his moral crusade against modern psychiatry:

> By showing what man has done, and continues to do so, to his fellow man *in the name of help* I hope to add to our understanding of what man is, where coercion, however well-justified by self-flattering rhetoric, leads him, and what might yet become of him were he to replace control of the other with self-control. (1970a, p. xviii)

Thus relativism suggests that *any* social phenomenon may be labelled deviant or built into an illness through professional fiat. The scope of phenomena which thus is assumed to qualify for labelling tends to be unlimited. Indeed, it resembles rather closely the well-known list of topics which define social pathology since the early twentieth century. Marijuana or heroin use (Becker, 1953 and 1963, Ray 1964), premarital sex (I. L. Reiss, 1970), homosexuality (Humphreys, 1970; Szasz, 1970a), drug addiction (Schur, 1964; Duster, 1970; J. Young, 1970), mental subnormality (Dexter, 1964; Mercer, 1965; Edgerton, 1967), mental illness (Lemert, 1951, p. 387ff. and 1962/67b; Sampson, Messinger and Towne, 1961/64; Scheff, 1966a, 1974; Mohavedi, 1975), blindness (Lemert, 1951, p. 101ff.; R. A. Scott, 1969 and 1970), speech defects (Lemert, 1951, p. 143ff.), prostitution (Lemert, 1951, p. 236ff.; A. J. Reiss, 1964), alcoholism (Lemert, 1951, p. 338f.; Lemert 1962/1967c; Trice and Roman, 1970), political radicalism (Lemert, 1951, p. 175ff.; Goffman, 1963, p. 143ff.) as well as more 'medical' phenomena such as epilepsy (P. West, 1976 and 1985), migraine (MacIntire and Oldman, 1977), or tonsillitis (Bloor, 1976b) have been demonstrated to befit the vagaries of a basically arbitrary application of illness labels.

Intrinsic qualities – that is, the physical or mental state of the individual – are not accepted as a sufficiently clear-cut dividing line between health and illness, or normality and deviance. *External* criteria set the social definition of an illness. These are judgmental: since no entrenched hierarchy of moral values is said to exist which could shape the diagnostic categories (Lemert, Goffman), they are established by *political* fiat. 'It is . . . true', asserts Becker, 'that the questions of what rules are to be enforced, what behavior regarded as deviant, and which people labeled as outsiders must . . . be regarded as political' (1963, p. 7). In this context, 'political' has two meanings. One is that it refers to repressive agencies of social control. Becker contends that treatment ideologies are instigated by social reformers but 'the final outcome of the moral crusade is a police force' (1963, p. 156). Likewise, Szasz accuses psychiatry of incarcerating unsuspecting victims: 'The institutional psychiatrist is a duly authorized agent of the Therapeutic State; his client is the State and its agency, Institutional Psychiatry. This is why he can, and indeed must, accuse persons of mental illness, prove them insane, and finally cure their minds by imprisoning their bodies' (1970a, p. 239).

In this context any use of power or privilege in society is deemed amoral. This, however, makes it more rather than less difficult to qualify the criticism of 'professional power'. Short of rejecting modern society as a whole, the sociologist is left with no criteria to distinguish between the status quo and practices in particular societies. Not even Fascist discrimination and crime against arbitrarily defined outgroups may be denounced. One cannot but detect a trace of cynicism in a statement such as: 'Marihuana [*sic*] smokers, witches, usurers, nationalists, internationalists and the Jews have all been variously defined as deviants in different societies. The definitions have been of great consequence to them' (Rock, 1973, p. 20).

The second meaning of 'political' refers to bargaining and negotiation. Gerson (1976a) detects the political element in illness in the negotiability of diagnosis as well as treatment. Cunning and the ability to put pressure upon others are perceived as the political side of the doctor's as well as the patient's participation in medical encounters. Wiener (1980) discovers the *Politics of Alcoholism* in the process of how the arenas for public policy against alcohol abuse are set over a period of two decades in the US. In this, a collective definition of the supposedly vast amount of hidden alcoholism is shown to be the creation of a number of specially established agencies aiming at mobilisation of resources. Wiener introduces her study as an 'exploration of the collective definition of the social problem of alcohol abuse' (1980, p. 8). She shows that welfare politics (denoting what might be 'politics with a capital P') is intricately related to 'turf securing' (which might be 'politics with a small p').

The relativistic aspect of this view is that no moral limitations are introduced regarding actors' practices: that is, no limitations seem to curtail the claims to legitimacy of what an authority declares as sick or treatable. In other words, these relativist views, by stressing the political nature of illness categorisations, inadvertently promote the idea that individuals, in the last instance, cannot resist the authorities defining their condition as sickness and determining a mode of treatment.

Such apparent political acquiescence, however, seems to be at odds with the plea for more concern for individuals and more active involvement in their favour. In his Presidential Address to the SSSP (1967), Becker endorses the researcher's identification with the underdog ('Whose Side Are We On?'). He deems such partisanship morally justified since in a political situation of opposing values it seems that there is no answer to the question of bias or truth: 'Almost all the topics that sociologists study, at least those that have some relation to the real world around us, are seen by society as morality plays and we shall find ourselves, willy-nilly, taking part in those plays on one side or the other' (Becker, 1967, p. 131). This, however, does not solve the problem of relativism. On the contrary, such liberalism has a relativist tinge. Gouldner, therefore, ridicules Becker's claim that underdog research, *per se*, is political. Instead, he discovers a more mundane political function of labelling theory on the level of national political struggle. Becker's claim for identification with the underdog, Gouldner states, serves to disavow the conservative caretaking ideologies of the local welfare and police departments. Instead, it favours the more cosmopolitan control strategies of the federal bureaucracies in Washington, DC. A 'blind or unexamined alliance between sociologists and upper bureaucrats of the welfare state', he maintains, favours repression under the guise of 'the market research of liberalism' (Gouldner, 1968, p. 115). However, Gouldner proves unable to substantiate his argument through a thorough analysis of Becker's texts, and Becker criticises him not for this omission but for the surmise that he, Becker, suffers from 'fear of emotion' (1974, p. 63).

The incapacity to rise beyond a politically acquiescent relativism seems to be deplored by many of labelling theory's critics. For instance, Alexander Liazos' unjust accusation of voyeurism may nevertheless make a valid point: 'As a result of the fascination with 'nuts, sluts, and preverts' and their identities and subcultures, little attention has been paid to the unethical, illegal, and destructive actions of powerful individuals, groups, and institutions in our society' (Liazos, 1972/75, p. 259).[19]

What such critics overlook is the tradition into which the interactionist sociology of deviance belongs. Since the early 1920s, social pathology in the US has been interested in the betterment and integration into society as useful members of those whose depersonalisation unnecessarily made them victims of their life circumstances (Mills, 1943; Horton and Leslie, 1955/70). The sociologists' interest in social problems is governed by their wish to understand how the afflicted are frequently driven into their fate by no fault of their own. Because of this 'other-directedness', vices such as alcoholism or drug addiction are seen as curable through help from benevolent competent welfare agencies. It is this tradition in which interactionist sociology stands, enacted in the catalogue of topics dealt with in Lemert's *Social Pathology*. Its political impetus is geared towards the underdog, the 'remaking of the personality' in the interest of 'social reorganization'. This is to be done by incorporating more of society's members into the ranks of productive normal citizens. In their *Social Pathology*, published in 1925, Queen and Mann justly point at the relativity of what is labelled normal:

> We are by no means prepared to state what is a 'normal' family, a 'normal' amount of employment, a 'normal' body or a 'normal'

mind . . . When, through failure to meet any difficulty, a person 'goes to pieces' or a group loses its morale, then it not only fails to solve the problem in hand, but tends to lose the capacity to meet new situations as they appear. It is such a condition as this that we would describe as socially pathological. (1925, pp. 658–9)

The reformist fervour derived therefrom is shared or replicated by the 'symbolic-interactionist' approach in the 1960s. It may be debated whether Goffman ever aimed at reforming psychiatric inpatient services (Sedgwick, 1982a, p. 62). Maybe, in fact, this is an unanticipated consequence of his work. But it is unquestionable that the reform of mental hospitals has been greatly helped by the widespread positive reception of Goffman's acid description of total institutions. Psychiatrists as well as welfare state officials acknowledge their debt to social science regarding the recent changes in psychiatric treatment (Wing, 1978; Bloor and McKega. ney, 1980). The spirit which, in the 1960s, triggered off the unprecendented optimism connected with the Office of Economic Opportunities also pervades the political partisanship which the 'symbolic-interactionist' study of illness takes. Thus, in spite of the naiveté connected with the relativist notion, its activist potential in the 1960s was undeniable. It propelled sociology for approximately a decade to become the source of advice and analysis which welfare-state officials used in the interest of counteracting the ills and woes of modern society. Disillusionment, in due course, has been unavoidable.

Two models of illness

In accordance with the general view that illness is defined through processes of normative evaluation, aetiology and theraphy are conceptualised in terms of how the 'societal reaction' takes place and what its consequences are for the individual. In short, the aetiology of illness *is* the occurrence of the 'societal reaction'; accordingly therapy is the process (or, rather, the way in which people are being processed) when the 'societal reaction' has taken place.

However, there is a marked difference between two models of the aetiology–therapy relationship. The *labelling* and *antipsychiatry* literature propagates a *crisis model* where the 'societal reaction' is viewed as public crisis, and changes it produces are pictured as the irreversible consequences of a once-and-for-all impact. Therapy appears as a strategy to maintain the changes in role-status and identity brought about by the crisis. Medicine is seen as the application of diverse therapeutic ideologies under the auspices of *professional dominance*. Their success depends not so much on the quality of clinical expertise as on the blessings of an undeniable 'placebo effect'.

In contrast, the *negotiation model* hypothesises a piecemeal process of acquisition of the ill status and/or an open exchange between patient and doctor (nurse) in medical settings which may or may not be dominated by professional authority. Accordingly, therapy appears as an application of clinical knowledge (which may or may not present therapeutic ideology). What is important is that this application involves negotiations of the division of labour defining routine work in institutions. Continuous compromises are envisaged between an individual's needs or wishes, on the one hand, and what he or she does or is made to do, on the other. The 'negotiated order' characterising any system of social roles is shown to incorporate frequent adaptation to external and internal forces impinging upon a situation. In recent years this has been extended to the study of 'trajectories': that is, temporal structures linking work routines with the course of an illness while treated.

These two models – the crisis model and the negotiation model – seem different enough to be presented as separate. Each has a notion of aetiology, and also of therapy; both are derived from the general idea that illness is an outcome of social construction impinging on its recognition as well as treatment. While the crisis model comprises mostly the labelling and the anti-psychiatry literature, the negotiation model comprises the approach of 'grounded theory' and interactionist writings presented by British medical sociologists since the middle 1970s.

Chapter 6
The Crisis Model

As social but not biological deviance, illness means deviation from normative standards, and becoming ill is being categorised – 'labelled' – accordingly. The elements of labelling, however, are not created by the 'societal reaction'. Instead, so to speak, it acts as a *catalyst* helping to integrate existing elements into a pattern they would not otherwise form. Two classes of factors – the classificatory label and the behaviour being classified – are brought together. Neither the label alone nor the symptom represent anything but normal life. Their unification due to 'societal reaction' – often a crisis event – triggers off alternative role-taking accompanying 'secondary deviation'. This, in its aetiological phase, is described in three stages: initially, the independent existence of a ubiquitous stereotype, on the one hand, and 'normal', although often strange or symptomatic behaviours, on the other hand; then, 'public crisis' allowing for the stereotype to be applied to the behaviour; and, finally, alternative role-taking accompanying retrospective reinterpretation of the person's past together with internalisation of an illness-centred identity.

Role-taking including identity formation is perceived as socially organised since it takes place through professional help, mostly within treatment organisation. An anti-professional bias is inherent in this 'individualistic' standpoint (Thio, 1973) identifying with the patient. That a label of illness is conferred, with concomitant imputation of (sick) role, is taken to mean that therapy marks a transition to second-class citizen status.

In this vein, treatment is but socialisation into a deviancy role. It amounts to little more than applying treatment ideologies which owe their success to the credulity of a more or less captive population of health-service users. While individual practitioners may adhere to treatment ideologies, these are most efficiently put into practice by specialised organisations such as blindness agencies, mental hospitals, subnormality asylums, or voluntary associations such as *Alcoholics Anonymous*.

The three stages of aetiology

The state of normality

The stereotype. A well-entrenched, however derogatory, imagery of a wide range of deviations and diasabilities (Lemert, 1951, p. 87ff.) is seen as commonplace in our social world. Scheff asserts that 'everyone in a society learns the symptoms of mental disorder vicariously, through the imagery that is conveyed, unintentionally, in everyday life' (1966a, p. 80, emphasis omitted). Similarly, Robert Scott holds that, 'a part of the socialization experience in any society involves learning attitudes, beliefs, and values about stigmatized people such as the blind' (1969, p. 16). Such imagery is mostly unfavourable to the afflicted, and, in fact, discriminatory: 'The ethical and moral overtones of concepts such as "constitutionally inferior", "psychopathic", and "neurotic" or "psychotic" are ubiquitous' (Lemert, 1951, p. 404). Three sources of learning of such derogatory imagery are named: one is that during socialisation in childhood typifications are learned (Scheff, 1966a, p. 64; Scott, 1969, p. 16); another is folklore and smalltalk in everyday encounters that reinforce the stereotype (Scheff, 1966a, pp. 67ff., 82; Scott, 1969, p. 16); and a third is public communication media such as newspapers and television which are sources of vicarious reinforcement (Scheff, 1966a, pp. 67–80; Rock, 1973, pp. 37–47). Stereotyped images of 'the' blind, prostitute, or cripple (Goffman, 1963, Ch. 1) are learned during socialisation also by those to whom they (eventually) apply.

Some recent debate has focused on the question of whether classificatory typifications must necessarily carry a negative meaning to convey stigma. Winick (1982) holds against Becker and Goffman that, since 1968, the contents of the public image of the schizophrenic has changed from 'crazy' to 'bizarre' to 'person with problems'. In this, Winick argues, 'destigmatization of mental illness over the last decades' may be seen (1982, p. 244). One may also argue that although mental illness has lost some of its previous imagery, its negative connotation as an illness label is still undisputed. In Freidson's (1970a) terms, the issue is that medical knowledge contains the diagnostic entity of, say, schizophrenia. Through the 'nosological category' which justifies the idea that a certain state of mind constitutes illness, a stereotype defining a stigmatisable group in society emerges.

The behaviour. A discrepancy is noted between the numbers of those who display certain symptoms or show certain behaviours, on the one hand, and those who are diagnosed on the basis of such symptoms or behaviours, on the other. Freidson (1970a, Ch. 13) focuses on the variability of individual responses to pain and physical handicaps in order to make clear that the use of medical services is independent from the experience of symptomatic signs. Goffman (1959/61, p. 134) distinguishes between 'those offenses which could have been used as grounds for hospitalizing the offender' as opposed to 'those that are so used.'

While it is generally accepted that there is a considerable gap between the number of those who *could* be categorised as ill or disabled, and those who actually *are*, one question begs a clear-cut answer. It is whether categorisation – wherever it occurs – focuses on strange or impaired behaviour, or whether the incriminated behaviour falls within the range of normality. The problem is that of 'primary deviation'.

This question is crucial because it is the illness nature of mental disturbance – focused upon as 'primary deviation' – which is cited by the critics of the labelling approach to justify the treatment provided by modern psychiatric hospitals (Gove, 1970a, 1970b, 1974a, 1974b, 1982b). When electroconvulsive therapy and drugs with long-term side effects (not to mention sensory deprivations linked with 'institutional neurosis' as analysed by Barton in 1959 and Wing and Brown in 1970) are applied to persons who are as good as normal, most hospital treatment appears unethical. If the only thing from which patients suffer is the need to have been hospitalised (Goffman, 1961), the physical or psychological damage which could result from surgical or drug treatment appears unjustified under almost any angle. The question of 'primary deviation' has an eminently political connotation. It contains the answer to the problem of whether clinical expertise concerns patients' welfare, or whether medicine is an onslaught upon patients' personal liberty. This has been discussed by numerous, often polemical books focusing on the issue (Coulter, 1973; Clare, 1975/80; Pearson, 1975; Scull, 1977).

In principle, two arguments are raised. A group of writers holds that the behaviour which leads to stigmatisation is basically non-conspicuous and displays no noticeable features warranting its labelling; this will be referred to as the *non-conspicuousness approach*. Other writers contend that 'primary deviation' exists but may be analysed as rational behaviour occurring in an irrational environment; this will be referred to as the *life-problem approach*.

The Non-Conspicuousness Approach.   The distinction between an act and its meaning or label is behind the idea of 'residual rule-breaking'. Behaviour which – as the pure act of doing something or not doing it – cannot but be called normal (i.e., everybody does it or could do it) is nevertheless taken as a reason for labelling someone as sick. What distinguishes normal from symptomatic behaviour is not its contents – what the person, in fact, does – but its *context*. That the application of the label is arbitrary is derived from the fact that 'relative to the rate of treated mental illness, the rate of unrecorded residual rule-breaking is extremely high' (Scheff, 1966a, p. 47).

Scheff introduces three hypotheses which concretise the non-conspicuousness assumption: a *selectivity* hypothesis stipulates that there is more untreated than treated mental disorder; a *diversity* hypothesis stipulates that psychiatric symptoms do not display a homogeneous origin but, on the contrary, stem from a diversity of different origins (with the act of labelling being the only homogenising aspect of the heterogeneous symptoms as viewed by Goffman, 1961, pp. 134–5); and third, a *relativity* hypothesis stipulates that most residual rule-breaking is denied, and only if – by chance – a 'societal reaction' occurs does mental illness becomes manifest (Scheff, 1966a, pp. 39–54).

Becker assumes that the marijuana user first commits the act (i.e., one-off smoking of marijuana) in a non-intended and tentative fashion, and only when the environment teaches the user the techniques to enjoy the drug (presupposing the person is introduced into a group of dope smokers) will the new user acquire the motivation to proceed with the deviant habit (which eventually may lead to public labelling: Becker, 1963, pp. 41–58, esp. 46ff.). At this stage, the deviance may be of a *secret* nature (1963, p. 20): that is, although the individual engages in stigmatised behaviour, no public reaction has so far occurred.

It has been widely debated – if the 'societal reaction' is crucial for the transition to deviance – whether any 'secret' (i.e., pre-crisis) deviance can exist. If labelling does not occur through external normative evaluation alone, but also implies applying socially given stereotypes to one's own behaviour by the actor him- or herself, secret deviance is no epistemological problem (Lorber, 1967). However, this presupposes that deviance is not only a conceptual category used by doctors who diagnose, or by social scientists who deny its grounding in social reality. Deviance, if perceived by the actor, denotes a dichotomous categorisation between normal and abnormal used by all bona-fide members of a given society. In this vein, Pollner holds against Becker that two categories of deviance should be separated: namely, the one used by everyday actors taking for granted that the distinction between normal and deviant is grounded in the nature of the social world, stigmatising their fellow-humans accordingly; and also that of the social scientist denying the ontological character of the distinction and stipulating that its cognitive grid has no basis in the 'real' society. Only the latter, Pollner assures us, implies that 'secret' deviance is a logically contradictory problem (1974, p. 38).

Becker maintains that the 'residual' rule-breaking labelled mental illness has a double origin. One is that it is rule-breaking which cannot be accounted for in terms of other more mundane labels such as bad manners or crime. Furthermore, it would not appear as deviant were it not for the out-of-place context in which it occurs: muttering to oneself, for instance, is socially acceptable in prayer but not at a party where it may appear 'sick'. Scheff follows Szasz in the idea that the categories of residual deviance change over history but he goes beyond Szasz when he states that norms of decorum and decency are being violated:

> The typical norm governing decency or reality . . . literally 'goes without saying' and its violation is unthinkable for most of [a society's] members. For the convenience of the society in construing those instances of unnamable rule-breaking which are called to its attention, these violations may be lumped together into a residual category: witchcraft, spirit possession, or, in our own society, mental illness. (Scheff 1966, p. 34)

The most extreme formulation of the non-conspicuousness approach may be found in Rosenhan's 'experiment'. He sent eight persons to seek admission to 12 mental institutions in California on the grounds that they heard voices muttering 'empty', 'hollow' and 'thud'. All 12 pseudopatients, Rosenhan reports, were admitted and hospitalised for between 7 and 52 days, and it was their fellow-patients (*sic*) rather than staff who detected their sanity (Rosenhan, 1973, reprinted in Scheff, 1975 and in Grusky and Pollner, 1981). Despite the grave deficiencies in the design of Rosenhan's study (see R. L. Spitzer, 1976), Wing (1978), from the standpoint of concerned psychiatrist, raises the issue that Rosenhan's experiment may be credited with exposing psychiatry's practice (as opposed to theory) of prematurely hospitalising patients who might be able to manage in the community.

Of course, in the last instance, the margin is fluid regarding what constitutes normality and what goes beyond. The non-conspicuousness approach has to argue the point whether to do away with pathology altogether benefits anybody. Should Lemert be followed when he exclaims: 'Rare, indeed, is the person who at one time or another has not committed a felony. To ascribe this to mental pathology is to make the term lose its meaning, for most of us would have to be called "episodic psychopaths"' (1951, p. 19)? The Life-Problem Approach. 'Auditory hallucinations are often reported by normal persons, who hear voices of dead relatives, usually as a nocturnal occurrence . . . Delusions of uxorial infidelity, of approaching economic disaster, that one has been "framed", or that other people are insane or "need a psychiatrist" are all commonplace reactions in our society' (Lemert, 1951, pp. 425–6). In accordance with this earlier statement, Lemert (1962/67a) proposes that a person's diagnosed paranoia originates in the production of collusive clues by a persecutory environment. He refers to a case of conspiratorial exclusion of a particular research worker experiencing derogatory practices from team colleagues and their subsequent denial of exclusionary action. He reports eventual public scandal pushing the victimised outcast into a career of diagnosed paranoia (1962/67a, esp. p. 207).

Thus accepting a more-than-arbitrary nature of who and what is subjected to the illness label, Lemert implies that 'primary psychotic reactions' 'may be a reaction to intrafamilial conflict' or they 'may be acquired directly through learning from parents' (1951, p. 427). The latter is said to hold, in particular, for overaggressiveness, neurotic fears or similar symptoms. In this vein, Lemert suggests a psychological explanation for why some people – having suffered from 'societal reaction' – accommodate themselves with stigmatised identities which they then occupy. These 'negative identities', he surmises, 'may offer temporarily or relatively stable solutions to life problems despite the fact that they represent a lower order of human existence' (1967, p. 48). Elsewhere, he explains what these life-problems are. For instance, 'the crippled workman who becomes a beggar and accepts the dole' is an example for 'Freud's illustration of advantage through illness' (Lemert, 1967, p. 63, footnote 51); that is, the cripple's handicap appears as the life problem which can be 'solved' by drifting into unemployment and begging. By the same token, this allows the cripple to draw advantage from the impairment psychologically ('accepting the dole') and materially in that it may supply a residual income. That life problems are behind the behaviour which is being diagnosed is also argued by Thomas Szasz. Szasz stipulates that 'psychosocial, ethical and legal deviations' (1970b, p. 17) are ubiquitous, and they mirror conflicting personal needs, opinions, social aspirations, values and so on. That 'problems in living' are behind diagnosed illnesses has a double meaning: on the one hand, hysteria may be seen as 'non-discursive' communication of a need to be helped (Szasz, 1961, p. 128ff.), and interpersonal conflicts may be muffled by 'fighting the battle of stomach acid and chronic fatigue instead of facing up to marital conflict' (Szasz, 1970b, p. 23). On the other hand, there is a cosmic discrepancy behind such substitute suffering: namely, the incidence of illness is due to the discrepancy between mankind's ever-increasing need to control the world, and mankind's growing incapacity or unwillingness to publicly and collectively take the responsibility for its actions (1970b, pp. 21–2).[20]

Such cosmic as well as personal 'problems in living', Szasz contends, are camouflaged by their being diagnosed as illness. Much of Szasz' effort goes into the demonstration that a 'thing' – illness – is inserted into a vacuum where awareness of conflicts and discrepancies would have been more adequate. Such reification – a 'thing' taken for reality – is what Szasz criticises when he states that schizophrenia, or mental illness in general, represents a myth (Szasz, 1960, 1961). The reason given is that the same function that the label of illness serves in modern society has been served in history by other similarly vague labels (which lacked an 'objective' basis of measurable organic lesions or deficiencies): namely, witchcraft, heresy or sorcery (Szasz, 1970a). Freidson (1970a), who liberally quotes from Szasz throughout his *Profession of Medicine*, uses a passage from *The Myth of Mental Illness* (1961, pp. 44–5) to castigate modern medicine's expansion. He agrees with Szasz that modern medicine acquires the social-control function which law or religion had in historical societies, but cannot make a justified claim to scientific accuracy:

> Starting with such things as syphilis, tuberculosis, typhoid fever, and carcinomas and fractures we have created the class 'illness'. At first, this class was composed of only a few items . . . Then, with increasing zeal, physicians and especially psychiatrists began to call 'illness' . . . anything and everything in which they could detect any sign of malfunctioning, based on no matter what norm. (Freidson, 1970a, pp. 248–9)

A life-problem argument is also put forward by Laing. His anti-psychiatry is developed during the period from 1962 onwards (i.e., excluding the early books *Self and Other* and *The Divided Self* which attempt a phenomenological description of schizophrenia: see Gerhardt, 1978). Laing states:

> In the context of our present pervasive madness that we call normality, sanity, freedom, all our frames of reference are ambiguous and equivocal. A man who prefers to be dead rather than Red is normal. A man

who says he has lost his soul is mad. A man who says that men are machines may be a great scientist. A man who says he *is* a machine is 'depersonalized' in psychiatric jargon. (Laing, 1959/65, pp. 11–12)

Laing argues that life problems are due to a mechanism of categorisation which makes idiosyncratic patterns of family relationships become dangerous. The mechanism is called *mapping*, and its two stages are called internalisation and externalisation. While internalisation produces a cognitive representation of a family pattern in the child's mind (establishing a cognitive pattern called 'family'), externalisation achieves the reimposition of this 'family' pattern upon the outside world. He clarifies:

> The re-projection of the 'family' is not simply a matter of projecting an 'internal' object onto an external person. It is superimposition of one set of relations onto another: the two sets may match more or less. Only if they mis-match sufficiently in the eyes of others, is the operation regarded as psychotic. That is, the operation is not regarded as psychotic *per se*. (Laing, 1969, p. 9)

What distinguishes the psychotic from the normal is the *character of the family* into which an individual happens to be born. If relationships within one's family happen to be strange and unrealistic, and expose a child or adolescent to contradictory definitions which, at the same time, are being denied, schizophrenic breakdown may occur. Laing stresses on various occasions that the family structure is at the root of the schizophrenic process although he hastens to add that the family is not to be regarded as a causal agent producing schizophrenia (Laing, 1959/65, pp. 189–90). In general, his question in the analysis of case histories of schizophrenic adolescents is: 'to what extent is the experience and behaviour of that person, who has already begun a career as a diagnosed "schizophrenic" patient, intelligible in the light of the praxis and process of his or her family nexus?' (Laing and Esterton, 1964, p. 24). He answers this by pointing out that the experiences and behaviour of diagnosed schizophrenics are to be seen as strategies to cope with and make tolerable an intolerable family situation (Laing, 1969). Schizophrenia thus becomes an act of breaking loose and establishing a purified new reality freed from the ambiguities of 'normal madness' (where, for instance, to be dead is preferred to being a Communist). He introduces schizophrenia as *death–rebirth process* characterised as '*X experience*': 'as a movement in, down, back, turning at the nadir, and then out up, forward into the world . . . It appears to be a sort of death–

rebirth sequence, from which, if it is sucessfully negotiated, the person returns to the world feeling new-born' (Laing, 1969, pp. 51–2 but see Siegler, Osmond and Mann, 1969, for the dangers of equating psychedelic and psychotic experience).

Laing has *two* notions of schizophrenia. Whereas the one promotes the idea that schizophrenia is a real or natural phenomenon and should be permitted by society for those who need liberation from stifling family settings, the second notion reveals that the usually diagnosed schizophrenia is a construction by psychiatry. The latter is exposed as a falsely causal image meant to account for allegedly disturbed behaviour: 'This suggests research into the origins of schizophrenia is hunting a hare whose tracks are in the mind of the hunters' (1969, p. 44). From this perspective, it is only a short step to assuming that the ubiquity of the behaviour inviting its classification as schizophrenic is a function of the ubiquity of the family as a social institution (this triggers Cooper's plea for *The Death of the Family*, 1971). The *normal* processes of 'mapping' in the family are said to generate liberation attempts by adolescents whose families practise particularly restrictive image control.

Anti-psychiatry's double notion of schizophrenia makes it possible that, on the one hand, behaviour which becomes an object of labelling is seen as a 'life problem' (and, from this perspective, schizophrenia is said not to exist); at the same time, in its idealised version of death–rebirth experience, schizophrenia is hailed as a liberating experience which could change the world ('The Bird of Paradise').

In this vein, deviance diagnosed as schizophrenic is understood to be less 'residual' than 'rational': That is, the irrationality is in the environment (the family, the society), and the individual suffering from it to the point of mental breakdown appears more rational than his or her 'normal' contemporaries. Those who tolerate society's contradictions without emotional repercussions are deemed inferior to those who cannot sustain the world's moral discrepancies and fall ill.

The 'societal reaction'

The cycle of denial, the 'psychotic process' and the 'clinical iceberg'. That symptoms cannot systematically be related to diagnosis is documented by numerous studies. Freidson (1970a) cites Zborowski (1952), Apple (1960) and Zola (1966) to demonstrate that cultural attitudes interfere with 'objective' perception and evaluation of symptoms. In a study of wives whose husbands are hospitalised for schizophrenia, Yarrow *et al.* (1955) find that husbands' symptoms are disregarded or interpreted away by distressed wives over considerable periods of time (see also C. C. Schwartz, 1957; Sampson, Messinger and Towne, 1962). Lemert sees such normalisation as an effect of the stigmatising label: 'The family of the heavy-drinking man erects perceptual defenses against seeing his action as alcoholism because they, like him, are distressed by this ascription of meaning' (1967, p. 52; see also 1962/67b). That symptomatic behaviour would *normally* arouse denial calls for the introduction of an additional element, one not implicated in the nature of the symptomatic behaviour, which triggers off the process of illness labelling. Scheff opposes Gove who insists on the aetiological significance of 'primary deviation', saying: 'The master question which labelling theory raises with respect to commitment rates is . . . At what point and under what conditions does the process of denial stop and labeling begin?' (Scheff, 1974, p. 448).

The answer is not unambiguous. On the one hand, *contextual* public recognition is said to render the symptomatic behaviour conspicuous which, in turn, leads to the crisis behaviour's labelling. On the other hand, the idea of one-off public crisis is partly contradicted by the idea of a 'sequence of interaction leading to secondary deviation' (Lemert, 1951, p. 77). The latter envisages a cycle of gradually increasing norm-breaking and responsive sanctioning constituting a so-called deviant career (Becker, 1963, p. 23ff.), which eventually leads to the acquisition of a deviant identity. This gradual deterioration of behavioural performance is what Lemert conceptualises as 'psychotic process' when he elaborates:

> At each step in the psychotic process there is an interplay between the internal and external limits and the symbolic process, with social failures leading to a distortion of the anticipatory reactions, which attenuate communication and make for more social failures. Because of these failures, subtle or outright rejections and segregational responses toward the deviant increase. (Lemert, 1951, p. 428)

Indeed, it could be argued that the 'psychotic process' proceeds over long periods of time and goes through various cycles of denial and deterioration until the person is 'ripe' for being labelled mentally ill. This would be similar to symptoms representing the 'clinical iceberg' (Wadsworth, Butterfield and Blaney, 1971): namely, signs of sickness not perceived as serious enough to warrant a visit to the doctor (although there are subcultural variations regarding what symptoms and with what severity are brought to medical attention). In all, the crucial question is the role of the *contingencies* in 'public crisis'.

The 'public crisis': context and contingency.   Diagnosis, according to Freidson, is where medicine's power to 'create illness as a social meaning' (1970a, p. 245) comes into its own. This entails the 'variable character of the problem at issue, the ambiguity and arbitrariness of, if not the knowledge, then at least the concepts to which the knowledge is attached' (1970a, p. 308). What counts is the *ceremonial* form in which the application of medical knowledge happens. The idea is that diagnosis thus becomes *functionally equivalent to a collective reaction in a primitive society*. Becker assures us: 'You can commit clan incest and suffer from no more than gossip as long as no one makes a public accusation; but you will be driven to your death if the accusation is made' (1963, pp. 11–2).

What, then, is the specific feature of a public reaction? In an article on *status degradation ceremonies*, Garfinkel (1956a) maintains that 'degradation ceremonies' affect the normality–abnormality attribution.[21] In other words, they determine whether a person is accepted as a normal competent actor. In this sense, the 'degradation ceremony' produces a shift between the basic constitutive *normal* identity, and the new reduced *total* identity. Garfinkel stresses the pervasive character of such a shift:

> The work of the denunciation effects the recasting of the objective character of the perceived other: the other person becomes in the eyes of his condemners literally a different and *new* person. It is not that the new attributes are added to the old 'nucleus'. He is not changed, he is reconstituted. The former identity, at best, receives the accent of mere appearance. In the social calculus of reality representations and test, the former identity stands as accidental; the new identity is the 'basic reality'. What he is now is what, 'after all', he was all along.' (1956a, pp. 421–2)

Such 'degradation ceremonies' are pictured in the literature on labelling *either* as single crisis events producing shock reactions in the individual and the environment, *or* as a sequence of stages making for an ordered process of identity loss and change. These two views are promoted by different authors, although some who emphasise one may also allow for the other as an additional aspect. However, the two views are not reconciled into the hypothesis, say, that *successful degradation* presupposes a crisis as well as subsequent validation.

The idea that 'societal reaction' happens as public crisis and produces shock in the individual is demonstrated for blindness.

Scott, in his account of the *Making of Blind Men*, insists that 'the overwhelming majority of people who are classified as blind according to this definition [i.e., the Snellen measure] can, in fact, see' (1969, p. 42). Accordingly, the person with poor vision is severely upset when an ophthalmologist at a certain point in time feels unable to do any more for his or her client. This, maintains Scott, *produces* the client's blindness as an official reality. In principle, the ophthalmologist's decision is not based on 'objective' reality since there is no complete absence of vision in most of those pronounced blind. The quasi-official character means that from now on the client's 'problems are no longer medical ones of vision but psychological and social problems of adjustment to blindness' (Scott, 1969, p. 73). This is further elucidated by the fact that the ophthalmologist, when determining that a patient has reached the blindness stage, refers the patient to a welfare authority rather than offering further intensified treatment.

Some authors believe that the 'societal reaction' does not come without warning. Either the individual has become sensitised to the possibility of a serious breakdown of communication by previous experiences of exclusion and collusion (Lemert, 1962/67a), or the individual has, in fact, been doing something utterly foolish or reprehensible – such as appearing nude on a motorway – which triggers off the public reaction. In such cases, the individual is described as being 'in a confused and suggestible state' (Scheff, 1966a, p. 121), realising how much havoc he or she has created. Scheff elaborates a double spiral of mutual meaning attribution which explains the public-crisis impact:

> When gross rule-breaking is publicly recognized and made an issue, the rule-breaker may be profoundly confused, anxious, and ashamed. In this crisis it seems reasonable to assume that the rule-breaker will be suggestible to the cues that he gets from the reactions of others toward him. But those around him are also in a crisis; the incomprehensible nature of the rule-breaking, and the seeming need for immediate action lead them to take collective action against the rule-breaker on the basis of the attitude which all share – the traditional stereotype of insanity. The rule-breaker is sensitive to the cues provided by these others and begins to think of himself in terms of the stereotyped role of insanity, which is part of his own role vocabulary also, since he, like those reacting to him, learned it early in childhood. In this situation his behavior may begin to follow the pattern suggested by his own stereotypes and the reactions of others. That is, when a residual rule-breaker organizes his behavior within the framework of mental disorder, and when his organization is validated by others, particularly prestigeful others such as physicians, he is 'hooked' and will proceed on a career of chronic deviance. (Scheff, 1966a, p. 88)

What astonishes, at first sight, is the crucial role attributed to the physician. Although the physician may not share the confusion and shock which Scheff attributes to the immediate environment, it is the diagnosis and categorisation provided by the physician which settles the label. Scheff's argument is consistent if he assumes that the physician shares with patients as well as those present in the crisis situation the culturally stereotyped label of the lunatic or insane. That is, Scheff must think that pre-medical imagery is also operative in medical personnel.

Goffman, on the other hand, sees the label applied not by a physician but by the hospital as an institution. Goffman's view is that a person's identity is a function of institutional, or environmental, processes of attribution ('this special kind of institutional arrangement does not so much support the self as constitute it': 1961, p. 168). That is, he hypothesises a reciprocity 'between the self and its significant society' (1961, p. 127). If the significant society submits individuals to systematic efforts of diminishing or destroying their identity, this makes them eventually unable to retain their original (or any) self. Goffman maintains for a patient who has just been committed to a mental hospital, and whose past experiences now retrospectively appear as those of a pre-patient:

> The pre-patient's career may be seen in terms of an extrusory model; he starts out with relationships and rights, and ends up, at the beginning of his hospital stay, with hardly any of either. The moral aspects of this career, then, typically begin with the experience of abandonment, disloyalty, and embitterment. This is the case even though to others it may be obvious that he was in need of treatment, and even though in the hospital he may soon come to agree. (1961, p. 133)

Goffman pictures a 'betrayal funnel' (p. 140) into which the patient is manouvred while being handled and/or dealt with by different agencies or 'significant figures' (Goffman, 1961). In this view, a 'degradation ceremony' (p. 139) may be but one of a number of humiliating events which the individual experiences during the last stages of his or her 'pre-patient career'. That the potential patient has to appear in front of a mental health commission is, for Scheff, *the* crisis event which erodes the person's civic identity (since more often than not he or she is committed to a mental hospital); for Goffman, however, the commitment jury only represents one among a number of significant others who finally accomplish a person's loss of identity (see also Lemert, 1951, p. 414ff. and Richard Dewey, 1913, quoted there). The main impact, according to Goffman, does not occur prior to hospitalisation but only as soon as the person enters the hospital; it is not

until then that the mortification and alienation set in which systematically undercut a person's identity and replace it by an illness-
related self. The end-point is virtual loss of any clear-cut identity,
manifesting itself in the practice of 'the amoral arts of shameless-
ness' (1961, p. 169).

What parameters determine the 'societal reaction'? If neither
the incriminated symptom nor the classificatory label can claim to
be causal, and if the consequences of 'societal reaction' are as
grave as Scheff and Goffman maintain, can the sociologist nevertheless find a systematic relationship between the occasion of
labelling and its object? Goffman argues: 'in the degree that the
"mentally ill" outside hospitals numerically approach or surpass
those inside hospitals, one could say that mental patients distinctively suffer not from mental illness, but from contingencies'
(1961, p. 135).

What contingencies are envisaged? Lemert mentions *visibility* of
the symptom held against a community's *tolerance level*, yielding a
'tolerance quotient' (Lemert, 1951, pp. 404–9). Scheff adds to
these a third factor, namely the *power* of the rule-breaker (but he
partly neutralises his emphasis on environmental contingencies by
stressing two parameters concerning the incriminated behaviour
itself: namely, the amount and degree of the rule-breaking: Scheff,
1966a, p. 96ff.). Goffman completes this list by 'socio-economic
status, . . . proximity to a mental hospital, amount of treatment
facilities available' (1961, p. 134ff.), and he leaves room for more:
'For information about other contingencies one must rely on
atrocity tales' (p. 135).

Some of these contingencies have been confirmed by research.
Several studies focus on the relationship between socio-economic
status and the chance to be labelled psychotic or neurotic (Hollingshead and Redlich, 1958; Dohrenwend and Dohrenwend,
1969; see also R. Cochrane, 1983). The issue of visibility is dealt
with, for instance, in Clausen and Yarrow (1955), and Greenley
(1972, 1979). Mishler (1981), in a partly edited book also focusing
on non-psychiatric illness, draws together evidence that *context* (as
defined through contingencies) determines the variability of treatment chances.

In terms of explanatory theory, as d'Arcy (1976) aptly shows,
the notion of contingency is at the heart of the labelling perspective. 'Societal reaction' needs the contingency postulate to clarify
what causal nexus the crisis model suggests:

> If illness is defined . . . as social deprivation – as a social status – then
> the contingencies have theoretical significance. They are theoretically

significant for they are the determinants of why and how people come to be labelled sick. In this sociological context the contingencies assume theoretical importance because they are the causal nexus. (d'Arcy, 1976, p. 46)

D'Arcy complains that despite such theoretical impact, the conception of contingency remains vague and no attempt at a proper hypothesis is made. It remains unclear, he remarks, which contingencies affect which persons' perceived or actual chances of being submitted to an illness labelling, and in what way. It seems that much confusion and inconsistency in the literature is based on this.

Is the publicly occurring one-off shock possibly the prototype of the 'societal reaction'? Or does the 'societal reaction' presuppose an additional socialisation through an institutional or any significant environment to produce the 'total' identity change triggered off by the crisis? Since it is as yet undecided whether both elements together constitute the effective aetiological force, or whether each of them alone will also do, a diversity of heterogeneous hypotheses have arisen on what labelling is and should be. For instance, Trice and Roman (1970) show that the work of Alcoholics Anonymous, and the treatment of recidivism, imply processes of 'delabelling' and 'relabelling'. Daniels (1970a) maintains that the diagnosis of mental illness in military personnel takes into account the 'consequences that a specific diagnosis label may have for the career of the patient' (1970b, p. 183). Rogers and Buffalo (1971) also refer to the possibility that an individual does not accept the label that has been attached, and they recount nine different ways in which an individual may disavow or refute a label.

It is likely that a 'societal reaction' – one which incorporates a 'degradation ceremony' and instigates a negative status change – may consist of *both* elements in conjunction. That is, neither a public crisis alone nor solely an institutional socialisation towards the role of mental illness may produce the relevant changes in the individual. Thus people evading hospitalisation after a public degradation may have a better chance of avoiding the label altogether (this is the *raison d'être* of community psychiatry). Rosenhan's pseudopatients during their hospital stay did not develop the symptoms or mannerisms of *institutional neurosis* (Barton, 1959), let alone those of schizophrenia; they were spared a public crisis prior to their admission. Trice and Roman (1970) refute the irreversibility of the alcoholism label; they focus on a population which is not treated in mental or other institutions but by a self-help organisation. Daniels (1970a) focuses on the fact that in some cases where a psychiatrist considers hospitalisation after a public crisis, extramedical reasons may make him or her refrain from suggesting it; that is, the process of labelling is stopped by the psychiatrist even after the patient has been referred following public degradation. Finally, Rogers and Buffalo's (1971) types suggest that if identity change goes together with public crisis (or, in medical circumstances, diagnosis), 'repudiation' of a label can no longer be effective; strategies such as 'channelling', 'reinterpretation', 'redefinition' or 'alteration' are then futile.

From this angle, the debate between Scheff and Gove loses much of its acumen. Gove maintains two main points against the 'societal-reaction' explanation of illness: first, that there is 'primary deviation' evoking the public reaction, and, second, that the latter does not necessarily set forth a process of role attribution and identity change (see Gove, 1970a, 1970b, 1972, 1975, 1975/80, 1982b; Akers, 1968, 1972; Scheff, 1974; Horvitz, 1979). The first issue is clarified by saying that whether or not a 'societal reaction' occurs is independent of whether or not a 'cycle of denial' takes place; what matters is whether degradation is staged. On the second point one may say that if public crisis and role attribution (identity deterioration) represent two distinct aspects of 'societal reaction' independent from each other but only together producing lasting stigmatisation, then Gove's criticism is reduced to a helpful suggestion.

The state of illness or disability

That interactionism presents a *role* model has rarely been recognised. Parsons, who introduces the sick role as part of the complementarity relation between doctor and patient, has often been reproached for not focusing on chronic illness (Mechanic, 1959; Gallagher, 1976). Moreover, his concept of sick role has been mistaken for a conceptualisation of deviance (Gerhardt, 1979a; also see above, Part I). It seems to have escaped the *critical* interest of Parsons' critics that what they implicitly would like Parsons to have produced (namely, a sick-role concept of deviance applying to chronic illness) has in fact been introduced by the labelling approach. The interactionists' role concept, at first sight, looks rather like that of Parsons. Scheff, for instance, focuses on received expectations in a relationship of presumed complementarity, and he suggests that the pattern of a patient's symptomatic behaviour (written 'symptomatic') is 'in conformity with the stereotyped expectations of others' (1966a, p. 92). Thus, for Scheff, it is received normative expectations which make for the 'sick role' (p.

93). Similarly, Scott holds that blindness constitutes an imputed set of role expectations: 'Helplessness, dependency, melancholy, docility, gravity of inner thought, aestheticism – these are the things that commonsense views tell us to expect from the blind' (R. A. Scott, 1969, p. 4). This is where the similarity ends. The labelling protagonists deviate from Parsons in two points. They do *not* envisage temporary incumbency of the sick role. Rather, once people have entered the sick role, institutionalised processes of social control – above all engineered by medical and welfare agencies – are seen to help people to internalise the respective role-expectations into their selves and thus make their role incumbency permanent. Such presumed permanency of role-taking conceptually relates sickness to disability. Freidson (1966, 1970a) envisages disability as a life-long status of deviance. Other authors like Haber and Smith (1971) combine a Parsonian notion of (in)capacity with the interactionist thesis of 'secondary deviation': 'disability', they define, ' is a form of social adaptation to incapacity which organizes behavior in terms of a distinctive pattern of expectations characterized by Lemert . . . as "secondary deviation"' (1971, pp. 89–90).

The second aspect in which labelling theory's idea of illness deviates from Parsons' role model concerns the question of *motivation*. Although some authors see the patient seeking the sick status as committing him- or herself to a mental hospital to establish an unconsciously motivated claim against a sceptical family or environment (Erikson, 1957), most authors do not follow this idea. Becker, for instance, holds (contrary to Parsons) that the sequence from motivation to social act ought to be reversed. At the outset, he suggests, is a certain culturally or historically facilitating or inhibiting 'climate' which also influences whether, in case of narcotics use, drug-induced psychoses occur (Becker, 1968). Motivation, he claims, stands at the *end* of a labelling process, and it emerges from vicarious and gradually more purposive committing of the act (including being incorporated into the appropriate subculture). At first, the act happens by chance, beyond motivation, and motivation only represents the last stage of deviancy accomplishment (Becker, 1963, pp. 30–8).

This view on the motivational question is shared by all authors hypothesising that processes of *identity change* follow the occurrence of a public crisis. That such identity formation is *learning* seems to make sense if the whole process is understood as role acquisition. One version explains it in terms of psychology's stimulus–response paradigm: 'Given rewards for disturbed behavior, that disturbed behavior may become integral to a role-making process out of which an identity as a disturbed child may be reinforced' (M. Schwartz, Fearn and Shryker, 1966/72, p. 521).

Elsewhere, a more interactionist view of the learning process is promulgated. Lemert distinguishes between a 'societal definition' (the externally imputed role) and a 'self definition' (the internalised role), and the latter is defined as acceptance of the former:

> The adjusted sociopathic person is simply one who accepts his status, role, and self-definition . . . [Such acceptance] frees a fund of energy which hitherto has been consumed in a continuous struggle to repudiate the societal definition . . . Even today in our society if a blind person can accept the unrealistic and sentimental attitudes of the public toward his handicap, he can exploit them very profitably and live very comfortably in the community. He becomes a professional blind man. (1951, p. 96ff.)

The imputed definition is societal and refers to the organisational side of label construction. To be sure, Rosenhan's quasi-experiment as well as Scott's carefully collected evidence documenting that stigma production is engineered through professional experts (R. A. Scott, 1970) focus on organisational goings-on. Illness and disability labels – *because* they are implemented by medical and welfare agencies – succumb to professional politics pursued by, and pressure-group interests served by, service agencies. The blindness role, maintains R. A. Scott (1969), is geared towards and internalised by 'acceptable' categories of the blind such as young people and able-bodied men; often others are excluded from attention as well as help. Similarly, Lemert holds that even access to roles organised around disapproved behaviour may be restricted by 'age, sex, physical characteristics, nativity, kinship, religious affiliation, economic positions, and societal class' (1951, p. 81). He points in the direction of a two-tier division even with stigmatised populations: those who *fit the label* may pursue a *career* of, say, a 'professional blind man' (Lemert, 1951, p. 97). A more recent study focuses on mentally ill in the community who 'make it crazy' (Estroff, 1981). Others with less desirable characteristics in terms of age or presence of multiple disease may find it difficult to avoid being taken advantage of in the medical or other settings ('*Unkindest Cut*', Millman, 1977).

The introduction of identity change as a sequel to 'societal reaction' complements the deviancy-focused *role theory*. What characterises roles in the labelling and anti-psychiatry approaches when contrasted with Parsons' model? D'Arcy points out that the assumption that not everyone who has symptoms of mental disorder ends up being labelled mentally ill *logically* presupposes that

mental illness is an *ascribed* status (1976, p. 45). This corresponds
with what has been described as 'master status' (Hughes 1945;
Schur, 1971, p. 70). Illness then becomes a 'total moral state which
reflects the substantial self [of the sick person] . . . [Illness] is . . .
regarded as . . . an indication of [the sick person's] essence'
(Rock, 1973, p. 32).

The notion of 'master status' (Hughes, 1945) means that with the
'sharp rite of transition' and the 'ceremonies which accompany this
change of status' (Erikson, 1962/64, p. 16), the individual's range
of actual and/or accessible roles changes drastically. This entails,
on the one hand, that a new range of 'subsidiary roles' (Lemert,
1951, p. 90) are selected which appear compatible with the person's sick 'master status'; second, it means that existing roles such
as 'familial and occupational status' (Scheff, 1966a, p. 118)
undergo dramatic reinterpretations. This becomes drastic when
the discharged mental patient finds it difficult to slot back into an
inconspicuous family and occupational life because 'his welcome
back into the community is a qualified and watchful one under the
best of conditions' (Lemert, 1951, p. 441; also Scheff, 1966a, p.
87ff.; Miller and Dawson, 1973).

It is at this point that the moral indignation becomes understandable which propels Freidson's heavy criticism of the medical
profession's power to '*create*' illness. If the 'deviant illness roles'
(Freidson, 1970a, p. 261) are '*master statuses*' of quasi-ascribed
nature, the suffering induced by illness must appear as a burden
additional to the loss of normalcy rights.

Dynamically, the 'master status' has two sides. A process of
'validating identity' (Schur, 1971, p. 70) leads to *retrospective
reinterpretation* of a person's past life and personality. Kitsuse
describes this for the issue of homosexuality:

> When an individual's sexual 'normality' is called into question, by
> whatever form of evidence, the imputation of homosexuality is docu-
> mented by retrospective interpretations of the deviant's behavior, a
> process by which the subject reinterprets the individual's past behavior
> in the light of the new information concerning his sexual deviance.
> (Kitsuse, 1962/64, p. 96)

The message is one of *once a thief, always a thief*. As regards the
example used, homosexuality, the reader of the 1980s thinks that
more bias against it was held during the 1960s than today. But the
reader also may feel that recently the debate around Acquired
Immune Deficiency Syndrome (AIDS) has shown that 'master
status'-homosexuality labels may have mellowed but not disappeared.

The second dynamic aspect of 'master status' relates to the *interiorisation* of behavioural rules and self-conceptions. Erikson refers to 'an act of social placement, assigning . . . a special role (like that of prisoner or patient) which redefines his position in society' (1964, p. 16). In other words, marginality and the reduced chance to achieve full participation in society's privileges become core aspects of a person's self-perception. Scheff ventures that such redefinition of the self induces increased likelihood of illness since a person with a sick-role identity, 'may feel that he has reached his "breaking point" under circumstances which would be endured by a person with a "normal" self-conception' (1966a, p. 92). In the same vein, Kaplan, Martin and Robbins (1982) discover that self-derogation may be a sequel of drug use which, in turn, becomes a motive for continued adolescent drug consumption.

The argument has come full circle. Because the individual occupies an illness 'master status' and performs the role related to it, and because the nature of this role facilitates deterioration of normal behavioural controls, the individual in a labelled social position ('sick role') does what he or she is supposed to do: act sick. Thus, sickness is now seen to be produced by the role, not vice versa. The disabling symptoms or pain may be present but are seen to derive also from the individual's incumbency of the sick role. For instance, Mishler (1981) interprets Posner's (1977) findings about diabetes in a way which suggests that taking the prescribed insulin is often a cause of coma: 'These results suggest that a significant complication of adult-onset diabetes may be . . . treatment-induced' (Mishler, 1981, p. 150). This view, however, may be too unspecific. For example, Greenley (1979), in a longitudinal study of 31 hospitalised schizophrenics and their closest relatives (significant others) could not find that received role expectations (at admission) influence symptom incidence (illness behaviour at follow-up). But he finds that a supportive attitude of close kin enhances the degree to which a patient is expected to improve positively during hospitalisation (see also Greenley 1980): that is, the iatrogenic impact of the role is here not corroborated.

Returning to the notion of role, and the relationship between the Parsonian and the interactionist model, what emerges from the previous discussion is that there seem to be two points where the two conceptions differ.

1. Both focus upon the sick role as a *status-role* (Gerhardt, 1971), albeit in a different way. Parsons defines all roles as status roles (1951a, p. 38) and envisages the sick role as one among various structural forms in society; his focus is on medical practice

which helps to overcome the sick status. The interactionists (especially the labelling theorists) define the sick role as master status; they concentrate on the individual's experiences when acquiring it.

2. The question of *motivation* is given contrasting answers. While Parsons introduces a psychodynamically based model of unconscious motivation, the labelling theorists maintain that motivation is a consequence rather than a cause of role incumbency. However, both approaches agree that eventually motivation and normative expectations merge into a person's identity. In some ways, it may be said that Parsons perceives more problems in such mergers than the labelling literature (in fact, Parsons is concerned about how such mergers can be avoided).

The general connotation of sick role is that Parsons' *social niche* is converted into a hermetic *iron cage* which the individual, once trapped in it, may actually never leave. Illness as a 'negative identity' and a socially stigmatised 'master status' does not allow for the return to normal life as if nothing had happened.

Therapy and the impact of institutions

Aetiology in the crisis model is an acquisition of an illness label through ceremonial status passage. In the light of this, therapy is treatment but the patient does not reacquire normality. Parsons, in his deviancy model, focuses on social control administered using psychoanalysis on an unconscious level to return the patient to normal duties. Labelling theory and anti-psychiatry assume that the social control exerted by the medical profession forces or educates the patient into becoming a fully-fledged deviant. The function of therapy, then, is to ensure that the incumbency of the sick role is *not* transitory.

Medical work, in this perspective, appears as the application of clinical ideologies. Therapy allegedly is no more than the practical use of treatment doctrines. Their effect for the patient is doubtful at best. To be sure, it is argued that the application of treatment (treatment ideologies) to an often captive patient population produces rather than reduces the prevalence of illness. Such iatrogenic effect of therapy, however, does not contradict the fact that most patients feel better after treatment. It is suggested that the latter is due to a universal 'placebo effect'.

Labelling theory's and anti-psychiatry's anti-professional bias mirror the institution-critical attitude pervading much of the political spirit of the 1960s. Becker emphatically makes the connection between war crimes committed by US Marines in 1968 and the defaults of school psychiatrists acting on behalf of educational authorities:

> Even if no general is ever brought to trial for the killings at My Lai, those events shook such faith as people had in the moral correctness of the military action in Vietnam and those at the highest level responsible for it. Similarly, when we understand how school psychiatrists operate as agents of school officials rather than of their patients (Szasz, 1967), we lose some of whatever faith we had in the institutions of conventional psychiatry. (Becker, 1974, p. 61)

Behind Becker's statement is the political credo that any agency or person acting for the state or an established authority comes suspiciously close to conniving with adversaries of the 'underdog'. From this angle, the patient occupying the sick role is but another underdog deserving the sociologist's unconditional partisanship.

It ought to be clear that the basic identification is with the patient as apparently powerless and beleaguered victim. The view on therapy takes the side of the patient in a medical scene where doctors' and patients' interests, in principle, are deemed irreconcilable.

The patient's position is considered all the weaker because therapy joins forces with public policy. For instance, campaigns against alcoholism and drug abuse are reinforced by public policy and become official law. Medical treatment thus becomes part of the state's curtailing of individual freedom. The self-styled humanistic sociology (Matza, 1969, p. 105) turns against 'professional dominance' because it merges with *Legislation of Morality* (Duster, 1970).

The crisis model, when dealing with therapy, mainly focuses on three issues:

(a) identification of treatment and treatment ideologies;
(b) the idea that illness is produced through treatment;
(c) the idea that individuality (normality) is comparatively untouched by illness as well as its treatment.

These may be discussed in some detail.

Identification of treatment and treatment ideologies

A 'naturalistic' description of 'total' institutions (whether hospitals, 'homes', or welfare institutions for the blind or disabled or others), according to Goffman, points to the following:

First, all aspects of iife are conducted in the same place and under the same single authority. Second, each phase of the member's daily activity is carried on in the immediate company of a large batch of others, all of whom are treated alike and required to do the same thing together. Third, all phases of the day's activities are tightly scheduled. (1961, p. 6)

In the second place, after 'breakdown of the barriers ordinarily separating [the] three spheres of life', Goffman stresses the rigid 'basic split between a large managed group, conveniently called inmates, and a small supervisory staff. Inmates typically live in the institution and have restricted contact with the world outside the walls; staff often operate on an eight-hour day and are socially integrated into the outside world' (1961, p. 7).

These two features, breakdown of communication barriers and establishment of rigid authority split, connect with what Scott analyses as the double function of blindness agencies. They serve as ragbag dumping grounds for the unwanted stigmatised population, and they channel the public's general expectation that something 'be done'. The latter depends on the fact that neither the agency nor the disabled get too much into the public limelight while attracting some publicity. This ensures that everybody feels that the disabled and the sick are cared for without stirring undue attention (R. A. Scott, 1969, pp. 92, 97).

This leads to a rather shattering analysis of what happens in actual treatment agencies. Lemert presents a deplorable overall picture:

In a climate of political insecurity, with a mediocre-to-poor staff constantly going and coming, with authority-minded, medically trained psychiatrists in charge, the totalitarian pattern of the ancient hospital is conserved despite the more democratic trends beginning to be manifest in the treatment of sociopathic deviants by social workers and clinicians in many welfare agencies. (Lemert, 1951, p. 417)

The two functions which therapy is meant to serve are: *discipline* as instigated through a reward-and-punishment system, and, second, loss and partial *reconstruction of one's identity* as engineered through the staged sequence of mortification experiences.

Discipline, Goffman assures us, is vital because 'state mental hospitals . . . function . . . in terms of a "ward system". Drastically reduced living conditions are allocated through punishments and rewards, expressed more or less in the language of penal institutions' (Goffman, 1961, p. 206); and Lemert elucidates that 'the supervening elements in patient–staff interaction in the mental hospital are restraint and punishment. These are . . . strongly suggested if not fully symbolized by most things called "therapy"' (1951, p. 418).

Scheff (1966b) makes it clear that 'ward system', in this context, means *work system* but, seen in terms of what actually gets done: 'Often there is considerable difference between the official version of the work done in an organization and what actually gets done' (1966b, p. 146).

Reconstruction of the patient's identity, as a second accomplishment of therapy, is related to what Freidson (1971) addresses as the 'depersonalization of the client in the medical organization' (1971, p. 35) and which he pictures vividly: 'Simply to be strapped on a rolling table and wheeled down corridors, into and out of elevators, and, finally, into an operating room for the scrutiny of all is to be treated like an object without the consciousness of a person' (1971, p. 36). Such experiences which imply mortification are, according to Goffman, advertised to the (mental) patient as 'intentional parts of his treatment' (1961, p. 149). To make it plain that this means nothing which may be changed easily, Goffman argues that the 'stringent punishments' (p. 148) effecting the patient's depersonalisation and loss of accustomed self-esteem and ego-identity are what, in fact, represent the main contents of organisational life within mental hospitals. Treatment merely serves the purpose of reaching this aim. When R. A. Scott recognises two distinct treatment ideologies for the blind – the restorative approach staging a self-concept for the patient of 'death' and reconstitution, and the accommodative approach coaching people into becoming dependent and willingly accepting help (1969, p. 88) – it remains taken for granted that both ideologies serve the same function. This is to replace whatever treatment might be institutionally conceivable (but not given by the institution) with the deliberate reshaping of the blind's malleable self-concept. The aim is that they accept their blindness identity rather than ask for additional treatment or extra help.

That medical treatment would always represent merely the application of a treatment ideology is explained by Freidson (1970a and 1970b, 1971) as due to the very nature of professional work.

The crux of the matter is that expertise is not mere knowledge. It is the practice of knowledge, organized socially and serving as the focus for the practitioner's commitment. The worker develops around his work an ideology and, with the best of intentions, an 'imperialism' that stresses the technical superiority of his work and his capacity to perform it. The 'imperialist' perspective, built into the individual perspective through training and practice, cannot be overcome by ethical dedication to the public interest . . . The issue is who is to determine what the goals are to be pursued. Accountability for effective and humane services must, in some way, be more responsive to the client himself. (Freidson, 1971, pp. 39–40)

The criticism of medical treatment (that it is a realisation of treatment ideology) also pervades the idea that the doctor – a representative of the medical profession – is a *moral entrepreneur*. Becker (1963, pp. 47–63) is the first to use the term. He claims that moral entrepreneurship logically concurs with the illness label's being conferred by medical personnel on a person's condition for social-control purposes. Freidson (1970a, p. 252) bases on Becker's idea the claim that that illness tends to be diagnosed where laymen see only problems must be fought in the interest of the patient's dignity. In a paper presented at the First Social Science and Medicine Conference at Aberdeen in 1968, Kosa (1970) argued that, in Weber's terms, the medical profession's moral entrepreneurship entailed *charisma* (which was later analysed further by Horobin, 1985). Kosa found, however, that this applied more to fee-for-service health care (such as in the US) than state-funded systems (such as in the Soviet Union and, to a certain extent, the UK). He also found a relationship between charisma and quality of care. It appeared to him that the quality of medical services deteriorated in bureaucratic systems entailing less charisma. The ensuing dilemma between the need for good quality of care, and the need to protect the patients' dignity (suggesting that charisma be overcome) was 'solved' by Kosa with an appeal to social-science research.

To sum up, treatment in the understanding of the crisis model is a moral enterprise. Professional knowledge providing multiple and often contradictory explanations fosters ideologies whose use engages medicine in social control of a moralist kind. Application of an ideology cannot be regarded as patient-centred. This holds, in particular, since ward systems – denoting what actually happens on a ward – are seen to represent organisational principles favouring punitive rather than supportive attitudes *vis-à-vis* the patient. The function of treatment ideologies is *social control*, a repressive and segregative endeavour splitting the world into good and bad. 'Thus', asserts Rock, 'a twofold process is at work in the defining process of control agencies; not only does it reduce ambiguity and make the moral world simpler, it also makes moral actors discrete and clearly distinguishable' (1973, p. 74).

In this vein, the ex-patient after being treated (submitted to application of clinical knowledge) is supposedly not in the same category as his or her normal environment. The 'cured' mental patient, Lemert maintains, is expected to succeed despite wide-spread suspicion and discrimination (1951, p. 434; see also Lamy, 1973). He may become a victim of irresponsible medical treatment or outright economic exploitation (Lemert, 1951, p. 413ff.; see also Miller and Dawson, 1973). The post-hospital environment 'brings off' the deviant person's newly-acquired self-definition but does not forget the stigmatised 'master status'. A *self-fulfilling prophecy* engendered in the 'common belief "once insane, always insane" may always come to be seen as adequate in the long run' (Lemert, 1951, p. 434). Possibly, especially for the mentally ill, the danger is that, 'outside of hospitals at least, [they] tend to be threatened psychologically by the presence of others with a comparable status' (Lemert, 1967, p. 47).

The iatrogenic effect of the treatment and/or institution

If therapy is implementing treatment ideology, and no benefit for the patient ensues, then the question becomes: how is the difference between hospitalised and non-hospitalised patients or persons accounted for? How can it be explained that those in hospital apparently are more ill than those living outside? In other words: if the reason for being hospitalised is not that a person is ill (more ill than others who are not), why is it that illness is usually found in those who are treated and symptoms are less obvious or less recognised (if this is so) among the untreated? The answer is that an *iatrogenic* effect of treatment is assumed. In the literature from the early 1960s delineating the crisis model it is usually maintained that the institution produces illness. Matza sums up the views of Becker and Goffman:

> Their irony, stated simply, is that systems of control and the agents that man them are implicated in the process by which others become deviant. The very effect to prevent, intervene, arrest and "cure" persons of their alleged pathologies may, according to the neoChicagoan view, precipitate or seriously aggravate the tendency society wishes to guard against. (1969, p. 80).

Later authors extend the iatrogenic effect to non-institutional treatment; for instance, Loseke and Cahill (1984) argue that, by having presented themselves to 'experts on battered women' and later returned to their husbands several times (as most people do in the process of separating from a spouse), wives who have been beaten by their husbands are exposed to a second degrading experience: namely, their (normal) course of separation–reunion decisions is taken by the 'experts on battered women' whom they consult as a sign of weakness and irresponsibility: 'In a sense, battered women may now be victimized twice, first by their mates and then by experts who claim to speak on their behalf' (1984. p. 306).

In what way, one may ask, does treatment produce illness (deviance)? Four arguments are put forward to substantiate this claim.

The exclusion argument.   The idea is that treatment in institutions, because it severs the deviant from his or her indigenous social world, destroys communication channels which could help patients to be reintegrated into their families or jobs after discharge. The 'dual moral ideologies' (1967, p. 49) which Lemert finds – rejection and rehabilitation – serve the function, at the same time, of excluding the 'alcoholics, drug addicts, criminals, physically handicapped persons, and the poor' (Lemert, 1967, p. 49) from mainstream social life, and to integrate them into society, albeit on a low-status level, through philanthropy (Matza, 1969; also Mead, 1918).

Another version of the argument is presented for instance by J. Ryan (1976). She states that only by setting standards of 'mental age' defining 'normal intelligence' would 'illnesses' such as mental subnormality and stupidity be 'produced'. The mentally retarded are excluded from mainstream education and employment while they are, at the same time, integrated into society through special schools and sheltered workshops. These sever relations with normal peers who could provide needed learning incentives.

The deviant identity argument.   Loss of capacity for self-help, it is argued, destroys an individual's non-deviant identity. The self, organised around his or her sick role, becomes insufficient for independent functioning. 'Organizational systems', maintains R. A. Scott, 'that are constructed so as to discourage dependence in fact produce independent blind people; systems that foster dependency by creating accommodative environments produce blind people who cannot function outside . . . them' (R. A. Scott, 1969, p. 116).

In the same vein, Scull (1972) argues that changes in the British pattern of drug addiction around 1960 were brought about by organisational changes. These responded to new groups of addicts more prone to or already with deviant identities. As long as mainly housewives, middle-aged doctors, and so on were 'customers' of opiate-prescribing general practitioners, centralised services were not needed to control the habit nationally. When large numbers of young junkies started to obtain drugs not merely for personal use but also for selling, the state had to alter its policy. The new restrictive system, however, failed to make the new users abandon their habit.

The vicious circle argument.   This in almost pure form states that hospitals produce the deviations which they treat. The paranoid person, argues Lemert, when exposed to 'staff practices of ignoring explicit meanings in statements and actions of patients and reacting to inferred or imputed meanings' (1962/67a, p. 209), tends to react with fresh suspicions of collusive mystifications directed against him or her. In general, Lemert maintains, 'conflicts and faulty communication among staff and custody people' (Lemert, 1967, pp. 45–6) produce patient feelings of hopelessness in a meaningless world. These may increase the degree of disturbed behaviour as well as the number of suicide attempts. In this situation, Lemert states – and Goffman makes the same point (1961, p. 167) – the patient is at a double risk: he or she is expected to stabilise his or her emotional-expressive behaviour which has been reprehensible; nevertheless, he or she is also exposed to the most rigid system of moral orthodoxy where even a small lapse may be interpreted as a symptom of unsuccessful recovery. Worse still, Lemert adds, 'even more defeating is the official suspicion of the conforming patient, that he may be shamming, or that his is only an "institutional cure"' (1967, p. 45).

The interference argument.   Another argument presupposes a dual nature of illness; while one is its genuine authentic form, the other is a contaminated, deflected or in some way tampered-with form; hence, it is inauthentic and artificial. According to Laing, schizophrenia in its second form happens when its first form has been inhibited by hospital treatment. In other words: institutionally-treated schizophrenia occurs as the inauthentic version of the birth–rebirth process which schizophrenia essentially is supposed to be (Laing, 1969, p. 52).

The four arguments suggesting an iatrogenic effect of treatment do not answer the question, however, of how the patient manages to feel better. Freidson (1970a) provides this answer. The patient, he states, 'would not be likely to seek help if he did not believe a physician could help him', and the physician, in turn, 'would not undertake help if he did not feel he could do something effective' (1970a, p. 263). Freidson goes on to say that mutual belief in the accomplishments of clinical practice, however, has been shown in numerous studies to be a potent factor determining what has been named the *placebo effect*. Beecher (1959) as well as Shapiro (1961) are cited to emphasise that the 'placebo effect' – deriving from joint trust in the effectiveness of a clinician's action – works in favour of whatever treatment happens to be administered. Freidson explains: 'In consequence, the patient feels better and the physician feels that his ministrations are responsible for the patient's improvement. This accomplishment occurs far more independently of the chemical or physical agents used in treatment than the patient or physician believes' (1970a, p. 264).

No doubt, such improvement of the patient's condition is interpersonally *constructed*: 'The practicing physician's philosophy of treatment is thus supported by the evidence of his wish-ridden senses, which tell him that his patient has improved . . . The patients . . . oblige . . . by feeling and reporting improvement' (Freidson, 1970a). In the light of such universal 'placebo effect', it appears that iatrogenic consequences of treatment can easily go unnoticed since the patients as well as their doctors have reason not to perceive them.

The undercurrent of presumptive normality

The crisis model claims that pathology in the health field does not exist. Rather, diversity is all that is to be found. In this, pathology means *morally* deficient in terms of – usually – mental capacity. If only diversity exists, the distinction between normality and pathology is itself false. This leaves those who are labelled sick as morally incriminated. Sociological thinking which sides with the underdog has to prove that *nobody*, in the last instance, may rightly be judged anything else but normal. The aim must be to show that an undercurrent of normality runs through even the most blatant façade of sickness. Or, to use a term of Laing's, even in the most 'delapidated hebephrenic' a normal person is to be detected by the concerned sociologist (psychiatrist).

That illness itself is identified, under treatment conditions, as a possible iatrogenic consequence of medical practice, makes it all the more likely that both normality and diagnosed illness can be present in a person. If the argument is that normality does not exclude 'primary deviation', and that treated abnormality may be nothing but environmentally labelled symptomatology, the apparent normality of even the sickest inmates of total institutions can be demonstrated. The issue is, from the standpoint of the sociologist arguing in the patient's interest, that the person must be understood as, (in principle) indestructible by treatment which may be forced upon him or her.

Goffman makes one feel as if the person's identity resembles a buttercup breaking through concrete: 'Our status is backed by the solid buildings of the world, while our sense of personal identity often resides in the cracks' (1961, p. 320). Manning hails Goffman as advocate of the endangered tradition of civility in modern mass society; 'In society, as [Goffman's] ironic use of the term "trouble-maker" indicates, he implies that it is the "troublemaker" who validly and legitimately responds to an oppressive degrading situation' (Manning, 1976, p. 24).

Goffman uses mental patients as examples of civilised behaviour (1956a). He devotes a whole essay ('The Underlife of a Public Institution') to hospitalised mental patients' attempts to 'work the system' and undercut ward routines while seemingly adhering to them. In fact, Goffman detects two layers of patients' behaviour: namely, that of psychosis where they 'remained entirely mute, were incontinent, hallucinated, and practised other classical symptoms' and that of their conforming to ward routine where they would (with very few expections) 'line up for food, take their shower, go to bed, or get up on time' (Goffman, 1961, p. 209, footnote 57).

This ability to conduct apparently undisturbed everyday activities in the face of florid symptomatology motivates Braginski and Braginski to investigate the question whether it is true that mental patients are unable to manipulate their environment. Goffman detects mental patients' relative normality in that they are capable of interpersonal manipulation. Braginski and Braginski show that mental patients are able to adapt their behavioural performance to what they perceive as hospital authorities' expectations relative to their own, the patients', interest either to be discharged or transferred to an open ward (Braginski, Grosse and Ring, 1966/73; Braginski and Braginski, 1973). However, as Price (1973) documents, this only holds for patients less severely disturbed; moreover, it only applies to those tending to present themselves as generally healthy, not those whom Price calls 'sick-presenters'.

Braginski and Braginski hold that patients' ability to manipulate is an indicator of their residual sanity. But one could also argue that the changeability of their manipulativeness is an aspect of their disease. The more severely ill they are, one could argue, the less they manage to be 'sick presenters' or stage their performance in a means–end related way. The diversity of their self-presentation while they do the one as well as the other may be explained by the typical symptoms of schizophrenia; that is, that such patients find it difficult to maintain a unified and authentic identity.

Recent discussion has taken up this point, but it does so without focusing on the normality issue. Pathology is acknowledged for the patients but a different one from that of the medical view. The two separate perspectives are deemed irreconcilable. A difference is perceived between 'the medical profession's ideology', on the one hand, and 'the patient's ideology', on the other. While the former 'denies the existence of structural conflict between doctors and patients, as well as the marketplace aspect of the exchange', the latter focuses on 'the possibility of excessive treatment . . . because it assumes that doctors and patients have different interests' (Betz and O'Connell, 1983, p. 91). These are never to be completely reconciled. Freidson (1986), with the arrival of *Health Maintenance Organizations* and more control over medical work through government-funded treatment programmes, perceives a marked loss for the medical profession of autonomy and power. But its detachment from the world of the patient remains in the 1980s what it is said to have been in the 1970s and before.

The question has also been raised of whether 'revolving-door' psychiatry, and deinstitutionalisation in the US and elsewhere have altered the propects of the mentally ill drastically. Does their non-pathological identity no longer need to be confined to the 'cracks . . . [of] the solid buildings of the world' (Goffman, 1961, p. 320)? Grusky and Pollner's (1981) textbook, for instance, selects contributions suggesting that not much has changed for the better despite psychiatric reform over the last decades. On the other hand, Morrissey (1982) – among many authors – claims that the effect of total institutions on patients has become minimised because patients' length of stay in hospital has been reduced considerably since 1955.

Both sides of the debate argue that they discuss the societal-reaction perspective, either by corroborating it or by contradicting it. Both arguments take for granted that the societal-reaction standpoint, or the crisis model of interactionist thinking, is based on systematic analysis of empirical facts. These facts are either seen as still prevalent despite reformist measures, or are judged to have been overcome because of improved circumstances due to reformist efforts.

However, it may be argued that the crisis model intends not so much an empirical analysis but presents a theoretical idea illustrated by selected empirical observations. The problem at the heart of this endeavour is how the perspective of the individual may be held against that of the society in such a way that society's order and maintenance is not automatically favoured over the individual's freedom. In other words Lemert, who wants to explain how 'social disorganization' and 'personal disorganization' are linked with each other, comes up with the solution of showing how the 'societal reaction' can 'produce' diagnosed deviance of patients. In this, he wishes to take the side of the individual whose deviance may be but in the eye of the 'symbolically reacting' beholder. But, inadvertently, Lemert's work and also the labelling and anti-psychiatry perspectives which follow most of his ideas, remain curiously concerned with the social order. Deviance, it turns out, is more or less arbitrarily constructed by society's ruling classes or cultural elites, and individuals remain relatively powerless against redefinition of their individuality as deviance. Moreover, few strategies are outlined, suggesting that those people or patients are deemed helpless against their more or less innocent acts being thus reconstructed.

The sociologist then is regretfully helpless as an ally of the 'underdog' on whose side he or she stands. Eventually, it seems, all the sociologist can do is insist on the sick individual's unaffected normality in the face of diagnosed illness and institutional treatment. At least, such partisanship may inspire the patient to become an active and critical consumer of health care. Freidson warns:

> Patently, if a patient does not (as do some of the better educated) deliberately select a 'school' [of clinical thought]; and if, once among the proponents of such a school, he adopts no active, aggressive voice in his treatment, the opinions of the medical men into whose hands he has fallen determine much of what will happen to him. (1970a, p. 263)

Chapter 7
The Negotiation Model

While labelling theory was highly visible between the early 1960s and late 1970s, a second interactionist model existed all along. It focused on 'societal reaction' with the proviso that negotiation universally constitutes the social order (Strauss, 1978a).

The work by F. Davis on deviance disavowal and functional uncertainty in diagnosis (1960, 1961) and by Roth on time structures in hospital treatment (1962, 1963a) was published only shortly before the idea of 'negotiated order' was first ventured (Strauss et al., 1963, 1964a).

After Strauss' move to the University of California, San Francisco, a prolific cooperation started between him and his new associates focusing on the topic of death and dying. Their work yielded a novel theoretical as well as methodological stance ('substantive theory', 'grounded theory'), together with insightful observations on hospital procedures (Glaser and Strauss, 1964a, 1964b; Quint and Strauss, 1964; Strauss, Glaser and Quint, 1964b; Glaser, 1965; Glaser and Strauss, 1965a, 1965b, 1965c; Glaser, 1966; Glaser and Strauss, 1967, 1968; Strauss and Glaser, 1970). During the 1970s the approach gained momentum by extending its scope to chronic illness (Strauss and Glaser, 1975). One of the recent books by Strauss et al. (1985) draws together ten years' efforts to combine the two topics: namely, organisation of work routines in hospitals, and chronic illness.

Issues of interpersonally constituted medical reality are also discussed in Britain. In the mid-1970s, several books explored the possibilities of an interactionist view of the doctor–patient relationship (Stimson and Webb, 1975; Wadsworth and Robinson, 1976; A. Davis and Horobin, 1977; Davis, 1979). In 1976, the British Sociological Association devoted its Annual Conference to the sociological analysis of health, illness, and health care. This resulted in two volumes of papers mostly based on interactionist thinking (Dingwall et al., 1977; Stacey et al., 1977). Since 1979, the journal *Sociology of Health and Illness* has become a fruitful forum for further elaborating the negotiation model.

The main idea is that rules and roles are not fixed givens but represent the outcome of negotiations between participants in a structural setting. Every social form, it is surmised, would break down were it not maintained through continuous tacit consensus between interactants to keep it intact. Such consensus, in principle, is achieved through bargaining on the basis of interactants' mutual task or efficiency orientations.

Strauss (1978a, p. ix) makes it clear that stability of social forms is to be seen as precarious outcome of negotiations between more or less inimical partners:

> Rules and roles are always breaking down – and when they do not, they do not miraculously remain intact without some effort, including negotiation effort, to maintain them. What we can assent to is that when individuals or groups or organisations of any size work together 'to get things done' then agreement is required about such matters as what, how, when, where and how much. Continued agreement itself may be something to be worked at. Even enemies may have to negotiate, to work together to arrive at their quite discrepant ends.

'Symbolic interactionism' denotes that the orientational side of interaction is reconciled through negotiation. According to Blumer, this concerns *meanings* which individuals give to their behaviour *vis-à-vis* others: 'The actor selects, checks, suspends, regroups, and transforms the meanings in the light of the situation in which he is placed and the direction of his action' (Blumer, 1969, p. 5). Meanings are organised in 'definitions of the situation' which structure the actors' understanding of their surrounding world. This reliance on the well-known 'Thomas theorem' (Thomas, 1925) is not meant as taking refuge to subjectivism but, rather, as a way of 'bringing men back in'. Glaser and Strauss (1967) base their claim for qualitative research in sociology on their assumption that valid sociological theory has to be derived in an inductive way from observational data. These, in turn, reveal interactive reality to be 'grounded' in 'definitions of the situation' making the behaviour of interactants accountable. The 'substantive theory' which Glaser and Strauss aim at elucidates in terms of action strategies and routines 'a substantive, or empirical, area of sociological inquiry, such as patient care' (1967, p. 32).

Negotiation, in essence, is conceptualised as *bargaining*. Where a preliminary consensus has been reached – that is, when a more or less fragile consensus comes to maintain rules and roles – bargaining may be replaced by routine. But such agreements and arrangements are precarious, and bargaining can be reintroduced by any interactant at any time into an encounter. Strauss (1978a) cites Schelling's *Essay on Bargaining* (1956/60) when he wants to clarify the 'mechanics' of negotiation. Schelling is interested in the *economic metaphor*. His model involves a seller and a buyer who wish to arrive at a price for a house. Schelling highlights the aspect of conflict as well as that of reflexivity in the interchange between the two business partners when he explains his 'tactical approach to the analysis of bargaining':

> The subject includes both explicit bargaining and the tacit kind in which adversaries watch and interpret each other's behavior, each aware that his own actions are being interpreted and anticipated, each acting with a view to the expectations that he creates . . . We shall be concerned with what might be called the 'distributional' aspect of bargaining: the situations in which a better bargain for one means less for the other. When the business is finally sold to the one interested buyer, what price does it go for? When two dynamite trucks meet on a road wide enough for one, who backs up? These are situations that ultimately involve an element of pure bargaining – bargaining in which each party is guided mainly by his expectations of what the other will accept. But with each guided by expectations and knowing that the other is too, expectations become compounded. A bargain is struck when somebody makes a final, sufficient concession. (1956/60, p. 21)

The two interactants, in principle, are of equal strength and bargaining power (if only because of an underdog's moral right not to be defeated).

The idea of the tactical juxtaposition of two partners manipulating each other while they reflexively take into account each other's expected responses has been introduced into sociology by Goffman's concept of 'strategic interaction'. It focuses on the enactment of rules in game situations which are the outcome of bargaining:

> Two or more parties . . . find themselves in a well-structured situation of mutual impingement where each party must make a move and where every possible move carries fateful implications for all of the parties. In this situation, each player must influence his own decision by his knowing that the other players are likely to try to dope out his decision in advance, and may even appreciate that he knows this is likely. Courses of action or moves will then be made in the light of one's thoughts about the others' thoughts about oneself. An exchange of moves made on the basis of this kind of orientation to self and others can be called strategic interaction. (1969a, pp. 100–1)

In this, an *image of man* is involved which distinguishes the negotiation model of illness explanation from the crisis model. The latter makes an implicit assumption of *passivity* on the part of the individual who is exposed to the experience of mortification and categorisation by a stigmatising agency in the crisis situation; this triggers off a status passage into 'second-class citizenship'. The negotiation model assumes that individuals *actively* manipulate their environment following two principles: they use their 'definition of the situation' as guidelines to purposes which they consider right and advantageous; in this, they take into account other participants' perceived 'definitions of the situations' as well as the others' interests, tactics, strategies and past behaviours. In this way, individuals are seen to *produce* rather than react to the rules and roles governing their situational conduct (Turner, 1962).

Shryker, in a critical appraisal of Blumer's interactionist teachings which may also hold good for the negotiation model of illness explanation deriving from it, states that 'the image of man in those writings is of a totally self-conscious creature whose choices are organized through maximally reflective processes' (1980, p. 141). Illness, in this view, is the outcome of a process of social construction. At the base is negotiation on various levels. The personal level includes the patient and his or her family ('significant others'), on the one hand, and the patient and his or her doctor, on the other. The institutional level concerns professions and semi-professions engaging in diagnosis and treatment. Sociology endeavours to show that illness is a socially constructed reality in that the former ultimately is submitted to the latter. Robinson (1976, p. 139) emphasises this for alcoholism:

> 'Alcoholism' and 'becoming an alcoholic' are *in essence* that set of practices enforced when people employ such notions in the course of their everyday lives. This is not to say that alcoholism and the alcoholic are not as well a product of biochemical apparatus and processes: they are, of course. But biochemical and physiological states and processes are 'noticed', 'recognised', 'assessed', 'responded to', 'treated' and so on, and such activities occur in specific social contexts.'

As in the crisis model, diagnosis is the crucial transition from person to patient where the person's condition is categorised and evaluated in terms of potentially stigmatising labels. But the doctor and patient are engaged in bargaining, and this means that, *in principle* , they are considered equal rather than unequal 'business partners'. Differences in their 'bargaining power' are taken to indicate the doctor's 'professional dominance' and criticised as unnecessarily granting supremacy to the doctor's perspective. Since such inequality in 'market rights' indeed jeopardises the patient's legitimate interests, the idea is to overcome 'professional dominance', or mitigate it by strengthening the patient's side.

Various studies show that patients rarely succumb passively to the doctor's dictum in the long run. As soon as the patient has left the doctor's office, such research documents, the patient resumes control of the illness reality. While the doctor–patient encounter is the core of the diagnostic endeavour, the social act of diagnosis is a *succession* of phases. In this, the doctor's decision is a response to the patient's self-presentation, and the patient's compliance or non-compliance is a function of both the patient's and the patient's significant others' response to the diagnostic decision and encounter.

The three stages of the *aetiology process* involve normality where doctors as well as patients develop their distinctive 'definition of the situation', the former with regard to how medical theory is translated into medical practice, and the latter with regard to how symptoms are interpreted prior to seeking medical care. The diagnosis brings the two 'parties' together in an effort to arrive at an illness as a common symbolic reality. Following on from there, illness or disability represent structured sequences of career stages which, in terms of practical work routines, form 'trajectories'. Unlike the crisis model, no reconstitution of identity accompanying chronic-illness incumbency is emphasised; equally unlike the crisis model, coping endeavours are conceptualised not under the perspective of deviance but, rather, under that of normalisation.

Treatment is viewed as mediated by treatment ideologies, but these are part of either a hospital or a home regimen. In hospitals as well as with regard to coping with chronic illness at home, *negotiated order* is emphasised which makes for a continuous give and take between interactants. In this the patient is introduced as fully responsible participant of the bargaining processes setting the stage for what gets done by whom, and so on. The aspect of *management* which this entails is highlighted both for hospital care and living at home of the chronically sick: they organise their lives in a way allowing for as good a reconciliation between incapacity and autonomy as they can muster.

The three stages of aetiology

Normality as uncertainty

The knowledge–practice gap (doctor's side).   A well-entrenched, however unnoticed, gap is revealed between generalised medical knowledge defining the range of symptoms signifying a certain disease, or warranting a certain treatment, and the range of symptoms actually taken by any specific doctor to suggest a particular diagnosis, or justify a particular treatment. The uncertainty relationship between the standardised medical knowledge on the one hand, and the individual knowledge application on the other, is either acknowledged as inevitable or criticised as putting into question the medical profession's expertise. The former of these two viewpoints suggests that uncertainty disavowal by the individual doctor in the practice setting is normal and inevitable. The latter viewpoint argues that such disavowal is to the detriment of the patient which is why uncertainty awareness ought to be demanded.

Arguing the case of uncertainty disavowal, Bloor (1976 a) depicts a conspicuous variation of symptoms which ear, nose and throat (ENT) specialists invariably diagnose as sufficient cause for tonsillectomy. He cites the eighteenth-century philosopher Bishop Berkeley to explain the ENT specialists' decisions. Since 'all ideas are intrinsically specific in character' (Bloor, 1976 b, p. 54), medical knowledge also must be specific and thus varies from doctor to doctor when used. Medical knowledge, when applied, aquires variability according to the context(s) into which it must fit. But only through such context-specific application can it be made practical: Bloor clarifies that without every doctor's *rules of thumb* which select from and redefine items of the generalised corpus of knowledge, no doctor would be able to *practise* medicine:

> The corpus of medical knowledge, accessible to all practitioners by reason of its enshrinement in texts and teaching, is simply an utilitarian guide to the comprehension of biophysical phenomena, it is a selective schema whose elements owe their addition, elimination, and perpetuation over time to their pragmatic utility . . . Consequently, for each general name of a disease entity, symptom or sign present in the corpus of medical knowledge the practitioner must construct for his own practical use representative particular ideas which stand for these general names and which have that degree of particularity which enables their unproblematic application. (1976 b, p. 58–9)

Strictly speaking, the 'false' certainty with which the doctor uses his particular criteria as if they were identical with (and, in fact, were) the general ones is prior to any negotiation process. F. Davis (1960) describes how uncertainty is often feigned by doctors when they feel that their patients' quest for clear-cut diagnosis jeopardises their wish not to tell everything they suspect or know about a patient's condition. But this is a different matter from the uncertainty to which Bloor refers. He points out that experience, which is the basis of expertise, results in a specification process of knowledge. Discrepancies exist between the individual doctors' interpretations and the standardised corpus of knowledge of which the doctors are unaware; in fact, while each may in practice use an idiosyncratic set of diagnostic and therapeutic rules, all believe that they are using the same rules in identical manner.

Many medical sociologists consider this as 'false consciousness' which ought to be overcome. They argue that the diversity of criteria signifying a certain disease can only be due to the situational or contextual constructedness of knowledge in society. In this, medicine is no exception to the general variability of 'definitions of the situation' and, therefore, should not claim objective truth for its knowledge. Dingwall (1976, p. 11) states that 'scientific and medical knowledge may be seen as just another set of ideas validated by social consensus'. This entails that doctors, like everyone else, depend on contextual categories of knowledge which are negotiated. David Hughes writes about an accident department: 'Staff members in the casualty setting like anyone else . . . are continuously engaged in a task of making their environment meaningful and intelligible by ordering their experience in terms of familiar categories' (1977, p. 130). This context-specificity, in turn, is taken by some authors to mean 'that the world is socially constructed and is infinitely malleable' (Fears, 1977, p. 79).

The issue is *categorisation*. In their early studies on death in hospital settings, Glaser and Strauss (1965c, 1968) point out that *social value* makes a difference when it is decided whether and what emergency measures are taken, or when a death disturbs a ward atmosphere more than usually. Such social value may relate to age when a child, gender when a young mother, or prestige when a well-known personality is involved. In the same vein, Jeffrey (1979) discovers a distinction made by staff of accident and emergency departments between 'good' and 'bad' patients; the former mean 'medically interesting' or 'clinically rewarding' while the latter category refers to 'trivia, drunks, overdoses and tramps'. Elaborating further on this distinction, Dingwall and Murray (1983) argue that a middle category of ordinarily processed patients ought to be added such that three distinct frames exist for the 'rule of clinical priority'. These are the 'bureaucratic frame', the 'clinical frame', and 'special frames', of which one is for vagrants, suicide attempts, and so on, and another is for children.

It is noteworthy that these categories exist as part of the staff's professional orientation *prior* to the situational contexts in which they are used. The labels of 'good' and 'problem' patient which Lorber (1975) finds enacted in a ward setting by nurses and doctors exist in the medical personnel's 'definition of the situation' as part of their work orientation. As such, these categorisations are present prior to actual application of the labels.

Symptoms and lay theories (patient's side).   The pre-diagnosis stage of illness is liable to be interpreted by patient and environment along the lines of normal world views. For instance, Schneider and Conrad (1983) report that epileptics prior to their being diagnosed have a variety of inexplicable experiences for which they also have names: 'What our respondents, after diagnosis, came to call seizures are made up of a great variety of feelings, sensations, movements, sounds, and sights . . . [which may be called] "strange feelings", "headaches", "spaciness", "black-outs", and "dizzy spells"' (1983, p. 56). At the same time, such 'people with symptoms' usually have an image of epilepsy as a 'terrible' illness deriving from the 'worst cases' as presented on television (1983, p. 148ff.). Scambler and Hopkins (1986) who also investigate epilepsy find that the name of the illness is frightening, and the to-be-diagnosed expect that 'epileptic' denotes a highly stigmatised social status. This attitude of the afflicted is rather similar to that of the general public. West (1985) finds that a generalised image of epilepsy exists carrying strong stigma connotations.

This finding sounds similar to what, for instance, Scheff (1966a) writes about mental illness. But Scheff suggests that the label is automatically applied in the *crisis situation*, and invokes stigma through diagnosis. However, the cited studies on epilepsy find that undergoing diagnosis does not necessarily entail a negative status passage: 'A medical, and hence authoritative, diagnosis of epilepsy does not indeed confer the social status of epileptic' (Scambler and Hopkins, 1986, p. 31).

Uncertainty, to be sure, prevails in the pre-diagnosis period with regard to meaning of symptoms since the person is troubled with a variety of inexplicable or worrying experiences. Bury (1982) reports about younger patients with rheumatoid arthritis that they often misjudge their symptoms for considerable time periods because they 'know' that arthritis is a disease of the elderly. Cowie (1976) discovers that even after having had a heart attack his respondents often misinterpret their pain and discomfort. Only when previous illnesses or biographical events appear to them to explain why a heart attack could be 'reasonable' or 'understandable', do they recognise what their symptoms mean: 'When patients could not reconstruct their past unambiguously and with reference to these "causes", they claimed not to understand how or why they had a heart attack' (1976, p. 95).

It is not so much denial, then, which takes place; rather, it is classification in 'wrong' – that is, lay – terms. In order to convert the 'lay judgment' into a medical diagnosis and have symptoms properly assessed, *negotiation* within the world of lay judgment may become a trigger. A person's *significant others* are found by various studies to be crucial influences on the decision to consult a doctor. In his research on ENT patients, Zola (1973) shows that family members' insisting that a relative see a doctor triggers the use of medical services, additional to life style-related incapacities. Albrecht (1977) reports that significant others decide (or demand) when and whether treatment of occlusal problems is needed. Locker (1981), following on from Robinson's (1971) model of utility calculations pitching further endurance of symptoms against anticipated consequences of medical treatment, describes a multi-phase process of 'the pathway from symptom to illness'. Zola (1973) calls this the 'pathway from person to patient'. Elaborate deliberations are documented which weigh between treatment and self-management, taking into account potential severity and possible prognosis of symptoms.

When medical care is sought, *categorisations* regulate which kind of care is needed, and whether or not emergency services are appropriate. Calnan (1983) explores the reasons which make a patient with a 'minor cut' or 'minor ailment' decide that the first choice of treatment should be an Accident and Emergency Department as compared to a GP. Calnan interviews his respondents at an Accident and Emergency Unit, and therefore those whose first choice would have been a GP (due to the nature of their complaint or because they are on a GP's list) give *additional* reasons why, in this particular instance, they have deviated from what they 'normally would have done'.

In sum, three aspects of the normality stage of an illness may be distinguished. Symptoms jeopardising physical or psychological well-being may be overlooked or underrated ('normalised') for considerable time periods. They may be found inexplicable but are given names and may be incorporated into a person's life style. Also, lay theories help to strengthen such disregard since one's own symptoms frequently appear weak compared with those in the general image of an illness. Finally, categories of appropriateness of treatment agencies for particular ailments are part of the lay public's corpus of knowledge.

These three aspects of normality together make for a picture of health where identity and interaction are closely linked. The 'definitions of the situation' which govern interaction are lay theories. They explain behaviour and structure routine actions such that the individuals' social identities are realised. Negotiations putting into practice 'definitions of a situation' are conducted with personal utilities in mind; that is, individuals realise their identities by promoting their own best interests in exchange with others whom they know to do the same. Social life depends upon reciprocal interlocking of 'definitions of the situation'.

In everyday life (and this is also the normality or pre-diagnosis stage of illness), the doctor's world and the patient's world are apart. They both contain strategies for the resolution of uncertainty dilemmas. For the doctor, these are (so to speak) latent until the actual encounter with the patient occurs. The patient, however, constantly uses 'normalising' (that is, he or she makes sense of symptoms in a 'pre-medical' way). Only when this is given up is medical care sought.

Diagnosis

The diagnostic encounter as a locus of 'societal reaction' brings together person (patient) and doctor, in an interaction conceived as negotiation. The bargaining process's outcome is diagnosis. Three phases may be distinguished. A legitimation phase determines whether *normal* sickness status is negotiated; deciding and telling is what usually figures as diagnosis; and it is through the third, validation, that the diagnosis 'works'.

Legitimation.   Jeffrey (1979), analysing 'deviant' patient categories in emergency departments, comes to the conclusion that they underscore 'normal' sick-role criteria. The less attentive treatment rendered to 'trivia, drunks, overdoses and tramps' is found rational in the light of Parsons' four criteria for the sick role: 'Rules broken by rubbish' (1979, p. 98) are that patients must not be responsible for their illness, must have occupational and family duties from which they then can be temporarily relieved, and so on. Thus, 'rubbish' patients define 'illegitimate illness' which, in turn, strengthens the criteria of the 'normal' sick role: 'Part of the work done by Casualty staff is the production of deviance as the obverse of the production of legitimate illness' (1979, p. 106).

Other classifications applied in the legitimation stage are normality versus abnormality of the general condition of the patient in question. Silverman (1981) shows that children with Down's syndrome are put into a completely different action frame from

normal children by cardiologists advising mothers on the appropriate treatment for their child's congestive heart failure. While
parents with normal children would be expected to accept cardiac
surgery, those with Down's syndrome children are expected to
agree with the cardiologist that surgery is not advisable. Hilliard
(1981) makes it clear that this side of the encounter ensures that
'roles [are] negotiated discursively' (1981, p. 318). That is, such
dichotomies as normal/abnormal, patently ill/not patently ill, my
(own) child/any child, member of the family/outside family and so
on denote frames of argumentation which are used by doctors to
manouvre mothers into the appropriate understanding of the
(normal versus deviant) sick role. This is then used to explain to
the mothers in what way an envisaged treatment is reasonable in
the prevailing circumstances:

> Two strategies . . . appear to resolve the problem of whether to define
> the status of the child under treatment as 'normal' or 'abnormal'. In
> one, the child's normality in a home context is stressed, and kept
> separate from the abnormal status it must occupy in an actual treatment
> situation. In the other, by contrast, it is during episodes of hospitalis-
> ation that the child's essential normality is most easily maintained, as it
> is compared with surrounding examples of 'abnormal sickness'. (Hill-
> iard, 1981, p. 324)

Bargaining, the use of such strategies, involves on the patient's
(or patient's mother's) side that he or she has an interest in being
classified as a bona-fide patient. Doctors are willing to grant this
for the ongoing diagnostic encounter if they become convinced
that the patient's credentials warrant 'normal sickness' status.
Such legitimation of one's patienthood through a doctor's judgment is precarious. Strong (1977), using Goffman's idea that
presentation of self in everyday life depends on strategies and
tactics of face-work, sees the patient as being in a weaker position
than the doctor. While the latter makes dealing with patients a
life-long occupation, the former's use of medical or social services
is but a short episode of otherwise busy daily schedules ('medical
errands'). This asymmetry in the degree of habitualisation of the
encounter makes for three features which put the patient in a
position where he or she is far from equal.

1. *Depersonalisation*: that is, the comparative non-significance of
   each patient's case for the doctor's overall work-load, involving
   the awkward task that patients have to tell their story in an
   appealing and competent way while often being allocated only
   very little time to do so.

2. *Confidence in the doctor's judgment* must be anticipatorily
   demonstrated by optimising one's impression upon the doctor
   who, in return, is to acknowledge the patient's unquestionably
   legitimate claim to patienthood; Strong ventures that this is
   why patients often present themselves in terms of status credentials ('wave the old school tie').
3. *Failure* is never completely ruled out and means the continuous
   threat of feeling a fool. This leads to painful and often counter-
   productive self-monitoring, with the added possiblity of being
   denied one's well-rehearsed requests because the doctor
   wrongly suspects cunning or malingering (Strong, 1977, pp.
   43–52).

In spite of these vicissitudes, patients usually manage to convince their doctors that theirs is a legitimate claim to bona-fide
patient status. Thus the stage is set for bargaining about the
diagnostic label.

Deciding and telling. 'Bargaining power', 'bargaining strength'
and 'bargaining skill', asserts Schelling, are with the powerful 'if
those qualities are defined to mean only that negotiations are won
by those who win' (1956/60, p. 22). The more realistic approach
ascertains 'whether and how commitments can be taken' (1956/60,
p. 26); in particular, *self-commitment* is vital for successful negotiation:

> If each does not know the other's true reservation price there is an
> initial stage in which each tries to discover the other's and misrepresent
> his own, as in ordinary bargaining. But the process of discovery and
> revelation becomes quickly merged with the process of creating and
> discovering commitments; the commitments permanently change, for
> all practical purposes, the 'true' reservation prices. If one party has, and
> the other has not, the belief in a binding ceremony, the latter pursues
> the 'ordinary' bargaining technique of *asserting* his reservation price,
> while the former proceeds to *make* his. (1956/60, p. 27)

Thus 'institutional and structural characteristics of the negotiation', including the advantages of a 'restrictive agenda', make for
the 'ceremonial' quality of the move. This, in turn, ensures controllability of the outcome through binding self-commitment.

In the exchange, threat and promise are 'weapons' with which
interactants may cause their partners to give up territory. Eventually, a state of 'limited war' can result; but usually this will be
avoided by reaching an agreement. Nicholson, in an overview of
political-science conflict analysis, describes the outcome of bar-

gaining as one party giving in after tactics and manoeuvring have been unsuccessful:

> In view of the guesswork which goes on, it is quite possible that, at the beginning of the negotiations, both think they can force the other into a position which, at the moment, he will not consider. The one who first becomes so pessimistic about the expected time before concession that he thinks that it is no longer worth while continuing the fight, gives in and accepts his rival's last offer. (Nicholson, 1970, p. 79)

The negotiation paradigm's conceptualisation of the labelling aspect of diagnosis follows this format. Gerson (1976a) highlights the political side of illness as bargaining during diagnostic encounters. Scheff (1968), in a much-quoted article on medical reality construction, uncovers a 'subterranean' nature of bargaining in diagnosis since 'neither physicians nor patients recognize the offers and responses process as being bargaining' (1968, p. 7). Balint (1957) speaks of symptoms being offered by the patient to the doctor who responds with a diagnosis each time that the patient presents himself, a seemingly endless chain of reciprocal dependency. Similarly, Scheff (1968, p. 12) speaks of negotiation which 'takes the form of a series of offers and responses that continue until an offer (definition of the situation) is reached that is acceptable to both parties'.

In this, the odds are against the patient. Scheff (1968, p. 5) states that a 'hidden agenda' brings off the professionally medical 'definition of the situation'. Strong and Davis (1978, p. 174) find the 'hidden agenda' in paediatric settings, and Strong (1979c) makes it the focus of the *Ceremonial Order of the Clinic*. He finds 'medical dominance' behind 'ceremonial order' which follows a 'bureaucratic format'. Webb and Stimson (1976) see the doctor's control of the consultation rooted in his better situational repertoire of strategies and tactics ('management'):

> [The doctor] provides entry and exit clues for the patient . . . and in general controls the course of the dialogue. He may interrupt and change the subject. Often these changes are marked or accompanied by non-verbal cues, such as the doctor diverting his attention elsewhere, rising from his chair, picking up or laying down his pen. It is because the doctor regularly and routinely holds consultations that he develops a routine and a range of strategies that he may call upon in his interaction with the patient. The patient is not usually as experienced in 'managing' the consultation or in 'managing' doctors. (1976, p. 116)

Anderson and Helm (1979) find that social upbringing affects necessary game-playing capacities: 'The education, ideology, and ability of the patient to "play the game well" is frequently a function of ethnicity and social class' (1979, p. 264). Other authors point to *language* as a medium of the doctor's power (Hughes 1982). In particular, medical vocabulary can be confusing to the patient feeling unable to question a diagnostic category couched in Latin. Mishler (1984) discusses in detail that medical discourse works to the disadvantage of the patient whose needs are not met and whose definition of the situation is not honoured.

Drass (1982), however, points out that opportunity for 'negotiation of discourse' varies for history taking, examination and problem discussion in the diagnostic encounter. The latter offers most opportunities for patients to air their views while the second offers least. The threefold distinction is usually not made in literature exemplifying the doctor's power by excerpts from discourse taken from any of the phases. Diagnosis is often not seen predominantly as a medical task where clinical knowledge is used and physical examination is imperative. The very instance of categorisation, that a patient's symptoms are subsumed under a generalised illness entity, is frequently taken as a sign of the patient's degradation. Anderson and Helm (1979, p. 265) find that 'objectification' results from 'the use of typification in diagnosis' which tends to 'anonymize and normalize the patient'. Here, doctors who do their work properly are criticised for not giving the patient equal say in the diagnostic decision.

Under this perspective of imperative equality but actual prevailing inequality (where the doctor's expertise is invalidated), every move of the doctor during clinical investigation must appear as undue medical control. At the same time, every one of the patient's moves going along with, rather than contradicting, the doctor's 'definition of the situation' must appear as undue subservience. Emerson (1970) describes a skewed balance between the doctor's definition of reality and the patient's counterdefinition in gynaecological examinations. She writes: 'The physician is in a position to bargain with the patient in order to obtain . . . cooperation. He can offer attention and acknowledgement as a person. At times he does so' (1970, p. 79). The doctor's taking into account of the patient's counterdefinition of reality, she says, mainly helps to neutralise possible interferences from the patient which might otherwise threaten the prevailing medical definition. Reflexive reassurance of the patient is but a strategy to safeguard the encounter: 'The foremost technique in neutralizing threatening events is to sustain a nonchalant demeanor even if the patient is blushing with embarrassment, blanching from fear, or moaning in pain' (1970, p. 88).

Another study tells of strategies and tactics to inveigle the patient into accepting the news of impending death. Clark and LaBeff (1982) couch their findings in the language of bargaining, with an explicit reference to reflexivity and reciprocity:

> We found that deliverers typically develop preparing and staging tactics before delivering bad news. Once prepared, the deliverers construct various 'telling' strategies, ranging from direct to conditional delivery. Moreover, it seems most deliverers recognize the importance of reacting to cues provided by the receivers which, in turn, influence the direction of the delivery. (1982, p. 379)

Thus deciding upon a diagnostic label is seen as unduly medically controlled. In this one-sided picture of the encounter, successful strategies of patients are rarely mentioned. It is even rare that patients' attempts to inveigle the doctor into changing a diagnosis are recognised. Scambler and Hopkins (1986) reported that their respondents tried to negotiate for a diagnosis less threatening than epilepsy; in this, uncertainty as a strategy is used by *both* parties similar to what F. Davis (1960) observed for the doctor:

> Paradoxically . . ., while uncertainty was without doubt an anathema to most of our respondents (the majority of whom wanted to know exactly what was wrong with them, at least until they were told), they, as well as their doctors, were able to – and did – capitalize on it. They used real or feigned uncertainty as 'tools of negotiation' when trying to disavow the diagnosis of epilepsy. (Scambler and Hopkins, 1986, p. 32).

Returning to the negotiation model's view of medical practice, we can now see how the *legitimation* and *deciding and telling* phases fit into the picture of bargaining process. 'Legitimation' puts the patient into a strong bargaining position since he or she mostly manages to be accepted as a patient; in Schelling's words, the patient makes a move which the physician cannot resist such that the physician must grant bona-fide patienthood. 'Deciding and telling', however, obviously reverses the strength of the parties. Now doctors are in a position where they make a move which the patient cannot resist. It is in this way that clinical examination proves to be the unquestionable core of the diagnostic endeavour.

Validation. In offer-response terms, diagnosis of disease is a doctor's offer to which the patient responds by validating it. Only validation makes the diagnostic categorisation (be)come 'true'. Without validation, diagnosis would fail to have an influence on behavioural conduct, self-perception, or life expectancy.

In their five-stage model of a visit to the doctor Stimson and Webb (1975) find, following upon the consultation, a stage of account formation. In it, the patient discusses with his 'significant others' what the doctor has said and done. Whether or not patients will follow the doctor's orders depends on how their friends and relatives evaluate the doctor's decisions. Compliance is jeopardised if the doctor's diagnosis is deemed false or problematic.

The accounting stage consists of stories which the patient tells about what was experienced in the doctor's consulting room. These stories also have the function of redressing the balance of power between the two interactants of the consultation. Baruch (1981) describes these stories as *'moral tales'*. They serve to reaffirm the moral integrity of parents whose children are chronically ill. Often, they are 'atrocity stories': that is, they emphasise that what happened during the visit to the doctor contradicts an average person's sense of moral value. In general, says Baruch, four features of discourse establish the parents' moral adequacy: emotionality (justifying their being upset), child-rearing practices (parents being the ones who know best), unreasonableness of priorities in outpatient clinics (making for unnecessary suffering, waiting, etc.), and not comprehending medical terminology (such that they could not get their own back in the conversation with the doctor).

As regards the chronically ill themselves, validation serves to make them accept their fate. Waddell (1982) describes five *techniques of neutralisation* with which parents with children with cystic fibrosis overcome the uncertainties which jeopardise their faith and hope. Sykes and Matza (1957) introduce the idea of techniques of neutralisation to demonstrate how criminals protect their personal identity by 'explaining away' those aspects of their deeds which threaten their sense of moral integrity. Among them, one of the techniques is telling atrocity stories which Goffman (1961, p. 135) also reports for hospitalised mental patients. Waddell finds that in cases of cystic fibrosis, the uncertain aetiology is *reduced* to the history of the diagnosis, the genetic uncertainty is converted to hope for further research, the uniqueness of each case is cited to explain the relative ineffectiveness of diet regimens, the comparison with other, worse cases helps to overcome adverse reactions from the social environment, and emphasising the lack of an alternative to therapy helps to decrease uncertainty stemming from the reduced life expectancy.

Chronic illness: management and self

The crisis model conceptualises illness (disability) as 'master status', changing the patient's whole life style and identity for the worse. In contrast, the negotiation model conceptualises illness and disability as a *challenge* to life style and identity, and the governing analytical perspective is 'management': that is, maximum relative normality in the face of incapacitation or stigmatisation is understood to be the aim of patients' coping strategies which, in turn, partly protect and preserve patients' identity.

Negotiation, for one, accompanies progress during a patient's illness career. The career is conceived as an ordered sequence of phases moving towards a recognisable end-point, with benchmarks or turning-points separating the phases from each other. While F. Davis (1963), without explicitly using the notion, describes career as the adaptation of polio victims to their incapacity until settling back into a somewhat normal life, Roth (1963a) analyses a succession of stages (and how patients try to negotiate them) during hospitalisation for tuberculosis. Glaser and Strauss (1968) understand the dying process such that medical work necessitated by a patient's condition follows a 'dying trajectory'. In other words, while there are 'prescribed schedules when the patient must be fed, bathed, turned in bed, given drugs' (1968, p. 2), such work is different, to a certain extent, when the initial definition of a dying trajectory pronounces it to be quick or lingering (and the actual course of events may or may not follow this definition). The work also changes when, for instance, the 'nothing-more-to-do' phase has been reached and the patient's 'significant others' may have abandoned him ('social death'). To be sure, management of the dying trajectory has several dimensions: 'Medical and custodial management of the dying patient is one thing, but what about the management of the patient's day-in, day-out behavior during his lingering dying? And what of the responses of his family, of other patients, and of the personnel themselves?' (1968, p. 61).

Shifting from the topic of dying to that of chronic illness and quality of life, 'grounded theory' after 1972 produces the same perspective. Again, management problems are in the forefront of analysis. Management of regimens, the trajectory and medical crises are now prime topics. The general line of the argument is that the patient negotiates as much normality as can be mustered; *normalisation* is introduced as *basic strategy*:

> The chief business of a chronically ill person is not just to stay alive or keep his symptoms under control, but to live as normally as possible despite his symptoms and his disease. How normal he can make his life (and that of his family) depends not only on the social arrangements he and they can make but on just how intrusive are his symptoms, his regimens, and the knowledge that others have of his disease and of its

fatal potential. If none is very intrusive on interactional or social relations, then the tactics for keeping things normal need not be especially ingenious or elaborate. But when regimen, symptom, or knowledge of the disease turns out to be intrusive, then the sick person has to work very hard at creating some semblance of normal life for himself. (Strauss and Glaser, 1975, p. 58)

Research in the field of 'grounded theory' produces an amazing array of what are called tactics or strategies of symptom control or management. For instance, Reif (1973) describes *Strategies for Managing Life* with ulcerative colitis, consisting of preventive, protective and corrective ways of dealing with what are euphemistically called 'pollution problems'. In another study, Wiener (1975) shows that patients with rheumatoid arthritis have a repertoire of strategies to accomplish 'covering-up', 'keeping-up', 'justifying inaction', 'pacing', and so on.

The normalising effort is also shown to extend to the meaning which the illness is given. G. Williams (1984) emphasises that chronically ill patients undertake a restructuring of their biographies such that their being sick becomes a reasonable and explicable outcome of past privations or challenging circumstances. Stories are presented to the interviewer which document *narrative reconstruction* of the patient's past and 'that identified "causes" represent not only putative efficient connexions between the disease and antecedent factors but also narrative reference points between the individual and society' (1984, p. 175). For example, a mother derives her rheumatoid arthritis from continuous overwork for her family, or a worker charges his ex-employer with having neglected safety regulations. Behind this is the view that chronic illness means a major *disruption* of the afflicted's biography. Bury (1982) describes in detail the cycle of disruption and reconstitution of 'taken-for-granted assumptions and behaviours' as well as 'explanatory systems' which Williams (1984) also envisages.

Bury concentrates on patients' *response* to the disruption, their mobilising of resources which overcome or neutralise as many threats to their previous life style as possible. Normalisation in the management of chronic illness is most successful if it is based on acknowledging the reality of illness. Schneider and Conrad (1983) describe the breakdown of previous control of one's body, and adoption of interpretive and behavioural strategies which help to control seizures; a particular 'seizure theory' as well as 'anticipatory defenses' and 'emergency measures' serve this purpose (1983, pp. 125–46).

To be sure, such normalising, especially if no overt stigma is experienced, amounts to 'living with a concealed or spoiled identity' (Scambler and Hopkins, 1986, p. 34): that is, in spite of elaborate strategies which may be adopted to overcome the loss of capacities and opportunities, damage to the self is unavoidable. Charmaz (1983) makes it clear that *loss of self* is inevitable in chronic illness. Jobling (1977), telling his own story of how he admirably coped with his psoriasis and became a university lecturer, nevertheless has this to say about how he felt when he realised that his condition was chronic: 'My self-conception was spoiled and the consequent feeling of self-stigmatisation was marked. I was in effect a different person from the one I had thought myself to be' (1977, p. 77).

Scambler and Hopkins (1986, pp. 37–8) find that felt stigma precedes stigma experienced from others ('enacted stigma'). Charmaz (1983, pp. 16–9) suggests that since interactions which, prior to the illness, were a source of positive self-image are now precluded due to incapacitation, crucial areas of the patient's self are doomed: 'As they suffer losses of self from the consequences of chronic illness and experience diminished control over their lives and their futures, affected individuals commonly not only lose self-esteem, but even self-identity. Hence, suffering such losses results in a diminished self.' Reduction of the patient's scope of activity, therefore, is seen as a reason why the self crumbles. Since it is through the 'looking-glass' effect of others' positive evaluation of one's actions and personal value that the self is constituted, losing contacts through social isolation due to illness-related incapacitation also destroys the person's identity. It is not so much deviant reconstituted identity which is understood to result from chronic illness but, rather, deterioration of any worthwhile identity. Bitter accounts are reported of others' motives for their basically inexplicable withdrawal. M. Davis (1973) describes vividly how multiple sclerosis patients feel:

> One man now in a wheelchair and very socially isolated, described why he thought others no longer came to see him. He said, 'I think sometimes people don't come to see me because I'm gruesome. It's not pleasant to feel you're gruesome'. Others explained to themselves why friends no longer visited or even phoned by telling themselves that 'nobody wants to see their friends go downhill', or that people are 'too busy with their own lives'. Still others felt that people were frightened that it might happen to them and that staying away kept the frightening possibility 'out of mind'. (1973, pp. 20–1)

To sum up, the normalisation perspective determines the view of illness as disability. Successful coping is discovered in strategies and tactics of illness management, but no positive effect of identity-constitutive interaction is revealed; rather, destruction of self appears inevitable. The idea of deviant identity is not adopted, and normal identities are understood as the sole worthwhile reference points of patients' self-image. Accordingly, consequences of illness-related incapacities are depicted as self-loss.

Therapy and the management of treatment

Aetiology, in the negotiation model, is a three-stage process of retaining as much as possible of one's normal social identity. The uncertainty state consists of strategies of reconciling clinical theory and daily practices on the doctor's side, and lay theories and everyday practices on the patient's side. When the two meet in a consultation, the patient succumbs to the doctor's diagnosis but subsequently validates the doctor's 'offer' by checking it against the opinion of, and also forming his or her own by telling stories to, relatives and friends. Such resurrection to relative strength of an other-than-ill identity is accomplished through various strategies of normalisation habitually used by the chronically ill and disabled. That is, bargaining strikes the most advantageous deal in interpersonal exchanges with others who do the same.

The basic idea is that patients' negotiative capacity is unaffected by their illness. This may mean that it prevails until patients are near death. But the literature also endorses negotiation: human beings should ask for and be granted a certain dignity of living (as well as dying). This is meant as a criticism interpreting observed practices beyond the occasion of death (Glaser and Strauss, 1968; Strauss and Glaser, 1975). Aetiology, in principle, never makes one lose one's normality, understood as whatever holistic qualities characterise the human actor: reflexivity, intentionality, capacity to react to and exchange with others.

The notion of therapy grants that the patient's realm of activity may be jeopardised by a physical condition. But a person's social identity, to be sure, is judged intact enough to make him or her capable of maintaining, and of being entitled to treatment according to, human dignity and social identity. In this vein, the patient is just another actor like nurses and doctors, and uses the same negotiation strategies as any other (normal) member of society.

Therapy comes to be understood as the management of treatment. The term 'management' implies that the patient takes an active part, or should be allowed one. Therapy takes place in two contexts, hospital and home. Where therapy is done in *hospitals* all members of the medical team (including the patient) are taken as working together to achieve the goal of the patient's getting better. However, the most important place where therapy occurs is *at home*. There, the patient manages both the regimen and the various infringements of illness on his or her life style more or less as a competent circumspect actor. The work aspect of this is recognised by the central role accrued to *resources*.

Three issues seem noteworthy, namely:

(a) that hospital treatment is understood as a social construction of a work arena around illness. In this, various 'definitions of the situation' abound, and 'treatment ideologies' are among them;

(b) that coping with chronic illness at home is the core process which sociologists are advised to analyse; through this, the crisis model's focus on professional dominance is not shared;

(c) the problem of acute illness is judged to be but a derivative of that of chronic illness in modern society: through this, the Parsonian theory's alleged predilection for acute illness is effectively overcome.

The social construction of hospital treatment

Hospital treatment, above all, is work organised towards a common goal on the basis of a flexible division of labour. In the introduction of their *Social Organization of Medical Work* (1985), Strauss *et al.* stress that a hospital represents a multitude of worksites rather than a monolithic system of prescriptive regulations:

> A useful way of conceiving of the hospital is as a large number of work sites . . . A hospital consists of variegated workshops – places where different kinds of work are going on, where very different resources (space, skills, ratios of labor force, equipment, drugs, supplies, and the like) are required to carry out that work, where the divisions of labor are amazingly different, though all of this is in the direct or indirect service of managing patients' illnesses. (1985, pp. 5–6)

The focus is on *what happens* in treatment encounters. This 'naturalistic' side of events highlights what actually can be protocoled by a participant observer. It marks the analytical interest in tasks done by everybody as well as how everybody feels about what is being done. Multiplicity characterising each separate worksite is a *prima facie* reason why *negotiation* is unavoidable. Hall, Pill and Clough (1976) state succinctly:

If we apply a problem solving perspective we must recognise that all the social actors are engaged jointly in this activity: their problems and their definitions of the situation may well differ, but inasmuch as they are constrained in the solution of their problems by the need to interact with others and establish some point of contact with their definition of reality, they enter a situation of negotiation and compromise. (1976, p. 148)

To negotiate one's 'turf', however, is, in Turner's terms (1962), 'role making'. Strong and Davis remark: 'Thus . . . being a doctor, a therapist or a patient is not something that you just passively *are*, it is something that you have to *do*, something that has to be managed and pulled off' (1978, p. 124). In this vein, J. Roth (1962, 1963a and 1963b) calls attention to the strategies of tuberculosis patients who wish to negotiate with their doctors a length of hospital stay which they consider acceptable. Medical personnel wish to avoid being cornered by patients over treatment decisions and dates of discharge. The reference issue serving both patients and doctors to make their bargaining look reasonable is a *timetable* of successive treatment stages. Roth relates:

Trying to 'make a deal' with the doctors is a game played by many patients who are looking for ways to speed up their timetable. Often these efforts fail. Some physicians uncompromisingly declare that they will not bargain with the patients on matters of treatment, although close observation shows that they often do. A patient who tells the doctor that he will stay in the hospital for six more months if the doctor will give him a pass every week may receive the same scornful rebuke that he would if he openly offered a judge five dollars for dismissing a traffic violation. However, despite the frequent resistance of bargaining on the part of the physicians, the fact remains that many such deals are made, and on occasion it is even the physician who suggests them. (1963a, pp. 52–3)

It is clear that Roth perceives paramount *conflict* between the two sides involved in the treatment. Their strategies which he enumerates elaborately in an article focusing on 'Staff and Inmate Tactics' (J. Roth, 1984) are directed *against* each other's perceived privileges and 'politics'. In contrast, for instance, Webb (1977), when describing experiences of living-in on a ward with her ten-month-old son, focuses on much subtler forms of bargaining which may beg the question of whether conflict prevails:

Mothers become skilled at formally acknowledging the staff as the decision-makers whilst among themselves sharing knowledge about how to work the system. 'Bargaining' is perhaps too crude a form to describe the subtleties of nuance, change in tone, looks, gestures and stance which characterized strategic interaction in these situations. (1977, pp. 178–9)

The issue is: is there conflict between the interactants who 'pull off' medical treatment together ? Or is conflict stifled by the particular kind of 'Meadian "fluidity"' which Strauss (1978b, p. 122) cites to account for constant redefinition of work responsibilities which he stresses under a 'social world perspective':

> The Meadian emphasis on the endless formation of universes of discourse – with which groups are coterminous – is extremely valuable, yielding a metaphor of groups emerging, evolving, developing, splintering, disintegrating, or pulling themselves together, or parts of them falling away and perhaps coalescing with segments of other groups to form new groups, in opposition, often, to the old. (1978b, pp. 121–2)

In other words, Strauss suggests that the social *order* of the hospital is constituted by constant *change* of rules or constant regrouping of people who work together. It is the sum total of nascent and transient 'definitions of the situation' by all concerned and comprising all of the hospital's worksites which constitutes the hospital's social order. F. Davis (1963, p. 19) refers to this as the 'paradox of ordering reality versus the unreality of order'. Kriesberg (1968), in a paper dedicated to Hughes, citing Strauss *et al.*'s 'The Hospital and its Negotiated Order' (1963), stresses that infinite change thus defines the structure of social organisations: 'The game of remaking an organisation continues as long as the organisation exists' (Kriesberg 1968, p. 156).

To focus on ever-changing rules which are followed, in the extreme case, only in one single situation between consciously negotiating interactants, brings up rather than solves the problem of how the *structure* of an organisation persists. In the second instance, this raises the question of how *conflict* can persist in an organisation. If through constant renegotiation of rules and roles the individuals' talents and 'bargaining potentials' are channelled into realisation through situational 'deals', how can structural conflict survive in an organisation?

The question regarding structure is comparatively easy to answer although the theoretical problem may not be solved satisfactorily. If constant change allows for maximum expression of bickering and bargaining over temporal arrangements with other interactants, stability of an organisational structure and even its very existence appear to be endangered. If no minimally lasting system of at least a set of basic rules guarantees the structure of an organisation, any change of rules and relations could threaten the organisation's collapse, or dissolve it into an arena of fighting factions. A shared purpose integrating the sum total of worksites, and an overall goal of the hospital as an organisation, does seem to be acknowledged by Strauss and his associates. This provides an anchor for structure. The aim of everyone who works in the hospital is 'getting patients somewhat better' (Strauss *et al.*, 1964a, p. 292), although this aim 'becomes fragmented in actual implementation'. The goal, while providing the joint orientation of otherwise widely differing status groups, is general enough to involve everybody, and specific enough to allow for contextual interpretations at the various worksites. Thus the structure of the hospital as an organisation is guaranteed through a highly generalised value pattern serving as an orientation for every member. But diversity of worksites and multiplicity of professional groups interacting in them are not accounted for. In other words, it remains unclear whether conflict 'is left' within the organisational structure of the hospital. Or does unlimited bargaining and change within the 'negotiated order' do away with conflict?

To answer this question, the notion of *work* may be important. Hospitals are made up of worksites, and they comprise a wide variety of *types* of work such as, for instance, safety (clinical) work, pain work, kin work, and so on. Usually, work offers an opportunity to 'get things done', including such humane accomplishments as ascertaining integrity of body and soul. Strauss *et al.* (1982a, 1985), for instance, point to 'sentimental work' as a way of making an input into a situation, safeguarding one's own or somebody else's humaneness, dignity, or identity. They specify:

> Among the sub-types of sentimental work, then, are: interactional work and moral rules, trust work, composure work, biographical work, identity work, awareness context work, and rectification work. Picture these types of work in dramaturgical terms: they are actions done during the medical scenes; sometimes they are front and centre, more often they are at the margins of the main line (medical-nursing, technical) of action. Sometimes they are so marginal that they are barely discernible to any audience, as virtually the only actor who is aware of the sentimental action is the actor doing it. (1982a, p. 266)

Such work, to be sure, is capable of reducing conflict. For instance, Strauss *et al.* (1982b, 1985) focus on the work which hospitalised patients do to ameliorate their potential frustration or suffering. Monitoring their own responses because they otherwise have to criticise staff for unfriendliness, or accuse them of mishandling technical equipment, patients commit actions which secure their own satisfaction. In fact, much conflict at hospitals could be avoided, say Strauss *et al.*, if patients' active participation in clinical work were not frequently overlooked by staff. The ideal is a structure of fully reciprocal cooperation where each participant is acknowledged in doing his or her share:

> Clear recognition of patients' work as part of the total division and organisation of labor could result in a decrease of tension and conflict between patients and staff members, contributing also toward more effective medical and nursing care, as well as more effective teaching of the patients themselves. The larger theoretical issue for the social scientist is that whenever a client is worked on or with by any servicing agent, then that client can become part of the division of labour in getting the work done, even though neither may recognise the client's efforts as constituting work. (1982b, p. 977)

It is obvious that Strauss *et al.* perceive conflict as endemic in hospitals. Despite frequent negotiations producing flexible rules and task ranges, the multiple worksites appear ripe with discrepancies and dissatisfactions. These seem to be the main forces driving towards constant reformulation and renegotiation of situational work schemes. Of course, technical innovations also play a part in renegotiation of tasks and procedures (see Strauss *et al.*, 1985, on 'safety work'), but the division of labour was less spasmodic if they were the prime source of change of organisational task arrangements.

How can the omnipresence of conflict and change in the 'web of negotiation' (Strauss *et al.*, 1963, p. 159) be kept from ending up in a state of *homo homini lupus* where everyone maximises his or her own gain at the expense of everyone else? Is the term 'negotiative order' a misnomer because centripetal forces constituting the social order of a hospital run counter to centrifugal forces which negotiation (with its corollary of segmentation) unleashes?

The problem seems solved by introducing temporal structures uniting the physiological course of a disease with the work it entails. In Strauss *et al.*'s earlier writings, these temporal structures are called 'career' (following E. C. Hughes, 1958), but in their later work, they are named 'trajectory'. To quote:

> Trajectory is a term coined by the authors to refer not only to the physiological unfolding of a patient's disease but to the total *organisation of work* done over that course, plus the *impact* on those involved with that work and its organisation. For different illnesses, the trajectory will involve different kinds of skills and other resources, a different parcelling out of tasks among the workers (including, perhaps, kin and the patient), and involving quite different relationships – instrumental and expressive both – among the workers. (1985, p. 8)

Where do these trajectories come from? How do they build up into patterns of particular medical or nursing action? Does clinical medicine at last come into the picture? It seems that it is here that the negotiation approach misses a chance to ground itself in the 'definition of the situation' of those working in hospital as clinically responsible medics. Clearly they are convinced that medical knowledge is specific to diseases which they treat, and that progress in clinical procedures including use of equipment to make them safe and effective constitutes a reality *sui generis*. The 'definition of the situation' of doctors bargaining over tasks and managing worksites leaves no doubt, it would appear, that clinical medicine commands its own reality in the hospital. However, instead of acknowledging clinical expertise, medical *ideologies* are introduced. They constitute what is called a 'philosophy of care' (M. Z. Davis, 1980, p. 47), embodied by an 'ideology bearer' (Davis, 1980, p. 45).

In her book entitled *The Politics of Alcoholism*, Wiener (1980) shows how a specific *arena* develops into the 'treatment philosophy' that alcoholism is a disease. Between 1960 and the late 1970s, she argues, a social movement springs up which effectively launches this 'social construction of reality' leading to public recognition and policy relevance. She phrases her problem as follows:

> In 1970, the year of publication of *Precarious Politics: Alcoholism and Public Policy*, the main obstacle to public support for alcoholism programs (as seen by its author, Dan Beauchamp) lay in demonstrating an invisible problem . . . Five years after the passage of the above act, [the former Senator Harold] Hughes could point to counsellors, scientists, 'think-tank' personnel, administrators, government funding agencies, lobbyists, associations, consultants, evaluators, technical assistants. Eight years after passage, this arena had grown from an 'invisible' state to federal budget appropriation of $ 161,467,000. What had happened in the intervening years to make such growth possible? (1980, p. 3)

Wiener purports to show how a powerful treatment ideology arises which commands research markets and becomes prevalent both in expert and lay definitions of the disease. She leaves no doubt that what emerges as *ideology* cannot claim independent objective proof to be superior to previous 'treatment philosophies': rather, agencies created to deal with alcoholism, Wiener states, are most interested in (re)defining alcohol abuse such that they become indispensable in fighting it. How the disease of alcoholism is defined appears, then, related to expansion and reputation of agencies originally created to treat it.

The crisis model recognises hierarchical separation between 'staff' and 'inmates' in institutions and sees illness as a product of the institutional set-up meant to treat it. In the negotiation model, 'treatment philosophy' is given a bad name of possibly being iatrogenic. Illness is 'constructed' through ideology defining it for the sake of treatment. The crisis model locates the sociological interest in illness wholly beyond the physiological reality of illness. In the negotiation model, this separation is not so clear. To a certain extent, physiological aspects of an illness enter into the sociological viewpoint. Physical symptoms, the pathology of physiological events, partly define the specific type of trajectory for a particular patient. When hospitalised, patients are given an envisaged trajectory with steps and stages for work serving the purpose of 'getting better' or 'getting home'. This means cooperative efforts at treatment, or crisis and breakdown of communication described as 'cumulative mess trajectory' (Strauss *et al.*, 1985, p. 160ff.). To accomplish physiological improvement until eventual discharge is aimed at by all who work on the patient (including the patient). It could be argued that thus 'treatment philosophy' (or a multitude of more or less conflicting 'treatment philosophies') is not wholly beyond what pathophysiological or clinical reality a treated illness represents.

Coping in everyday life

Between the crisis model and the negotiation model, the analytical focus shifts from the hospital as the main locale of treatment (supposedly also a potential source of iatrogenic illness) to life outside the hospital which is where (chronically ill) patients spend much more time than in the hospital. Medical treatment and the doctor–patient relationship thus become but one among a number of problems to which the patient attends, and one among many relationships which he or she keeps up. In Schneider and Conrad's narrative about epileptics' experiences, doctors appear as necessary but often not respected:

> People with epilepsy need physicians to tell them what is wrong, to prescribe an effective course of treatment, to monitor medication levels and effectiveness, and to provide information about their condition. They must (and some want to) depend on their physician. At the same time, however, many spoke of being dissatisfied with the effectiveness of the treatment and with their personal rapport with doctors. (1983, p. 211)

Other authors make it clear that criticism of doctors would be ill-advised since the patient depends on them. Bury (1982) states, replying to possible critics who might cite his respondents' experiences as proof of alienation between doctors and patients: 'My study provides no ground for assuming that these problems indicate any generalised disillusionment with medicine as a system of knowledge and explanation' (1982, p. 179). The patients' management of their illness is deemed, in principle, independent from what the doctor does for them. The doctor is one source of help among an array of resources. MacIntire and Oldman (1977, p. 59) state, for migraine sufferers, that 'coping and treatment are . . . dominated by different sets of relevances'.

Relevances for coping in everyday life are viewed from two angles. Impairment reducing vital resources and, accordingly, coping characterise a life riddled with constraints. This is here addressed as the *resources problem*. Furthermore, illness or disability jeopardise a person's moral stance in interpersonal exchanges; accordingly, coping denotes management of stigma. This will be described as a *sociability problem*. Both, under a negotiation view, picture the individual relentlessly attempting to control both body and environment. This constant confrontation between willingness and possibility in any given situation begs the question of whether the self or the environment, as it were, will make the offer that the other cannot refuse. The interchange between self and environment is guided by a strong urge for normalisation, the force behind the bargaining.

The resources problem.   The attitude of 'grounded theory' has been to look at the *work* with which the chronically ill organise their lives. What matters are vital resources which individuals have at their disposal. These are mundane media of environmental and self-management such as mobility, energy, skill, strength, time and body control (Reif, 1973, p. 83; Strauss and Glaser, 1975, p. 24; Wiener, 1975, pp. 72, 79) as well as societal resources such as money (Strauss and Glaser, 1975, p. 26; Suczek, 1975; Gerson, 1976b, p. 799ff.), and integration into a network of friends and social activities (Strauss and Glaser, 1975, p. 26; Bury, 1982, p. 175ff.; Schneider and Conrad, 1983, Ch. 5). Chronic illness poses a severe threat to resources. While resource reduction is inevitable, what differs is its amount, duration, and mode. For instance, in the case of rheumatoid arthritis, the available mobility, energy, skill and strength are different for each individual and, moreover, change constantly such that the patient has to adapt to uncertainty from one day to the next as to what reduction in fact is to be expected:

For example, [arthritic patients] may have reduced mobility but no impairment of skill, reduced energy but no interference with mobility, reduced energy one day but renewed energy the next day. Loss of skill will remain fairly constant if it is caused by deformity, but is variable if caused by swelling. (Wiener, 1975, p. 72)

In this situation, the individuals devise management strategies allowing them to redress the balance on a lower but realistic level. Negotiation enters the endeavour in the guise of 'balancing decisions' (Wiener, 1975, p. 80) which continually rearrange the importance of a commitment in view of the energy spent on it: 'One must decide what the options are, must decide between them by calculating consequences, must face the consequences whatever . . . they actually turn out to be; and one cannot rest easily or for long on previous definitions and decisions about options' (Weiner, 1975, p. 80). To continuously renegotiate the balance between resources and effort implies that no item stays unquestioned, not even the medical regimen, as Strauss and Glaser state: 'It is no wonder, then, that every regimen – and every item in it – is actually or potentially on trial. So are the people who recommend the regimen' (1975, p. 21).

The problem is for individuals to redesign their life styles in a way compatible with their illness and treatment (Strauss and Glaser, 1975, p. 36; Reif, 1973/75, p. 83ff.). Three main foci of such adaptation emerge: (a) the management of the regimen (which may be time-consuming as in renal dialysis, or painful and repugnant as with ulcerative colitis, and which may deeply involve family members as described by Corbin and Strauss, 1985); (b) the reordering of one's time perspective and outlook in life; and (c) fending off the danger of social isolation (Strauss and Glaser, 1975, p. 60ff.; Bury, 1982, p. 175ff.). The aim is to retain a network of friends or a workplace where a certain amount of shielding can be enjoyed against stigmatisation from 'uninformed' outsiders. This, however, may also produce feelings of being stifled by those who chaperone. Schneider and Conrad find that 'our repondents found it difficult to resist such parental help without risking the relationship itself' (1983, p. 102).

On the other hand, the reduction of resources also gives rise to the reconstitution of what Strauss (1978b) calls 'social world'. In an article focusing on 'the social organization of older people' from this 'social world perspective', Unruh (1980) gives some ideas as to what such reconstitution entails. He argues that in older people's social world, organisations are not monolithic blocks of fixed status hierarchies but ever-changing structures of informal and formal relations around (transitory) common goals or (more or less stable) groups of activists ('insiders'). Such 'social worlds' as Unruh describes are less occupational and more those of leisure activities. It may be argued that life and life style are unproblematically malleable here but not elsewhere. For example, Blaxter and Cyster (1984) show that patients diagnosed with alcohol-related liver disease find it difficult to 'understand' that this entails distinctively making changes in their choice of 'social world'. A sizeable number of patients 'prefer' to see no connection between liver disease and life style, and they claim that information and instruction received from their GP was far from decisive.

The sociability problem.   A separate approach analysing coping in everyday life goes back to Goffman's *Stigma* (1963). Its basic idea is that sociability – reproducing society in interpersonal encounters – is managed achievement and calls for continuous effort from social participants. Goffman initially distinguishes between social and personal identity, and both are merged in ego identity: 'The concept of social identity allowed us to consider stigmatisation. The concept of personal identity allowed us to consider the role of information control in stigma management. The idea of ego identity allows us to consider what the individual may feel about stigma and its management' (1963, p. 130).

Personal identity is achieved through two aspects of stigma management, namely, the handling of discredited versus discreditable aspects of the person. Whereas the former means that being different has been disclosed and stigma is virulent, the latter relates to strategies of concealing a stigmatisable feature. For the discredited, the main problem is tension management in social contacts; for the discreditable it is information control with the added complication of how closely to draw the circle of the informed among friends and acquaintances: 'To display or not to display; to tell or not to tell; to let on or not to let on; to lie or not to lie; and in each case to whom, how, when, and where' (Goffman, 1963, p. 57).

Goffman's analysis is relieved from its pessimistic overtones in the 'grounded theory' approach. Charmaz (1983) argues that identities result from interactions in which others corroborate a person's 'me's'. If a patient can no longer carry out activities which make others respond favourably within an interaction, the respective aspects of his or her definition of self become discredited (and deteriorate or wither away). This may go so far that self-pity is produced. That is, as Charmaz (1980) describes:

When the chronically ill judge their illnesses to be personal inadequacies, or some sort of failing, then conditions exist for them to be overly scrutinising of others to see if they can make any similar devaluating judgment. Subsequently, if the scrutinizing so bears out, they are apt to magnify any further indication of tacit judgments. In short, these persons become highly self-conscious and direct attention to the *possibility* of devaluating judgements then construe any response as evidence of such a judgement. This insidious process works only to further feelings of separateness and envy that give rise to self-pity. (1980, p. 134)

To be sure, this process is reversible, such as when the illness is in remission or gets better, when affirmation comes forward from others, or when the afflicted reacts against it (1980, p. 140ff.). Thus strategies of identity reconstitution are focused upon, rather than solely the devastating effects of being discredited. G. Williams (1984) points at reconstruction of the meaningfulness of one's life (including accountability of one's illness) as a strategy to redress the balance. Williams shows how stories are incorporated into the individual's self-presentation giving rational (understandable) accounts of the illness as well as of the fact that the person's basic social identities remain unaffected. Schneider and Conrad (1983) report that epileptics develop an elaborate set of strategies (including 'strategic selective disclosing') of information release to keep control over the stigma side of their illness. In particular, strategies of maintaining control over the possible occasions of when a seizure would occur, and what to do on such occasion, function to reinforce the epileptic's self as that of a competent – and insofar normal – actor.

In this the patient's family is either mentioned as a protective milieu which becomes a mediator with the outside environment, or as an arena for concern regarding the patient's freedom to make his or her own mistakes. In this, the negotiation model takes a more liberal and less doomed view than the crisis approach. For instance, while Schneider and Conrad (1983) distinguish between a 'closed parental style' and an 'open parental style' of handling an epileptic's potentially self-endangering life style, Goffman has this to say about the family's plight:

In the case of incurable disorders that are messy or severely incapacitating, the compensative work required by the well members may cost them the life chances their peers enjoy, blunt their personal careers, paint their lives with tragedy, and turn all their feelings to bitterness. But the fact that all this hardship can be contained shows how clearly the way has been marked for the unfortunate family, a way that obliges them to closed ranks and somehow make do as long as the illness lasts. (1969b, p. 367)

The problem of acute illness

Although it may be a misconception that Talcott Parsons' approach is unable to account for chronic illness (see above), protagonists of negotiation claim that their analysis is better able than Parsons' to account for chronic disease. Conrad, in an overview of recent literature, claims that Parsons' idea of sick role avails to no 'insider perspective' (1987, p. 2; see also Schneider and Conrad, 1983, pp. 9–15). It is noteworthy that Conrad identifies 'outsider perspectives' with 'a medical or social theoretical perspective', in contrast to which he endorses a subjectivity stance. 'There is a tendency here to take a doctor-centered view of illness', he says about the 'outsider approach':

> making receipt of medical care the center of research attention and giving short shrift to the experience of illness. An insider perspective, on the other hand, . . . focuses specifically on the perspective of people with illness and attempts to examine the illness experience in a more inductive manner. (Conrad, 1987, p. 2)

Thus it is held that chronic sickness can only be analysed from a perspective which 'takes the role of the sick', to paraphrase a term from G. H. Mead. Furthermore, it is also held that this is the only standpoint which does justice from a medical-sociology point of view to the *societal* reality of sickness.

Why, one is inclined to ask, can the analytical perspective focusing on the sick role not produce an adequate picture of the experience of illness? The answer provided is twofold. Namely, the sick role allegedly only helps to analyse illness as transient status; furthermore, it only concentrates on the doctor's side of the doctor–patient relationship but does not allow for, as it were, the 'side of the underdog'.

What are the connotations of illness as a transient as opposed to permanent experience, in this view? Gerson (1976 b, p. 804) argues that chronic patients need the doctor's emotional involvement as well as a higher quality of 'administrative and ancillary services'. Together, these govern the hospital staff's obligation 'to be rather more concerned emotionally with the welfare of each patient'. However, in the modern technologically equipped hospital basically geared towards dealing with acute conditions, the emotional involvement of medical staff is said to be neglected. In modern medical care where the sick role means transient status, surgical treatment takes priority over 'biographical work'.

This seemingly anti-Parsonian argument presented by, among others, Gerson and Conrad appears rather similar to what Parsons himself writes. In Chapter 2 above, it is argued that Parsons advocates the doctor taking into account the patient's emotional reaction to the illness. Parsons borrows from L. J. Henderson the term *sentiment* to pinpoint where modern medicine apparently performs unsatisfactorily. Strauss *et al.* (1982a, 1985) plead for 'sentimental work' by medical and other personnel, also an area where patients contribute considerably to their own treatment. Controversy over who sides with the patient, then, appears to be but a serious misunderstanding. On the one hand, the 'symbolic-interactionist' approach demonstrates that a negotiation of senti-mental tasks takes place in medical encounters. On the other hand, Parsons' incapacity approach pleads for doctors to incorpor-ate the sentiment dimension into their professional perspective. Are these two approaches really talking about two different things? Are they not approaching the same goal from opposite directions?

They probably do so less than it appears at first sight. The issue that only *chronic* illness provides an adequate target for the 'insider perspective' of the inductively proceeding sociological analysis entails two claims. One is that illness, where it becomes sociologically relevant, *is* a permanent status and should not be trivialised by emphasising its transient acute versions. The reasons given for this, if they may be called reasons at all, are not convinc-ing, however. One is that the most prevalent form of illness in modern society is chronic rather than acute (Strauss *et al.*, 1985, Ch. 2). Apart from the fact that this may not hold statistically, emphasising it in connection with *hospital* treatment may be incon-sequential when it is held elsewhere that chronic diseases call for a shift of the analytical perspective towards management of life *outside* the hospital. If the patient's life problems are brought to attention there seems no need to insist that they only prevail with chronic but not acute conditions. (Besides, the boundary between acute and chronic may be far from clear-cut in serial illness episodes over time, as Gerhardt, 1976b, points out.)

The second claim – that only chronic illness is analytically adequate – is more convincing, albeit political. By analysing sick-ness where it is at its worst – namely where, in effect, it becomes permanent like a 'master status' – the negotiation approach feels that it does not forsake the patient's legitimate interests. Only where chronic patients are taken seriously in their suffering and thus, so to speak, acknowledged in their role as society's under-dogs, leading the lives of second-class citizens, can medical sociology avoid serving the interests of professional institutions. Conrad's (1987) plea for 'insider perspective' makes this clear as do, for example, Locker (1983) and Fitzpatrick *et al.* (1984), among many others.

The sociologist analysing social reality from the point of view of institutions, and the doctor treating patients according to the best possible standards of modern clinical medicine, are seen to do the same wrong thing. They are seen to realise the same unwanted option: Acute illness, analysable using the notion of sick role, gives an opportunity for the well-trained technologically open-minded clinician to demonstrate skill and efficiency.

To claim the sentimental as a layer of medical-sociological interest in illness means something different for Parsons and for the negotiation approach. For Parsons, it means more taking into account by the medical personnel of the patients' fears and wishes (i.e., their emotional responses to being treated). For the negotiation approach, it means that a totally new power arrangement is called for in doctor–patient encounters. As Wiener *et al.* (1980) point out in their essay on the problem of patient power, it is not just new wine in old bottles which is needed:

> We would assert that people's rights do need to be recognized and respected by health professionals. Issues like informed consent and access to medical records do not even begin to deal with the realities of the medical scene. Citizen rights aside, while many option points do entail judgments and decisions that patients are not qualified to make, it would certainly move us toward better health care if the health professionals had a heightened awareness that patients are already making decisions, and that with more guidance and sharing of knowledge and responsibility this patient work could be better informed and effective. To scoff at contentions of patient power or to argue past them is only to invite further 'encroachments' on professional work and authority; but lay misunderstandings and oversimplifications of the complex contexts in which health professionals and technicians do their work only bring bitterness and retaliatory action. It is not that we need more tolerance of the counter positions, but that both need to be transcended. (1980, p. 38)

Chapter 8
'Symbolic Interactionism' and the Two Models of Illness

As a label conferred on a person/patient by a medical agent, or as a way of life into which a chronically ill person has to settle, illness takes on two different forms in the crisis and the negotiation models. Both claim to derive from 'symbolic interactionism' which, in turn, claims to evolve from the thought of G. H. Mead.

The two approaches emerge over a time period of some 35 years. Their patterns of development are remarkably different. After about a decade of concept formation, the crisis model (as labelling theory and as anti-psychiatry) plunges into an unexpected exposure to the limelight of worldwide emulation. Its heyday in the 1960s is followed by falling into disrepute in the 1970s. A barrage of critical onslaught from nearly every other theoretical perspective in the early 1970s marks the change. Gouldner's sarcastic remarks concerning Goffman and others in his *The Coming Crisis of Western Sociology* (1970) find credibility just like Dahrendorf's did against Parsons 12 years earlier. After this, a decade of arguments and counter-arguments follows which eventually peters out when even the protagonists lose interest. In contradistinction, the negotiation model neither becomes the predominant thought in deviance research at any point in time, nor does it attract the vigorous criticism which thoroughly destroys the prospects of the labelling approach. In fact, there does not seem to be a single *analytical* article which attempts to understand critically the argument presented by the non-labelling version of the interactionist paradigm. In particular, the newer 'social world perspective' and the not so new 'negotiated order' notion of Strauss and his associates have never been submitted to impartial analytical scrutiny.

The fate of anti-psychiatry has only partly been comparable. Laing and his co-workers abandoned 'their' anti-psychiatry in the early 1970s when they adopted psychotherapy in the privately funded *Philadelphia Association*. Szasz' work ceased to be cited by interactionist medical sociologists some time during the 1970s, but found new followers among those who admired Illich's (1975) strictures against modern technological medicine. His polemic against academic psychiatry continued unabated, also taking on psychotherapy (1978), while insightful demonstrations of his misconceptions concomitantly seemed worthwhile (Begelman, 1971; M. Roth, 1976; Pies, 1979; Goldstein, 1980).

The concluding chapter of this part attempts three things. First, it goes back to the two explanatory models in order to determine their relationship with each other as well as with 'Chicago sociology', and the work of G. H. Mead.

From this vantage point, the question will be raised as to what the contribution of the idea of professional construction of illness is towards general sociological theory. Here, as in the concluding section of Part I, the problem of what social order means in the context of illness is of pivotal importance. For the interactionists, the stance towards social order proves to be one of taking sides against the orderliness of fixed normative regulations or established authorities. Their partisanship with the underdog has to be seen in the light of their juxtaposing society and individual. Behind this is a sensitivity for possible loss of citizenship rights through the state. As mentioned above, for contemporary American society, this highlights that poverty is a real danger to the individual with unequal opportunities in the educational and labour markets.

The final part of the chapter is devoted to the problem of pathology. Since diversity avowedly replaces pathology as a rationale of sociological analysis, the problem arises of whether losing the normality–pathology continuum has serious consequences for research. It will be argued that it does, on the grounds that sociology here blinds itself to distinctions which are relevant for society's members. If the 'symbolic interactionist' approach wishes to avoid contradicting its own 'naturalistic' and 'grounded' orientation, it seems that it has to take account of the patients' as well as the doctors' world. In these, normality and pathology are clearly real realms structuring their 'definition of the situation'.

The two models revisited

The crisis model states that the aetiology of an illness is due to professional construction. In a situation of suffering, the person gives him– or herself up and submits to the expertise of the medical practitioner. This implies that the patient waives the right to say 'no' to surgery, drug treatment or incarceration in a treatment institution. Accordingly, therapy consists of validating the status passage which illness (deviance) entails. This suggests that therapy – particularly in institutions – is the application of clinical ideologies. They educate the patient into surrendering to the clinician's 'definition of the situation'. For psychiatric disorders, blindness, alcoholism or drug addiction, among others, this works towards acquiring a 'new' identity.

The negotiaton model also states that the aetiology of illness is due to professional construction. Doctors apply the framework of generalised patient typification as well as categories of clinical knowledge in the situation of diagnosis. They may bargain with the patient over the meaning of symptoms, particularly when chronic illness is suspected. The patient validates the doctor's diagnosis (and subsequent regimen) through his or her everyday environment, and then proceeds to rearrange his or her life such that as much mastery as possible of normal tasks remains feasible. Therapy, in this vein, consists of occasional or unavoidable use of medical services by the chronically ill. As regards hospitals, their generalised treatment purpose filters through to a multitude of work arenas. Ever-changing rules are negotiated between staff and (albeit frequently unnoticed) patients such that treatment can proceed in an orderly fashion. Treatment in hospitals is organised into work–person interchange patterns over time ('trajectories'). The standpoints taken by both paradigms on aetiology and treatment may be entered into a four-cell table which looks like that shown in Figure 8.1.

	Aetiology	*Therapy*
Crisis	Becoming ill is an irreversible status passage which is assimilated by the individual through identity changes.	The hospital functions as a total institution, and medicine is as repressive (punitive) as are law or religion regarding outsiders (outgroups).
Negotiation	Becoming (chronically) ill is a loss of capacity, subsequent upon diagnosis, and it leads to the loss of normal self while the individual struggles to keep as normal as possible.	The hospital functions as a negotiated order of only here and now relevant divisions of labour, and medicine is constituted of practices (ideologies) of how to treat particular disorders.

Figure 8.1 *Aetiology and therapy as viewed by two interactionist models*

The two paradigms have in common that they conceptualise illness as an interactive process. In this, *reflexivity* is the main feature characterising how the problem of self is approached. They differ at first sight, with regard to how they conceptualise social process related to *relativity*.

Reflexivity, in the crisis model, means that an interactive process leads to the identity changes which illness (deviance) entails. The person – whether or not after a cycle of 'primary deviance' – is confronted with the 'societal reaction' of significant others who interpret for him or her the meaning of that person's behaviour or suffering. The person proceeds to internalise the image of him– or herself – in Mead's terms, acquiring a 'me' – which matches with the judgment received from the environment. That he or she does so is grounded in the human capacity of viewing one's own person and behaviour from the standpoint of the 'generalised other' whom, in this case, medicine as an institution embodies.

Reflexivity, in the negotiation paradigm, is implied in the way in which bargaining is envisaged. For instance, diagnosis as well as treatment are pictured as a process of offer met by, or outdone by, counter-offer in a situation of strategic interaction: that is, where both partners know that the other knows that they wish to maximise their gain by mystifying their position. That agreements are reached at all in this situation of universal gamble is due to the consensus among interactants that decisions must be reached, or tasks must get done. Therefore the interactants arrive at temporary agreements setting situational rule interpretations which are limited to specific work routines or persons involved.

Relativity, in Mead's posthumously published writings, is defined through the insight that everything is in motion (including the observer) while the relationships between moving objects may stay the same (1938, p. 549ff.). With regard to societal processes, this refers to the emergence of social control which is closely linked to self-control. Mead writes:

> If we conceive life as a process and not as a series of physiochemical situations . . . we realize that each individual has a world that differs in some degree from that of any other member of the community . . . and the life of the community is the sum of all these stratifications . . . If the objects that answer to the complex social act can exist spatiotemporally in the experience of different members of the society, as stimuli that set free not only their own responses, but also as stimuli to the responses of those who share in the composite act, a principle of coordination might be found which would not depend upon physiological differentiation . . . Social control depends, then, upon the degree to which individuals in society are able to assume the attitudes of the others who are involved with them in common endeavour . . . Besides property, all of the institu-

tions are such objects, and serve to control individuals who find in them the organization of their own social responses. (1924/64, pp. 275–91)

Mead makes it clear that the relativity standpoint entails that neither is the institution the creator of the individual's motives, nor is the individual without impact upon the change of institutions (1934, p. 263). In other words, apart from 'oppressive, stereotyped, and ultra-conservative institutions . . . which by their more or less rigid and inflexible unprogressiveness blot out individuality' (1934, p. 262), individuals are seen to be part of, rather than adversaries to, the constantly changing scene of social institutions. This ascertains two things; first, that institutions represent society's members' common reaction of control which is built into their selves, and, second, that stratification prevails in society between ingroups and outgroups. Mead explains:

> The institution represents a common response on the part of all members of the community to a particular situation. This common response is one which, of course, varies with the character of the individual. In the case of theft the response of the sheriff is different from that of the attorney-general, from that of the judge and the jurors, and so forth; and yet they all are responses which maintain property, which involve the recognition of the property rights in others . . . In general, the self has answered definitely to that organization of the social response which constitutes the community as such; the degree to which the self is developed depends on the community, upon the degree to which the individual calls out that institutionalized group of responses in himself. The criminal as such is the individual who lives in a very small group, and then makes depredations upon the larger community of which he is not a member. He is taking the property that belongs to others, but he himself does not belong to the community that recognizes and preserves the rights of property. (1934, pp. 261, 265)

Thus, for Mead, self and society belong together through the relativity of the individual standpoint. The latter, however, is mediated by the basic fact of whether the individual belongs to an ingroup or an outgroup within a society. Institutions function to represent a community's values. They also embody the 'generalised other' which is part of every self among the society's members. In this, little room is left for sympathy for the 'underdog' or criminal who violates what for Mead is the basic principle of sociality: namely, respect for others on a reciprocal scale.

The negotiation model's notion of relativity differs comparatively little from that of Mead. Strauss and his associates, for instance, focus on the division of labour within hospitals, or the doctor/nurse/patient triad. They show how different interactants *work together* towards achieving a given task. This marks the communality aspect of social control. The relativity aspect of shifting standpoints but stable relationships is addressed in the notion of trajectory. Trajectory means individual patients' as well as each illness type's intertwinement of work, person and their relationship over time. In this way, each individual trajectory is unique but the pattern which trajectories of a certain type follow may only be revised over long time periods because of medical or technological progress. To be sure, all this takes place in hospitals which are communities *sui generis*, similar to ingroups; outgroups or other institutions may have different but comparable set-ups. The latter may be more repressive or more egalitarian.

The crisis model's notion of relativity, however, is more difficult to reconcile with Mead's notion. Their understanding of social control is of a more repressive kind than that of the negotiation approach. In the latter, consensual aspects of mutual 'taking the role of the other' – mediated by a 'generalised other'-related treatment target – seem to take precedence. In the former, what Mead called the 'oppressive stereotyped' nature of some seems to be generalised to all institutions. Thus, the social-control functions of social institutions *per se* seem to bear witness to their stifling impact upon the individual.

These two interpretations of Mead's original idea are forecasted by two areas of sociological thought deriving from the teachings of 'Chicago sociology'. In the overview of the principles of sociology then developed, edited by Park in 1939, it becomes clear that more than one line of thought derives from Simmel's reciprocity scheme and Cooley's 'looking-glass' and social-process ideas. The participant-observation empirical work merges with several streams of social philosophy to produce a set of insights about society in general. E. C. Hughes' chapter on institutions and Blumer's on collective behaviour mark the range within which interactionist thought is established. Blumer stresses 'that individuals are acting *together* in some fashion; that there is some division of labor between them; and that there is some fitting together of the different lines of individual conduct . . . This conduct is collective in character' (1939, p. 221). In contrast, Hughes on institutions stresses repressive aspects: 'Processes of institutional control are well illustrated by the professions. The members of a full-fledged profession possess a technique and a body of knowledge . . . The services offered are such that the client is not supposed to be able to judge their value' (1939, pp. 334–6).

Of the two scholars, only Blumer is known to be a student of Mead's. In fact, after Mead's death Blumer was asked to teach the psychology course at Chicago's philosophy department, Mead's established domain for 30 years. Hughes, however, is not known to owe an acclaimed intellectual debt to Mead. On second thoughts, this distinction should not be overrated. It might be too easy to say that while the negotiation approach's view of social control and social organisation owes everything to Mead through the mediation of Blumer, the crisis model is more directly related to Hughes' less idealistic ideas about society's disunity and inner cleavages. The volume of papers presented to Hughes by his former students (Becker *et al.*, 1968) contains contributions from both groups. There seems to be every reason to believe that the protagonists of both approaches were eager students of both professors in their formative years at Chicago.

One difference, however, remains regarding the way in which both models deal with social control: their respective *images of man*. While the labelling approach puts forward a *passivity* concept, the 'grounded theory' approach uses a strategic reciprocity concept focusing on *actively* shaping one's environment.

The labelling perspective has been widely commented on in that the 'labellee', or patient, is perceived as hardly having any choice except to accept being stigmatised. This has been characterised by Schervish (1973, p. 47) as 'pessimistic and fatalistic assumptions that an imputed labelee is both *passive* and stands alone as an *individual*'. In contradistinction, the 'grounded theory' approach makes every effort to redress the balance towards the individual's capacity for rational choice in social conduct. E. A. Weinstein and Deutschberger (1964) attribute to Thibaut and Kelley's *The Social Psychology of Groups* (1959) the progress made in social psychology linking 'tasks, bargains, and identities in social interaction' to an image of humans who actively pursue their interests. They write:

> This perspective is geared to the systematic study of the concrete ways in which an individual attempts to administer any of the innumerable encounters which make up his daily life. It does not deal with 'goals' or 'purposes' or 'needs' in the abstract, but with an individual's adaptation of his goals to the circumstances of the encounter as expressed in the form of the specific performances he requires from others. It keeps clearly in focus that all of the participants are engaged in the pursuit of interpersonal tasks so that the interaction cannot be thought of solely as something ego does with or to an alter. (1964, p. 455)

It may be said that the 'grounded-theory' approach, in similar fashion, bases its views on human beings as conscious rational actors. Strategic interaction relies on an image of each person as having a sense of the other as a person who can be understood by 'taking the role of the other'. Accordingly, individuals are pictured planning their active pursuits in a way that refrains from hurting others, be it only because they can thus avoid being hurt by them at other times.

The contribution to general sociological theory

The image of mankind as proposed by the labelling approach is that of victims suffering in a world divided into ingroups and outgroups. Gouldner (1968, p. 105) states sarcastically but adequately: 'The essential point about the underdog is that he suffers, and that his suffering is naked and visible. It is this that makes and should make a demand upon us.' This *grass-roots view*, so to speak, may be discovered behind some of the dilemmas and contradictions with which the labelling approach has justly been charged. Two of these are of particular importance for the argument here: the problem of social order, and the problem of moral issues in sociology.

As regards the problem of social order, Gibbs (1966, p. 14) criticises the 'new conception of deviant behavior' because it rejects an explanation whereby criminal conduct is identified through norms (see also Gibbs 1972). In his view, societal norms appear as non-arbitrated, non-interpreted rules enshrined in statutory regulations: that is, the notion of social order behind Gibbs' preference for the 'old' explanation of deviance tends to be based on normative determinism (otherwise he would not hold against Becker, Erikson and Kitsuse that *his* is a view where deviant acts are identified with reference to norms). Inherent in such 'mechanistic' view (Mechanic, 1970) is the idea that deviance – be it illness or crime – is behaviour which violates the social order. Thus rectifying deviance is considered an act of social control, beneficial to society as a whole. Against critics such as Gibbs, Becker defends himself in his paper presented at the annual meetings of the British Sociological Association in April 1971. He ridicules his adversaries' opinion that interactionist theories are subversive. He writes: 'These critics think the principled determination to treat official and conventional viewpoints as things to be studied, instead of accepting them as fact or self-evident truth, a mischievous assault on the social order (Bordua, 1967)' (Becker, 1971, p. 19).

So, whereas from the publication of Becker's *Outsiders* (1963) onwards the labelling approach is charged with putting in question or rejecting the social order outright, the accused themselves reject this. However, they rarely respond by seriously repudiating their opponents' arguments (which frequently are but polemical statements). Instead, they often prefer to see their critics as conservatives or ridicule them as advocates of 'conventional morality' (Becker, 1971, p. 19). Where a more serious rejection of counter-arguments is attempted, professed allegiance to the social order is muffled at best. Thus in a rebuke of, among others, Gibbs (1966), Kitsuse (1972) states that:

> logically, the production of deviants *need not* have anything at all to do with their acts or behavior. Nor is it theoretically necessary that some act or behavior *even be imputed* to those who are socially differentiated as deviant by the treatment others accord him. He may be treated as deviant simply for what he is *conceived to be*. (1972, p. 240)

Such statements give an impression that norms which set deviancy standards are seen as arbitrary. In this light, it must appear as if Becker, Kitsuse and Erikson were implying that even theft or mental illness were defined by ruling classes in a haphazard fashion as violations of norms upholding an unjust social order. Against this, Becker (1971, p. 19) defends himself and the labelling theory by refuting that they 'willfully [refuse] to accept [the] definitions [of conventional morality] of what is and is not deviant'.

In his defence against his critics, Becker argues that all he wants is to point out that it needs a silent majority to tolerate that a minority is prosecuted (the issue of 'tacit cooperation'), and a collective-behaviour scene of consensus about what supposedly constitutes deviance to have designated rule-breakers punished by the authorities ('overt cooperation'). He writes: 'In its simplest form, the theory insists that we look at all the people involved in any episode of alleged deviance. When we do, we discover that these activities require the overt or tacit cooperation of many people and groups to occur as they do' (Becker, 1971, pp. 6–7). The dilemma is heightened by Becker, and also others, drawing attention to the *political* nature of the standards which define who is prosecuted (or treated) as deviant in a society or era. Consequently the problem arises whether, in principle, rules which embody and defend morality are politically stipulated. If their claim to represent objective standards of goodness proves to be only the claim of the righteous to power, they must be revealed to be nothing but legally executed standards in the interest of the state or some ruling circle.

Thus, on the one side, labelling theory is taken to attack the social order on the grounds that its rules allegedly are merely the self-protective stipulations of established authorities. On the other side, the allegation derived therefrom – namely, that it favours amorality or fosters chaos – is vigorously rejected by all protagonists of labelling theory. They claim to hold morality *against* the state or punitive institutions. But they insist that this does not jeopardise the social order as such. What they propose avowedly strengthens rather than weakens the moral acumen of the social fabric. They come out in favour of indigenous rights of any citizen to dignity and self-determination, no matter what race or mental condition. The fervour with which such moral impetus is phrased belies the accusation of supporting amoral aberrations. Becker concludes his introduction to the collection of papers entitled *The Other Side*, edited in 1964: 'If the papers of this collection err being sentimental, it is in the direction of unconventional sentimentality. But this, after all, is the lesser evil' (1964, p. 5).

The second problem area where a dilemma is obvious concerns the stance of sociology. On the one hand, which Gouldner (1968) rightly depicts as methodologically problematic, the labelling approach comes out with partisanship for the underdog. On the other hand, as Gouldner also notices, this standpoint wishes to be morally neutral although not expressedly value-free. How can a stance, at the same time, identify itself with one side in the ingroup –outgroup, or mainstream–underdog division, *and* take a disinterested look from above the divided factions? How can sociologists at one and the same time be scientific in terms of disinterested research *and* favour, if only in their souls, the beleaguered underdog?

The answer has two sides to it. On the one hand, such a contradictory standpoint seems possible if sociologists refrain from *any* value judgment, and even bracket evaluative classifications that might exist in their minds or society. Thus they favour the underdog by *resisting* the dominant dichotomous evaluative pattern which disadvantages or excludes underdogs. In this vein a standpoint arises which makes no claim whatsoever for any moral category to have any truth to it, except that it exists. That is, the underdog–partisan standpoint which the social researcher takes is characterised by deliberate neutrality against the claim to right and wrong of any prevalent norm. From this vantage point, a statement like the following is possible (it is made in a book entitled '*Heroin, Deviance, and Morality*', based on research devised in 1969): 'By morality we simply mean the process of defining any object in the world as good or evil or similar evaluative dualism . . . Using our definition, Adolf Hitler was probably every bit as actively moral as Mahatma Gandhi' (Lidz and Walker, 1980, p. 23).

The other aspects of solving the dilemma is that a *two-tier nature of society* seems to be taken for granted in labelling theory. In it, only two layers of status seem to be assumed. On top are the ruling classes and the state, assisted by institutions like medicine, law or religion, who command the power to determine and enforce mainstream social reality. Underneath are a mass of deprived and despised deviants who are prey to the 'definition of the situation' imposed upon them by their omnipotent adversaries. Becker suggests in *Outsiders* the racial divide in American society as an example of this:

> The law is differently applied to Negroes and whites. It is well known that a Negro believed to have attacked a white woman is much more likely to be punished than a white man who commits the same offense; it is only slightly less well known that a Negro who murders another Negro is much less likely to be punished than a white man who commits murder . . . Some rules are enforced only when they result in certain consequences. (1963, p. 13)

That is, the difference in status between black and white in the America of the early 1960s is taken as a dichotomous racial structure where the life of those in the lower stratum is generally less valued than that of those in the upper stratum. Jurisdiction about homicide and rape is used as an example to point out that a Manichaeist status system exists.

On the basis of this assumption (that a dichotomous status system prevails) it is conceivable that the partisan of the underdog must reject *any* evaluative categorisation that exists in society. To use a Marxian metaphor: in such a dichotomous society, the 'underclass' represents but the negation of the ruling class. The researcher who wishes to be on the side of the 'underclass' must relinquish *any* normative orientation of his or her surrounding society because it may be tinged by whatever safeguards the power of the ruling class.

On the other hand, seriously to harbour a Manichaeist world view about modern society might appear to border upon naiveté. Did not, in the early 1960s, Martin Luther King spur a vigorous Civil Rights Movement which eventually helped to improve the educational, occupational and voting chances of the non-white population? Did not, after John F. Kennedy became President of the US in 1960, a wave of goodwill towards Greater Society sweep the country? Was it not followed by admirable efforts to close the gap between rich and poor (partly identical with that between

white and non-white) through state-sponsored action, particularly
the Office for Economic Opportunities?

It may contribute a new aspect of the ongoing debate about the
political message of labelling theory if their work is looked at from
a different angle. In 1962, E. C. Hughes first published an article
written in 1948. Its title was *Good People and Dirty Work*, and its
topic was the pleas of ignorance by German survivors of the Nazi
regime of the atrocities committed in concentration camps and by
the *Einsatzgruppen*. Hughes argued that such 'dirty work' could
not have taken place had not the 'silent majority' connived by tacit
cooperation. However, Hughes refrained from accusing the surviving population of repressing knowledge, or of having partici-
pated in the crimes. He wrote:

> The common people of Germany knew that the camps existed; most
> knew people who had disappeared into them; some saw the victims,
> walking skeletons in rags, being transported in trucks or trains, or being
> herded on a road from station to camp or to work in fields or factories
> near the camps. Many knew people who had been released from
> concentration camps; such released persons kept their counsel on pain
> of death. But secrecy was cultivated and supported by fear and terror.
> In the absence of a determined and heroic will to know and publish the
> truth, and in the absence of all the instruments of the opposition, the
> degree of knowledge was undoubtedly low, in spite of the fact that all
> knew that something both stupendous and horrible was going on; and in
> spite of the fact that Hitler's *Mein Kampf* and the utterances of his aides
> said that no fate was too horrible for the Jews and other wrong-headed
> or inferior people. (1962/64, p. 29)

Hughes goes on to point out that such (at best) involuntary
support of the murders by not enquiring into why people disappeared is related to a normal mechanism of intergroup relations. It
is the divide between ingroup and outgroup. Hughes makes it
plain that the Nazi state created a society with dichotomous status
incumbency, depending on Aryan versus Jewish 'race'. Subsequently, the extermination of the designated Jewish race (and
other so-called subhumans) becomes the 'dirty work' which the
'good people' only need to tolerate. They do this by not knowing
or not realising that they know 'too much'.

As regards the mechanism of intergroup relations at which
Hughes hints, a book published one year before his long-
abandoned article gives abundant horrible detail. Hilberg's *The
Destruction of European Jews* (1961) stipulates a three-stage
(basic) pattern which is inherent in the destruction process of
continent-wide range. He writes:

A destruction process has an inherent pattern. There is only one way in which a scattered group can effectively be destroyed. Three steps are organic in the operation:

Definition

Concentration (or seizure)

Annihilation

. . . If a group seeks merely the destruction of hostile institutions, the limit of its most drastic action would be drawn with the complete destruction of the bearers of the institutions. The Germans, however, did not draw the line with the destruction of Jewry. They attacked still other victims, some of whom were thought to be like Jews, some of whom were quite unlike Jews, and some of whom were Germans. The Nazi destruction process was, in short, not aimed at institutions; it was aimed at people. The Jews were only the first caught in its path. (1961/64, p. 275)

Fascist society in Germany, and particularly how the mass murders became possible through a process of designating/segregating/killing, were being debated worldwide when, in 1960, Adolf Eichmann was kidnapped by the Israeli secret police and brought to trial in Jerusalem. For two years, stories of unbelievable atrocity entered newspaper and television news. The question was asked many times: how could a civilised country with a history of legal process (Weber's *Rechtsstaat*), if not respect for human dignity, engage in the persecution and systematic murder of a 'race'? Before the 1935 so-called Nuremberg Laws, this 'race' did not even exist in many Germans' categorisations, let alone the state's legislation. It is pointed out repeatedly that German anti-Semitism prior to the Nazis coming to power may have been *less* widespread in the general population than in countries like, say, Poland or France. At any rate, Jews were better integrated into German society, at the time, than in many other European countries where segregation and exclusion from educational and occupational realms were more widespread.

The issue is introduced among the topics which define 'social pathology' in American sociology. Rosenberg, Gerver and Horton (1964), in a reader on *Mass Society in Crisis* (second edition 1971), bring together a large section on Nazi crimes as one point where 'social problems and social pathology' warrant a perspective beyond drug addiction or premarital sex. Mental hospitals, mass terror in concentration camps as well as by the state such as is seen, for instance, in Algeria, South Africa or China, genocide, thermonuclear war as threatened by the destruction of Hiroshima and Nagasaki in 1945: these represent 'extreme conditions' equally to be dealt with by sociology as the 'endemic conditions' which crime, drug addiction, mental illness, slum living or unemployment entail.

In an article entitled 'An American Death Camp' which is reprinted in the 'solutions' section of the book and taken from *Politics* (1948), Orlans says the following:

> Nothing . . . is clearer than that the Germans are ordinary human beings, that regimentation is a normal aspect of industrial society, and that the carnage of Auschwitz was as consistent and logical an outgrowth of such a society as are subways, burlesque, and packaged meat. At any rate, this is the contention of this article. To support it, two courses are open: either one can prove that the Germans are normal human beings and that their death camps operated as do other social institutions; or one can show that other people, generally accepted as normal – e.g., ourselves – have institutions which, in their own way, can be regarded as incipient death camps. I have adopted the latter course, and the institution I am going to describe is an American state insane asylum. (1948/64, p. 614)

The description which follows of life in the asylum, and of the dichotomous structure of attentents and inmates, reads as Goffman's analysis foreshadowed.

The hypothesis is ventured here that labelling theory which, in the early 1960s acquired unexpected acclamation through the book *Outsiders*, captures the spirit of what it is like, and how the sociologist ought to behave, in a Fascist society. Through the atrocities resurfacing as news worldwide during the Eichmann trial in Jerusalem, the possibility of a (or any) civilised society turning Fascist (with the police turning murderous) may have been reflected upon by many concerned citizens. One answer is that the developmental pattern must be studied and understood which facilitated the fateful change of German society (if it was not proto-Fascist all along, which is also frequently argued). This can help to understand what made mass murder possible. In this vein, Hilberg's book furnishes a theory of Fascism as a Manichaeist socio-political system which designates or creates underdog categories to abreact its people-destructive tendencies. It is this spirit of wilful and apparently inconsequential senseless definition of any group or so-called race as an outgroup to be segregated which labelling theory may be seen to catch in its affirmative and nevertheless vague formulations. When Becker (1963) states that only by making laws which prohibit marijuana use would 'dope fiends' be turned into criminals (see also Duster, 1970), the moral indignation which the statement entails is only plausible if it is seen against the background of widespread awareness, at the time, of the segregation of Jews from German mainstream society by the so-called Nuremberg Laws 28 years earlier. When Becker (1967) haplessly pleads to take into account the human dignity of the underdog, he pictures the 'established order' in a way which makes sense against the background of the still-looming knowledge that Jews, 25 years earlier, had no one to turn to in their plight.

It is through the ready identification of its present-day society in the US or Europe with the (one hopes) destroyed Manichaeist status system of Fascist society of yesteryear that labelling theory creates most forceful opposition. Among irritated social-science colleagues, what is criticised most strongly are the allegations of whim or irrational power in the application of exclusionary 'master statuses'. Labelling theory's high hopes but meagre accomplishments regarding its capacity to understand political processes of outgroup creation have often been castigated in the secondary literature. But it may be mentioned in defence of the image of mankind (i.e., that of the deprived sufferer) and of the image of institutions (i.e., that of agents responsible for incarceration and exploitation in the guise of treatment) that these seemingly wild and far-off characterisations of the contemporary social world make perfectly good sense when the contemporary world is taken to be the German Third Reich. After all, only 12 years of the behemoth (Neumann, 1942/66) have eradicated in modern mankind the self-image cherished since the Renaissance. It is no longer uncontroversial that to be human makes humaneness a pledge to be realised by the nation state over time. The labelling approach, with its sometimes odd-sounding generalisations about institution –client dichotomies, is a forerunner rather than a backwater. It takes up the challenge to incorporate into social theory the knowledge of the horrendous, if not horrific, possibilities of social order and social process. Hardly any other general explanatory paradigm has so far ventured explicitly to envisage these possibilities as being within the range of *normal* societal evolution.

It is not argued here that this is a conscious endeavour. Rather, it is argued that partly because of their own sensitivity for the details of the abundant terror 'stories', the protagonists of interactionist thinking do not shun this side of pathology. In 1963, an intellectual climate prevailed of both being stunned by the reported atrocities and feeling urged to understand why it all happened. This may have promoted the sales of a book entitled

Outsiders. But this book does, in fact, contain insights which are able to tackle the then debated issues of dichotomous ingroup–outgroup politics. The problem of arbitrary designation of underdogs by law or medicine is not left out of the picture. This may have convinced many among the then fast-growing number of sociology students in the 1960s that here was something that could help them understand their own troubled world.

Medicine, from the start, had a stake in this for several reasons. For one, it may well have been one of the ugly facts which became known again to many in the early 1960s that murder in the concentration camps was termed 'special treatment' in the meticulous name lists which were kept. Furthermore, it occupied the public worldwide for many years that the so-called selection between gas-chamber and camp candidates upon arrival at Auschwitz was made by the infamous physician, Dr Mengele; this fact must have been widely commented on during the Eichmann trial and afterwards.

As regards another reason, a book published in 1979 by Chorover provides a preliminary answer. Under the title *From Genesis to Genocide*, he argues that to invite biology, and medicine in its wake, to define who is and is not to have rights in a society (be they rights for education or sexual intercourse) means to enter the road to genocide. Using Nazi quasi-medical 'race hygiene' as an example, Chorover warns against natural science as a Trojan horse which may carry a barrage of undemocratic principles of selection and exclusion of the unfittest. Naturally, the 'medical model' of natural science explanations is seen as far less uncontroversial in the interest of democracy than many unsuspecting citizens think.

Last, anti-psychiatry creates a strong bridge between the view that medicine has to change, and the self-styled emancipatory sociology. Quinney, in an introductory chapter to his then forthcoming book, *Social Theory in a Radical Age* (which is included in a volume edited by R. A. Scott and Douglas, 1972), quotes Laing (1967) to show how deeply identified every sociologist must be with the patient view as pictured by Laing. The quotation reads: 'We wish to die leaving our imprints burned into the hearts of others. What would life be if there were no one to remember us, to think of us when we are absent, to keep us alive when we are dead?' (1972, p. 326).

Labelling theory makes a most important contribution to general sociological theory. It makes it known what it is or would be like to devise theoretical conjectures from a non-partisan viewpoint within a Fascist society. The uncompromising 'taking the role of the other' for the underdog leads the way, and the disclosure of the powerprone process of outgroup 'creation' and 'treatment' follows from it.

The negotiation approach, at first sight, appears to be less involved. It might warrant a separate analysis whether the negotiation model often addresses the same issues, albeit in less polemical or exaggerated fashion. Some points may show that the two approaches are possibly not too far apart. Both take sides for the patient; both conceptualise treatment as the application of politically relative clinical ideology. But the analysis shall not be attempted here in detail. Suffice it to say that with regard to the most salient issue, both interactionist models agree on their strictly patient-oriented view of medical care.

The place of pathology

Turning to the question of whether, from the interactionist standpoint, anti-Semitism represents an illness, it emerges that the question may have to be rephrased.

Parsons ventures that psychiatric disturbances are at the heart of the sociological concern for illness. The reason he gives is that the sickness-induced incapacity to play normal roles is due to emotional disturbances necessitating psychotherapeutic care (if only on an unconscious level). The labelling approach repudiates the notion that psychiatric disturbances have a sociologically relevant psychological origin. To substantiate this claim, it points to the discrepancies between the prevalence of disturbed behaviour and the incidence of treatment by psychiatry. It concludes that patients suffer most from contingencies which are wholly of a societal, rather than psychological nature. The 'grounded theory' approach equally rejects the idea that psychological disturbance could be at the root of being treated. In this, psychiatric illness does not occupy as much space or receive as much attention as does other chronic illness. With the latter, it would be difficult to argue that the symptoms leading to diagnosis are only in the eye of the beholder of the 'societal reaction'. The sociological interest in illness is geared towards the deterioration of identity after being diagnosed. Related topics are the social organisation of treatment institutions or the social organisation of life at home, given permanent (chronic) sick status incumbency.

Both approaches stress the *constructive* nature of illness throughout. How far this emphasis on social construction entails that whatever is 'behind' the construction is not 'real' remains remarkably vague, however. This suggests that the linkage between the manipulative side of the political, and the constructive side of the social, may be quite strong. In fact, illness is addressed as political where it is negotiated by clients and where it emerges as a diagnostic entity through the action of social groups. It is also viewed as constructive where treatment ideologies are concerned, and where political interests come into play (e.g., where alcohol or drug abuse are defined through socio-political movements).

In these terms anti-Semitism could easily be identified as a disease of society at large. Since reaction to an otherwise possibly harmless human characteristic is often introduced as a perfectly realistic crucial entry point into the disenfranchised 'master status' of sickness, anti-Semitism might well qualify as pathological. This would not be contradictory to the history of the interactionist paradigm. Its strong connections with the tradition of *social pathology* in American sociology are obvious. Its roots in 'Chicago sociology' strengthen rather than weaken the background of 'responsibility ethics' (*Verantwortungsethik*), to use a Weberian term. As early as 1899, G. H. Mead commented on the 'Working Hypothesis of Social Reform', and Park (1935) focused on 'Social Planning and Human Nature' with the following statement:

> Social problems are not wholly solved by changing the form or structure of society. It is necessary that the new social order should be understood, accepted and eventually incorporated into the habits, traditions, and mores of the community. In this way it becomes a part of the routine and of the conventions of an established social order which, because it is customary and unconscious, may be said to enforce itself. Thus, the social worker's task of securing the cooperation of the client in the program of his own rehabilitation is typical of the problem which arises everywhere in the effort to make social programs effective. (1935/55, p. 42)

It may appear tragic that 'symbolic interactionism' never rises beyond this individualistic view on social change. Although, in 1935, the goings-on in Nazi Germany may have been known somewhat across the Atlantic, the model of dealing with social pathology is the social worker. The scale in which social pathology is tackled is that of aberrations like alcoholism, delinquency, unemployment or poverty. The wider connotations of social pathology do not become envisaged: namely that a whole society can acquire pathological features. Later, after the Second World War, they entered *indirectly* into the notion of that curiously forbidding, rigidly punitive social order which informs the authors of *Asylums* and *Outsiders*.

Thus, pathology as a *societal* problem is not addressed from the interactionist point of view. Nevertheless, in a way, labelling theory gets closer to envisaging a Fascist society than many other conceptual approaches. That interactionism fails to *discuss* the problem, while *visualising* it, is due to its unrelenting partisanship for the oppressed individual envisaged in a hostile organisational world.

From this vantage point, pathology as a dimension of illness is deliberately left out of the picture. Rather, *diversity* is all that counts. The emphatic taking of the underdog's side precludes taking into account pathology in illness. The sociological interest is defined as one which – *sine ira et studio* (not propelled by anger or zest) – ought to look at *what happens* to anyone and everyone who is ill, and how they come to be seen as, and see themselves as, occupying a sick status in the first place.

To replace the aspect of pathology by that of divergency, with regard to medical issues, has two immediate consequences. The work of the doctor whose job it is to identify pathology and treat it appears wrongly geared. In fact, the 'medical model' of illness definition is seen as merely power-prone self-indulgence securing a field of uncontrolled professional autonomy. Furthermore, no systematic distinction holds between illnesses where the pathology label is justified and those where it ought to be rethought. While some authors such as Scheff (1975) wish to exclude infectious diseases from the argument because of their lack of variation through societal definition, other authors such as Freidson (1970a) make no such reservations. Eventually, the fact that every diagnostic category is reproached for being liable to societal variation in its definition and use makes it difficult to find a *systematic* reason why *some* definitions of illnesses should be revoked or revised. If every illness is deviance, and deviance is the modern form of defining outgroups, how can some aberrations or diseases be called legitimate and others illegitimate? The answer given by the interactionist paradigm is that they cannot: that is, all illness is to be seen as but a form of the diversity of representations which life can take. All is possible, and none, eventually, ought to be treated as pathological.

As honourable as the interactionists' motives may be for sticking to their emphasis on diversity in the patient's interest, an unanticipated follow-up problem arises. If no systematic distinction can be made between the pathological and the basically-just-divergent, no scientifically grounded reason can be formulated as to why any society ought to refrain from extending the illness label even to such 'aberrations' as being Jewish or being an internationalist (Rock, 1973, p. 20). In this way, by running away from tackling the issue of pathology, the interactionist paradigm invites back the very problem which it attempts to solve with such admirable moral vigour.

Where does this leave us? First, the division between pathological and normal ought to be reinstated. Medical sociology is ill-advised to replace the principle of pathology by that of diversity. As the brief reference to the impasse into which interactionism has manouvred itself with regard to the problem of pathology may have shown, not much is won but the most important issue is lost if the normality–pathology distinction is eliminated.

On the other hand, as soon as it is reinstated, it can easily be pointed out that what does define normality and pathology regarding particular diseases and individual doctors' practices may be liable to considerable fluctuation. These can be investigated by sociologists. But there is no need to derive from this variability that the claim of medicine to objective truth is ill-founded. Rather, it seems that scientific truth, whatever it is in respect to concrete items of the world, is liable to historical change as well as to the relativity of ever-moving standpoints (which G. H. Mead was quite fascinated by).

If the idea of pathology is reinstated, another problem also looks different. Interactionist thought in medical sociology finds it difficult to accept that a sociology *in* medicine does not, at the same time, have to be a sociology *of* medicine, to use Straus' (1957) terms. But when pathology is accepted as belonging to the *medical* realm where clinical knowledge and expertise are vital and sufficient sources of diagnosis and treatment, a new understanding of what is social in medicine becomes feasible. In my own work on patient careers, this point has been argued in two ways. One is theoretical, and one is methodological; both are derived from, and feed back into, empirical research.

It appears that illness has two sides to it, one medical and one going beyond medical jurisdiction. One has been called disease, the other illness. The former relates to the ever-increasing realm of known pathophysiological lesions which, for instance, are catalogued in the WHO's inventory of diagnostic categories. The latter is a unitary, or at least relatively undifferentiated, absence or reduction of participation in normal active life, mediated through such transient quasi-occupational statuses as 'sick leave' or similar transitory familial statuses to bridge the gap to one's normal identities. It is the latter rather than the former to which temporal patterns of illness management belong, the patient career focusing on reciprocity structures and reflexivity patterns (Gerhardt, 1976a and 1976b). The course of the occupational and private-life impact of an illness can be distinguished from the course of the disease, and both analysed in their intertwinement as *relative*.

Ten years after its initial formulation, a refined version of the argument addresses also the methodological problem involved (Gerhardt, 1986). Careers, temporal patterns of development along treatment, occupational, financial, and family status lines, are all now understood as a two-faced structure. On the one hand, they constitute courses of *status development* which the (chronically) ill person musters. On the other hand, they also constitute *idealised typified* patterns of what patients and everybody else in their society consider a 'career' in the literal sense of the word. Experiencing the social side of illness, or coping with the threat to their family's financial and rehabilitation potential, are judged by the patients as deviation from or in relation to idealised typified career patterns. Researchers base their investigations on these evaluations. The Weberian conception of ideal type as methodological device helps to understand career structures and analyse illness experiences in their biographical context.[22]

In this way, the problem becomes less imminent of whether perceiving pathology addresses the patients' experiential dimension on the wrong level. The patient sees deviation: namely, comparative digression from a typified standard of health or excellence, the idealised career as societal form. The sociologist must not pretend that deviance does not exist in order to analyse each patient's career in its own right. In fact, deviation from the ideal-type case becomes the methodological principle common both to the patient's and the researcher's perspectives. One uses it to make sense of his or her life, and the other to make sense of the data showing how the other makes sense of his or her life. Suffice to say that medical sociology finds ample ground for fruitful *qualitative* research even when it refrains from repudiating pathology.

Part III
The Phenomenological Paradigm: Illness as Intersubjectively Constructed Reality

Ethnomethodology, cognitive sociology and conversational analysis

Introduction: the Weberian legacy

In the euphoria of revolutionary spirit accompanying the 1968 uprising of peaceniks and beatniks in sociology departments on both sides of the Atlantic,[23] phenomenology became the epitome of anti-elitist theorising. That sociology and everyday reasoning should both use the same documentary method of interpretation in order to make sense of what goes on in the world was understood to mean that the distinction between the analytical level of science and emprical level of everyday life could be given up. The radically democratic implication of such apparent verisimilitude between social science and common-sense *Verstehen* fitted into the self-image of the then radical student movement. Its aim of establishing true egalitarian life chances in society presupposed that social science became the mouthpiece of the hitherto suppressed working classes.

When, in 1972, Filmer *et al.*'s reader *New Directions in Sociological Theory* hailed the revolutionary impact of ethnomethodological theorising, Goldthorpe (1973) angrily retorted in his review of this (as well as of Douglas' reader *Understanding Everyday Life*, 1970) that there was nothing revolutionary about ethnomethodology. Perhaps, Goldthorpe implied, it may be said that like all revolutions this (mistaken) one attempted to offer an untenable position (regarding the notorious *hermeneutic circle*) in place of the tenable but less comprehensible traditional position.

Indeed, it seems that phenomenology became entangled in the student movement by chance. Berger and Luckmann's *The Social Construction of Reality* (1966) was born, as they confide in the preface, out of a certain yodel sung on the Swiss mountain Chesaplana. The groundwork for the ethnomethodology books which

179

happened to come out around 1968 was laid much earlier (in fact, most of the crucial research seems to have been done in the 1950s and early 1960s). Nevertheless, the enthusiastic response which *Studies in Ethnomethodology* (Garfinkel, 1967a) and *The Social Organization of Juvenile Justice* (Cicourel, 1968) met (after *Method and Measurement in Sociology* (Cicourel, 1964) paved the way) seems to signify that there was something revolutionary about phenomenology or ethnomethodology in spite of its lack of political intentions.

Vis-à-vis the then traditional sociology still involved with the ramifications of systems thinking, the new micro-perspectice appeared to be the long-awaited revelation about the real nature of social process. Until then, throughout the 1960s, studies such as Goffman's *Asylums* (1961) and Becker's *Outsiders* (1963) had been considered as political statements in favour of the folk perspective, emphatically stated in the latter's 1967 SSSP Presidential Address (Becker, 1967). The closeness of 'symbolic interactionism' and ethnomethodology was soon acknowledged: in 1969 (and again 1970), Denzin proposed a level on which the two theoretical approaches could be integrated. Throughout the 1970s, various attempts were made to demonstrate that no irreconcilable cleavage existed between the two micro approaches, particularly in the light of their both focusing upon face-to-face interaction rather than structural norms and values (Weingarten, Sack and Schenkein, 1976).

In this vein, a sharp line is drawn between the two interpretive approaches, on the one hand, and a normative paradigm represented by Parsons' social-system theory on the other (Wilson, 1970). In fact, a schism between 'two sociologies' is diagnosed (Dawe, 1970). Throughout the 1970s, particularly until revived Marxism as politically activist conception took over, ethnomethodology and structural functionalism remained metaphors for leftist versus rightist standpoints. Although such distinction has been overcome meanwhile, and both phenomenology and structural functionalism now tend to be deemed politically non-leftist, the perceived cleavage between interactionist-interpretive, and systems-normative, paradigms in sociological theory has not lost its acumen. In 1981, in her introduction to a reader on research methodology, Knorr-Cetina diagnosed a change in sociologists' interests 'from the normative order to the cognitive order' (1981, p. 2) since the 1950s. She echoed Dahrendorf (1958a) and Wrong (1961) in her view that Parsons' was but a standpoint of normative determinism which crumbles in front of the question of what constitutes social action:

Yet as critics have pointed out, despite the elaborate 'action frame of reference' social action with Parsons remains a residual category: it is conceived as not more than the execution of a normatively pre-established harmony through individual agents who, in contrast to Durkheim, are seen as internally (rather than externally) controlled by society. (Knorr-Cetina, 1981, p. 3)

However, Knorr-Cetina seems to overlook that Garfinkel's thought has its origins in his thorough study of Parsons' work while being a graduate student at Harvard from 1946 onwards. In fact, Garfinkel participates in what Parsons later terms the 'golden age' for graduate students (1970b). He refers to the formative period of the Department of Social Relations (incorporating sociology, cultural anthropology, social and clinical psychology), newly founded after the Second World War and quickly becoming a centre for interdisciplinary theory (leading up to the integrative volume edited with Shils, *Toward a General Theory of Action*, published in 1951). In 1952, Garfinkel received his PhD from Harvard, with Parsons as his supervisor, for a hitherto unpublished dissertation on the topic of 'Perception of the Other'. Judging from rare references in later secondary literature, Garfinkel at this time knew not only Parsons' theory whose solutions of the intersubjectivity problem he analysed and then attempted to overcome, but also Schütz's work which he heavily endorsed (Heritage, 1984).[24] In 1954, Garfinkel claims, he developed his idea of 'observable-reportable' jurors' accounting practices from Bales's categories of interaction that were developed, in turn, in co-operation with Parsons (Garfinkel, 1974).

The problem which Garfinkel primarily addressed in his dissertation – keeping in mind that *perception of the other*, or the issue of intersubjectivity, is a domain of the hermeneutical or *Verstehen* perspective in sociology (Outhwaite, 1976) – was that of *how social order is possible*. To be sure, this question was raised at the outset of the first major outline of interpretive sociology by G. Simmel (1908), it informed Weber's elaborate reflections in *Economy and Society* on the interconnections between subjective meaning formation in social action and authoritative rules formation in economic and political associations (1922/68), and it prevailed in Parsons' anti-Hobbesian conjecture that the structure of social action depends on the actors' shared normative orientations (1937). Garfinkel, who acknowledged that Parsons legitimately derived his approach from Weber, set out to formulate an alternative notion of the generalised social system which was solely based on the actors' situational experiences:

At least two important theoretical developments stem from the re-searches of Max Weber. One development, already well worked, seeks to arrive at a generalized social system by uniting a theory that treats the structuring of experiences with another theory designed to answer the question 'What is man?' Speaking loosely, a synthesis is attempted between the facts of social structure and the facts of personality. The other development, not yet adequately exploited, seeks a generalized social system built solely from the analysis of experience structures. (Garfinkel, 1952, p. 1)

John Heritage (1984, p. 9), quoting this passage, goes on to say: 'The objective of the dissertation was "to go as far as possible in exploring a theoretical vocabulary to transform [the second deve-lopment] into a working scheme for experimental investigation of the social order"'. In this endeavour, the attempt to take actors' experienced observable actions (including reasons given thereon) as basic sociological data has been overwhelmingly recognised by the secondary literature. This, however, is done at the expense of, on the one hand, Garfinkel's acknowledging of the Weberian legacy which he shares with Parsons and, on the other hand, Garfinkel's avowed indebtedness to Parsons regarding such crucial concepts as 'bona-fide member', 'collectivity' and, of course, 'so-cial system' (e.g., 1959, pp. 52, 53; 1967a, pp. 57, 76). In a sense the way in which Garfinkel phrases his central interest in his dissertation sounds remarkably Parsonian: he wants to explore: 'how men, isolated yet simultaneously in an odd communion, go about the business of constructing, testing, maintaining, altering, validating, questioning, defining an order *together*' (Garfinkel, 1952, p. 114; citing Heritage 1984, p. 71).

The anti-Parsonian element in this concerns the *level* at which an explanation is sought for social action and social organisation. McHugh (1968) makes it clear that while Parsons locates the social order on an *analytical* level of norms and values shared by actors as a condition *sine qua non* of the sociological conceptualisation of social systems, Garfinkel locates the social order on an *empirical* level of actors' actual experienced and observable behaviour. This means that subjectively constructed situational meanings become the condition *sine qua non* of the sociological notion of any social collectivity. In this vein, where Parsons intends but heuristic state-ments on the hermetic consistency of rule use and norm validity, Garfinkel tries to prove that the hermetic consistency of rule use is a fact. However, he clarifies that this is a fact with which we comfortably seem to live under the *proviso* of an 'iceberg phe-nomenon'. He writes in 1956:

Sociological inquiry accepts almost as a truism that the ability of a person to act 'rationally' – *i.e.* the ability of a person *in conducting his everyday affairs* to calculate, to project alternative plans of action, to select before the actual fall of events the conditions under which he will follow one plan or another, to give priority in a selection of means to their technical efficacy – depends upon the fact that the person who is going to 'act rationally' or 'realistically' must be able literally to take for granted, to take under trust, a vast array of features of the social order. In order to treat rationally the one-tenth of his situation that, like an iceberg, appears above the water, he must be able to treat the nine-tenths that lies below as an unquestioned, and even more interestingly as an unquestionable, background of matters that are demonstrably relevant to his calculations but which appear without being noticed. (1956b, pp. 186–7)

Of course, this is where Schütz's reflections on the sociological relevance of Husserl's idea of 'natural attitude' come into the picture (see, e.g., Schütz, 1945b, 1959). Schütz, mainly in his articles on common sense and scientific knowledge (1953, 1954) develops further the conjecture that everyday routine activities are based on *Verstehen* (using the ideations of 'et-cetera-clause', and 'reciprocity of perspectives'). As such, lay persons' reasoning is structurally similar to the second-order *Verstehen* as practised by scientists. The principle of taken-for-granted world of routine activities based on assumptions of calculability and controllability is the epitome of rationality in everyday life (1943). This, in fact, follows directly from and attempts to supersede Weber's idea that rationality governs modern life. In Schütz's critical appreciation of Weber, such rationality is recognised behind the use of ideal types which contemporaries need to make themselves understandable and the social order intelligible (Schütz, 1932/67).

It appears that Garfinkel's recourse to Weber is mediated through how Schütz attempted to overcome what he felt was Weber's fault. Weber, Schütz argues, puts undue focus on a solely analytical level of *Verstehen*. What matters is to look at the use of *Verstehen* also in the everyday world. On the other hand, Garfinkel's (as well as, incidentally, Parsons') main problem with Weber is that of the *motivatedness* of behaviour (Parsons, 1937, 1940). Garfinkel, who became Parsons' student, directs his avowed Weberian partisanship against his mentor Parsons. Parsons' incorporation of the psychoanalytic concept of unconscious motivation into the realm of action theory appears to clash with the imperative legacy of Max Weber:

In sociology, in the social sciences generally, as well as in the inquiries of everyday life, a prominent problem is that of achieving a unified conception of events that have as their special formal property that their present character will have been decided by a future possible outcome. Motivated actions, for example, have precisely this troublesome property. It is a matter of great theoretical and methodological import that Max Weber should have defined sociology as the study of human activities insofar as they are governed in their course by the subjective meanings attached to them. In this programmatic statement, Weber provided for this troublesome feature as an essential property of sociology's fundamental occurrences. (Garfinkel, 1959, p. 64)

Without hesitation, Garfinkel goes on from there to describe the *documentary method* of interpretation which is the core of the ethnomethodological endeavour. However, it is not Weber but (with reference to Dilthey and Troeltsch)[25] Mannheim who, in an article published 1923 (and first translated in 1952) explains that among methods of understanding the meanings of works of art and other 'cultural objectifications', documentary interpretation best serves adequately to elucidate how an object or an idea is a document of, and, at the same time, serves to clarify, an underlying *Weltanschauung*. This quality of reciprocal enlightening of each other between a 'surface structure' and a 'deep structure', as it were, is what Garfinkel as well as Cicourel stress about the documentary method of interpretation. Garfinkel explains:

> The method consists of treating an actual appearance as 'the document of', as 'pointing to', as 'standing on behalf of' a presupposed underlying pattern derived from its individual documentary evidences, but the individual documentary evidences, in their turn, are interpreted on the basis of 'what is known' about the underlying pattern. Each is used to elaborate the other. (1967a, p. 78)

In contradistinction, Cicourel is concerned with what he terms 'interpretive procedures'. They convey the same properties to social action as Schütz's 'natural attitude' which also defines Garfinkel's common-sense knowledge of social structures. In other words, these 'interpretive procedures' give to any behaviour the characteristics of reciprocity of perspectives, et-cetera clause, normal-form orientation, retrospective–prospective structure, and so on (Zimmerman and Pollner, 1970, p. 95). Cicourel states:

> The interpretive procedures and their reflexive features provide continuous instructions to participants such that members can be said to be programming each others' actions as the scene unfolds . . . the participants' interpretive procedures and reflexive features become instructions by processing the behavioral scene of appearances, physical movements, objects, gestures, sounds, into inferences that permit action. (1973, p. 58 emphasis omitted)

Cicourel makes the point (directed against Parsons) that normative rules represent but a surface structure of varying moral imperatives while the issue beyond is of crucial interest. Interpretative
procedures constitute the *invariant* features at the root of any
effort of making sense of, and conveying meaning to, normative
rules in ongoing social interaction.

Related to Garfinkel's as well as Cicourel's work is a third
attempt to discover invariant methodical principles behind the
multiplicity of interactional endeavours. What has become known
as 'conversational analysis' was originally based on the writings of
the late Harvey Sacks. This branch of ethnomethodology seeks to
point out that a 'fine structure' of formal properties characterises
verbal as well as non-verbal interchanges. Thus, context-neutral
stable features as well as context-related flexible properties of
story-telling and turn-taking in conversations, of openings and
closings of encounters, or recipiency and silences and so on are discovered (Schegloff, 1968; Sacks, 1972b; Schegloff and Sacks, 1973;
Speier, 1973; Sacks, Schegloff and Jefferson, 1974; Coulter, 1976).

In essence, the phenomenological perspective is based on two
assumptions about social behaviour:

1. The *indexicality* principle: the idea is that social action may be
   seen as the merger of an act or utterance, on one hand, and an
   account or pattern attribution on the other. Only through
   taking the act as an index of, or a document of, a pattern or rule
   or procedure which it also helps to clarify and specify, is social
   action achieved as a subjectively meaningful accomplishment.
   As such, it is also intersubjectively valid because, at the same
   time, it has to make sense to others. Two issues thus characterise indexicality. The disjuncture between act and account,
   utterance and pattern, leaves room for several options regarding their situational reconciliation. Futhermore, involvement of
   others in subjective meaning construction entails that it is
   through their accounting that utterances or acts acquire the
   meaning which they 'have' (i.e., become what they 'are'). In
   this, comparisons or attributions are made taking an individual
   case to be a representation of, or a deviation from, an idealised
   'normal-form' pattern.
2. The *praxeology* principle is rarely mentioned in the secondary literature. The idea is that social facts may by treated by
   the sociologist not as more or less stable (and, therefore,
   measurable) features of a social system but, rather, as an
   accomplishment of collective action achieved in methodical
   fashion. It becomes the sociologist's task to find out how it

actually functions that an observable piece of reality is brought about in the interplay between knowledge, routine and intent of the people involved. Garfinkel speaks of the 'praxeological rule of the sociological attitude' in terms of what Mehan and Wood (1975) call the dramaturgical potential of ethnomethodology: that is, its emphasis on practice and doing (see also Garfinkel and Sacks, 1970): 'The praxeological rule states that any and all properties whatsoever of a social system that a sociologist might elect to study and account for are to be treated as technical values which the personnel of the system achieve by their actual modes of play' (Garfinkel, 1956b, p. 191).

Indexicality and praxeology make for a paradoxical view of social action. In the first instance, a dynamic approach to reality is suggested where ongoing interactive practices replace stable characteristics of social institutions. At the same time, invariant properties of reality construction are to be identified and aptly demonstrated.

The problem which this tackles is, no doubt, that of motivation. Parsons takes refuge in psychoanalytical thought in order to account for the fact that not all of a person's actions can be called rational by the standards of social-systems integration; this, in particular, applies to illness and other forms of deviance. Garfinkel, on the other hand, holds against Parsons that no reliance on unconscious activities is necessary in order to account for the rational nature of seemingly irrational conduct. The complementary interest of the sociologist to the psychoanalyst's concern for the unconscious, asserts Garfinkel, deliberately using a Parsonian term, is 'common culture'. And he goes on to say:

Sociologically speaking, 'common culture' refers to *socially sanctioned grounds of inference and action* that people use in everyday life, and which they assume that other members of the group use in the same way. Such socially-sanctioned-facts-of-life-that-any-*bona-fide*-member-of-the-group-knows depict, among other things: distributions of income, motives of persons, the distributions among persons in the community of honor, competence, responsibility, goodwill, the presence of good and evil purposes behind the apparent workings of things, the actual and potential disorder, misery, poverty, illness, unemployment, trouble in the society as well as the effective remedies, the chances and the reasons that particular persons will be victims, and so on. (1956b, p. 185)

Thus ethnomethodology sets out to supersede Parsons. It wants to show that social systems are but the outcome of continuous processes of accounting and accomplishing whereby individuals take patterned choices and make interpersonally monitored decisions. Intersubjectivity, in this view, does not come about through shared properties of a common culture but, rather, it is presupposed in the 'natural attitude' bestowing trust upon social encounters. Motivation, in this vein, needs not to be unconscious in order to be beyond the realm of what an actor can consciously control and comprehensibly report on. Rather, motivation becomes an aspect of the 'natural attitude'. It is an incentive to action where the broader issue is the taken-for-granted character of well-entrenched routines. Legitimation of behaviour through others is no longer primarily an issue of social control. Rather, the 'natural attitude' automatically accepts others as agents rendering a person's behaviour situationally and/or morally appropriate (or the opposite).

This, in effect, is the point where the problem of motivation turns out to be the apex of the analysis of illness. It is the key to the analysis of *trouble*. Garfinkel, to be sure, claims that his use of the term 'trouble' derives directly from Weber where he is said to focus on 'the discrepancy between "destiny" and "merit"' (1967a, p. 105).

Chapter 9
The Phenomenological Notion of Illness

Medical issues never occupy as much of the forefront of phenomenology's concerns as, in contrast, problems of medical practice are core matters for structural functionalism, and mental patients' plight spurs on 'symbolic interactionism's' partisanship. In fact, it is not even sickness but *suicide* which serves as the conceptual model for the clarification of ethnomethodology's illness explanation.

In the mid-1950s, Garfinkel (who was then Assistant Professor at UCLA's Department of Anthropology and Sociology) became part of an interdisciplinary effort to establish and monitor a Suicide Prevention Center. It originated in the joint endeavour of a psychiatrist and a psychologist with hospital as well as university affiliation, backed up by cooperation from the Los Angeles Coroner's Office and funded by consecutive grants from the National Institute of Mental Health and American Public Health Service (from 1955 onwards, but the Rand Corporation was also helpful). The work done by Garfinkel at the Center was not honoured for over a decade by an offer to contribute to one of the numerous books edited by the two co-directors of the Center (Shneidman and Farberow, 1957; Farberow and Shneidman, 1961; Farberow, 1963 and 1967), nor was a reference included in the otherwise comprehensive bibliography compiled by one of them (Farberow, 1969). It is unclear whether Garfinkel was given a chance to present a paper at one of at least four conferences on suicide prevention held during the period of slightly more than a decade; none is included in the conference proceedings. It was only in the same year as *Studies in Ethnomethodology* was published that an article by Garfinkel was included in another volume produced by one of the Center's co-directors (Shneidman, 1967). Nevertheless, he had been working with the Suicide Prevention Center for well over a decade by that time.

188

In fact, the same volume contained an article by Sacks following on from his PhD dissertation which was partly supervised by Garfinkel[26] based on tape-reçorded telephone-conversation material elicited at the Center. While Sacks analysed the cognitive categories relevant for persons in trouble regarding those available to help, Garfinkel focused on the process of reasoning when officials connected with the Suicide Prevention Team decided upon a verdict solving doubtful cases where homicide, accident and suicide overlap.[27] The topic of practical account formation in cases of suicide where relatives and insurance companies may have interests at stake is also dealt with in a monograph on suicide appearing in the same year (Douglas, 1967). That its author acknowledged a 'great intellectual debt' to Garfinkel and Sacks for the most innovative part of his book (Part IV) signified that the ethnomethodological perspective upon suicide as a socially meaningful action had by then become a well developed approach.

In fact, the topic continued to be attractive during the 1970s and beyond (J. M. Atkinson, 1968, 1978). In 1983, D. E. Smith emphasised that the main point is that of intersubjective accomplishment. Under the title 'No One Commits Suicide', she argued that it is through others' eventual categorisation of a dead person's presumed behaviour that verdicts of suicide are validated.

As for illness (disability) studies, it was not until the mid-1970s that two books with phenomenological intent were published, both from British authors (Voysey, 1975; Dingwall, 1976). Meanwhile, among the mostly California-based American ethnomethodologists, the UCLA group took up the topic of how institutions (such as the police or psychiatric emergency services) dealt with (mostly mental) illness (e.g., Bittner, 1976; R. Emerson and Pollner, 1976), the San Diego group around Cicourel started to analyse communication structures in medical interviewing (Cicourel, 1973b, 1975, 1976; Shuy, 1976), and the group working with Sacks at UC Irvine completed the groundwork for what later (particularly in England) became 'pure' conversational analysis of medical encounters (Heath, 1981, 1984).

All three branches have developed since then into rich sources of insight into illness and therapy. Today, in the American context, much of contemporary ethnomethodological effort goes into deciphering the production of knowledge in science (Garfinkel, Lynch and Livingston, 1981, 1983). The emergence and use of clinical knowledge, as it were, have become a British domain (P. Atkinson, 1981a; P. Atkinson and Heath, 1981). Furthermore, 'cognitive sociology' has contributed considerably to the understanding of clinical reasoning (Cicourel, 1981a, 1981b, 1982, 1983a,

1983b, 1984). It is also in England that secondary literature on ethnomethodology has continued to appear while the latest major book on this topic in the US dates from more than a decade ago (Mehan and Wood, 1975; Benson and Hughes, 1983; Heritage, 1984). Also, West German researchers have recently published insightful studies on hospital work (Fengler and Fengler, 1983; Gück, Matt and Weingarten, 1983).

The basic idea in ethnomethodology (phenomenology) regarding illness (which it shares with suicide) is that it drastically diminishes a person's moral status (including its virtual or literal elimination). Competence as an agent of moral conduct and social control, in turn, constitutes the essential presupposition of membership in society. Voysey explains what is at stake:

> When moral character is *not* imputed, the entity concerned is not regarded as a person. Since the ascription of intellectual character is a necessary condition of that of moral character, and to the extent that the ascription of moral character is influenced by physical characteristics, then the disabled individual may not be regarded as a person. (1975, p. 32)

Illness, as latent absence or impending reduction of moral quality of the person, is liable to invite normalisation efforts. They use repair strategies guaranteeing as much normality as the sick person's family and friends may feel necessary to function as an intact membership group. In this way, illness belongs to a broad category of disturbing occurrences (accidents or achievements) which breach the taken-for-granted peace of everyday routines. In other words, illness (together with crime and other 'unusual' goings-on) constitutes *trouble*.

The notion of trouble is important for the phenomenological approach for two reasons. On one hand, trouble offers an opportunity for social institutions (as well as individual members or collectivities) to strengthen the 'fabric' of their orientational commitments. The latter can be brought to bear upon deviant persons through the discretionary use of more or less punitive measures. In fact, Garfinkel in his famous experiments (1962, 1963, 1967a) uses the deliberate creation of trouble as a means to study what it entails to be normal. What he encounters is that 'victims' of his experimenter-students' rule-breaking express anger easily converted into a fully-fledged rebuff; for instance one of the 'victims' whose greeting 'How are you?' is experimentally answered by requests for further clarification as if it were a literal question retorts eventually, 'Quite frankly, I don't care how you are'. On the other hand, to a certain extent, trouble is an issue which is 'in the eye of the beholder': that is, the alternative of the 'cultural dope' who all but follows normative demands is the rational actor using hindsight and situational sensitivity to negotiate as much accountable normality as can be mustered. In this respect, trouble is endemic in everyday life and invites mechanisms of consensus formation entrenched in the social order.

In one way, therefore, illness incumbency is an intersubjective and situational accomplishment. The unwell (or, as Lynch (1983) summarily says, the 'troublemakers') are subject to practices from their fellow members accruing to the troublemakers whatever moral status they deem the ill people fit to sustain in their condition.

On the other hand, this also has an institutional side to it. Trouble invites the discretionary use of official routines in dealing with it. In this vein, the trouble's nature, severity and cause are determined by rational institutional procedures (see, for instance, Cicourel's *Juvenile Justice* (1968) and his work on medical history-taking). This, to be sure, brings reality construction into play as official decision-making about moral competence. It relates to persons who have become conspicuous or incapacitated among their membership collectivity. Garfinkel, in describing the principle of reasoning for deliberations among the Suicide Prevention Center's staff about the nature of a presumably suicidal death (a procedure called 'psychological autopsy') has this to say (which also concerns the task of medicine in case of illness):

> Every kind of inquiry without exception would consist of organized artful practices whereby the rational properties of indexical expressions – of proverbs, advice, partial description, elliptical expressions, passing remarks, fables, tales, and the rest are demonstrated . . . The managed production of this phenomenon in every aspect, from every perspective, and in every stage must retain the character for members of serious, practical tasks, subject to every exigency of organizationally situated conduct. (1967b, p. 186)

The dual nature of illness

Biological processes behind illness incumbency are not mentioned. Whether or not this entails, as Dingwall (1976) argues, that a distinction between physical and social phenomena is made against the background of cultural relativity of illness categories, may be left unanswered. Rather, since phenomenology's aim is to produce a theory of social systems based on the structure of actors' experiences, what counts are the invariant features of actors' meaning construction. In this, any physical or mental incapacity figures as a source of trouble. It is recognised by one's environment and made the issue of normalisation by the individual as well as the collectivity to which he or she belongs. This, no doubt, may even entail the notorious degradation ceremonies which Garfinkel (1956a) vividly invokes:

> Max Scheler argued that there is no society that does not provide in the very features of its organization the conditions sufficient for inducing shame. It will be treated here as axiomatic that there is no society whose social structure does not provide, in its routine features, the conditions of identity degradation . . . Just as the structural conditions of shame are universal to all societies by the very fact of their being organized, so the structural conditions of status degradation are universal to all societies. (1956a, p. 420)

In this, it seems, biological and social deviance both appear of the same origin: namely, both constitute features dealt with by the 'natural attitude'. Illness, on the one hand, is a category which the 'natural attitude' allows for and can accommodate through categories of deviance (Pollner, 1974). But, on the other hand, illness as a source of trouble endangering the 'natural attitude' must be neutralised by normalisation efforts or outright therapeutic measures.

This dual nature of illness comes out in its manifesting, at the same time, a state of fault or failure (i.e., troublemaking), and a category of accounts serving to legitimise deficiencies of attributed moral status. For instance, Cicourel's (1968) reconstruction of how deed and normative rule are brought together as indexical expressions in juvenile justice includes a case where the label of illness constitutes a possibility of opting out of police jurisdiction for a middle-class family. Likewise, D. Smith (1976) presupposes that mental illness is but one of a number of explanations given for strange behaviour. Garfinkel (1967a), in reporting on his experiments, finds that some of the student experimenters who break the rules of ritual conduct are deemed ill by their bewildered 'victims'.

Nevertheless, not every stigmatisation sticks. In fact, Voysey (1975) makes it clear that the family with a disabled child gives elaborate accounts documenting that, in spite of the handicapped member, it is a normal modern family: that is, what counts is not so much whether or not an illness category is rightly applied but rather whether or not an entitlement to moral competence in interaction can convincingly be legitimised. In this, the dual nature of normality becomes clear: it signifies, at the same time, the scope of interactional competence defined by others' reactions and the realm of negotiated participation accomplished through one's own 'definition of the situation'.

The issue of political impact

Criticising the stigma notion, it has been stated above that 'symbolic interactionism's' siding with disenfranchised groups presupposes that they see the world as split into irreconcilable halves while implicitly endorsing the power of dominant institutions or groups (Gouldner, 1968). Phenomenology does not make this claim. In fact, while mundane reasoning is found with every member of society, and sociologists are explicitly included, the same mode of consciousness is deemed to prevail among the learned and the uneducated. This resembles whatever democratic version of sociology students were longing for in the late 1960s. Ethnomethodology, at the time, found itself quite unexpectedly hailed as revolutionary. In fact, Garfinkel, Cicourel and Sacks have never claimed a political, let alone a radical, stance. Only work by Molotch in the early 1970s introduces an attempt to demystify authority practices but no consistent approach has sprung from it (Molotch and Lester, 1973, 1974).

What is it, then, that is of political relevance? Among students around 1968 were activists who burnt their draft papers for Vietnam and were sentenced to jail for it. In Germany, at the time, the Nazi provocation of the Second World War was compared with the Gulf of Tonking (apparently equally staged) incident resulting in the invasion of Cambodia as a 'retaliatory' measure. What the students were afraid of was inadvertently becoming accomplices of a war particularly cruel to the non-military population. Simply by going about their daily business of studying as if nothing was happening, they felt that they were colluding with those responsible for the napalm bombings. The fabric of everyday life providing for the *natural attitude's* explicit exclusion of foreign or far-away troubles was resented by these students. They felt that it was their responsibility to realise that normal taken-for-granted activities in industrial societies are only possible because wars are deliberately staged in Third World countries. Thus the treacherous quality of the taken-for-granted world (i.e., that it hides the invisible part of an iceberg of endemic war crimes elsewhere) was resented by many students.

Through this awareness of close interconnectedness between war in Vietnam and affluence and peace in the US, Germany or

Britain, a level of political control became visible exceeding what hitherto had been perceived. In one of his lectures in 1970, Sacks put this attitude into words while addressing the accounting structures of interaction:

> I will be saying some things about why the study of storytelling should be of interest to anybody. And the loosest message is that the world you live in is much more finely organized than you would imagine. Now the pileup of evidence about that would serve to give a great deal of flesh to that assertion, and you would not have to stay around after today to have caught that message, and to have been armed with some materials that could permit you to wander around noticing things that you might not have noticed, and find them ghastly. (Sacks, 1970/84, p. 414)

Such awareness of a nearly inescapable social structuring of one's situational conduct has repercussions on how much institutional taken-for-granted routines a person wishes to tolerate. Ethnomethodology, during the 1960s, investigated official agencies' dubious selection procedures (Cicourel and Kitsuse, 1963) and produced evidence of the doubtful validity of official statistics (Kitsuse and Cicourel, 1963). This contributed for many to a feeling that they were being processed by institutions who had a right to judge them while they, in turn, were more or less deprived of the right to judge and possibly sanction the policies and practices of the institutions. This, to be sure, added a perception of helplessness to many students' radical consciousness. Voysey, in her account of the role of official agents as compared with the individuals' influence on the attribution of normality or stigma, sums up this mentality in a most insightful statement. She writes:

> Official agents both construct and maintain an absolute public morality. Individuals may believe that there is an absolute morality governing their lives and act in accordance with it, even if privately they do not agree with its rules. They may believe others do agree, or not know that they disagree, since in most relationships they lack knowledge of each other's personal beliefs and background. It is safer, therefore, not publicly to challenge or violate the public morality. Even if an individual suspects that most others do agree with him in his opposition to some aspect of public morality, public commitment is risky, since the official agents have established organized interests and legal sanctions. Of course, some suffer the consequences, but for most there is more incentive in acting as if they agree with the public morality in cooperating with others to maintain a public fiction of morality and normality. An individual, then, does not have to be normal in the sense that he judges himself in terms of absolute moral categories; rather, he has to maintain a respectable appearance. Whether or not he agrees with the

official morality is irrelevant, since it is to this that he is held accountable for those of his actions that are public or 'private' but held to have
consequences for the public realm. (Voysey, 1975, p. 42)

The metaphor of latent or *everyday Fascism* was created by a
German writer living in California in the late 1960s (Lettau, 1971).
It alluded to the insight that modern pluralism was but a combination of surface liberalism with, on a 'deep' level, monolithic
capitalism (Offe, 1970/76). Equally, it was remembered that in
Nazi Germany *not* being imprisoned or sent to a concentration
camp for such 'crimes' as homosexuality, gipsy descent, Jewish-
ness, being a Jehovah's witness or undermining the nation's war
efforts had to be accomplished through public conformity with the
National Socialist ideology, notwithstanding one's private beliefs.
Thus, 25–30 years earlier, when everybody knew what it meant
that 'some suffered the consequences', most Germans at the time
managed to keep their reservations against the regime secret or in
private. This, however, created a widespread ambiguity towards
post-war accusations of collective guilt. Many survivors, at the
same time, felt guilty as well as not guilty. That is, they had known
'in private' what publicly they were not supposed to know; but also
they had disbelieved their knowledge because Nazi newspapers had
frequently denounced (but explicitly mentioned) realistic reports
from concentration camps. This had been introduced as *atrocity
propaganda* allegedly set up by the allied powers to undermine the
German war effort.
  In Voysey's passage, it seems that the personal and political
dangers for the population of a state's monopoly over trouble (i.e.,
defining its categories as well as its consequences) are most clearly
addressed. At this point, the phenomenological approach to illness
(disability) emulates what social and political science – with the
intensity of eyewitness-experience – explain about the use of
underdog categories for maintaining the social cohesion of Fascist
societies (Neumann, 1942/66; Kogon, 1946).

One model of illness

Although what originates in the 1960s as ethnomethodology is
later divided into three branches (Attewell, 1974; Weingarten,
Sack and Schenkein, 1976; Benson and Hughes, 1983), the same
explanatory model is used. Garfinkel's work is now solely credited
with the name *ethnomethodolody* while Cicourel has termed his
approach *cognitive sociology*; *conversational analysis* is frequently

understood as a separate field. However, all three approaches use the idea of indexicality to describe the everyday world, and that of praxeology to mark the sociologist's attitude. They conceptualise illness as *trouble* which can be reacted to in two distinguishable ways. Either the sick person's environment is shown to use neutralisation practices to reduce potential blunders, together with discriminatory practices to reduce participation. Or the trouble is diagnosed and dealt with by an expert (in the case of illness usually, but not always, a doctor). In general, medical help is perceived as organised in a linguistic domain and knowledge frame of its own. Frequently, clashes between the doctor's world and the patient's world are described where more often than not the patient is shown to become subdued. In some writings on doctor–patient communication (incidentally, mostly where women writers comment on experiences of women patients), this leads to implicit or explicit criticism of the doctor's not taking the patient seriously.

In their views upon therapy, all three approaches are mainly concerned with verbal (and, occasionally, video-taped gestural) material which comes out of medical encounters. In particular, medical records as institutional devices as well as conversations during ward rounds, private consultations and group psychotherapy are made the target of reality construction analysis. The aim is, in all three approaches, to demonstrate what intrinsic rationality prevails in clinical settings. This may, to be sure, sometimes entail that such rationality is explicitly or implicitly criticised as one of professional dominance where that of mutuality and reciprocity is deemed more appropriate.

Chapter 10
The Trouble Model

The three steps of aetiology

The normality stage

Contradictions and misconceptions within 'symbolic interaction-ism's' (particularly the labelling approach's) model of deviance frequently help to clarify the phenomenological stance. For in-stance, Pollner (1974) shows that Becker (1963), although denying intrinsic validity of stigmatising labels, creates the category of 'secret deviance' and thus implicitly admits that acts may be deemed deviant by rule violators not (yet) blamed by others. This, argues Pollner, documents that deviance is as much a members' category as it is one of official agents. In the same vein, R. Emerson (1973) maintains that the sequence that residual rule-breaking precedes identification of deviance, particularly mental illness, need not always apply. In the case of mass murder, he says, initially this may not be seen as a rule violation at all, 'yet questions of mental illness are almost inevitably raised in such cases' (1973, p. 7). Moreover, Emerson goes on to say, the relation-ships between an act ('violation') and the rule of which it is a violation is far from fixed: 'Consider the act of "shoplifting" as managed in the juvenile court: committed by an upper middle class youth, this offense often indicates mental illness to court personnel; yet the "same act" committed by a lower class young-ster is typically seen as a minor, crime-like delinquency' (1973,p. 8).

It is precisely this quality of non-predictability of relationship between violation and rule, on the one hand, and rule violation and subsequent sanctioning, on the other, which incites Becker to take the standpoint that only by deliberately siding with the underdog can the sociologist avoid inadvertently colluding with social-control agents and legitimising apparent injustice. How-ever, the phenomenological approach takes such fluidity between rule and behaviour as normal. In fact, as has been shown above,the interactionist paradigm also allows for disjuncture between rule and violation; nevertheless, this is considered wrong and the paradigm holds that this is what gives contingencies a casual role in the genesis of illness incumbency which should not be underestimated. Phenomenology, in turn, comes to the conclusion that 'nothing unusual is happening' unless somebody in a situation successfully brings off the stance that 'something unusual is happening'. As J. Emerson (1969/70) emphasises, it is more difficult in a situation to maintain a 'something unusual' stance. If not everybody present corroborates it, the person claiming that a rule has been broken and remedial actions are due may be left to ridicule or embarrassment; those pleading for inconspicuousness have a situational advantage:

> The 'nothing unusual' advocate capitalizes on the ambiguity of events. In the movie the music swells up to signal 'something unusual' . . . and should the audience miss [the] cues, they can hardly miss the camera zooming in upon the actors' reactions to the unexpected event. In real life people almost expect the concomitants found in the movies, and their absence creates uncertainty about the meaning of the situation. (J. Emerson, 1969/70, p. 15)

In this context, the question arises as to whether the scope of variability is unlimited for the putting together of behaviour or utterance, on the one hand, with a rule or pattern (which may be followed or violated), on the other hand. Is there a limit to what accounts can do for a behaviour by telling a story, making it intelligible through clever remarks or 'sad tales'? Does presupposing rationality suggest that, to quote a German proverb, 'where no judge is, there is no crime'?

In their insightful essay on *accounts* as safeguards of social order, M. B. Scott and Lyman (1968) state that 'they prevent conflicts from arising by verbally bridging the gap between action and expectation' (1968, p. 46). Through the account (which may be an excuse for an apparent misdemeanour, or a justification of a disavowed wrongdoing), a behaviour is retrospectively recognised as what it supposedly is and has always been; it thus becomes, for all intents and purposes, the calculable piece of intersubjective reality. One limit to such peacekeeping in social interchange is that background expectations should not have been violated. For instance,

> We learn the meaning of 'a married couple' by indicating that they are two people of opposite sex who have a legitimate right to engage in

sexual intercourse and maintain their own children in their own household. When such taken-for-granted phenomena are called into question, the inquirer (if a member of the same culture group) is regarded as 'just fooling around', or perhaps even being sick. (M. B. Scott and Lyman, 1968, p. 46).

The other limit is that accounts can fail to become intersubjectively validated; they may not be honoured. This may, on the one hand, be due to a person's low rank in a group but, on the other hand, it may also derive from inability to master the more subtle clues such as linguistic style:

> The idiomatic form of an account is expected to be socially suited to the circle in which it is introduced, according to norms of culture, subculture, and situation. The acceptance or refusal of an offered account in part depends on the appropriateness of the idiom employed. Failure to employ the proper linguistic style often results in a dishonoring of the account or calls for further accounts. (M. B. Scott and Lyman, 1968, p. 57) [see also Lyman and Scott 1970]).

In the same vein, conversational validation of behaviour often leads to peaceful reconciliation between action and expectation; attributions of responsibility are continuously made. In particular, this includes the attribution of blame (Pomerantz, 1978). How much responsibility and/or blame is to be taken by a person or role incumbent for a particular behaviour, Watson (1978) argues, is only partially open to negotiation. In fact, if responsibilities which 'normally' belong to a person or role are not claimed by those entitled, this is also specially accountable.

In all, everyday interaction where 'nothing unusual' is happening may be far from a reassuring or pleasant interchange making for mutual identity corroboration. Rather, in the first instance, 'being ordinary' is the result of a continuous effort of avoiding falling into the traps of doing something outrageous. Sacks describes as the accomplishment of 'doing "being ordinary"' that it defeats underlying temptations to 'act out'. Anyone not doing that, of course, would become an object of stories, becoming exposed to anything from notoriety to repute:

> So it seems plain enough that people monitor the scenes they are in for their storyable characteristics. And yet the awesome, overwhelming fact is that they come away with *no* storyable characteristics. Presumably, any of us with any wit could make of this half-hour, or of the next, a rather large array of things to say. But there is the job of being an ordinary person, and that job includes attending the world, yourself, others, objects, so as to see how it is a usual scene. And when offering

what transpired, you present it in its usual fashion: 'Nothing much'. (1970/84, p.417)

On the interpersonal level, everyday interaction consists of a sequence of troubles. People get themselves into trouble or others may be to blame, and troubles are 'solved by a broad range of reconciliatory or help-inducing measures including, in the last instance, the acrimonious *cooling the mark out* or *degradation ceremonies* (Goffman, 1952; Garfinkel, 1956a). Conversational strategies of dealing with trouble are aptly described by various authors (J. Emerson, 1969a, 1969/1970b; Jefferson, 1984a, 1984b). Beyond talk, remedy action plays a role. R. M. Emerson and Messinger (1977) argue that only through the remedy perceived to deal effectively with a trouble is the latter's nature satisfactorily understood by those involved. For instance, they quote an example from Freidson (1961) where the eventual relief of a husband's cold-like symptoms through hay-fever medication which he received from a doctor successfully corroborated the wife's persistent opinion that her husband had an allergy. Among the spouses, then, the remedy retrospectively settled the dispute over the nature and cause of the trouble. The analysing sociologist (i.e., Freidson), Emerson and Messinger point out, shared this perspective although the eventual diagnosis took three years of unsuccessful visits to a doctor: 'Conceptually, the definition of a trouble can be seen as the emergent product, as well as the initial precipitant, of remedial actions' (1977, p. 123).

It is noteworthy, in this context, that trouble in everyday life occurs in cycles of attributed causes and remedies without necessarily exhausting the realm where normality applies. Emerson and Messinger point at reciprocal blame attribution as one way of keeping the trouble–remedy cycle contained:

> A husband may complain to his wife about her staying out nights, for example, but the wife need neither see nor acknowledge her behavior as a problem. When confronted by her spouse's rebuke or threat, she may identify his behavior as the trouble – as unreasonable insistance that she stay home. (R. M. Emerson and Messinger, 1977, p. 125)

The constraints of 'doing "being ordinary"' may well include the vicissitudes of endless trouble–remedy cycles. What incorporates these under the umbrella of normality is that *no help* is being invited. That is, no intervention from 'third parties' occurs to assist in defining and/or solving the problem at hand.

Even the latter, in special circumstances, can entail that normality prevails. Daniels (1970a), in an account of how psychiatrists in Vietnam during the war distinguished between those to whom they gave the label of war neurosis, and those who they felt had no claim to this diagnosis, has this to say about the task of military psychiatry:

> The world of military service is a harsh one; and so those who come to the clinic must revise their underlying assumptions or 'background expectancies' (Garfinkel, 1967) about the world that they carry from civilian life. Much higher standards of endurance are taken for granted in military settings than might be the case at home. Psychiatrists and their agents reaffirm this reality when they refuse to recognize the legitimacy of illness as an excuse. They help to substantiate this reality; for if they were sympathetic or lenient in expectations of performance the military world would not, in fact, be so harsh. (1970a, p. 172)

Cycles of help

Benevolent and malevolent network support. The question arises of how normality cycles containing trouble within the confines of lay advice and admonishing are kept from worsening. No clear-cut answer can be given. Boundaries are fluid between where friends, neighbours or clergymen provide the necessary support or interference to take care of a trouble, and where official agents are involved. The latter, to be sure, can vary in sanctions available from marriage counsellors to mental hospitals. Even if no doctor is consulted but subsequently professional help is likely, a case is not left to the vagaries of nature. The phenomenological approach makes it clear that it is primarily the membership group in which a person lives whose reactions upon strange or inapt behaviour are the first 'line of defence' of the social order against illness. In fact, the aetiology of psychiatric illness is described by various authors as one of gradually excluding a member from responsible duties when mental difficulties arise; concomitantly, accounting takes place which secures the rationality of others' discriminatory practices.

D.Smith (1976) extracts from an account of how a person, K, comes to be judged mentally ill that it is not a factual process of losing one's psychiatric health but a factual account of *what happened* which is the basis of the aetiological process. Others, primarily, says Smith, construct a reasonable account of what makes sense of K's experiences or behaviour. This is done in a way providing justifications for the accrued label such that K's apparently unreasonable actions and how they are perceived as strange and eventually sick by more and more members of K's membership community can be understood by any hearer/reader. At first, as the data from the narrative of one of Smith's students suggest, K is a pretty girl and a fellow student, but then things start to go wrong. But, Smith cautions, the account which produces evidence for what, actually, is a 'factual account' should not be mistaken as simply recollecting past experiences:

> The actual events are not facts. It is the use of proper procedure for categorizing events which transforms them into facts. A fact is something which is already categorized, which is already worked up so that it conforms to the model of what that fact should be like. To describe something as a fact or treat something as a fact implies that the events themselves – what happened – entitle or authorize the teller of the tale to treat that categorization as ineluctable. (D. Smith, 1976, p. 35)

In this vein, Smith constructs a chain of account producers and recipients: first is *Angela* who originally was K's friend and tells the story of how K became mentally ill (or became seen as such); second, Angela's and K's flat mate, *Trudi*; third, Angela's *mother* and *Aunt Betti* who became suspicious of K's behaviour; fourth, a *woman friend* of the family who was consulted for advice; fifth, the *student interviewer* who extracted the story from her friend Angela; sixth, the *professor* and respondent to the interviewer's written account which was an assignment for a sociology class; seventh, the *reader/hearer* of the interview as now presented in the article to the sociological public. Smith argues that such concatenated levels of public assertion constitute the accomplishment of being ill: that is, reasonably not being held responsible for one's actions or failures to act. In this way, moral competence comes to be gradually reduced and eventually completely denied in cases of oncoming mental illness. In this the question of whether or not mental illness is involved as psychological deterioration is deliberately left open. 'Whether K is really mentally ill or not is irrelevant to the analysis', Smith maintains (1976, p. 28), and she sums up (assuming that all persons involved are female):

> The credibility of the account and the reader/hearer's obedience to the restrictions on search procedures as well as her authorization of the teller of the tale, depends upon Angela *et al.* as K's friends. The contradictory interpretation provides a context for much of what is reported of K after Angela and Trudi had decided 'she just could not cope' and found themselves 'discussing her foibles in her absence'. The friendship version of their relationship depends upon successfully defining K as 'mentally ill'. Conversely defining K as 'mentally ill' depends upon preserving that version. So I take it as crucial that it is K's statement about 'the little black sheep and the lambs' which receives the gloss from the teller of the tale. 'This was really completely out of

touch'. The social organization of the account can be seen as playing a crucial part of the construction of the fact that 'K is mentally ill'. (D. Smith 1976, p. 52)

While Smith neither commits herself to K's 'real' illness nor to an unsubstantiated labelling process, Lynch's (1983) data allow for an actual worsening of an afflicted person's behaviour. When somebody produces 'crazy' behaviour, that person's membership group(s) (family, friends, classmates, etc.) react(s) with what Lynch terms 'accomodation practices'. That is, Lynch's informants document through their stories that the immediate social environment has layers of accomodation practices available which are apt to contain the craziness while, at the same time, possibly aggravating it. For instance, a member of a rock band who (among many other items of disturbing behaviour) played particularly loudly and *'awful'* during concerts in order to be heard better by the audience than the others, was neutralised by the sound mixer's turning down this player's microphone in the concert hall and on the radio. On the other hand, this 'difficult' band member was sent fake love letters by another which the flattered addressee read out aloud in the dressing room, thus making himself a laughing stock among the others when he was not present. Lynch clarifies: 'Accomodation practices are interactional techniques that people use to manage pesons they view as persistent sources of trouble. Accomodation implies attempts to "live with" persistent and ineradicable troubles' (Lynch, 1983, p. 152).

In all, Lynch distinguishes three main practices, namely: (a) minimising contact with the troublemaker (avoiding, ignoring/not taking seriously); (b) directly managing the troublemaker's actions (humouring, screening/monitoring, taking over/excluding from most responsibilities, orienting to local prospects of normality/ taking someone on his or her good days, practical jokes and retaliations (see above); (c) influencing the reaction of the troublemaker (turning one into a notorious character, shadowing, advanced noticing, hiding and diluting, covering for/covering up). This impressive catalogue documents how much illness as well as normality are but an achievement of collective cooperation. Lynch explains:

Taken as a whole, accomodation practices reveal *the organizational construction of the normal individual*. The individual is relied upon both in commonsense reasoning and social theory as a source of compliance with the standards of the larger society. The normal individual successfully adapts to the constraints imposed by social structure. Troublemakers are viewed as persons who, for various reasons, could not be given full *responsibility* for maintaining normality. Instead, the burden of maintaining the individual's normal behavior and appearance was taken up by others. Troublemakers were not overtly sanctioned; instead, they were shaped and guided through the superficial performances of ordinary action. Their integration into society was not a cumulative mastery learned 'from inside'; it was a constant project executed by others from the 'outside'. (Lynch 1983, p. 161)

Of course, this is what others' help is all about. In his account of how apparently suicidal persons come to set themselves up as suicide candidates, Sacks explores what it means when callers on the telephone to the Suicide Prevention Center say about themselves that they have nobody to turn to. What, asks Sacks, are the boundaries of categories of persons liable to help those wanting to take their own lives. This entails the question of who dodges their responsibilities by not being available in a person's suicidal crisis. Conversations between a caller (C) and a staff member (S) at the Suicide Prevention Center may run as follows:

S1 Have you ever been married, Miss M--?
C1 No.
S2 And you're out here kind of on your own and things not going well?
C2 That's it.
S3 You have no one out here?
C3 Well, I have cousins, but you know they're cousins. They're third or fourth cousins. (Sacks, 1967, p. 207)

Help in a suicidal crisis, it turns out, is to be provided by the next of kin (namely, spouses, parents and children) in the first instance. In the last instance, professional help from doctors or other health or counselling personnel can be commissioned if a suicide candidate is willing to go along with their conditions of advice or treatment. That is, while the family's help may involve lesser expectations of reasonable conduct on the part of the suicidal, bringing in professional help involves commitments towards more reasonable actions in the future. Sacks, by referring to the adequate categories of relatives as *R*, with *p* standing for proper, and using the letter *K* for experts with professional knowledge, comes to point out another aspect of how problematic switching from *R* to *K* is:

Since the conclusion 'no one to turn to' is arrived at by reference to Rp, it might be supposed that the replacement of R by K would in principle undercut the possibility of arriving at the conclusion. However, to remove the appropriateness of R may serve to undercut the obligatory character of the search for help. Furthermore, insofar as the use of K is seen as not merely conditional on need of help, but need of help plus ability to pay, those who lack the latter might see themselves in even a weaker position if they saw K as exclusively appropriate. (Sacks, 1967, p. 222)

All this is part of *micro-politics* of trouble, as R. M. Emerson and Messinger maintain (1977), in the realm where outside intervention is sought. The relational network involves, they point out, four roles. The first is that of *complainant* who announces the trouble by seeking remedial action. As in the case of relatives of someone suicidal who seek advice on the telephone from the Suicide Prevention Center, the 'complainant role may be distinct from the role of *victim*' (1977, p. 126). Third is the role of 'remedy agent or *troubleshooter*', and 'finally, one party to the trouble may come to be designated the *troublemaker* responsible' (1977, p. 126). Only in the case of non-psychiatric ailments diagnosed by a doctor would, in fact, complainant, victim and troublemaker be the same person; that is , the latter two categories would be more or less irrelevant. In the case of a psychopathic condition, for instance, where violence is involved the complainant may well be the victim, and the troublemaker the patient. In case of crime, however, the four roles could be filled by different persons altogether.

At this point, it seems, peacekeeping by the police (including control of crime) and attending to illness by the medical profession (or semi-professionals or community services) are seen as tasks with basically the same social structure. In fact, phenomenological studies find it difficult to distinguish sharply between the function of the police and the courts, on the one hand, and those of doctors and medical services on the other. Research shows how,as it were, 'medically responsibly' the police handle psychiatric cases which they encounter answering emergency calls (Bittner, 1976). At the same time, emergency psychiatric teams of a community mental hospital engage predominantly in 'police-equivalent' peacekeeping functions (if only their actual work load, not its idealised image of heroic intervention and help are considered) (R. M. Emerson and Pollner, 1976).

In any event, 'when an outside party moves from giving advice to active intervention the structure of the trouble undergoes significant change' (R. M. Emerson and Messinger, 1977, p. 126). What becomes different? Two issues are noteworthy: the trouble is now formulated as a coherent whole describing adequately a patient's or wrongdoer's complaint or deed, and this then retrospectively ascertains what has been the case all along. In particular, attributing such an account to what so far may have been an act or utterance of ambivalent moral stature leads to the formulation of a 'history of the trouble' (1977, p. 128). In medicine as in social or police work, taking the history of (and thus deciding upon the proper genesis of) a complaint or trouble fixes for all intents and purposes what, from now on, is the to-be-treated condition or to-be-dealt-with misdemeanour or misbehaviour. Furthermore, designation through diagnosis (and remedial action following on from it) of the nature of the illness (or other deviance) may start the individual on an odyssey of remedial help-getting or even help-suffering from sequential official agents. These may take refuge in referrals when they have exhausted their means (including those of general versus special hospitals). In Emerson and Messinger's words:

> In moving through a circuit of troubleshooters, an initially ambiguous trouble tends to crystallize, as new ways and means of dealing with the problem are sought out and implemented and prior ways are determined to be ineffective and rejected. In this process, an individual may be definitely assigned the role of troublemaker and explicitly identified as deviant. As full-scale deviant remedies are tried and found to fail, the troublemaker may be referred to specialists in other areas of deviance, the nature of his or her trouble undergoing reinterpretation as new ways of eliminating, reducing, or confining the troublemaking are implemented. (R. M. Emerson and Messinger, 1977, p. 127)

At this point, Lorber's (1975) and Murcott's (1981) focusing on the issue of 'bad' or 'problem' patients comes to mind. But normal medical practice is also of interest. For instance, patients with severe angina are often submitted to coronary artery bypass surgery which, in the case of failure, may be followed by more surgery (maybe eventually heart transplantation). It is not unheard of, to take a more extreme example, that hysterectomies may be performed as placebo measures for women patients where 'nothing else' seems to make a physician feel that the patient can be helped.

Diagnosis and history-taking. At an uncertain point, help provided by one's environment already containing conjectures regarding *what is the matter* leads to the step of asking for help from a professional, such as a doctor. Diagnosis is interesting from the sociological standpoint for two reasons. It involves a reasoning process which includes taking a history of a complaint from a patient; this can be traced to the doctor's contextual use of idealised typified textbook knowledge of disease categories; particularly interesting, in this connection, are instances where history-taking is insufficient or flawed but nevertheless leads to an appropriate diagnosis, or where the diagnosis later turns out to be wrong but its emergence and use were or could have been appropriate under the situational circumstances. Furthermore, the history-taking leading up to diagnosis is, as a method of eliciting evidence to corroborate a hypothesis, similar to the method of interviewing used in sociological research. Thus, queries raised against interviewing in social research, particularly with respect to how important language as a variable is (Cicourel, 1970), also apply to the standard format of medical history-taking.

On both points 'cognitive sociology' has contributed most useful empirical work. For instance, in the earliest of what by now has become a sequence of insightful papers on the topic, Cicourel (1973b) argues that it is far from clear when comparing the transcript of a doctor–patient interview with the doctor's eventual production of a medical history how the former is translated into the latter. Rather, a coding process seems to go on responding to cues on different levels while eventually producing only a short verbal account of an originally long, sometimes incomprehensible, partly garbled conversation. In this paper, Cicourel attempts to name the problem:

> The processing of information seems to occur at several levels simultaneously despite the fact that our representation of what we are thinking, feeling, or perceiving is being channeled into a verbal coding that is oral and/or written and thus linear. This coding does not adequately represent the information we experience, but what we experience at different levels is important for what we say next to each other because our talk relies on this assumption. (1973b, p. 27)

The problem is addressed in another paper two years later by recourse to linguistic processes. Using the same example as in the 1973 paper and also a resident's interview with a 15-year-old suspected epileptic and his mother and uncle (the latter acting as an interpreter for the former who only speaks Spanish), Cicourel comes to disentangle the syntactic structures of the stories presented. From work by the San Diego linguist, D. Rumelhart, on how summaries of recognition are made according to a schema for stories, Cicourel sets out to prove that a 'bottom-up or data-driven organization of the discourse material suggests that the participants' focus on topics or events was influenced by local conditions of the interview' (1975' p. 59). These are, in particular, the patient's understanding of hospital procedures and organisation, and the physician's organisation of the information elicited according to a cognitive scheme derived from textbook knowledge. These supposedly structure the interview although this may be far from obvious for the unsuspecting researcher following the sequence of questions and answers in the tape-recorded interview. 'The physicians' questions and remarks have an organized structure to them that suggests their orientation to hypothesis-driven conceptions that motivate the questions and that enable them to decode responses and fit them into preexisting categories based on prior training and knowledge' (1975, p. 59).

What schemes of diagnostic relevance are behind the question-and-answer sequence revealed in the history-taking interview is further explored in a paper (Cicourel, 1984) on 'Diagnostic Reasoning in Medicine: The Role of Clinical Discourse and Comprehension'. In the case whose material is analysed, it occurs that a misdiagnosis is made. Two transcripts are available: one from a 'training fellow's' history-taking of a presumptive rheumatoid-arthritis patient, and another from the 'training fellow's' report to his attendant physician on the diagnostic observations and conjectures allegedly corroborating the diagnosis. Midway through this reporting, when the 'training fellow' has just mentioned some important information (on which the correct diagnosis should have been based), the telephone rings; through analysing the tape over a year later together with the previously attending physician, Cicourel can substantiate the point that contextual contingencies may at times interfere with, and have a deleterious effect on, the genesis of a clinically correct diagnosis (although, as he aptly shows, the mode of reasoning of the 'training fellow' was quite professional).

Finally, in a paper published in 1982, Cicourel uses evidence produced by two interviews conducted 16 months apart. The patient had a hysterectomy following a positive pap smear and biopsy for cancer, but also received a laboratory test result mailed to her immediately after the operation which assured her of the absence of malignancy in the tissue from the biopsy. Cicourel analyses the remarkable cognitive dissonance in the case. While the patient, on the one hand, harboured deep-seated suspicions against doctors' practices in general (and maintained a contagion-theory of cancer), she also followed her doctors' advice, kept her appointments and went through with her operation. How, asks Cicourel, can her account contradict another account of the same illness in the same patient, and the person live with the resulting reality disjuncture?

Cicourel argues from the point of view of concomitant linguistic structures. Would not the woman, he implies, have to give up her diversity of partly irreconcilable but equally adhered-to accounts?

Or else how can her conflicting views not lead to contradictory or failing action, such as troublemaking at the hospital or non-compliance regarding doctors' orders? To be sure, a Freudian would tend to argue in the same way; that is, that conflicting unconscious tendencies or conflict between consciously maintained and unconsciously held views result in 'psychopathology of everyday life' indicating apparent disjunctures of reality construction. This, no doubt, would also be how Parsons would argue; he would surmise that unconscious motivation to fall ill or retain illness can interfere with a patient's avowed wish to become well; at the intersection of these tendencies, failure to follow doctor's orders can result. This is the reason, in Parsons' view, why doctors need to practise 'unconscious psychotherapy' to control patients' motives on both levels of their action.

Several authors following Cicourel emphasise that patients' views and doctors' views clash anyway. The woman's adhering to medical as well as non-medical trouble–remedy structuring, or act–account association, is but a usual phenomenon practised by most in order to minimise conflict with doctors without totally subscribing to their views. For instance, Shuy (1976) argues in a special issue of *Primary Care* on health care for women that communication problems between doctor and patient are endemic in medical interviews. Three factors, Shuy argues, contribute to produce the patient's frequent feeling of being misunderstood or dissatisfied. First, the interview is fraught with emotion from the patient's side while the doctor attempts to practise affective neutrality; furthermore, medical jargon used by the doctor deliberately clouds important issues such that the patient fails to comprehend what is said; and, third, the difference between social classes leads to a *restricted code* being used by lower-class patients, and an *elaborated code* being used by middle-class doctors which does little to bridge the gap between them. Equally, the volume edited by Fisher and Todd (1983) contains various contributions elucidating this clash between the doctor's world and the patient's world. Using verbatim transcripts, for instance, C. West (1983) gives evidence of how self-initiated questions are treated as problematic by patients tending to stutter although being verbally fluent elsewhere.

However, that the doctors' dominance or conceit prevails in the context of medical diagnosis seems to make an inadequate point. What diagnosis is intended to achieve is an adequate categorisation of symptoms in clinical terms such that clarification of the lesion together with its history also presupposes a programme of therapy. In this respect, as Cicourel rightly observes, only the medical model can be right, and the patient's lay notions ought to give way to professional expertise. While most contributors to Fisher and Todd's book on linguistic structures suggest that psychotherapeutic views on the importance of communication for medical treatment ought to be adopted openly or implicitly, Cicourel favours more of a 'medical model'. It may be of no small importance in this respect that, between the early 1970s and the mid-1980s, Cicourel held a joint professorship at University of California San Diego (UCSD) School of Medicine and the Sociology Department. He therefore had a constant chance to observe clinical work and also to discuss his observations and insights with those concerned. It may be said that he comprehends the process of medical practice better than many sociologists whose interviewing or interview-analysis is more or less cut off from medical settings. How act and account are joined together in diagnostic reasoning is shown by Cicourel without wishing thereby to criticise doctors' alleged communicative failures.

From this vantage point, many sociologists' tendency to see communicative defaults becomes problematic. For example, Paget (1983) uses the transcript of a case mainly as evidence to blame the doctor for not listening to a woman patient but tending to take her complaint as psychosomatic ('nerves'); it is argued that this is what male doctors often do with female patients. However, it occurs to the clinically competent reader of Paget's interpretation that she misses an important point: that is, the examining doctor who conducts the interview fails to realise that the patient's complaints could, in fact, mean new metastatic growth since the patient has recently been operated on for cancer. Here, the doctor displays insufficient *clinical* expertise and should be criticised for this rather than for his apparent 'macho' attitude.[28]

In all, psychosomatic interpretations of a complaint for which help is sought, as Emerson and Messinger remark, may be but a stage in a cycle of troubles. Authors like Paget (1983) or C. West (1983), however, regard them as the resolution of a cycle of troubles. That psychosomatic interpretations have gained credibility over the last decades is beyond question. Analysing the diagnostic process can increase their chance to be taken for real while, in fact, they represent but a dominant ideology of the *medicalisation of troubles*: 'What begins as a personal trouble can be redefined and treated as a relational one and vice versa. With bodily illness, for example, a psychosomatic diagnosis can transform any physical symptom, such as chest pains . . . into a product of some relational strain' (R. M. Emerson and Messinger, 1977, p. 124).

As mentioned above, in the analysis of how diagnosis comes about, a second line of argument may be discerned. It concerns the *use of language in interviews.* While much of phenomenological research is directed towards sequential analysis of doctor–patient conversations and does not particularly focus on the format of interviewing, some authors discuss it in more detail. Since sociology, over the last 50 years, has produced a rich literature on questionnaire construction, interviewer bias and related problems, it seems obvious that medical sociology should tackle the topic of medical interviewing from a methodological point of view. Few authors have written on the theme so far.

One of these, Shuy (1976, p. 377), reports a case where a patient is interrogated to discover whether tuberculosis, epilepsy, neurological or psychological disorders, allergies or multiple births ever occurred in the family, to which she responds with less and less emphasis in her voice until she becomes completely silent, shaking her head, and eventually gives no reaction at all until she confesses, to the last question, that she once had a retarded child. Shuy concludes that the patient felt the questions intruded upon her personal identity. He also cites a case where a doctor attempted to explain to a patient symptoms of what presumably is cystitis, or urinary tract infection, by using what he believes is the patient's own language; namely, the words 'belly', 'john', and 'wet your pants' (to which the patient reacts by being obviously hurt; Shuy, 1976, p. 386).

Medical interviewing, as Cicourel argues (1973/74a), does not benefit from a fixed-item list because it fails to allow for the specific case history to be explored in the interview. The fixed-item list, he surmises, is rather like the survey questionnaire which fails to take into account the contextual meanings and peculiarities of a case which are needed to elucidate its actual properties (as in the case of a newly married person whose illness background should be connected with the time when he was single); also, meanings of mundane categories as, for instance, whether one's children are legitimate can vary considerably with (sub)cultural background (Cicourel, 1974b). As with a survey questionnaire presupposing an ideal society member, fixed-item medical histories have three faults which mar their comprehension: first, accepted facts or beliefs are assumed in the world of the respondent which presumably can be elicited as answers to fixed-choice questions. Furthermore 'the standardized natural language sentences of the questionnaire are presumed to activate only the schematized knowledge in the respondent's memory that corresponds with the researcher's theoretical and substantive intentions' (1983b, p. 25). Then, the respondent's reasoning is taken to be adequately represented by the researcher's use of scaling or path analysis or cross-tabulations. Similarities between the standardised medical history and the survey questionnaire call for the transformation of the criticism into suggestions. What can be done to reform history-taking? Cicourel does not advocate that doctors forgo their clinical expertise: rather, he suggests:

> specifying the relationship between speech acts or textual materials, and the grammatical and text or discourse structure. The expert system should model the kinds of objects, events, or properties in the world of the text, and the kind of knowledge which tells the ideal reader that he or she is dealing with structures of expectations associated with a detective story, medical interview, a folk tale, a sales transaction, or an obituary, as told from the point of view of some observer in some temporal setting. (Cicourel, 1983, p. 34)

The state of illness (disability)

The legitimation of suffering.   Once a diagnosis is made and the patient enters into therapy, the issue becomes one of disavowing rather than internalising stigma. This, it is surmised, follows rules leading the individual along a thin edge between too much and too little.

Dingwall (1976) visualises being ill in terms of the taken-for-granted functioning of the body being put in question, and re-establishing it through remedial action:

> Disturbances affecting the body . . .present immediate and important problems for the interpretive scheme being employed by the individual in any situation. The automatic expectation of a stable and predictable relationship between a person and his body cannot be sustained. If he is to continue to sustain a presentation of himself to others as an essentially normal person, who is sufficiently reliable to act as competent partner in some encounter, then remedial action is called for. Such action is a three-stage process. First, it involves . . .'identifying' what is going on . . .Secondly, the sufferer takes a decision to act . . .Thirdly, the effects of the treatment are monitored until the sufferer decides he has returned to a normal level of functioning. This is not necessarily the same point at which he started . . .A new balance may be struck between body structure and function and the knowledge used to monitor them. Alternatively, the sufferer may conclude that the treatment is not working and that a new evaluation is called for, followed by a possible new initiative in action. (1976, pp. 98–9)

The phenomenological approach is particularly concerned with how knowledge aids structuring the social world. Such knowledge may be the individual's learned cultural categories at hand, or what is imposed by responsible official agents; the two, however, need not contradict each other. The latter may include medical helpers but also goes far beyond. Voysey (1975), in her account of how families come to 'accept' themselves as normal when they have a disabled child, distinguishes between three levels of the problem. Initially, the definition of the child's disability or that of the child as disabled becomes a rational construction by recollecting how it all happened: thus, types such as *gradual onset/clear diagnosis/certain prognosis* as opposed to, for instance, *sudden onset/unclear diagnosis/uncertain prognosis* help to order the parents' experiences and re-establish their capacity to make plans for the future. Then, by carefully monitoring public performance, including the child's presentation to others (and the child's being judged by them in terms of 'how bad') and by striving in private to focus on how to do things just like others, as well as being as realistic as possible, the parents attempt to strike a balance between denial and overconcern ('Mr. and Mrs. J consistently called their son "fat boy", yet claimed to others that he was "just sturdy", and in addition told the child to tell others "you're not fat"': Voysey, 1975, p. 155). Lastly, legitimations which 'not only define what "is" but . . .ascribe "cognitive validity" and "normative dignity"' (1975, p. 163) come to be furnished by official agents.

Such accounts glorify the sacrifice which a disabled person's relatives willingly make of much of their own private lives (often referring to religious values), or they point out that nothing can replace a family environment; this implies that sending somebody to any kind of home away from home is but cruel selfishness. In this way, medical doctors, social workers, voluntary associations and also the media and other sources publicise moral virtue and become of help in the legitimation of suffering. Elsewhere, Voysey (1972a) ventures:

> that although the general decline of religion as historically the most effective instrument of legitimation is substantiated in the field of disability, three main elements of the Judaeo–Christian tradition seem to persist in present-day 'common-sense' thought. These are: first, the prevalence of the 'masochistic attitude', which entails the affirmation of the reality of any social world through the 'acceptance' of one's fate, challenges to that world being seen as illegitimate; secondly, specific theodicies (justifications of God in the face of evil), notably the endurance of suffering as a way of achieving various forms of compensation in this world rather than the next; and thirdly, the belief in the possibility of miracles. (Voysey, 1972a p. 534)

In order rationally to construct a reasonable account of one's illness (or one's child's disability), together with an equally reasonable account of one's normality (in terms of basic interactive competence), public morality has to be merged with private fate. This is often done as a construction of the history of the disease or disability, either establishing an afflicted person's responsibility for the condition or accruing this responsibility to others (or to no one, or 'God's will').

G. Williams (1984) argues that *narrative reconstruction* of the aetiology of his research subjects' rheumatoid arthritis must be understood by the sociologist as rational meaning construction. It is an attempt, says Williams, to close the gap between experiences (suffering) and accounts (explanation), making illness appear not so much as incomprehensible disruption of one's world but, rather, as perfectly predictable albeit deplorable. Williams depicts three types of such narrative reconstruction: one former worker blames his illness on adverse working conditions which readily matches his Communist views; one middle-aged woman understands her illness as stemming from suppression of her real self while being a wife and mother; and one elderly single woman feels chosen by God through the medium of her illness. Williams concludes:

> The body is not only an object amongst other objects in the world, it is also that through which our consciousness reaches out towards and acts upon the world . . . However, consciousness is itself biographically framed, so that consciousness of the body and the interpretations of its states and responses will lead us to call upon images of the private and public lives we lead. Narrative reconstruction is an attempt to reconstitute and repair ruptures between body, self and world by linking-up and interpreting different aspects of biography in order to realign present and past and self with society. (1984, p. 197)

In this vein, the theoretical reconstruction of the life-event approach contained in Gerhardt 1979b (p. 214) argues that reconciliation between act and meaning pattern takes place on three distinct levels. While *physiological* coping is located on the level of body functioning (and its explanations), *psychological* coping focuses upon what sense it makes for the individual to be in the world and to experience his or her fate as unfortunate or unforgivable, and *social* coping relates to active changes with which individuals wish to shape their environment (in relation to themselves) through purposeful behaviour meant to forestall trouble in the foreseeable future.

Normalisation. To put it crudely, phenomenology's trouble model focuses on normalisation where interactionism's crisis model focuses on stigmatisation. This concerns both the meaning of illness for a person's overall societal status and the place of illness in modern society. Phenomenology's concern with the taken-for-granted world is linked to the conditions under which society's members take each other's identities and expectations for granted. This links up with conditions under which these members take themselves for granted: that is, their bodies' reliable functioning as well as their mental health (interactive competence ascertained through others' affirmative reactions).

Normality, in this vein, is not necessarily tied to absence of illness. Rather, it designates the state of affairs where everybody can get on with their business and the taken-for-granted world is not visibly shaken. This excludes, as one may suspect, not sickness but trouble. (That the two partly overlap will not be stressed further.) Therefore, it is as trouble that illness becomes a problem disturbing the social order. It is as an agent for remedial actions successfully containing the disruptive consequences of trouble that medicine becomes a safeguard of the social fabric.

Insofar as it is a deviation from normality (i.e., as a condition causing trouble) that illness becomes sociologically important, no clear-cut distinction between illness and crime is needed. Both, at first, put into question a person's moral competence as a fully-fledged member of the collectivity, and both call for sensitive handling on the side of so-called troubleshooters or remedial agents making an initial diagnosis. As the person's normality is called into doubt, it is through collective acceptance of residual or full moral competence (possibly following therapeutic or corrective measures) that renormalisation on the side of the sick and/or criminal is achieved.

Normalisation thus shapes the state of illness (disability). At its roots are conditions under which members are integrated into any environment as useful and reasonable. This even applies to those who, through death, are excluded for good from the community. With respect to those who take their own lives, Garfinkel (1967b) argues that suicides take place in society and have to be validated by society. That is, a verdict must represent a reasonable account, satisfying the needs of practical reasoning. D. E. Smith (1983), by distinguishing between 'killing oneself' and 'committing suicide', also refers to the necessary step from the former to the latter as an accounting accomplishment. If the act of self-destruction is to be understood a suicide – that is, subsumed under the idea of more or less 'normal' suicide (considering circumstances typical for different sexes, age groups, etc.) – the account must be reasonable. With respect to the non-suicidal, Sudnow (1967) points out that death and dying (when taking place in a hospital) are also 'social states of affairs'. That is, structured ecological and occupational considerations influence the occurrence and visibility of a death in a county hospital (where he made his observations). Extended into the stage of 'bad news' and mourning, death as a social accomplishment acquires normalised features. These make it possible for the bereaved, hospital staff, and others to close the gap in their personal environments without the need to account for contingent circumstances further.

Therapy and clinical practice

In the work relating to therapy, two main topics are tackled. One is that of *organisational routines*, in hospitals and elsewhere. Its focus, among other things, are medical records (which, at first sight, appear to be prime sources for the sociologist wanting to understand medicine and then turn out to provide only insufficient information). The other topic is *talk*. Its analysis takes two forms. One group of researchers looks at how the doctor–patient communication displays systematic features of conversation, such as standardised opening and closing sequences, and how recipiency is signalled by body language keeping the conversation afloat. The other group of researchers is more interested in whether the patient's ideas and identity have a chance to structure his or her treatment, or whether and how the doctor has exclusive control over the dialogue and also over the outcome of the encounter.

The latter line of research aligns itself, to a certain extent, with the critical stance against the medical model often taken by symbolic interactionist thought (and, incidentally, also Marxism). In this, dramaturgical aspects of the construction of social reality are stressed. The use of the theatrical metaphor, if only indirectly, conveys the message that an element of manipulation cannot be denied in the doctor–patient relationship. Equally, among some researchers focusing upon hospital routines, especially in the context of medical education, a tendency prevails to take clinical practice as an effort of staging reality in a carefully monitored way such that the doctor's world becomes separate from that of the patient. In this, Freidson's (1970a, 1970b) idea is taken up that medicine defines the conditions of its own use and even defines its own concept of what is illness.

On the other hand, not all research understands phenomenology as an offshoot from 'symbolic interactionism'. Rather, for instance, Garfinkel in his classic essay on medical records produces a non-interactionist (and, therefore, non-'patient prone') view of the issue. This stance takes the standpoint of clinical medicine (inasmuch as a non-clinically trained person can). In this vein, what from a 'patient prone' perspective might appear as 'bad' records can be shown to have a sound rationale in safeguarding the high quality of medical care rendered to the patient. Equally, what by patients' standards appear to be unreasonable features of, for instance, 'therapy talk' in group sessions can be shown to make perfectly good sense under the auspices of clinical perspective. Also, that openings of a GP consultation are marked by brief silences, and that talk and recipiency sustain each other through body language, adds to the understanding of the way in which five-minute consultations can produce effective medical care. In this, the phenomenological approach insisting on the principles of indexicality and praxeology clarifies the particulars of clinical practice. The *immediate* viewpoint taken is not, however, that of clinical judgment (Feinstein, 1967): rather, the reference point is social organisations' dealings with tasks and troubles, related to a hospital's or surgery's taken-for-granted routines, and rules or measures available to neutralise or remedy disruptions.

In all, it appears that the phenomenological concern with therapy focuses on two main issues:

(a) understanding that treatment is embedded in taken-for-granted practices of clinical medicine;
(b) realisation that talk is an important dimension of medical work. Submitting it to conversational analysis can contribute to the understanding of medical accomplishments.

Organisational routines and normal illness

One attempt has been made to define what the term organisation means 'from within': that is, when practices of daily routine are made the focus of the analysis together with tasks and values which these are to accomplish (Bittner, 1965). All subsequent literature including Garfinkel (1967a) and Cicourel (1968) relies on Bittner's argument although it is possibly circular. Bittner starts by criticising Max Weber:

Weber, of course, intended to achieve an idealized reconstruction of organisation from the perspective of the actor. He fell short of attaining this objective precisely to the extent that he failed to explore the underlying common-sense presuppositions of his theory. He failed to grasp that the meaning and warrant of the inventory of the properties of bureaucracy are inextricably embedded in what Alfred Schutz called the attitudes of everyday life and in socially sanctioned common-sense typifications. Thus, if the theory of bureaucracy is a theory at all, it is a refined and purified version of the actors' theorizing. (Bittner, 1965, p. 246)

Bittner goes on to demand that the real scenes of action be studied by observing those at work deemed competent by the public and themselves (and the researcher) to represent and embody a particular organisation. This, however, must not lead to a theory of organisation but rather to an outline of a programme of enquiry as to how to study organisations (1965, p. 248). One would think that this can only apply to particular organisations which are studied; because a programme of enquiry is related to tasks and troubles characterising work in particular organisations, research must focus on concrete agencies of one kind or another. All organisations have a scheme (possibly a goal or designation of purpose), and the researcher, says Bittner, 'will look for a way the scheme is brought to bear on whatever happens within the scope of its jurisdiction' (1965, p. 249). For example, Cicourel (1968) argues, typifications used in police work with young offenders are, to a certain extent, specific to the particular office where they are used. Equally, P. Atkinson (1981a), describing medical education in the first year of clinical studies, points out that his observations may be typical for Scotland and, even more specifically, for Edinburgh, while only certain aspects may apply in England and elsewhere.

Bittner, however, places little emphasis on such contextual specificity. He seems to assume that any particular organisation is but an indexical expression of a general scheme of organisation. He states that there is:

a rational organizational scheme . . . as a generalised formula to which all sorts of problems can be brought for solution . . . More important than the open capacity and applicability of the formula is, however, the fact that problems referred to the scheme for solution acquire through this reference a distinctive meaning that they would not otherwise have. (1965, p. 249; emphasis omitted)

Fortunately, this 'theory of organisation' has not been applied by phenomenological research in its generalised version (which offers nothing beyond ,for instance, a systems perspective enlightened by Weber's ideal-type conceptualisation of bureaucracy).[29] Research concentrating on organisational routines is concerned with taken-for-granted practices of, say, the police or a teaching hospital or a social-work office or an ex-drug users' halfway house (Sudnow, 1967; Garfinkel, 1967a: partly Zimmerman 1969a, 1969b; Wieder, 1970).

Among organisational routines practised in medical settings, *case records* have been variously studied. The earliest work by Garfinkel (1967a) focuses upon the poor informational quality of medical records and asks the question – renouncing the temptation to criticise the doctors – in what way this 'bad' quality makes sense as rational and reasonable. Through analysing the uses to which records are put, primarily their being part of clinical work, Garfinkel succeeds in understanding that only by being 'bad' from the perspective of an outside observer can the records fulfil their function as ongoing documentation of clinical practice. In this, the 'bad' quality of the records best serves the purpose of clinical work: namely, successfully completing the patient's therapy and restoring his or her health or working capacity.

The idea is that only on the basis of background knowledge of practices (experience) entrenched in the medic by clinical education can the case-folder's contents be understood as reasonable. In fact, any clinic member treating the patient in the course of therapy finds here the relevant information assembled in a way which promotes as well as presupposes clinical reasoning. 'The possible use of folder documents', says Garfinkel, 'might be said to follow the user's developing interests in using them; not the other way around' (1967a, p. 204). And he goes on to explain:

> Most important, the competent reader is aware that it is not only that which the folder contains that stands in a relationship of mutually qualifying and determining reference, but parts that are not in it belong to this too. These ineffable parts come to view in the light of known episodes, but then, in turn, the known episodes themselves are also, reciprocally, interpreted in the light of what one must reasonably assume to have gone on while the case progressed without having been made a matter of record. (1967a, p. 205)

In the pattern of illness behind such notions, explains P. Atkinson (1981b), *time* is of crucial importance. In other words, illness as well as treatment, in a hospital setting but also elsewhere, are understood as a sequence of stages and symptoms, developing in a more or less expectable, orderly fashion. Physiological stages and physical (mental) signs which the patient displays therefore combine to make a developmental pattern which is the relevant unit of clinical judgment. This is constantly brought to students' attention by their teaching consultants and tutors, observes Atkinson.

That this is so, of course, is due to the need for medical students to learn clinical judgment. Its peculiarities have been outlined by Feinstein (1967). He points out that medicine is neither a natural nor a social science but, rather, an applied science in its own right.[30] Its baseline of knowledge is that of experience, as he aptly points out:

> In observing the illness of sick people, in formulating principles of therapeutic management, and in evaluating the subsequent results, clinicians constantly classify the clinical behavior of disease. These observations, formulations, and evaluations constitute a clinician's *clinical experience*. The appraised events of the past are the background for the judgment with which he designs, executes and appraises his future activities in the bedside experiments of clinical care. (The procedures of 'experience' and 'experiment' are so closely related that the same word is used in some languages such as French, to represent both activities). A clinician achieves his 'experience' by observing the illness of his patients, by categorizing the observations, by analysing the contents of the categories, by storing the information in his memory, and by later retrieving the data selectively when he engages in the reasoning processes of judgment. The information stored in this rational background includes many types of classified data, but the particular distinction of a clinician's experience is an intellectual collection of data in which disease is classified according to its clinical behavior. (Feinstein, 1967, p. 142)

From this vantage point, illnesses can be seen as developmental entities that may follow a most likely course as well as a range of possible deviations from *normal form* in any individual case. The clinician's task is to judge the actual trajectory of an illness in a patient against the pattern of potential developments which it can take; accordingly, the prognosis may be influenced by his or her treatment. In this, the patient's singular physiological conditions have to be matched against the most likely or *normal form* developmental pattern of the diagnosed disease. The aim is to understand the individual case through its similarities with, and deviations from, the *normal* illness which is the basic entity of clinical knowledge.

The latter idea, to be sure, is here phrased in the ethnomethodologists' rather than Feinstein's language. Adapted from Sudnow's (1965) notion of 'normal crime', P. Atkinson (1981b) and also Rees (1981) use the idea of 'normal illness'. By this is meant a construction of crime or illness along the lines of typical pre-diagnosis histories and post-diagnosis trajectories, typical categories of persons who get involved in them, typical outcomes relative to typical features of the incumbent, and so on. Atkinson highlights the task which this presents for clinical teaching:

> In the course of clinical teaching there is a constant tension between the definitions of 'normal' illness and the particularities of individual patients' presenting complaints. They are, of course, dialectically related: the underlying disease pattern can be discerned only through the particular manifestations, while the signs and symptoms gain their significance from the pattern of disease which they are held to index. (P. Atkinson, 1981b, p. 51)

In Atkinson's monograph on how clinical expertise (experience) is acquired by fourth-year medical students (1981a), not much further clarification of the normal illness pattern is given. The construction and reconstruction of medical reality is there explained under the auspices that clinical practice has dramaturgical aspects to it. They are seen to be serving a glossing function and, in the last instance, promoting professional dominance (see also P. Atkinson, 1977, and Atkinson, Reid and Sheldrake, 1977). More enlightening, in this respect, is Rees' (1981) short account of how medical records are used to facilitate hospital routine. Rees investigates the use of records; he finds that original history-taking is usually done by doctors who have little experience (or advanced medical students, as often happens in Germany); that initiating a record starts a patient's diagnosis; that records are used on ward rounds to familiarise the staff with how the case is developing; and that they serve as cues for estimating prognosis in subsequent outpatient treatment. The 'normal illness' idea is taken up from Sudnow's finding that public defenders make use of typifications of 'normal crimes':

> In the construction of the 'official version' of what happened, the Public Defender selects those elements from his client's story which are held in common with a general category of offense, such as petty larceny. This enables him to typify this particular offense as a normal crime. The advantage of this designation is that such cases are well recognized within the institution and can be processed in a non-problematic, routine way. In this way, the allocation of a patient to a diagnostic group can be seen as administrative device designed to facilitate the further management of the case. (Rees, 1981, p. 57)

In this, Rees points out that the 'normal illness' typification facilitates the patients' being processed through hospital treatment. Diagnosis as based on *normal form* disease entity, and hospital routine consisting of the therapies and facilities available (with clinical practices resulting therefrom) are closely inter-related. The medical or case record, in fact, is the link between them. It documents what is important about the patient's condition and what has been done to him or her (and to it). But it also documents (by being 'boring' and seemingly insufficient) the process of *clinical work* of which, above all, it is a part.

The issue has also been discussed for record keeping in general practice. Heath (1982), reporting on a study about some 4000 consultations in an urban, general-practice health centre, produces evidence that GPs use medical records in remarkably similar fashion. Not only their 'bad' quality (making them readable only by the treating GP) but also their function of promoting as well as documenting the patient career is similar to what has been found for clinical practice in hospitals. Particularly interesting is an example where Heath shows what Garfinkel hints at when including in the record the items not mentioned there. Heath interprets an entry such as '14/4/73 c. "badly bruised" cert. 1/4 Brook Centre' thus: 'The Brook Centre is a temporary shelter for women who have been battered by their husbands. The reference to Brook Centre provides a rich source of information for a reader assessing the doctor's thoughts on the patient's problem' (1982, p. 63). Equally self-explanatory are entries such as: '12/6/74 c. "can't get up" Librium (30) (10 m.g.) r/f A.A.' which contains a referral to Alcoholics Anonymous. A case where the entry is '2/11/72 c. "tired and weepy" r/f G.C.' (the initials of a psychiatric social worker) is understood as having been adjudged by the GP as serious enough not to be submitted to diagnosis by himself.

Thus, medical records are seen to provide a structure for treatment routines and facilitate (or generate) the smooth flow of clinical work. That this is less critical of the social-control function of records which are kept in all organisations (Wheeler, 1969) is due to what standpoint phenomenological as opposed to interactionist research takes. Garfinkel maintains that when the sociologist takes the side of the patient or, in fact, any non-clinical stance, he or she will end up criticising those aspects of medical records as insufficient and unsatisfactory which are the very safeguard of the record's clinical usefulness. That is, as soon as records *can* be read and understood by anyone, their benefit for clinical work is lost. The reason is that only under the conditions of the background expectancies constituting clinical medicine can the records' documentary function for the therapeutic purpose (and nothing else) be maintained. This puts in question sociologists' frequent belief that only by making records understandable to outsiders of an organisation (including, above all, sociologists themselves) could an agency's professional or discretionary power be reasonable.

The form and function of medical talk

Conversational analysis of doctor–patient communication has mainly developed as a sequel to the work of Sacks, Jefferson and Schegloff. But 'cognitive sociology' has also contributed, if only insofar as both editors of a recent reader on the linguistic properties of doctor–patient communication have received their PhD from University of California San Diego (UCSD), with (apparently) Cicourel as supervisor (Fisher and Todd, 1983).

Conversational analysis engages in linguistic study of taped or video-taped conversation material in order to ascertain formal invariant elements. For instance, turn taking, time sequence, the organisation of silence and other features have been shown to make interaction meaningful by following a tight scheme of discernible rules.

Such research on medical encounters has produced, among others, the following findings and insights: Heath (1981) shows how the organisation of talk in consultations marks an opening sequence. This is achieved by a silence of usually a fraction of a second between the greetings and the doctor's question about what the patient's trouble is. In this vein, Turner (1972) observes that in group-therapy sessions the cleavage between ordinary talk and 'therapy talk' makes it possible that the analyst may discuss a matter with the sessions' members who are all present, referring to it using the words 'before we start'. Equally, Stimson and Webb (1975), albeit not in terms of linguistic analysis, contribute material on the formulae with which a session or consultation can be concluded by a doctor. Schegloff and Sacks deal with this matter in their essay 'Opening Up Closings' (1973).

The discourse between doctor and patient is referred to as *micro-political*: in Todd's words 'influenced by and . . . reinforcer of cultural values of the society in which it takes place' (1983, p. 160). Todd undertakes to prove that such micro-political structure favours the doctor over the patient. Her approach consists of three steps of analysing tapes about contraceptive advice rendered in a public-health clinic and by a private gynaecologist. She first uses speech act analysis to prove how much more is decided in the encounter by the doctor than the patient; second, she uses an analysis of sequential properties of speech to come to the same conclusion; and, third, she uses an analysis of frames (i.e., contrasting a medical and a social frame of topics tackled). This shows that the social frame (marriage, job and so on) is more often introduced by the patient, and if the doctor introduces a social frame it concerns issues such as pregnancies being problematic when a woman is single. Todd interprets her findings in terms of power relationships which are cemented by linguistic structures. Her own rhetorical question as to their origin receives a partisan answer:

> Why are such doctor–patient encounters so systematically repeated? What could hold such a system together? . . . Sexism and elitism are certainly involved, and feminist theories invite consideration of reproduction as a political and social phenomenon. But a full description of oppressive and exploitative aspects of the encounter does not completely explain the structure of doctor–patient interaction . . . The doctor's exclusion of the realms of life to which the patients refer has origins that predate the sixteenth and seventeenth centuries, but advances associated with the scientific revolution are probably chiefly responsible for this exclusion. (Todd, 1983, pp. 182–3)

An equally critical but less ideological standpoint is taken by Frankel's (1984) attempt to understand the medical encounter through sentence-by-sentence micro-interactional analysis. His aim in reconstructing linguistic regularities from examples of doctor–patient conversations is to prove that the doctor's supremacy is enhanced or possibly even generated by speech habits typical for medical encounters. Frankel is of the opinion that the doctor ought to follow up and take seriously each answer of a patient (and not just get on with completing a check list). Like Todd (1983, 1984), Frankel finds that doctors ask many more questions than patients, and they get theirs answered (and may acknowledge the answer received by an 'OK' or 'Uhhuh') while the patients often do not get fully-fledged answers to their questions, or may even be talked down to in the reply. Implicitly, it seems, Frankel advocates a change in the 'set of assumptions' governing health care from what he calls 'neutral' to what he calls 'affective' (1984, p. 160).[31]

As for the 'fine structure' not only of verbal interchange but also gaze and other gestures, Frankel (1983) provides an analysis of how touch and gaze are coordinated with talk in a most artful way between doctor, child-patient and onlooking mother. Equally, Heath (1984) shows how the doctor's posture and gaze are interpreted by the patient as acknowledging recipiency of what he or she has said and thus validation of what has been said. Both, doctor and patient, display recipiency as well as availability for the other's talk, and only in rare circumstances can the latter clash with the former. What Heath particularly points out from his audiovisual data (which he offers to post to readers on request) is that the doctor's turning away from the patient, reading case notes and so on is followed by stuttering on the patient's side which usually produces the doctor's gaze as signal of renewed recipiency. Also, in the opening sequence, the doctor's reading of the record while the patient enters provides an opportunity for the patient, Heath argues, to land on a chair and arrange his posture such that once the doctor's gaze has shifted towards the now 'ready' patient the consultation can start.

Similar research has been conducted in Germany with more 'micro-political' and less 'micro-analytical' intent. Gück, Matt and Weingarten (1983) produce linguistic evidence from ward rounds in various intensive care units. They come to the conclusion that the structural organisation of talk during ward rounds may be evidence that this is predominantly a doctor-shaped encounter. Where patients enter into it with self-initiated speech at all and do not simply answer a doctor's question with minimum words, they are compelled to fit their statements into a strictly medical framework. This amounts to usually not more than one sentence since otherwise they risk being cut off by the doctors who may start talking among themselves while the patient has not yet finished.

In these studies, with the exception of Heath, a critical overtone against clinical practice is present. C. West (1984a) explicitly concerns herself with 'Medical Misfires: Mishearings, Misgivings, and Misunderstandings in Physician–Patient Dialogue'. Fisher (1984) ventures that institutional authority explains the skewed structure of discourse. The crucial issue critically pointed out by her and various other authors is *asymmetry*, implying 'control over topic and flow' for the doctor but none for the patient (1984, p. 217). She phrases the issue rather bluntly: 'When the patient asks questions . . ., the doctor, acting on the assumption that he knows what she needs to know, controls the information she receives. When the doctor asks questions . . ., the patient, acting on the assumption that full disclosure is appropriate, provides the information' (Fisher, 1984, p. 220).

The purpose of medical practice.

The analysis of talk follows two formats. On the one hand, Heath makes it clear how turn-taking takes place on finer levels even than verbal discourse. On the other hand, authors like Todd or Frankel put forward a partisan view favouring the patient's perspective in what is perceived as a male dominated, impersonal doctor-centred encounter.

Among the two views, the emphasis on the patients' rights and wrongs does not represent the standpoint of clinical practice. It is a view imputed to data transcribed from audio-tapes and video-tapes, but not necessarily following the sole intention of showing how prudently the interchange unfolds. Neither Garfinkel's stance on the good reasons for 'bad' records nor Cicourel's insights into coding during medical history-taking are used here. Rather, the authors derive their rationale of the material from their feeling that elitism or sexism should not occur in medical practice (or anywhere, for that matter). They surmise in this that emotionality would be appreciated by many as an atmosphere of friendliness. The disjuncture between the patient's and doctor's world is highlighted from a partisan sociologist point of view merging with the researchers' own more or less political standpoint.

Garfinkel explicitly cautions against such external viewpoints. He warns that the clinician who is responsible for the patient's diagnosis and therapy entertains a completely different perspective from the sociologist who looks at medical records or transcribed dialogue (1967a, p. 207). The 'artful practices' which accomplish medical interaction cannot be discovered if the sociologist 'knows' beforehand that his or her data represent the world of elitism and sexism. This limits the openness with which the researcher can learn through careful scrutiny of the reality-construction process how the interactants themselves make sense of their encounter. In other words, for Garfinkel, the sociologist's work consists of unravelling the taken-for-granted assumptions of the interaction such that the sociologist can understand how it comes about that the interactants attend to the situation in a way which he may and must observe. In short, inherent rationality of the action is presupposed, and the sociologist's task is to document it as one of mutual competent participation. Sociologists, in this, refrain from putting themselves on the pedestal of 'knowing better' than the interactants themselves.

In contrast some, especially in the case of feminist authors undertaking to analyse fragments of dialogue linguistically, argue that such logic of impartiality favours an unjust and unreasonable status quo. Critically refusing to accept the status quo has been suggested to American sociology by Wolff in an article written shortly after the Second World War. He surmises that by not asking certain questions sociology becomes a partisan of the status quo, however unjust it may be. For instance, blacks or others may be seriously disadvantaged: by taking existing realities for granted, sociology forgoes its chance to at least hint at 'man's tragic nature' as the origin of existing injustice and inequality. He clarifies:

I am not suggesting that the focus upon men's tragic nature ought to inform American sociology as one of its conceptions, but only that in so far as it does not, American sociology, for reasons which a sociocultural interpretation might reveal, is not objective in its orientation because [it is] overlooking one side of man which to at least some 'trained observers' is important. (K. Wolff, 1946, p. 551)

It may be argued that to analyse medical practice as 'artful contextual accomplishment', as Garfinkel, Cicourel and others do, means to indirectly strengthen the reality of sexist and elitist features of medical encounters. On the other hand, it may be held against such criticism that the purpose of clinical medicine is to get the patient better. So long as medical work achieves this aim, the scrutiny of individual practices by the sociologist under more or less Utopian principles of democratic dialogue or interchange can be called unfair or unsuitable.

In this vein, the question must be asked what the various authors perceive as the main purpose of medical practice. If it is the 'artful accomplishment' of clinical work of the highest possible standard of expertise, the sociologist making sense of the doctor's services clearly must emulate the *action rationale* acquired through medical education. If the purpose of medical work is defined as the patient's satisfaction, however, a different picture ensues. It has often been demonstrated and is widely accepted as a fact that clinical settings produce inequality between patients' and doctors' influence on relevant decisions. This skewed situation is taken to reduce patients' satisfaction, although recent research in Germany has shown that nurses perceive their patients as being dissatisfied with the unpleasantness of Intensive Care Unit (ICU) care while patients themselves, to a large extent, report high levels of satisfaction (Klapp, 1985). Be this as it may, what is important when distinguishing between the 'adherents'and 'opponents' of the status quo is that their ideas differ with regard to what the purpose of medical practice is. While some authors see it as primarily improvement of patients' condition, others see the patients' satisfaction as much more imperative.

The distinction, to a certain extent, is one between *medically* effective as opposed to *sociologically* approved criteria of successful doctor–patient interchange. In a recent polemic contrasting the viewpoints of medicine and sociology, Freidson (1983b) stresses that both harbour myths. Medicine, he says, entertains the myths that only doctors can make reliable and valid statements about medical and health care while sociology can be learned by everyone without training, and that medical sociology ought to have an ancillary function in medicine. Sociology, on the other hand, tends to confuse logical constructs and distinctions of theory with practical human activity, to promote the myth that a critical position truly helps actually to improve the character of human life, and to venture that since value-free sociology is impossible sociologists must not only choose their values but also actively engage in advancing them. Freidson suggests sidestepping both arrays of myths by introducing sociology into health care as a *research* endeavour, 'in its disciplined character – its systematic and self-conscious methods of data-collection and its theoretically organized methods of analysis' (1983b, p. 219).

The only difficulty with this may lie in the nature of medicine itself. Freidson assumes that, if the distinction is between the natural and the social sciences (leaving out the arts, in this context), medicine may gain from partly overcoming its narrowly natural-science based model of illness explanation, and adopt more social-science prone knowledge. But Wieland (1975) argues convincingly that medicine represents neither a natural science nor a social science (notwithstanding how much it allegedly is predisposed in either direction). Rather, medicine constitutes an *action science*: that is, a realm of practical decisions based on a distinction between pathological and normal that has its sources in experience and experiment. To put it differently, medicine can *rely* on natural and/or social sciences which foster reliable models for the explanation of clinical observation. But the core of medical work is the situational *use* of this knowledge in ever-changing, albeit routinised, circumstances. Such use functions to make sense of *individual* patients' symptoms or suffering under the guiding perspective of how to relieve or cure them. Garfinkel comes quite near to Wieland's clarification by emphasising the *practical* nature of the clinical endeavour, and its ongoing processual, but sociologically not amenable, character.

Chapter 11
Phenomenology and the Issues of Responsibility

Drawing together the insights which the phenomenological view suggests, it emerges that it presents a new idea of aetiology and' therapy. Structural functionalism and 'symbolic interactionism' are linked with each other in many ways, although often not noticed by their protagonists. For instance, the idea of the sick role is adopted in both approaches and it is incorporated into different conceptualisations of the social order which both use the system idea. In contradistinction, the phenomenological paradigm is only rarely concerned about the sick role. In fact, illness is frequently not distinguished from crime. Both are viewed under the perspective that it is the *same* social processes which make for their intersubjective construction.

The starting-point is normality where acts which may break the trust of others, or threaten to do so, are made amenable by 'techniques of neutralisation' or deeds of recompense. Normality may contain 'sick behaviour' in the sense that symptoms are incorporated into lower levels of everyday functioning. In normal everyday life, conflict may abound, or exploitation or degradation of others may be widespread. Only when *help* is sought would – structurally speaking – trouble become obvious. At this point, mechanisms of re-establishing trust are set in motion. Under the auspices that illness constitutes trouble – causing pain, suffering and anxiety – a *therapeutic trust* relationship helps to bridge the gap until the individual has overcome the condition causing the trouble. The theoretical stance of ethnomethodology places considerable emphasis on the fact that trouble as well as trust are related to modes of speaking about them. This, however, does not entail relativity in the sense that the knowledge used to produce either can be or should be seen as insufficient or unsatisfactory. Rather, every act needs accounting in order to be accepted as meaningful, and health-related interchange is no exception. Eventually, it comes down to stressing the importance of what Garfinkel calls conventionality. Conventionality as an aspect of making

229

sense of one's body and world governs the identification of trouble, and it also informs the establishing of trust.

To be sure, this is always an *interpersonal* process. 'Symbolic interactionism' stresses reflexivity: that is, the capacity of people to make themselves objects in thinking and imaging in order to conceptualise how reciprocity between ego and alter renders illness incumbency a *social* process. Phenomenology has a different notion. The key is the taken-for-granted nature of the everyday world. It acquires a curiously unchanging continuity as long as individuals react to each other under the idealised assumption that their perspectives are perfectly reciprocal. As soon as this presupposition constituting intersubjective reality construction is threatened, however, chaos looms large. Mechanisms of mending the broken fabric of the taken-for-granted world set in. Medicine as well as the law (plus judicial system) fulfil the function of re-establishing trust where trouble has proved unmanageable among those immediately concerned. Also, these professional institutions which re-establish trust (namely, trust in the general order of society and also trust in their functioning to establish this order) themselves provide and use trust to fulfil this purpose. This befits their nature that, as organisations, they consist of practices organised towards re-establishing trust-prone conditions. The knowledge which they apply is of an eminently practical kind, and ought to be understood from the standpoint that it serves to organise actions in an interpersonally rational and accountable way. Under these general assumptions, the literature analyses some aspects of hospital care, on the one hand, and talk as the main feature of general practice, on the other hand.

This chapter investigates implications and corollaries of this. First, the question is raised of how unitary the trouble–trust model is, then the contribution to general sociological theory is outlined. Finally, the crucial problem with the trouble–trust paradigm is discussed: namely, that it is meant to apply to illness and crime *alike*.

On the question of model(s)

Above, it has been argued that only one model of aetiology and therapy (the trouble approach) is used in the phenomenological theorising about topics of medical sociology. However, the point can also be made that, in fact, two explanatory models present themselves *in statu nascendi*.

Of these, the first may be called that of *clinical reasoning*. Its aetiology ideas are contained in, in the first instance, the many statements by Garfinkel on the ways in which jurors or members of the Suicide Prevention Team or students deciding upon the appropriateness of programmed advice go about assembling cues for the right way to perceive and define a problem, and how to resolve it in due course. In this, normality can be understood as artful management of one's own or other people's troubles which is part and parcel of one's private or professional life. Furthermore, Cicourel's elaborate reflections highlight the linguistic process of how the contents of a medical interview become coded in disease categories which, in turn, contain 'normal illness' as well as contextual contingent elements. This primarily concerns normality where health is converted into illness. In the event, the state of illness emerges as an issue of moral virtue defining an actor's perceived competence as a person. The clinical-reasoning conceptualisation of therapy brings out the autonomy of the decision-making process in professional medicine. It highlights the fact that practical matters of accomplishing rather than simply accounting are of importance (i.e., 'doing medicine' is what is referred to). The sociologist is a stranger to the world of clinical reasoning where he cannot help but take the perspective of the patient. The latter may be the object or even the subject of medicine but lacks the knowledge and training for effective, technologically competent self-treatment (which rules out 'democratic sharing' of appropriate treatment decisions). This entails that the doctor's responsibility for the patient's well-being is behind his or her apparent dominance in medical encounters. This standpoint can be brought off by a linguistic analysis of doctor–patient communication such as that by Heath (1981, 1982, 1984).

A second explanatory model may be called that of *micropolitics*. Its view upon normality and the cycles of help is such that continuous bickering and infighting are going on in our accustomed world. Such *homo homini lupus* experiences decide who imposes whose account regarding a trouble on whom, and in what way. The view is one of basic conflict. Consensus is merely a stalemate in conflictual relations, brought about by considerations of expediency or impression management helping to maintain the social order. In this the diagnosis of an illness equals fixing a label on someone who thus becomes a certified troublemaker. The state of illness, therefore, is one where the necessity of legitimising one's suffering as well as one's normalised competence is of prime importance. In the related view on therapy, dramaturgical and manipulative efforts play a major role. Medical records are interpreted as a means of controlling the patient, and placing stigma upon him or her even beyond that person's spell in hospital (or, for that matter, prison). Clinical experience is taken to be simply a mystification of perfectly simple and learnable techniques of handling patients' complaints and conditions. This is taken to mean that professional dominance finds many outlets. One example is doctor–patient communication where asymmetry is observed and studied on a linguistic micro-interactional level. Eventually, sexism and elitism as ideological attitudes of doctors are traced to defaults of the natural science-based cognitive model of modern medical thinking.

Both views, according to their own persuasion, emanate from Garfinkel's and Cicourel's writings which, in turn, derive from Schütz's philosophy of the social world. However, this may be questioned. Schütz in his article on rationality in the everyday world (1943) makes it plain that the taken-for-granted quality of 'what everyone knows' plays a major part in social encounters. It ascertains, for those actors involved, that a situation is governed by a reciprocity of mutual perspectives, by an assumption that they could at will repeat any present encounter in the future, and so on. Thus it is not through dramaturgical, let alone manipulative behaviour that the interactants convince each other of the seriousness of their motives. Also, it is not (only) through accounts which they give about what they are doing that interactants prove to themselves and others that theirs is rational acting. Rather, rationality is intrinsic in social action because it draws upon sizeable aspects of knowledge 'which everyone knows' (out of which, in due course, accounts may be constructed which document and ascertain one's professed sanity, reasonableness, etc.).

The micro-politics view on the aetiology-therapy process, it seems, misses out on these 'deep structure' criteria of action rationality. They insist that the sociologist using social-science knowledge is able to distinguish between appropriate and overly dominant behaviour, and judge what is rational and what is irrational. In this, the micro-politics view relies on *accounts* of actions seemingly offering their reasonable rationale. For instance, McCleary (1977) uses parole officers' accounts of what they do when he wishes to explain their discretionary use of clients' (criminal) records. Likewise, P. Atkinson (1981a) gives evidence on how clinical experience is acquired by quoting medical students' reports of their experiences. Finally, linguistic micro-interactional analyses of doctor–patient dialogue often quote verbatim material in a way that seems to make obvious the particularly 'male chauvinist' or 'professionally dominant' language of a physician.

However, it ought to be pointed out that accounts are only a part of the indexical structure. They do not, in fact, constitute its essence: that is, in principle, the act/utterance and the pattern/rule of which it is a document (be it realisation or violation) are two separate matters. They are linked together through a situation where interactants rely on taken-for-granted background knowledge when doing their duty and when acknowledging this. The accounts which they give to themselves or others in such encounters may serve to legitimise a particular documentary relationship chosen. Or an account may bridge a presumed inconsistency between an act and a rule (expectation) in such a way that no gap remains. That is, accounts are themselves devices which serve to confirm taken-for-granted background expectations. They fulfil this function by *not* putting into the focus of talk those aspects tacitly assumed to prevail in every reasonable encounter of a particular kind.

The micro-political view disregards this special quality of rationality of the everyday world. According to Schütz (1943), and Garfinkel's adaptation of Schütz's thought (1967a), such rationality provides motivation to action. But, at the same time, it ascertains that action motives do not lie open for preformulated questioning by a social researcher. No exhaustive understanding or unproblematic explanation is built into the linguistic part of the utterance accounting, ready for the inquisitive sociologist (or, for that matter, any investigator or co-actor who happens to want to know why someone did something to someone else).

Possibly, the *micro-political* view makes a rationality assumption. But it is important to point out that it is different from that which Schütz uses to promulgate the phenomenological perspective on social order. The *micro-political* view's conception of rationality is that of its sociologically explicable nature. It surmises that sexism, elitism and capitalism prevail, and its interest in medical goings-on is geared towards 'total' institutions or exploitative self-referent behaviour. It appears that the *micro-political* view more or less inadvertently assimilated Goffman's interactionist approach, including his partisan perspective presupposing maltreated or subdued patients (troublemakers). Occasionally, conflict-theory or Marxist thoughts are also used to belabour the point that interactants' interests are basically irreconcilable. It must be added, however, that secondary literature, such as Denzin (1969, 1970) and Churchill (1971), makes it easy for the micro-political view to mistake politically enlightened interactionism for consciously humane phenomenology.

In the remarks here on what the phenomenological perspective on illness explanation has to offer for general sociological theory, we shall concentrate on one of the two emergent models proposed. The following only relates to the 'clinical reasoning' view. What could be said on the general-sociology implications of the micro-political view might be somewhat similar to the comments on the interactionist crisis model in Part II, and the conflict-theory domination–deprivation model (see below, Part IV).

The contribution to general sociological theory

If the question is asked what the contribution is which the phenomenological viewpoint on illness makes to general sociology, the issue of *trouble* must be understood in its theoretical viability. First, institutions are defined through the *tasks* which they accomplish. These, in turn, are understood as ways of dealing with trouble. What, then, is trouble in such terms? For instance, to starve or to be homeless is trouble, and agriculture and housing, related to the food and construction industries, fulfil their tasks of forestalling such troubles. However, could not a poor family be unable to avail themselves of food and shelter? The industries' task fulfilment would then remain ineffective. To bridge such incongruency, in turn, is the task of yet another set of institutions: the welfare state. A concatenated system of organisations including, among others, the police and medicine, make for a chain of trouble-related task realms building up society's institutional structure.

In this, as Cicourel was the first to point out, a certain variability in the definitional scope with which troubles are diagnosed and assigned may be noted. To refer a trouble to the 'right' agency or put it on to the 'right' procedure of 'troubleshooting' is a discretionary act requiring high levels of professional expertise as well as on-the-job experience. Thus, the variability of contextual alignment of a trouble with an action type ('surface level') or a diagnosis-therapy course of action ('deep structure') makes it possible that a problem is solved in the best interest of the client as well as the wider social order.[32]

However, the theoretical import of trouble does not end here. For Garfinkel, trouble is the counterpart of *trust*. Trust is the prerequisite of those taken-for-granted sides of any situation which are embodied in the tacit background expectancies. They constitute the 'common culture' which is the very foundation of any and all social life. It is here, of course, that Garfinkel takes up the challenge to overcome his mentor Parsons' theory by providing the missing link: making sense of Parsons' thought *without* the ill-fated recourse to psychoanalytic thinking. At the outset of his second major outline of his ideas, the essay 'A Conception of, and Experiments with "Trust" as a Condition of Stable Concerted Actions' (1963, with a previous version having been presented at the 1957 Annual Conference of the American Sociological Association at Washington, DC), Garfinkel has this to say:

> Parsons' (1953) decision to incorporate the entirety of common culture into the superego has as its obvious interpretive consequence that the way a system of activities is organised means the same thing as the way its organisational characteristics are being produced and maintained. Structural phenomena such as income and occupational distributions, familial arrangements, class strata, and the statistical properties of language are emergent products of a vast amount of communicative, perceptual, judgmental, and other 'accommodative' work whereby persons, in concert, and encountering 'from within the society' the environments that the society confronts them with, establish, maintain, and restore, and alter the social structures that are the assembled products of temporally extended courses of action directed to these environments as persons 'know' them. Simultaneously these social structures are the conditions of persons' concerted management of these environments. (1963, pp. 187–8)

Following on from this direct recourse to Parsons to establish his own point of view as sequel to that of his mentor (just replacing the psychoanalytical by a phenomenological grounding of the idea of motivation), Garfinkel introduces the importance of *trust* in this. The starting-point is Durkheim's notion of anomie. He explains:

> To aid in locating events that must be altered to produce anomic states, I have conceived the phenomenon of trust. I shall begin by consulting games. From an analysis of their rules, the concept of the 'constitutive order of events' of a game will be developed . . . I shall extend what we learn about how trust is a condition of 'grasping' the events of games to the case of how trust is a condition for 'grasping' the events of daily life. (Garfinkel, 1963, p. 190)

No doubt trust, for Garfinkel, is a condition of, and also produces compliance with, rules (in games and everyday life). Only by trusting that another will comply with the rules just like ourselves do we feel able and willing to comply with games' rules. *This*, in Garfinkel's terms, is what produces norm conformity as well as reciprocal compliance with value orientation patterns in stable interaction. Only through introducing the concept of trust, Garfinkel suggests, could the clandestinely Hobbesian solution of the

Hobbesian problem of order have been avoided by Parsons in his *Structure of Social Action*. Besides, no psychoanalytical legitimation for the resultant image of residual conflict in the ego–alter dyad would have been necessary later.

Alas, Garfinkel has been widely misunderstood in his efforts to provide nothing but an uncontroversial theory of how the social order is possible. Instead, he has occasionally been labelled a 'dangerous man'.[33.] Or is there an understandable aspect to ethnomethodology's being perceived as dangerous, or anomie-producing? Of course, this label particularly prevailed in the heyday of phenomenology's 'revolutionary' impact (i.e., in the late 1960s and early 1970s).

Gouldner, in his *The Coming Crisis of Western Sociology* (1970), issued stern warnings against ethnomethodology. The experiments concerning trust which Garfinkel uses to prove his, so-to-speak, extra-Parsonian solution of the Parsonian problem were the target of Gouldner's warnings. He saw in these experiments a most despicable decay of decency in the sociologist's professional conduct. Garfinkel's experiments were judged as immoral and irresponsible.

No mention is made of this in the secondary literature on Garfinkel or on ethnomethodology in general. For instance, Heritage (1984) only hails Garfinkel's achievement to have focused on issues so mundane that 'a special effort of the imagination is required to notice them, let alone perceive their significance' (1984, p. 304). But it is also likely that the secondary literature's somewhat naive appraisal as well as occasionally wholesale condemnation miss the crucial point. It seems that Garfinkel's emphasis on the duality of trouble and trust relates to a theory of society and not just to interactive regularities. In this is indeed incorporated a view on the eminently political nature of everyday life and, in particular, the insight that society's influence on individual behaviour does not stop at the boundaries of the social system.

A book on National Socialism may serve as evidence of the implicitly political message in the trouble–trust view of social order. F. Weinstein's (psychoanalytically inclined) book entitled *The Dynamics of Nazism* (1980) investigates repercussions of the trusted and taken-for-granted everyday culture on the definition of action-prone wrong-doing, or trouble. He questions how the Nazi crimes could be tolerated by a, however partially informed, whole society. He argues that the *common-sense world* consisting of accounts rendering acts meaningful has a curiously tenacious quality safeguarding the sense of continuity of its members. Anti-Semitism, Weinstein maintains, was part of the common-sense world for wide circles of the population at the time, including many intellectuals. But so was the understanding that restraints were indispensable regarding what any human being could do to another if traditional values of decency and dignity were to be preserved. Thus, many even among the persecuted were not willing to believe until very late in the process that the Nazis meant what they proclaimed. Rather, they preferred to think that the Nazis boasted of atrocious intentions they would never put into practice. Weinstein explains:

> People accommodate events to their needs by common sense explanations in language made available by the culture . . . Most Germans just wanted the crisis resolved, and they took Hitler at his word: Standing above interests and parties, he would serve all of them alike. Thus, people saw the violence and they heard the threats, but they wanted to treat these things as isolated occurrences and not as part of a pattern, particularly if these occurrences did not threaten them. Ordinary German citizens had to make sense of the world they lived in, in terms they were familiar with, and so they told themselves that one cannot make an omelette without breaking eggs, one cannot clean house without chipping some porcelain, one cannot plane wood without shavings, the sickest cases get the strongest medicine, the devil is driven out by Beelzebub, and so on. It was mostly a matter of common sense: What was Hitler to do anyway, kill all the Jews? (F. Weinstein, 1980, p. 23–4).

By incorporating five well-known sayings which (except for the medical metaphor) are still used in present-day Germany, Weinstein captures the flavour of people's accounts from their diaries during the events and hapless recollections from exile (see 1980, p. 43). The accomplishment of Weinstein's book is that he does not treat these as the shortsighted self-interested protestations of a decaying bourgeois class. Instead, he suggests that accounting of one's surrounding world in terms of the taken-for-granted real and unreal is a mundane accomplishment of undeniable necessity. (In this, mass murder would clearly figure as unreal at the time because monstrosities of that order would not be accrued a chance of realisation among a nation of decent civilised citizens.) However, at the time, Weinstein argues, it was also accepted that renewal must happen if the prevailing crisis of society was to be overcome. The resultant array of ideas entered into the account structure justifying the common-sense world which otherwise threatened to fall apart and reveal an abyss of anomie and chaos:

> The ideas of blood, soil, folk, nation, expansionism, revanche, military prowess, cultural or racial superiority, etc., fed into and lent structure, coherence, and a sense of continuity in a situation in which people were

threatened by the loss of control over personal, social, and national destiny, a result of real environmental failure, the last and potentially most damaging in a series of failures reaching back to the defeat in the Great War. Those elements from the historical past that the Nazis used for their own ends may have been dramatic and available, but as with racism, they were not always the most important by any means. It was the effects of the unique, immediate situation that allowed culturally familiar expressions to be used as if the meanings were constant or everyone meant the same thing by them. (F. Weinstein, 1980, p. 78)

Phrased with Garfinkel's duality of trust and trouble, Weinstein argues as follows: trust was virtually preserved in this society which felt threatened by discontinuity and imminent economic, if not cultural, extinction through the definition of trouble being accepted (or at least not openly contradicted) which was put forward by the then imperative National Socialist authorities. That is, 'the' Jew had been designated as 'the' trouble because through Jewish striving towards world supremacy Germany had allegedly lost the First World War, was later impoverished through repara-tion payments and eventually suffered the consequences of 'Black Friday' on Wall Street after October 1929. At this point, Wein-stein brings in Hitler's personal teachings but makes it clear that they served the purpose of restoring trust by identifying the presumed source of trouble which needed eliminating:

Hitler tried to restore an ideological conception of the world sufficiently stable for people to experience society again as a safe, supportive, enhancing place, and he was quite deliberate in the way he appeared to people and what he told them. Thus, in his proclamation to the German nation, February 1, 1933, Hitler spoke of unity, energy, vitality, discip-line, honor, sacrifice, the legitimate suppression of enemies, the termi-nation of a chaotic era, the recovery of imperishable virtues that had given rise earlier to imperishable accomplishments . . . Hitler meant to save the Aryan race, and his radical posture to the world was so thoroughly rationalized, integrated, and controlled, and from his own standpoint scientifically justified, that there was no need to keep his anti-Semitism public at all times, to react to every 'provocation' or to rant before every audience . . . If Hitler's behavior can be conceived as pathological, it was a pathology of ideals . . . For the radical Nazis the present did not gain dignity from the past as such, but only from the eternal. The struggles of life made sense only as evidence of an abiding reality, that is, as the repetition of archaic struggles compelled by the blood and not by historically derived social conflict. Hence the image of the Eternal Jew seeking in his boundless arrogance to ruin Aryan blood. A struggle for the blood, and the space needed for it to flourish, was essential and primary, and everything else secondary. As Hitler put it, anything that is not race in this world is trash . . . But the remarkable feats of violence nevertheless failed to abate anxiety over penetration, contamination, and degeneration by World Jewry, a highly organized, demonic force. For no matter how many Jews they killed, the world still could not be brought in line with their wishes, and if that was so, if people resisted, then the Jews were still powerful and, relative to Germany's growing weakness, perhaps more powerful than ever. The killing in principle was endless. (F. Weinstein, 1980, pp. 82, 94, 102, 125, 147)

Weinstein's compelling account of the function for social stability of what he calls *ideology* (using Mannheim's term rather than Marx's) gives an example of how a trust–trouble view of society can prove helpful in understanding the complex goings-on of at least one society in the modern world. It seems feasible to generalise from Weinstein's insights using Garfinkel's formulations as a guideline. In this, the relative autonomy of the taken-for-granted world, and its curious elusiveness regarding the penetrating gaze of the social scientist, ought to be taken as to-be-explained features in their own right.

The argument here now returns to the *situational* aspect of trouble–trust disruptions in order to point out that another contribution of this to general sociological theory can be envisaged. Garfinkel argues that rationality is something which is not achieved by conscious planning and purposeful behaviour. Rather, rationality is often only a retrospectively recognisable feature of flexible situational decisions in more or less known circumstances. Thus the nature of society is such that it comes about through accepted practices and ideas which are used to produce routine actions. But these happen against a background of the constant danger of disruption which also looms large in the minds of those who follow everyday rules. In essence, although every bit of behaviour can be traced to society's mores (structural rules) being situationally accomplished, one may also argue that every bit of behaviour breaks new ground and reaffirms the mores if only by not negating them.

Maybe it was this dual idea which appealed to students in 1968: on the one hand, that every bit of behaviour may be found to display formal properties of structured social action and, on the other hand, that action results from decision-making in a process of flexible reaction to whatever others do.

Arendt writes in an essay entitled *On Violence* written in 1969:

Violence, being instrumental by nature, is rational to the extent that it is effective in reaching the end that must justify it. And since when we act we never know with any certainty the eventual consequences of what we are doing, violence can remain rational only if it pursues short-term goals . . . To ask the impossible in order to obtain the possible is not always counter-productive . . . Since the tactics of violence and disruption make sense only for short-term goals, it is even more likely, as was recently the case in the United States, that the established powers will yield to nonsensical and obviously damaging demands . . . if only such 'reforms' can be made with comparative ease, then that violence will be effective with respect to the relatively long-term objective of structural change. (Arendt, 1970, pp. 79–80)

In this statement lies an explanation of why ethnomethodology appealed to radical students. With its focus upon the dialectical relationship between *trouble* and *trust*, it constituted a rationale for what was in the students' minds. Many times their demonstrations had the purpose of creating trouble such that official agents would feel obliged to bring about reforms in order to re-establish trust in university education, for instance, or regarding various rules and regulations.

Also, as Arendt points out, everything beyond short-term goals did not have much chance although this was attempted with the same vigour. Arendt inadvertently touches upon the somewhat tragic fate which befell both the student movement as well as ethnomethodology. Ethnomethodology's seemingly 'revolutionary'touch was appreciated as long as the radical student movement lasted, but its serious contribution to the development of sociological thought never seems to have earned the praise which it justly deserves. Both the student movement and ethnomethodology, at the time, only managed to create trouble as a short-term disruption demanding ameliorative actions from official authorities, or that Sociology Departments adjust their practices to become more flexible or well-intentioned. But nothing more resulted in spite of the considerable ribbles.

The truly innovative achievement which Garfinkel obviously made during his time as a graduate student at Harvard was that he was the first to convert Schutz's phenomenology into a set of hypotheses for empirical research, and he also managed to find a way to design experimental and quasi-experimental projects serving this knowledge aim in a most cogent way. Through this, a long train of research endeavours has been set in motion. The starting point seems to be Garfinkel's PhD work (Cicourel, 1964, p. 235), then comes the research on jurors in the early 1950s which obviously took place before Garfinkel went to California (Heritage, 1984), then come the studies on suicide verdicts, and so on. Quickly students and colleagues gathered to join in the work. Scholars such as Cicourel, Sacks, Sudnow, Zimmerman, Pollner and many others began to share Garfinkel's interest in the early 1960s or earlier. In Europe, the spark caught fire in 1968, and in 1970 Silverman's book on organisations was the first to introduce the approach (although in a watered-down version), soon followed by research conducted by Voysey, Dingwall and others. In Germany, a special issue of the journal *Kölner Zeitschrift für Soziologie und Sozialpsychologie* published in 1973 documented a sizeable number of ongoing ethnomethodologically oriented research projects, mainly on psychiatric topics.

However, the phenomenological issue, that there is a taken-for-granted world not readily opening itself up to the investigative mind, is often ignored or bypassed in these studies. Interestingly enough, the problem is discussed extensively in Berger and Luckmann's adaptation of Schütz's (and, to a certain extent, Husserl's) standpoint in their book *The Social Construction of Reality* (1966), which does not even mention Garfinkel's pursuits. It is true, Berger and Luckmann's explorations would have been less hypothetico-deductive, as it were, and more empirical and/or inductive had they taken notice of Garfinkel's duality of trust and trouble. Phenomenological sociology derived from Berger and Luckmann's work kept itself remarkably distant from research for many years, and a merger of their views with Garfinkel's and Cicourel's insights is relatively unlikely even in the foreseeable future.

Nevertheless, it appears that both might profit from blurring their boundaries. Also, recent biographical research in sociology which owes much to the idea of social construction of reality (Bertaux, 1981) could fruitfully benefit from Garfinkel's methodological achievement.

Through his view on clinical as well as judicial reasoning as a way to put the individual case into the focus of professional decision-making, and by pointing out that such everyday activities are nothing other than what sociologists do to make sense of their observations, Garfinkel opens up for the social sciences a way of realising how much *Verstehen* is its basis.

In particular, it is case-oriented *Verstehen* which is of interest (of a first-order nature when accomplished in daily routines, of a second-order nature when used in the social sciences, as Schütz (1953) points out). Such *Verstehen*, explains Weber, is a way in which the sociologist can deal with historical or biographical data.[34] The *ideal type* is meant to facilitate the sociological endeavour of *Verstehen*. In many ways, it is a *normal form* construction.

It is at this point that the idea of 'normal illness' (and 'normal crime', for that matter) reveals itself as an adaptation of Weber's idea of the ideal type in social-science *Verstehen*. Together with the view that clinical reasoning follows its own *practical* logic (which is one of knowledge organised for action: i.e., uniting experience and expediency), the 'normal form' metaphor in phenomenological medical sociology paves the way for useful suggestions.

A closer connection with clinical medicine becomes conceivable. This is aptly demonstrated, among other things, by Cicourel's recent work. Furthermore, the theory of social order also implied in these ideas puts the medical issue, clad in the trouble–trust dichotomy, to the forefront.

In this theory of social order, illness is but an example of trouble, and medicine is but one of the many trust-re-establishing institutions (with medical treatment, in turn, heavily based on trust in the doctor–patient relationship). In any case, trust as a condition of, and accomplishment of, social relationships can be understood in general sociology through ethnomethodological or phenomenological research, using medical work as an example.

The place of criminology

One point of caution, however, needs to be added. It concerns the fact that crime, in phenomenological terms, is no different from illness (both denoting deviance cf. McHugh 1970a, 1970b). Both are seen as issues which mean trouble, and they invite the societal mechanisms of establishing trust (i.e., trouble control).

The problem may be elucidated by referring to the example of anti-Semitism. This time it is meant not as a prejudice kept by respectable citizens but enacted by individuals who belong to the Gestapo or SS, supervising as well as doing the killing. Ernst Simmel (1946) argues that such anti-Semitism is to be understood as mass psychopathology. Cohen (1953) offers an account of the psychological make-up not only of the inmates (victims) but also of the 'staff' (SS guards) of concentration camps. He wishes to make understandable the reports rendered retrospectively by either side of how they came to survive, or to kill. From this vantage point, for one, crime is viewed as illness (although the treatment suggested for the murderers is psychotherapy *in addition to* severe judicial punishment). However, if only from an ethical point of view, it feels intuitively wrong that crime should be identified with illness.

The reason is that crime and illness, in the everyday account structure, are rightly given contrasting attributes regarding the degree of individual *responsibility*. Although Freidson (1970a) makes it clear that some illnesses such as venereal disease are not exempted from the patient's being deemed responsible for the condition, by and large the distinction holds that illness labels exempt people from personal responsibility for the affliction while crime labels do not. The individual who is blamed for criminal conduct is, by definition, deemed to have had a choice to do otherwise. This also entails, as Aubert and Messinger (1958/72) aptly point out, different complementary standpoints for the *alter* (i.e., the one who reacts to someone who carries a sickness or criminal identity). They write:

> To react properly to illness, one must either understand the sickness naturalistically or one must know normatively what the patient 'can' and 'cannot' do. To react properly to the criminal one does not have to know more than in any other interaction-situation. We may also say that Alter always has the burden of proof in interaction with a sick person. In interaction with the criminal, Alter has no such burden of proof. (1958/72, p. 297)

This boils down to saying that there are two alternatives. When illness and crime are seen under the same perspective (namely, that of 'troublemaking'), the sick as well as the criminal are either both *not* seen as responsible for their action, or they are both deemed masters of their own conduct or fate. In a previous text (Gerhardt, 1985a), the implications of Becker's *underdog* perspective are investigated in terms of Enlightenment moral philosophy imperative for contemporary sociology's image of mankind. The heritage is that the individual emphatically is understood as free where freedom implies restraints (i.e., that one person's freedom is limited by that of the next person). When the criminal are identified with the sick and denied freedom of choice, this puts society into a role of a wholesale negative force encroaching upon individuals, preventing them from developing their culturally essential quality (i.e., the capacity to refrain from harming others). Floud (1975) makes it clear that this entails changes in the standards for justice in penal law: if the criminal may be proved simply a victim of adverse environmental circumstances, he or she can claim the right to corrective treatment rather than punishment. In this vein, recidivism emerges as a failure of the institution, not of the chronic criminal offender.

To be sure, the idea that crime might be seen as illness has been introduced because evidence seemed to allow the conclusion that treatment helped better than punishment. Interpersonal effort appeared to promise better results with juvenile delinquents and other offenders than harsh judicial punishment. This insight, for instance, is at the root of Philip A. Parsons' *Responsibility for Crime* (1909). It traces crime to insufficient or unsatisfactory circumstances of the criminal's socialisation. Prevention, which is here deemed society's best safeguard against crime, is the function of education rendered to the disadvantaged classes; nutrition for the poor and disenfranchised guarantees that they abstain from crime. Equally, Charles Richmond Henderson (1901), on whose ideas Parsons relies, propagates education and nutrition as adequate prevention of crime. He also warns that more drastic measures of combating crime which obviously were debated in his time have unwanted and unjustifiable consequences. He writes:

> Various methods of elimination have been proposed for cutting off the increase of the criminal classes by some scheme of elimination. The first of these, stated in its boldest form by McKim, is to kill all persons whose hereditary strain promises bad issue. Under this scheme all defectives and confirmed criminals would be placed in air-tight compartments and be put to death without pain by the introduction of some poisonous, but not unpleasant gas. Obvious objections to this plan are: that it would imply such a wholesale hardening of public feeling as would amount to a transformation of the entire community into a community of criminals . . . and that such a monstrous and colossal application of capital punishment would leave the social causes of crime untouched. (1901, p. 316–7)

Henderson, whose book first appeared in 1893, and who publicised his argument for some 30 years, advocated treatment for corrigible young offenders, and prevention for society as a whole (although he also suggested continued punishment for chronic criminal offender). Basically the idea is that since treatment appears to work, criminals (particularly if young and changeable) should be spared the pains of exclusion. Henderson also warned that those who punish (or condone the punishment) may themselves become entangled in guilt, particularly if the principle of complementarity between offence (guilt) and punishment were to be brushed aside. This attitude is later taken up by the psychoanalyst Alexander, who in a research monograph (Alexander and Healy, 1935) argued that the effect of adverse childhood circumstances can be corrected more effectively by psychotherapy than less treatment-oriented measures. Eventually, Friedlander (1960) likened delinquency and neurosis. She claimed: 'It has been found that there is no fundamental difference between unconscious conflicts underlying neurotic symptom formation and unconscious conflicts causing those delinquent actions which we might call "delinquent symptoms'" (1960, p. 116). At this point, there seems to be no clear demarcation line to the opposite stance regarding responsibility (namely, that crime as well as illness derives from conscious or unconscious wilfulness seems to be but a variant of the argument that responsibility ought not to be an issue). Indeed, if both crime and illness are what the individual bears responsibility for, the problematic impact falls on the illness side of the duality. There seem to be no *natural* boundaries, then, which exclude whatever counts as illness from becoming subject to 'troubleshooting' responding to crime in a particular society.

The extreme example of this, obviously, is race in Nazi terms. It was, at the same time, defined as deficiency of hereditary endowment embodied in inferior blood, and crime. It was like illness in that bodily features were concerned. It was understood as crime insofar as the Aryan race supposedly was contaminated by intermarriage and business or other contacts threatening Aryans' extinction through overpowering. Thus illness and crime were here merged to justify the incredible 'treatment' rendered. Less extreme examples can also illustrate what the dangers are in terms of account structures becoming part and parcel of common practices. When crime *and* illness are held both to be due to individual responsibility, nothing keeps the public from blaming the victim. In a mild version, current psychosomatic conjectures attributing cancer to the afflicted patient's previous repression of aggressive needs exemplify how mixed the blessings are which such 'explanations' entail (Sontag, 1978).

What conclusion can be drawn?

Neither identification of crime with illness as devoid of personal responsibility, nor that both are due to individual (conscious or unconscious)wilfulness appears to end up with a satisfactory image of mankind. In both versions, mankind is pitched against an overwhelming or uncontrollable society. The question, however, is setting the rights of the individual (even the chronic criminal offender) against the rightful interest of society in the prevention of crime (McCord, 1981). Where crime (like illness) is submitted to treatment, culminating in prevention as apparently the best kind of treatment, the *freedom of choice* is no longer upheld. This freedom of choice lies in the criminal act being a reaction to, or a conformist action within, a particular society. That criminals are denied responsibility for their misdeeds also means that they are not seen as able to make up for damage caused to others, and cannot choose to have insight into their wrongdoing. Likewise, where illness is taken as deed, no freedom of choice is granted to forgo treatment and cultivate one's weaknesses.

Moreover, another important conceptual issue is blurred in such identification. In their essay on the explicit and implicit meaning structures which, in most societies, distinguish the criminal from the ill, Aubert and Messinger (1958/72) argue that the more suggestive identification is that between the sick and the *victims* of crime. They write:

> A comparison of the victim of a crime and the sick, a victim of a disease, may add to the preceding analysis. There is in any society, it seems, a persistent need to 'explain' misfortunes . . . Since the crime, by definition, implies misfortune on the part of the victim . . ., there will be little spontaneous tendency to look for acts or choices made by the victim . . . It seems that the sick person has less to gain by such explanation and is so much the more open for the application of causal–genetic schemes, even though they may be very tenuous. (1958/72, pp. 294–5)

The whole argument thus seems to return to the question where medical sociology takes off: can illness (and crime, for that matter) be accounted for by a theory which makes plausible *how and why they happen*?

Cicourel (1972) argues that the 'how it happened' perspective in crime detection is one of basically illness-related enquiry. That police officers use this perspective in investigating crime gives it more of an illness semblance than might otherwise ensue. He says:

> My research on delinquency and juvenile justice convinced me that there are many juveniles who seemed to plan rule violations rather consistently; yet . . . group interaction . . . (for example, 'cruising' in a car at night . . .) is most susceptible to emergent outcomes that could not be anticipated . . . The after-the-fact interrogation by the police and probation officials or judge . . . concentrates upon a logical (from the adult point of view) reconstruction of 'what happened' . (1972, p. 156)

Thus techniques of 'troubleshooting' institutionalised in society may downplay rather than enhance differentiation of types of deviant acts. While some are due to free will, others cannot justifiably be so called. Where the boundary is may be more difficult to determine with some types of deviant acts than with others, but generally the distinction is meaningful, albeit only in *ethical* terms.

Moreover, the common-sense world of society's members also contains the differentiation. It distinguishes between harmful or incapacitating acts or experiences which one could have abstained from (where there *was* freedom of choice involved), and acts which were not so disposed. Ample proof for this distinction is the array of finely tuned excuses, repair strategies, and techniques of neutralisation used in everyday interaction when freedom of choice is wrongly imputed, or when it is wrongly denied to an act of ego's by an alter.

As a concluding point, this leads to suggesting a suitably reduced scope for medical sociology. To (re-)establish criminology as a field *outside* medical sociology – where it ought to remain – means contradicting the argument that medicine's 'professional dominance' in society calls for sociology's vigilance against its control. The argument is that since the medical system has acquired functions of the judicial system, sociology must castigate medicine for such a tendency towards dominance. Medical sociology, however, should realise, that by criticising more and more 'medical jurisdiction', it clandestinely extends its scope beyond its *terrain of expertise*. The phenomenological paradigm makes it clear (or at least its clinical-reasoning model of illness explanation does) how much sociology, if it sees itself fit to explain clinical medicine (and criticise such medicine, for that matter), encroaches upon a realm in which it can, at best, be dilettante.

Part IV
The Conflict-Theory Paradigm: Illness as Failure of Resources and Ideological Construct

Life-change research, social constructionism and political economy of health

Introduction: medical sociology has come of age

The *Maximum Feasible Misunderstanding* (Moynihan, 1970) between the state's welfare policy, on the one hand, and academics' efforts to help with democratising society on the other, did not leave sociology unscathed. In the wake of realising that favouring the franchisement of groups hitherto discriminated against is of no consequence for the afflicted, sociology raises a voice of disenchantment. It responds to the loss of meaningfulness of emancipatory activism by disclosing the reasons why political involvement is basically futile.

In the late 1960s and early 1970s, many sociologists proclaimed optimistically that change was feasible, and radical action needed (Colfax and Roach, 1971). In the mid-1970s it became clear that not only was a revolution not imminent (which would abolish inequality and overcome poverty) but conditions warranted less sense of progress than so far appeared justified. Particularly since the 1973–74 oil crisis and subsequent turn of the business cycle in economic development to a period of inflation and increasing unemployment, there seemed less and less reason for optimism. It became clear over the decade of the 1970s that not only had full equality not been achieved despite the political accomplishments of the 1960s, but that the welfare state had not been able substantially to change the distribution of wealth in society (A. B. Atkinson, 1972). Research proves that class inequality has remained nearly constant since the early twentieth century (Halsey, Heath and Ridge, 1980). Despite beliefs that ours is an open society, class barriers have not lost much of their impermeability (Goldthorpe, 1980). Whatever mobility is experienced by individuals is revealed

249

to be due to changes in the economic structure of the labour market rather than a loosening of social constraints (Sørensen, 1983).

Searching for reasons why its dreams about equality have proved futile, sociology discovers the same theoretical insights, albeit with more critical distance, which also inspired the political activism of the late 1960s and early 1970s. Karl Marx is re-established as one of sociology's founding fathers and classical theoreticians (Avineri, 1968; Giddens, 1971), but his work is taken to signify a point of departure rather than a credo.

In fact, while Marx is concerned with the social contradictions of *capitalist bourgeois society*, it is the capitalist *state* which now attracts sociology's attention. In this shift, orthodox Marxism is abandoned, and the '*critical theory of society*' is adopted.[35] In the early 1970s, one of Horkheimer and Adorno's former students, Habermas, developed a theory about the legitimation crisis of the modern state. It was devised along the lines of critical theory's thesis of disjuncture between the capitalist economy and the modern welfare state, on the one hand, and the latter's diminishing capacity to wield unconditional authority on the other (Habermas, 1971/73). While Habermas focused on the relative autonomy of cultural realms to explain the legitimation crisis of the state, O'Connor (1973) focused on the fiscal crisis of the state. He developed a theory of tripartite structure of the labour market in modern society where the state also became a major employer. In fact, O'Connor showed how entangled the modern state was in social contradictions. He diagnosed a financial catch-22 situation whereby the problems of reform become insoluble which are the *raison d'être* for the involvement of the state.

From this debate arises an interest of general sociology in how social contradictions abide. The issue becomes that of social conflict, and the question is how problems evolve such that they must remain unsolved.

The focus on conflict is first established by Coser (1956) and Dahrendorf (1959) in careful attempts to show how integration in society allows for cleavages that need not be dysfunctional. Coser emphasised how multiple dividing lines of conflict between status groups can add to the colour rather than the explosiveness of social relations and social life. Dahrendorf showed how class conflict is institutionalised in agreements of limited duration which may have a formal or informal contract nature. But it took until the mid-1970s before Collins' comprehensive *Conflict Sociology* overcame the preoccupation with harmony as the essence of social order. He emphasised Weber's insight that only because force is its ultimate means, and violence is its underlying rationale, can society as a whole or the state as its agent of control function through less obviously oppressive forms of constraint. In this vein, harmony between social forces was revealed to be a product of stifled conflict. Giddens wrote in his *Central Problems in Social Theory*: 'It should be acknowledged that some of the major traditions in social science are prone to underestimate how far force and violence (or its threat) can be successfully employed to forestall the emergence of conflict as overt struggle' (1979, p. 145).

In this awareness of domination and subjugation, knowledge is explicitly included. No longer is science excluded from the sociologist's gaze identifying the relativity of seemingly objective discoveries. The notion of *ideology* becomes prominent. Habermas (1968/71) ventured the hypothesis that science and technology, while claiming to be above social values are, in fact, far from value-free and must therefore be called ideological. Althusser (1974) extended the idea of ideology to institutions that are 'apparatus' promoting a world view suiting the dominant classes. In this vein, Giddens (1979) made it clear that ideologies are embedded in an interpretation of reality due to 'the capability of dominant groups or classes to make their own sectional interests appear to others as universal ones' (1979, p. 6); this then affects disenfranchised sections of society.

Thus conflict is identified as basic to social life. Inequality in society documents the fact that conflict is suppressed by those who are in power, and kept latent through means of intimidation and indoctrination. Conflict is not confined to the political, but extended to all realms of life. Or, rather, it may be said that every aspect of social life is recognised as politicised or potentially so. This is done through analysing social phenomena under the perspective that they represent repressed conflicts of interests. In this, the disenfranchised (i.e., the powerless) would be assumed to go along with the dominants' world view and suppress their own regarding power and equality because of false consciousness due to ideological indoctrination. In this context, Collins (1975) introduced the idea that Weber allegedly extended Marx's view of conflict (which relies on material production) to one that includes 'mental production' leading to unequal conditions of consciousness in society. Collins wrote:

> Weber also opens up yet another area of resources in these struggles for control, what might be called the 'means of emotional production'. It is these that underlie the power of religion and make it an important ally of the state; that transform classes into status groups . . . and that make 'legitimacy' a crucial focus for efforts of domination . . . For Weber retains a crucial emphasis: The creation of emotional solidarity does not supplant conflict, but is one of the main weapons used in

conflict. Emotional rituals can be used for domination within a group or organization; they are a vehicle by which alliances are formed in the struggle against other groups; and they can be used to impose a hierarchy of status prestige in which some groups dominate others by providing an ideal to emulate under inferior conditions. (1975, pp. 58–9)

It is at this point that medical sociology makes its entry into the scene of contemporary conceptualisations of society. It fully embraces the topics of ideology, domination, and inequality to understand society as a web (or an abyss) of conflict production. In their overview of current literature entitled *Sociological Approaches to Health and Medicine*, Morgan, Calnan and Manning give a summary of what they perceive as leading theoretical viewpoint in contemporary medical sociology:

The conflict perspective, rather than emphasizing the functionality of the differential distribution of rewards for society as a whole, encompasses a number of traditions which emphasize the role of competing interests in contributing to the prevailing distribution of resources between social groups. One approach is to regard the formation of contending groups as based on differences in life style associated with cultural traditions or political interests, and to see the distribution of resources as influenced by the power of various competing groups. A second major approach is provided by the marxist conception of class, which views social classes as groups characterized by an antagonistic relationship based on their relative positions in the social relations of production. (1985, p. 226)

When this was written in 1985, medical sociology had had over two decades of most successful growth. Regarding opportunities for serious research and also regarding its being accepted as part of medical education (in England, Switzerland, the US and West Germany, for instance), medical sociology gained respectability around 1970 or not much later. Levine and Scotch's volume on social stress, as well as Wing and Brown's study on schizophrenia and institutionalism – both eminently sociological conceptualisations of illness – were both published in 1970. They extended the discussion of how 'normal' mental illness is, after Srole *et al.'s Mental Illness in the Metropolis* (1962) and Leighton *et al.*'s work on the relationship between social disorganisation and mental disturbance (1963). How ubiquitous illness is was next asked for physical sickness by Wadsworth, Butterfield and Blaney (1971). They recognised symptoms as signs of illness as opposed to, or not always related to, illness behaviour. The distinction, first discussed by Koos (1954) and later promoted by Mechanic and Volkart

(1960) and refined by Zola (1970/73) – between illness and 'what the people do about it' – gives sociology the dignity of its own subject matter. At the end of the 1970s, the phenomenon of symptom ubiquity and medical-care selectivity became known as '*clinical iceberg*' (Hannay, 1979). It relates not only to use of medical services but also social-class differences of morbidity and mortality, as documented for the US by Kitagawa and Hauser (1973) and for the UK by N. Hart (1978). The latter study, developed into the famous Black Report named after the Department of Health and Social Security's (DHSS's) Chief Scientist at that time, Sir Douglas Black, became a milestone of inequality documentation (Townsend and Davidson, 1982).

In the years 1960–71, five journals were set up that still flourish today, mostly on topics concerning the organisation of care and illness behaviour: namely, the *Journal of Health and Social (Human) Behaviour* in 1960 (made an official publication of the American Sociological Association in 1967); *Medical Care* in 1963; *Social Science and Medicine* in 1967; and *Social Policy* and the *International Journal of Health Services* in 1970 and 1971 respectively. Comprehensive textbooks for medical and social-science students made vigorous efforts to explain empirically health and health care. Mechanic's *Medical Sociology* of 1968 (with an impressive revised edition in 1978), Susser and Watson (1971, revised edition of 1962, again revised 1985), Siegrist, 1974 (with second and third editions in 1975 and 1977), Tuckett, 1976, Patrick and Scambler, 1982 (revised 1986), and Morgan, Calnan and Manning (1985), to name but a few, covered a wide range of insights and findings. Indisputably, medical sociology is now a discipline in is own right. During this time and still today, various edited *readers* undertake to put together evidence concerning social aspects of health and medicine. For instance, Freeman, Levine, and Reeder (1972, revised edition of 1963), Jaco (1972, revised edition of 1958, revised again 1979), Cox and Mead (1975), J. Ehrenreich (1978), Conrad and Kern (1980), and Aiken and Mechanic (1986), just to name a few, take stock of the knowledge from different angles. They adopt a critical stance towards health conditions and delivery of care, but also attempt a descriptive account picturing the medical scene's contradictions and peculiarities. How much a general sense of self-assertiveness characterises the whole endeavour may be learned from Margot Jefferys' persuasion that medicine can no longer do without sociology. She writes:

> It seems to me impossible to argue that acquaintance with such findings
> and with the methods and conceptual frames of the discipline on which

they are based is not an essential ingredient in the preparation of the doctor for medical practice . . . He or she is at the very least for protection against the very real hazard of frustration and unhappiness when it proves difficult to implement medical measures: but above all it is needed if the medical and other health-related professions are to make their greatest potential contribution to the welfare of the popula-tion they are privileged to serve. (Patrick and Scambler, 1982, p. xi)

Such assurance that sociology is vital to medicine is far from standing alone. In fact, while Jefferys contends that sociology changes medicine while being incorporated into it, other authors voice the idea that medicine without sociology is but an ideological express-ion of class domination in modern society. In a book designated to expose the historical relativity and systematic one-sidedness of medical knowledge, Wright and Treacher (1982) show through various papers (most of which originally were presented at the British Sociological Association's Medical Sociology Group Con-ference in 1977) that medicine is but a social construction. The implication is that the claim to objectivity is revealed as untenable, and traditional assumptions regarding effectiveness of medical practice ought to be revised. From a different vantage point, McKeown (1965, 1975, 1979) offers the same argument. Based on an analysis of social epidemiological data on changes in morbidity and mortality since the nineteenth century (and earlier), he puts into question medicine's claim to have contributed significantly to the decline of infectious disease. He concludes that the mechanical image of the body giving rise to medical technology proves a serious impediment to medicine's efficiency and effectiveness. While McKeown favours a community-medicine approach to the problems of disease which is indirectly sociological, Wright and Treacher plead for a sociology derived from the work of Foucault. In this view, cultural relativity (which has by the early nineteenth century developed a clinical focus on disease as bodily lesion) is proof of the ideological nature of the medical undertaking. In due course, that medical practice is accepted by the public as seemingly effective and efficient in dealing with health matters must be traced to domination over the normal working-class population. In other words, medicine is revealed as an ideology stabilising the power of the state and society's other established authorities.

This critical view is shared by the political economy of health. It bases its debunking of modern medicine on Habermas' conjecture that science and technology are but expressions of ideology. In this, ideology is seen as somewhat similar to that *opiate of the people* which Marx saw in religion. In essence, the Marxist view stipulates that, far from having origins which can be located within the body, diseases must be seen as externally caused by societal relationships of deprivation and exploitation. Thus class conflict extends to medicine insofar as the medical profession is part of the ruling class whose ideologies doctors willingly or inadvertently impose upon their patients (Navarro, 1976; Waitzkin, 1983).

However, serious research has been able to document the conflict and ideology issues only in a much milder version. Inequality between classes is acknowledged as a vicissitude of life in modern society, and unemployment affects the unskilled strata of the working classes more severely than people of higher social standing (as does premature mortality, for that matter). Numerous studies find that more experiences of loss and failure are encountered by disenfranchised groups, and less social support is available to them to assist their coping with adversities (Dohrenwend and Dohrenwend, 1970; Brown and Harris, 1978). In this is involved an implicit criticism of medicine since it fails to acknowledge social causes of disease due to unequal life chances in society. In this context, the debate on self-help has gained momentum since the middle-1970s and is partly sponsored by the WHO (Robinson, 1980). If nothing else, it proves that sociologists keenly look for new and alternative ways of health care better suited to cater for the population's health needs than clinical medicine which is allegedly unable to serve them adequately.

It is blatantly obvious that the relationship between sociology and medicine has not developed into a harmonious side-by-side arrangement. Rather, much if not most present-day medical sociology holds that clinical medicine must change if it is to avoid the odium of cost ineffectiveness or even outright cruelty to patients. Medical sociology is often convinced that it offers answers to medicine's problems which the physicians do not wish to hear. It even sometimes seems to provoke conflict where is does not yet prevail. For instance, Conrad and Schneider's position may be found difficult to accept even by the most sociologically inclined doctor. They contend that:

> many medicalized services are not 'freely' chosen by clients; skid row or occupational alcoholism treatment, methadone maintenance, mental hospitalization, disability benefits, even medications for hyperactivity operate through the coercion of others such as courts, schools, or employers . . . It is essential to remember that demedicalization does not occur until a problem is no longer defined in medical terms and medical treatments are no longer seen as appropriate solution. Demedicalization can be said to have taken place, for example, if childbirth were defined as a family event with lay attendants, chronic drunkenness reconstituted an educational problem, or opiate addiction redesignated

as solely a legal–criminal issue, as happened in the 1920s. (1980a, pp. 78/77; emphasis omitted)

In fact, Conrad and Schneider's contention is part of an argument carried on in *Social Science and Medicine* as to whether sociology charges medicine with imperialist tendencies because it harbours intentions of professional imperialism itself (Strong, 1979a). Replies to Strong's article refute the accusation of sociological imperialism. They say that when he fails to see how imperialist medicine has become he must be taking a medicine-prone perspective rather than, from a patient-prone perspective, castigating the medicalisation of problem-solving in modern society (Waitzkin, 1979; Conrad and Schneider, 1980a).

In this situation, a sociological explanation clarifies the medicine-aversive stance of much medical sociology. In 1976, Armstrong first points out in an analysis of Reports of Royal Commissions on issues of medical care that 'medical hegemony' appears to decline since before the Second World War. In 1979, he diagnoses a 're-emergence of the sick man', paraphrasing Jewson's (1976) conclusion of the latter's disappearance from medical cosmology between 1770 and 1870. Contemporary general practice, Armstrong contends, undergoes a comeback after decades of characterisation by the degrading image that it is for those who 'fall off the ladder' of a career in hospital (specialty) medicine.[36] Biographical medicine, which is heavily indebted to the patient's whole person rather than diseased organs, becomes prevalent. In his book, published in 1983, Armstrong reveals how much his analysis is influenced by Foucault's perspective on *The Birth of the Clinic* (1963/75) in early nineteenth-century France but also *Discipline and Punish* (1975/1979). He uses the latter's insight that the clinical gaze of modern medicine also signifies the interest of the state and society in surveillance and domination. Armstrong extends Foucault's understanding into a view where medical sociology enters the picture. For instance, the pioneer role of the Peckham Health Centre in South London in the 1930s is explained in the following terms:

> Whereas for traditional hospital medicine, illness was a deviant status, to the Dispensary, as found at Peckham, it was normal. If everyone had pathology then everyone would need observing . . . The idea that everyone was ill was an important element in the operation of a generalised surveillance. The new social diseases of the twentieth century, tuberculosis, venereal disease and problems of childhood, had been reconstrued to focus medical attention on 'normal' people who were

nevertheless 'at risk'. The same notion can also be seen in the discovery of the neuroses which, at least in mild form, came to appear in almost everyone. The innovations of the Peckham centre effectively extended this principle to more traditional organic diseases by dissolving the clear boundary between the healthy and the diseased. This process was to be continued after World War II with the discovery, on the one hand of the 'clinical iceberg' by epidemiologists, and, on the other hand of 'illness behaviour' by medical sociologists. (1983, p. 37)

Thus medical sociology extends the clinical gaze into areas hitherto excluded from the realm of medicine. The notion of illness expands from organic lesions to what Armstrong addresses as *the space between the bodies* (1983, p. 8). Social relationships as well as life styles become relevant for medicine because they prove to be important aspects or precursors of illness. In this way, medical sociology becomes a vital contributor to the newly emerging fields of community and social medicine. But since clinical medicine moves more in the direction of biology and chemistry (if only as reaction to the emergence of community medicine, as Strong (1979a) argues), medical sociology fills a gap which the development of modern medicine creates. It fits into a niche, or bridges a gap, produced by the changes within the scope of clinical interest itself. In other words, medical sociology's origin and growth is itself revealed to be an aspect of the notorious medicalisation of life in modern society.

Under these auspices, the literature on social causes of disease takes on a new meaning. It points out where medicine develops over the next decades in terms of factors and processes that the medical effort may feel obliged to treat and/or control. It is ironic that medical sociology investigates far-reaching causes of illness because, at the same time, it accuses the medical profession of extending its realm further and further into non-medical fields of social behaviour. Thus it appears to denounce conceptions of treatment derived from its own analysis of illness.

This brings up the question of how to retain an extensive aetiological notion of treatment but deny implications for the definition of illness. If the wide range of phenomena figuring as illness-related under the sociological gaze were to be subject to treatment by medical personnel, the ominous medicalisation of society could neither be curtailed nor reversed.

As an alternative, therefore, sociology proposes to return to lay conceptions of treatment, either through self-help movements or through deprofessionalisation, if not demedicalisation, of health care. In the last instance, when social causes are identified as ones inherent in the structure of (capitalist) society as such, only more or less revolutionary changes seem able to solve the problem. At this point, to be sure, medical sociology at times fails to resist the temptation of seeing itself as a better healer of society's ills than medicine supposedly ever can.

Chapter 12
The Conflict Notion of Illness

Through Armstrong's analysis it emerges that the sociological focus on illness implies that practically everybody is sick. The divide between pathology and normality is torn down. Armstrong writes about the 'Sickness Survey' conducted around 1940, which he considers a predecessor of contemporary socio-medical research:

> In effect, the survey established the possibility of removing the abnormal/normal divide . . . The referent external to the population under study – the norm – which had for almost two centuries governed the analysis and distribution of bodies was replaced by the relative positions of all bodies . . . Illness was no longer the preserve of the medical profession but of the body's own perceptions. (1983, p. 51)

This means that the individual's judgment of feeling sick is to be taken as being as reliable as the clinical examination in detecting illness. Of course, at the time of the war efforts and a highly centralised structure of many state and social services (including the Emergency Health Service) the survey of social medicine also meant the physical examination of recruits, pupils, and so on. The method used was the same as that introduced by sociology: namely, the survey. It was intended to ascertain people's state of health and it became the major methodological approach. On this basis, the alliance between medical sociology and social medicine after the Second World War (see Koos, 1954; Commission on Chronic Illness, 1957/59) gradually eroded the distinction between pathology and normality. Originally, sociology adopted this distinction from clinical medicine but medical sociology gave it up when it partly joined the epidemiological endeavour of social medicine.

In what way, it may be asked, can it be said that hardly anyone in modern society is healthy? Zola, in the early 1970s, made the point that surveys have uncovered such a vast amount of untreated illness that the question must be asked why this is not treated. The answer which he provided contended that people refrained from seeing a doctor because of their being intimidated. He based his claim on the findings of epidemiological research (partly his own, e.g., Zola, 1966). He wrote: 'Given all the untreated medical complaints uncovered by medical surveys, seeking a doctor's help is a relatively infrequent response to symptoms. Delay is a statistical norm, fear and anxiety the psychological norm' (1973/83, p. 219).

In fact, in the early 1970s, several surveys reveal a noticeable number of symptoms which either are not treated at all or only through self-medication at home (Wadsworth, Butterfield and Blaney, 1971; Dunnell and Cartwright, 1972).These surveys find a proportion of between 5 and 10 per cent of the population who consider themselves free from symptoms or say that they are healthy. From this vantage point, Pflanz and Rohde (1970) argue against Parsons that his assumption that illness represents deviance, and health normality, may have to be reversed in the light of the statistical evidence presented by epidemiological research. The new insight achieved in the 1970s is that health is *not* a statistical norm, and illness is not an exception from normality; rather, illness seems to characterise the condition of nearly everybody in modern society to a degree hitherto unnoticed.

In the light if this insight, medical sociology begins to ask itself the question whether it wishes to be implicated in the plight of the majority of society's members, or should it not be concerned with how this plight could be alleviated? Should it not occupy itself with the conditions of *health*?

Sociology's change from the topic of illness to that of health became evident around the end of the 1970s and the beginning of the 1980s. In the US, Twaddle and Hessler (1977) were the first explicitly to put health on the agenda of the entire medical-sociological endeavour. Their initiative was mirrored in England by Stacey and Homans (1978), who argued that the sociology of health and illness ought to replace the sociology of medicine. While Patrick and Scambler (1982), when writing for a medical audience, took social causes of *disease* as their point of departure, Morgan, Calnan and Manning (1985) and N. Hart (1986a), who wrote for a sociological audience, used health rather than illness as their main focus. Both supplemented the topic of disease/health by that of medicine, understood in terms of the organisation of medical or health services. Pursuing such efforts further, the discipline itself aspired to change its name. In 1986, the International Sociological Association's Research Committee 15 (hitherto called Sociology of Medicine) during the 11th World Congress of

Sociology held in New Delhi, India, decided to change its name to Sociology of Health.

Various reasons are given for this change to health as main analytical interest. One is that *prevention* can be more effectively promulgated if more is known about the conditions of absence of sickness in a population (Hingson *et al.*, 1981). Stacey and Homans argue that the focus of health (and illness) helps to overcome undue 'connection with the medical profession' (1978, p. 295). They write: 'The contribution of sociology must be with the whole range of knowledge, belief, feeling, organization, institutions associated with health and illness and thus connected with the whole range of workers, professional, semi-professional, paraprofessional, unpaid workers and others who are involved in the health industry and including the patients in that industry' (Stacey and Homans, 1978).

Armstrong (1983) shows that the focus shifts from illness to health because the *community* becomes the reference for measurements of amounts of sickness. This is to say, the relevant amount of sickness is no longer that in the individual but that in the whole community. The basis of its measurement is what Sir John Ryle, in his autobiographical report on his work in the Medical Research Council's Committee on the codification of disease and in the Oxford Institute of Social Medicine (founded in 1942) terms 'living samples'. Armstrong comments: 'The source of these living samples could not be the hospital ward but must be the "welfare centres and nurseries, in schools and universities, in the armed forces, or the large communities"' (1983, p. 48).

Another reason given for the change to health as the sociological focus is the nature of disease in modern society. It is felt that while infective agents may have explained much of disease in the past, 'for most of the Western world, sources of morbidity and mortality now lie in the patterns of behaviour' (V. A. Brown, 1980, p. 195). Behaviour, to be sure, is not necessarily connected with illness and ought therefore to be the focus of a primary interest in non-illness. This insight is carried one step further. Namely, that health is embraced means that *holistic* rather than clinical medicine is envisaged. Brown, explaining what the altered orientation of health-care research entails, insists that health itself is a holistic concept: 'Healthy refers to the state of the whole person: the very word "health" means hale or whole. Writings on wellness are necessarily concerned with the physical, mental or social states of the individual, considered together, and the concepts of health available to individuals in a culture' (V. A. Brown, 1980, p. 196).

From the vantage point of partisanship for health, illness acquires two hitherto unanalysed features. First, that illness is ubiquitous means that it defines conditions of life in modern society which are obstacles to an attainable state of well-being. Life styles as well as environmental conditions in the urban and industrial world are discovered to harbour dangers to health warranting detailed study. The insight that everyone is ill becomes the presupposition that this may not always be openly recognised but is *potentially* so. The ubiquitous failure of (total) health, as documented by the survey data, becomes understood not necessarily as prevalence of actual but unnoticed illness but, rather, as potential illness. The propensity to fall ill is the most conspicuous corollary of socio-economic, ethnic, racial, married versus unmarried and other social statuses. Social factors characterising the individuals' position in society are understood to define a degree of general susceptibility to disease to which each group is prone. The person, insofar as he or she is a member thereof, is liable to be under the threat of potential illness. Morgan, Colnan, and Manning, in their overview over sociological approaches to health and medicine, sum up the idea as follows:

> A third model of disease causation, which complements and supplements the monocausal and multicausal models of disease, is the model of general susceptibility. This model which has gained increasing prominence over the last ten years, shifts the emphasis away from the identification of the causes of specific diseases to look at why certain groups in the population are more susceptible to disease in general. (1985, p. 21)

This entails that *epidemiology* becomes a basic science providing research on which medical sociology relies. (It also forms an analytical perspective often uncritically credited with securing objective facts.) In this, the image of man is that of '*homo sociologicus*'. That is, the individual is seen as an incumbent of multiple roles or statuses each of which may carry a certain risk or susceptibility to sickness or premature death.

The idea of 'homo sociologicus' is introduced by Dahrendorf (1958/68) to describe with a critical undertone sociology's image of mankind. Dahrendorf makes it clear, referring to Parsons' role theory and also Linton's writings on status and role (1936), that the individual is understood to follow the expectations of others (gradated from *must* through *should* to *can*). In this, the individual as a person is pitched against society such that, taking the perspective of the person, Dahrendorf speaks of society as a 'vexatious fact' (p. 34). This means that the person's unique needs are not met and cannot be. The reason is that society caters to all, condensed into an image of the average: that is, institutions function according to ideologies which are fitted to an impersonal average member instead of being geared towards the sum of individualised persons who are members. Dahrendorf surmises that, as long as sociology finds itself unable to go beyond the 'homo sociologicus' image of what the individual is, individuals and society will be conceptually irreconcilable. He writes about this, referring to the non-sociological aspects of mankind, with Robert Musil's term of 'tenth character':[37]

> *Homo sociologicus* can neither love nor hate, laugh nor cry. He remains a pale, incomplete, strange, artificial man. Yet he is more that the showpiece of an exhibit. He provides the standard by which our world – and indeed our friend, our colleague, our father, our brother – becomes comprehensible for us. The world of *homo sociologicus* may not be the world of our experience, but the two are strikingly similar. If we identify with *homo sociologicus* and his predetermined ways, our 'tenth character' rises in protest; but we are nonetheless constrained to follow his paths as they appear on the maps of sociology. (1958/68, p. 58)

It is this view of 'homo sociologicus' which constitutes the epidemiological idea of how participation in social life is associated with health risks. Illness, in this vein, is a potential contained in the incumbency of any social status. The individual's susceptibility to disease in general, or with reference to a particular disease or disease spectrum, must be understood accordingly. As 'homo sociologicus' means the constellation of role statuses held by a person, susceptibility to disease(s) refers to the sum total of particular risk factions associated with the various role statuses held by someone.

The second feature of illness deriving from the sociologist's partisanship for health is *political*. A Utopian aspect is that of universal well-being and equal yet extended longevity. To improve the situation where everybody, in principle, is not well means that perfect health and utmost life expectancy become the reference points from where any illness or premature mortality are criticised.

Medicine is grudgingly granted respect for its successes regarding reduction of morbidity and mortality over the last century. Areas where inequality is detected are taken as proof that medicine is not doing as much as it could. For instance, the class gradient of mortality (Kitagawa and Hauser, 1973; Townsend, 1974) and what is called 'inverse care law' (J. T. Hart, 1971) are felt to be partly due to medicine's failure to treat rich and poor, or middle-class and working-class patients in exactly the same manner (Tuckett, 1976; N. Hart, 1986a). The length of consultation, number of questions asked and other minutiae of seeking care are investigated under the proviso that they signify less favourable treatment conditions for the working class (Cartwright and O'Brien, 1976; Waitzkin and Stoeckle, 1976). In this seems to lie one key to the higher mortality rates of those in the lowest social strata. Another is related to life style and working conditions which are said to be underestimated in medical practice and by the clinical theory of disease. In the light of inequality and conflict in society in general, and the doctor–patient relationship in particular, sociology makes itself the advocate of the patient (person) when it strives to find reasons why better health does not prevail. Many sociologists feel justified in taking an anti-medicine view because they are convinced that the medical profession is far too entangled with the upper classes to do all it could for the benefit of the powerless.

This even is applied to countries where, as in Britain, the National Health Service has abolished blatant discrepancies in the care rendered to patients from different social classes. Blane (1982) charges the lack of satisfactory progress to a *logic of the vicious circle*. He writes:

> The Victorians were familiar with the vicious circle of 'poverty causes disease which causes poverty'. Although this may be reformulated to read 'limited opportunity to lead a healthy life combined with inadequate medical care is likely to result in illness and disability which may lead to further deprivation', the logic of the vicious circle remains. (Patrick and Scambler, 1982, pp. 122–3)

The double nature of illness

Under the impression that society is ripe with inequality causing experiences of deprivation and difficulties for large parts of the population, sociology is interested in how dismal, deficient or distressed living conditions influence disease. The relationship is no longer that a dual nature of illness is stipulated where medicine is responsible for the physiological or biological side while sociology investigates the social side. Instead, both are now seen as interrelated such that physiological lesions are traced to antecedent conditions characterising the social situation of the patient.

In this, two major lines of argument have been taken. The theories of *psychosomatic* origin of disease become relevant to sociology not only when Parsons incorporates Alexander's adaptations of Freud's work into his explanation of deviance; from the late 1950s onwards, research is published which brings together feelings of anxiety, hopelessness or helplessness with the onset of major illness. For instance, Weiner *et al.* (1957) argue that duodenal ulcers are brought about by states of anxiety which influence the acid level of gastric fluid. Schmale and Iker (1971) maintain that cervical cancer is facilitated, if not caused, by periods of extended hopelessness. Seligman (1975) concludes from research with animals and also depressed humans that sudden death may be related to psychosomatic breakdown. This hypothesis is also ventured by Parkes (1972) who follows up on his work on higher mortality rates among recently widowed men during a six-month period after the death of their spouses.

In 1977, Henry and Stevens tried to pull together the evidence they found in the biological and biochemical literature on physiological processes which accounted for the observed link between disease, on the one hand, and anxiety and hopelessness as responses to environmental deprivation, on the other hand. In particular, the propensity of the hormonal system, especially along two concatenated axes, to respond to environmental stimuli with pathological levels of hormone production provided a potent explanatory link between the person's psychic reaction and physiological lesion. Many authors are convinced that this physiological link, explored by what is called *psychoneuroimmunology* (Riley, 1981) eventually proves indispensable for medical sociology. For instance, McQueen and Siegrist (1982) maintained that psychoneuroendocrine influences on the cardiovascular system are responsible for the propensity of persons with Type-A behaviour patterns to develop heart disease. They outline in detail the relationship between neuroendocrine responses and cardiovascular pathology. Their basic idea is taken from Henry and Stevens (1977), and they argue that 'synergistic activation of two stress axes and possible effect of neurohormonal imbalance' (McQueen and Siegrist, 1982, p. 363) is at the root of heart disease, or, in their words, 'sympathetic adrenal-medullary and pituitary adrenal-cortical activation have been found in mechanisms leading to four well established precursors of IHD' (1982, p. 363; IHD means Ischaemic Heart Disease).

However, these views have not gone unchallenged. For one, Najman (1980), in his overview of sociological theories of illness causation, deems the biochemical explanation wanting. He writes:

> While there is some evidence to support the views put by the psychosomaticists, they have not to date been able to demonstrate the existence of the causal sequences they postulate. Specifically, they have not

shown that the biochemical and physiological changes which are a consequence of stress are of sufficient magnitude to cause the range of diseases involved. Nor have any researches successfully demonstrated that intervening in the stress process increases longevity. (1980, p. 234)

The other line of argument which puts the social in the forefront of the medical aspect of disease may be called *sociosomatic*. Najman characterises it in the following way: 'Sociosomatics argue that morbidity and mortality rates are significantly influenced by environmental and behavioral factors. These factors include exposure to industrial hazards, smoking, excessive alcohol consumption, diet, the inappropriate use of medical services, and extreme lifestyle' (1980, p. 234).

He goes on to say that, according to the sociosomatic hypothesis, health is a function of 'healthy' lifestyle and the individual is responsible for his or her own poor health. He overlooks the fact that a major contribution to the sociosomatic body of theories is made by the Marxist literature heavily criticising medicine for making the individual rather than society responsible for alcoholism, smoking, or other aspects of an unhealthy life style.

For instance, Brenner (1975) purports to show that heavy consumption of alcohol is related to high unemployment rates in the economy. Accordingly, mortality from cirrhosis of the liver as well as other morbidity related to alcoholism are traced to an origin beyond the individual's failing to adhere to a 'healthy' life style. To be sure, Brenner's analysis of the mechanism involved evokes a vague reference to adverse effects of economic and social stress. He establishes a link between negative business cycles and measures of ill health in the community, and he writes: 'The available evidence is that economic downturns are a very major source of economic and social stress and that they show substantial correlations with increases in suicide, mental hospital admissions, heart disease mortality, and infant mortality at least for the same period as is covered by this study' (1975, p. 1289).

In the light of findings such as this, Waitzkin (1979) holds against 'individualization of social problems' (1979, p. 606) as well as 'locating the source of the problem within the patient rather than society' (1979, p. 605) that this unduly camouflages the 'class patterns of oppression' in society (1979, p. 606).

One often-used picture of the mechanism behind the sociosomatic connection focuses on social support. In the mid-1970s, Cassel (1975, 1976) derived from the well-known fact that disease strikes selectively a hypothesis regarding *host resistance*. He argued that environmental conditions, including one's social network of friends and relatives, determined which among those exposed to a disease risk or noxious agent suffered as a result. Change and adaptation, he insisted, only led to illness if their destructive forces were not counteracted by protective circumstances. 'Environmental factors capable of producing profound effects on host susceptibility to environmental disease agents', he proposed, should be extended to the social world and, thus, included 'the presence of other members of the same species, or more generally, certain aspects of the social environment' (1976, p. 108). The general idea is further developed in a number of subsequent studies of which the most striking is Berkman and Syme's follow-up of the Alameda County sample group. They found that more of those who had few and poor social contacts at the time of the original study tended not to have survived until nine years later (Berkman and Syme, 1979; Elinson, 1985).

Although not much is known so far on the clinical rationale which could explain this link, it is evident from empirical research that changes in environmental conditions can have measurable effects on health. This has been demonstrated for selected causes in sufficient detail. For example, such mental-health failures as hospitalism for children (Spitz, 1958) and what Barton (1959) calls *institutional neurosis* are obviously brought about by environmental deficit. Wing and Brown (1970), calling the latter illness *institutionalism*, demonstrate through comparing three hospitals with different degrees of environmental impoverishment (subsequently differently 'opening-up') that institutionalism (institutional neurosis) responds to changes in the hospital milieu which improve personal expression, communication and the patient's participation.

These two lines of thought, the psychosomatic and the sociosomatic, have been followed by medical sociology in a large number of research projects. The aim is to get nearer to an explanation of disease where environmental conditions are clearly shown to be causal agents. Short of that, at least a trigger function of social circumstances is often documented. Both strive to put medicine into a subservient role *vis-à-vis* sociology. The idea is frequently that physiological processes no longer predominantly require the expertise of a clinician in order to be properly understood. Rather, the clinician should realise that environmental stimuli are behind pathophysiological events. The literature focusing on social stress as well as social support presupposes that these represent societal factors explaining the why if not the how of a particular disease occurrence. The doctor choosing to disregard them is judged prejudiced if not irresponsible. Such a strong 'hegemony' attitude of medical sociology over medicine regarding the idea of where illness comes from may bear witness to the change of the general disease paradigm which Armstrong (1976, 1979, 1983) invokes.

The medicalisation of politics and the politicisation of medicine

According to the labelling approach, what constitutes illness is relative to cultural meanings accrued to symptoms. A moral dimension prevails in the categorisation distinguishing normality from pathology. Such rejection of a 'natural' dividing line between moral and amoral, it has been argued above, leads to an understanding of any dividing line in a society as political. If the difference between health and illness is political, it is deemed subject to power and indoctrination and may depend on the wisdom of the government of the day. Expressions of political influence on illness are found in clinical theory and practice. Since logical or natural barriers cannot be invoked against extending the illness label into realms such as race, sexual behaviour or political opinion, contradicting or fighting it must be done on political grounds: that is, medical sociology comes to embrace moral standards explicitly different from those used by medical, societal or political authorities.

Like the labelling approach, conflict-theory views stress cultural relativity's political function. Fitzpatrick (1982), writing on social aspects of illness in a medical textbook, emphasises that symptoms as well as illness are *culturally* relative. Both respond to meaning structures entrenched in the society (or a particular social class or ethnic milieu). This insight is also behind the notion of illness behaviour which, from the perspective of medical care, defines the baseline of sociological interest in health matters (Mechanic, 1978). Hingson *et al.* (1981) point out in another textbook for medical students that since subpopulations like smokers must be taught how dangerous their behaviour is, the political aspect of illness is that prevention falls into the jurisdiction of governments attentive to social origins of disease.

The view that the demarcation line between health and illness is political is also stressed with more critical intent. In 1972 and again in 1975, Zola described medicine as an institution of social control since more and more realms of hitherto legally or religiously defined norms came under the jurisdiction of medicine. He criticised the fact that medicine acquired an aura of scientifically grounded neutrality while, in fact, being deeply political without knowing it. He warned of the dangers inherent in the increasing use of metaphors of health and illness for explaining social problems such as race riots, anti-war demonstrations, juvenile delinquency or the use of heroin or other drugs. He wrote:

> My concern is what happens when a problem and its bearers become tainted with the label 'illness' . . . Most cynically put, it could mean being satisfied with having millions of unemployed and then exploring how we can make these people less of a problem. What becomes operative in all such examples is a 'go-no-further-effect' and one largely due to that aspect of the medical model which locates the source of trouble as well as the treatment primarily in individuals. (1975, p. 86)

The 'socio-political impact of medicine' he said, is that it 'is quite capable of being used to achieve certain political aims (amoral interventions) or as a mask for certain value assumptions (moral interventions)' (1975, p. 86).

In fact, 'the rise of medicine to the position of dominant explanatory model for deviance in industrial society had already been diagnosed by Parsons in his essay 'Definitions of Health and Illness in the Light of the American Values and Social Structure' (1958). Parsons found modern concern with, in particular, mental health more prevalent than with crime or sin, and he stated that more and more aberrations came under the treatment frame of reference. In this, Parsons saw an achievement of liberal democracy overcoming more punitive forms of social control. Freidson (1970a, 1970b) argued that through this shift in importance between the judicial system exerting repressive sanctions and the medical system using reconciliatory measures, the latter more and more acquired connotations of the former. Rather than becoming more benign to the individual, society's institutions of social control became less fragmented and lost or closed niches which spared the patient punitive control.

In the second half of the 1970s, Conrad (1975, 1979) offered the same argument. He showed that through medicalisation of social control, redefining deviance 'from badness to sickness', medicine acquired a political role. It is used, argued Conrad and Schneider (1980b), more or less forcibly to treat those who would otherwise protest against intolerable living conditions or political repression. The political message is that medicine's power must be curtailed. Waitzkin (1983) endorsed McKeown's questioning effectiveness and efficiency of modern medicine (1979, pp. 190–8), and acknowledged for the physician what he called a *pastoral* role. Despite medicine's claim to be scientific and thus divorced from law and religion, he quoted Zola (1972, p. 487) as saying that modern medicine was 'nudging aside, if not incorporating, the more traditional institutions of religion and the law'. Waitzkin advocated for doctors a role far removed from technological excellence. He wrote: 'Even if their effectiveness is difficult to prove for large populations, medical professionals can offer nurturance, counseling, and emotional support for clients when they are ill or troubled. This service is analogous to what religious practitioners provided in less secularized societies' (1983, pp. 38–9).

This political nature of medicine on the background of medicalisation of large parts of modern society constitutes a historical necessity, insists Zola: 'This is not occurring through the political power physicians hold or can influence, but is largely an insidious and often undramatic phenomenon accomplished by "medicalizing" much of daily living, by making medicine and the labels "healthy" and "ill" *relevant* to an ever increasing part of human existence' (1972, p. 487). Such warnings imply that medicine's claims to heal and cure are deemed identical with self-righteousness. Freidson's scathing criticism of professional dominance, together with A. Cochrane's (1972) doubts about scientific testing of surgical and other procedures which echoes McKeown's (1965) and Dubos' (1959) refutation of the successes of technological medicine of the last century, serve to warrant fears of medical power. While medicine is called ineffective, the political implications of its unlimited growth appear daunting.

The idea that medicine is supposedly ineffective also inspires a second line of argument. It starts with showing how historically relative modern medical knowledge is. Although allegedly representing an apolitical truth universally applicable, medicine is said to mirror belief systems and typical social relationships of any era in which it is practised. This entails that it is far from immune against the particular structure of a society. Using the work of Foucault to prove how much medical knowledge owes to the invention of *clinical gaze* in the wake of the French Revolution, and how modern psychosomatic thinking is relative to present-day society, Figlio documents for various diseases the close relationship between medical theories and relations of production experienced by the workers who fall ill (1978, 1982). He justifies his approach in a constructionist-cum-Marxist way:

> In answer to the question, How do we historicise medicine?, my answer is that we treat its concepts as symbolic systems whose political function is to reinforce social relations necessary to the capitalist mode of production. The symbolic systems will make those relations appear natural, and this naturalness will both reinforce those relations and render the

symbolic system apparently autonomous from its social roots. Finally, they will conceal the origins of social relations in the mode of production, and thus hide the roots of structural domination and hierarchy in society. (1978, p. 170)

Therefore, the aim is to demystify medicine. This means that, first, its claim to political and value neutrality is rejected and its ideological character revealed. Second, it is shown to be a symbolic system embedded in the belief structure of the ruling classes. Third, the latters' supremacy is understood as one which turns the rules of the dominant classes into the dominant rules by threatening the powerless until they submit. This is done through the state. Therefore, fourth, the political issue in the forefront is the unholy alliance between state and ruling classes which facilitates the unchecked growth of the 'medical model'.

In this, the relationship between medicine and sociology takes on a new quality. Taylor and Rieger's (1984/5) rediscovery of the work of Virchow (1848), and also Waitzkin's endorsement of it (1981), serves to reformulate the scientific basis of medicine. While clinical theory hitherto bases its illness explanation on natural science models, medicine is now proclaimed a social science instead. In its concluding sections the report, which the 26-year old Virchow (who later wrote a seminal work on cellular pathology) filed with the Prussian government in the revolutionary months of 1848, attempts to draw a connection between the typhoid epidemic in Upper Silesia and the mining population's living conditions of abject poverty and powerlessness. He recommends better wages, education and transportation as a way of improving the material as well as spiritual well-being of the workers. To be sure, Virchow is aware of the fact that economic reform in Prussia including the introduction of modern industry has until then resulted from enlightened civil servants' forward-looking policies. So he pleads for their empathy with the workers to prevent more famine and disease. He writes (but his belief in the benevolent function of the emerging welfare state is curiously disregarded by his modern disciples):

The acumen and ability which civil servants have as a result of their detailed knowledge of the country and its needs will serve to increase the national wealth and to secure the welfare of each citizen. This being achieved, one can then think about achieving a state in which work not only provided men with food, clothes and shelter, but is enjoyable in itself and is combined with full opportunities for education. (Taylor and Rieger, 1984/85, p. 554)

What is emphasised about Virchow's beliefs is that he couples medical with social reform. In particular, his 'rhetorical but effective slogan: . . . Medicine is a social science, and politics nothing but medicine on a grand scale' (Taylor and Rieger, 1984/85, p. 548) is to contain a message that deserves reiterating after over 100 years of near oblivion. In the light of modern epidemiological findings on social inequality of health states, Virchow's opinion that medicine is a social science, and politics is medicine on a grand scale, is hailed as the *credo* of modern medical sociology. The new medical science, if it is a social science, should also be conscious of its political task. Medicine now becomes politicised in that medical measures are to contribute to the well-being of the population at large. Health care must then be a democratic right of everybody rather than the privilege of the well-insured or well-positioned few.

Such politicisation of medicine, it is argued, changes its focus from instrumental procedures to expressive care. Medical sociology, deemed an essential ingredient of the new social medicine, is warned not to overlook this change. Echoing Gold's (1977) opinion that the identity of medical sociology forecloses identification with clinical practice, Frankenberg (1986) writes: 'Indeed, I would wish to argue that the major danger for medical sociologists of taking their problems ready-made from the medical and, latterly, even from other healing professions is precisely either the undervaluing of the expressive or . . . its subordination to the instrumental' (1986, p. 623).

This warning is directed against basing medical sociology on the teachings of Parsons. In a recent article entitled 'The Medicalization of Social Control', O'Neill argues that a redirection of the welfare state has taken place over the last decades, absorbing class conflict through redefining political life in terms of client rather than citizen relationships. In this change, professional sociology has a stake since it gives advice to governments and thus acquires 'a quasi-medical function' (O'Neill, 1986, p. 362): 'The *therapeutic state* in turn employs the discourse of the social sciences according to a medico-legal model whose function is to pacify clients, or to produce docile citizens'.

O'Neill's revealing that Parsonian (together with Durkheimian and Freudian) social science is an instrument of repression is all but unambiguous. He extends the diagnosis of politicisation of medicine to incorporate medical-sociological thinking. Parsons' work is denounced as another quasi-medical approach where the bio-power over the body revealed by Foucault for the medical sciences is endorsed for the social sciences. Embracing instead the teachings of the women's health movement, anti-psychiatry, and holistic medicine, O'Neill sees:

> the clinicalization of the socio-psychic spaces in the American social order and the medicalization of the concept and techniques of social control . . . They open up a new field of power relations which we have called the therapeutic state and in which the life-sciences are the hegemonic modes of power/knowledge. (O'Neill, 1986, p. 363)

Thus, two arguments characterise the relationship between politics and medicine as seen by the conflict-theory approach. First, medicalisation of much of everyday life is diagnosed. This renders medicine one of the most potent agencies of social control. It calls for the demystification by sociology of the claim to value-free scientific rigour of modern clinical practice. Second, politicisation of medicine is demanded which implies that medicine is redefined as social science. If sociology becomes basic to medical knowledge this, in turn, entails that 'politics is nothing but medicine on a grand scale'. However, the politics in question frequently are far from the modern welfare state. The latter is criticised for the medicalisation of politics, namely, turning the political life of the citizen into an agency–client (or professional–patient) relationship. Politically astute medicine, an avowed social science, ought to focus not on instrumental but on expressive processes. An anti-technological impetus pervades the idea of how politics could become medicine-like on a community scale.

Two models of illness

The general idea is that illness answers to universal risk embedded in social status and environment. Since the risk is universal, a supplementary condition is needed which explains when and why one's susceptibility turns into sickness. This facilitating condition splits into two aspects if the nature of this link is discussed in more detail. In this, the question of what the role of the individual is *vis-à-vis* illness-inducing influences becomes crucial. Comaroff's definition may serve as a starting point:

> Illness is a particular expression of a universal feature of human existence, namely, the threat to personal viability and survival. This implies a partial or total eclipse of man's *social* being by his *natural* state . . . In short, illness touches upon universal paradoxes of human existence, which are mediated by particular cultural concepts and values. (1982, p. 51)

This can be conceptualised in two ways. First, a process is envisaged through which an individual is or may become the focus of medical attention (i.e., become a clinical case). This 'caseness' of the individual's experience allows for the investigation of forces and factors impinging upon him or her while becoming ill as well as while recuperating or undergoing rehabilitation. Cultural concepts and values refer to beliefs and hopes held, the social support received, actions taken to mitigate the person's plight, and the success of coping and help rendered; or, on the other hand, that the social being is overwhelmed by the natural state may refer to the society at large. This points at wholesale life circumstances as are embodied in the relationships of production (economic and otherwise) or in the power of the state. Here, illness is focused on as a collective experience, and individualisation of the focus is recognised as undue 'blaming of the victim'. It is the attitudes and actions of the community as a whole which count. The society thus becomes the locus of the 'universal paradoxes of human existence'. Through identification of unhealthy life styles or environmental influences as epidemiological or ecological phenomena, and through tracking down their connection with the prevailing economic system or political regime, medical sociology identifies social causes of disease. They are to be found in contradictions in the society's structure.

Along this dividing line, however, two models of illness explanation may be distinguished under the conflict theory paradigm. They may be more tentative than the ones distinguished for the structural-functionalist, interactionist and phenomenological paradigms. While the other paradigms developed longer ago and have been commented on in secondary literature, the conflict view has only developed over the last 15 years and has so far hardly been evaluated in its entirety in secondary literature. Of course, Marxism has been the target of non-Marxist criticism, and social constructionism has recently been debated (Bury, 1986, 1987). Also, life-change research has occasionally been submitted to critical comment (Gerhardt, 1979b, 1985b; Bebbington, Tennant and Hurry, 1985). By and large, secondary literature so far is scarce and has little influence on the sprawling variety of research with more or less eclectic theoretical leanings. The conception of the two models of illness explanation given here must be understood as a venture. As with the paradigms outlined in previous chapters, those in the conflict-theory frame also both contain a conception of aetiology and one of therapy.

The *loss* paradigm concentrates on the individual's experience during falling ill and recovery (or illness maintenance). The starting–point is the at-risk or susceptibility state which is contained in any major social status. It is understood to be the reverse of protective factors. The latter are particularly beneficial in the case of heightened vulnerability due to forces contained in the individual's biographical situation. The worst biographical events are changes which bring about the loss of a part of one's world or the loss of protective agents. This, in turn, threatens the breakdown of resistance resources. In this predicament social support acts as a buffer to resource failure. But when illness strikes, social support may also help to speed up recovery, and prevent further adverse effects of the illness or guard against incidence of further illness(es). Treatment, in this vein, is the strengthening of resources which act as social support. They help to restore the person's resistance against breakdown. It is in this function that self-help groups have an important role to play.

The *deprivation* paradigm is concerned with the plight of whole populations. Its focus is on the community whose life is ordered by a certain social structure including the economy and the state. The at-risk or susceptibility situation is contained in such issues as being exposed to environmental pollution with toxic waste, less than satisfactory road safety standards, stressful or dangerous conditions of work, violent family relations, or shortage of food or shelter. The process of becoming ill is divided into one of collective worsening of the general state of health, followed by a certain proportion of the endangered population seeking help for a disease. There are graded risks for different strata of the population, with the lowest social class having the highest mortality rates in most industrial societies. Treatment, according to this model of illness explanation, consists of societal rather than individual measures. Changes in modes of production, and also the welfare state, are seen by many authors as the most effective if not the only viable way of overcoming the propensity to illness in modern societies. It may be mentioned that protagonists of the deprivation paradigm also plead for the deprofessionalisation and demedicalisation of health care. Their views often follow an interpretation of Marxism which owes much to the work of Foucault.

These two models, the loss paradigm and the deprivation paradigm, seem so different that one may find it difficult to subsume them under the same heading of conflict theory. What unites them, however, is the firm belief that *inequality* is one of the major sources of suffering in modern society, and that inequality is an expression of covert or overt social conflict. Both views state that modern social science has a responsibility to alleviate the suffering induced by societal conflict, and that medical sociology can help to remedy medicine's alleged inability to give appropriate and effective health care. It is the latter, so to speak, more-than-scientific endeavour which seems to link together much of the last two decades' writing on illness in society.

Chapter 13
The Loss Model

As a biological breakdown engendered by societal influences, illness is conceptualised as a pattern of symptoms. That these cause suffering and incapacity concerning social functioning leads to sociologists being concerned that as much as possible of illness should be prevented. In this, illness denotes a biological state but the circumstances of its development, onset and manifestation are social. That is, the erosion of physiological capacities for unimpeded bodily functioning and deterioration of interpersonal capacities for psychological functioning occur through a socially structured environment impinging upon the individual. In this, personality may mean vulnerability to 'wear and tear' effects of biography, life style or hazardous surroundings. But more risks stem from the susceptibility to disease contained in each major social status (sex, age, class, etc.). However, vulnerability and susceptibility need not necessarily 'produce' disease. On the one hand, triggers or aggravating factors exacerbate risks implied in one's normal existence through class, sex, age and so on. On the other hand, buffering influences which neutralise risks must be inoperative or ineffective if illness strikes. These usually originate in other aspects of one's normal social existence, particularly the worlds of friends, family, and colleagues, for instance. Breakdown from disease results from a disequilibrium or negative balance between susceptibility and support. The most devastating trigger as well as a potent causal agent tipping the balance towards illness are experiences of social *loss*. They include loss of environment such as through migration, loss of role such as through bereavement, and other of similar impact. It is this illness-inducing effect of changes (or conflict) in the environment, and resulting lack of person–environment fit which makes real the risks contained in vulnerability and susceptibility.

277

The three stages of aetiology

The normality stage

Vulnerability and variability.   Propensity to illness is unequally distributed in society. Two classes of factors are documented through research to be foci of risk. They are, on the one hand, biographical vicissitudes and personality features (which may often be interrelated) and, on the other hand, role statuses which organise social inequality of resources and life chances: namely, sex, age, race and class, among others.

Biographical vicissitudes, for instance, are suspected by Hinkle and his collaborators (1956) of accounting for the higher incidence of past sickness disability among the subsample of healthy adult men (employees of a company) who are found to have the majority of illnesses. In a variety of studies, the Cornell University research group[38] proves that changes in life set-up are crucial for what they detect as 'clusters of illness' for certain years and certain people. In a later overview, Hinkle relates this to the nature of disease as well as biographical dynamics:

> In populations of similar people who share similar experiences over comparable periods of one or two decades, between the ages of 10 and 50, there will be a few people who have a great many episodes of disabling illness and days of disability, some who have a moderate number, many who have very little, and some who have none . . . The explanations . . . arise partly from arbitrary and empirical procedures that are used to define and classify the manifestations of illness . . . Some diseases such as coronary heart diseases are manifestations of other diseases such as arteriosclerosis . . . The occurrence of minor and transient episodes of illness increases the likelihood that major and life-endangering episodes of illness will occur . . . When people have preexisting susceptibilities to illness, or have established patterns of illness, the frequency of their illnesses and their number and kind are likely to change when there are significant changes in their social and interpersonal relationships. The apparent reasons for this have been mentioned several times. Changes in significant social and interpersonal relationships are very often accompanied by changes in habits, changes in patterns of activity, changes in the intake of food and medication, and changes in the exposure to potential sources of infection or trauma. They are also frequently associated with changes in mood and with physiological changes directly mediated by the central nervous system. Any or all of these might affect the frequency and severity of illness. (1974, pp. 38–40)

Biographical vicissitudes which may or may not be responsible for the incidence of illness interact with congenital or acquired predispositions towards metabolic, gastrointestinal, or cardiac 'vulnerabilities'. The Cornell team investigates large-scale biographical changes and trauma, such as emigration (immigration), forcible police interrogation, political revolution or dislocation of population groups, and their impact on the (always unequal) effect on health. The insight derived therefrom is that although life changes have an influence on health, the relationship is far from determinist:

> The effect of a social change, or a change in interpersonal relations, on the health of an individual cannot be defined solely by the nature of the change itself. The effect depends on the physical and psychological characteristics of the person who is exposed to the change and on the circumstances under which it is encountered. (Hinkle, 1974, p. 41)

The general notion behind the relationship is that of *life stresses* (H. G. Wolff, Wolf and Hare, 1950). It is noteworthy that this notion allows for an individualised reaction to any stressful event or experience; no environmental determinism results. The unique biographical quality of the life (and person) concerned is also partly addressed in Friedman and Rosenman's (1971) idea of coronary-prone (Type-A) behaviour. What Rosenman's questionnaire (published 1978) elicits, which the more frequently used *Jenkin's Activity Scale* does not, is a person's considerably idiosyncratic pattern of pushing him- or herself, interrupting others in conversation, showing signs of tension in facial and gestural expression, and so on. The latter may be a behavioural reaction to difficult life situations and must not represent a character trait. This entails that Type A in the original version is at least partly related to biographical vicissitudes producing (temporary) vulnerability to coronaries.

A third conception of vulnerability also acknowledges aspects of individual biographical dynamics. Following Weiss (1969), Brown and his associates find four factors defining a woman's increased vulnerability to depressive breakdown (only becoming effective once she encounters a severe life event: i.e., loss experience or extended difficulty). These are death of mother before the age of 11, lack of husband or boy-friend who may be regarded as a confidant, care for three or more children under 14 at home, and lack of employment outside the house. These are biographical vicissitudes which often characterise a woman's life situation at any time prior to the occurrence of a traumatising event or unsurmountable difficulty (G. W. Brown *et al.*, 1975; Brown and Harris, 1978; Gerhardt, 1979b).

While some conceptualisations of vulnerability leave room for individual variations defying environmental determinism, more of the variability idea is phrased in terms of 'homo sociologicus': the statuses most extensively dealt with in the literature, and proved relevant for differential incidence and prevalence of illness, are sex, age, race and class.

As regards *sex*, men are shown to be more endangered by accidents, heart disease and lung cancer as well as liver cirrhosis and suicide, particularly when unmarried (Gove, 1973a); besides, men's life expectancy is lower in industrialised societies. Women are more frequent users of health services and with some likelihood are also more ill while, with an upward trend, their life expectancy exceeds that of men considerably. The illness risk contained in the female gender is debated as one of sex versus feminine role. In other words, the question is whether women are more susceptible to disease in general (notwithstanding that certain specific diseases are more prevalent in men), or whether they tend to perceive more symptoms which they present to doctors, and doctors tend to recognise more symptoms and treat more as illness in women than in men. The issue is one of the *compatibility* hypothesis versus the *stress* hypothesis, as Nathanson (1975) phrases it: is the feminine role more compatible with illness perception and incumbency, or are female roles more strenuous such that more illness results? Gove and Hughes (1979), in a controversial article, argue the stresses of the nurturant role. Contradicting them, Mechanic (1980, referring to 1976) points out that only the illness-behaviour argument is supported by reliable data. Going beyond both points of view Verbrugge (1983), using newly collected data, shows that the incidence of diagnosed illness in men and women varies for both genders according to whether or not they combine multiple roles: namely, parenthood, partnership, and employment. In these terms, vulnerability emerges as a state of relative role deprivation rather than one due to use of sex-related stereotypes, be they accounted for by illness behaviour or doctors' propensity to diagnose.

Age in medicine usually means tripartite classification into childhood, adulthood and old age, the former and the latter subject to special disciplines (paediatrics and, more recently, geriatrics). Increased vulnerability of the growing or decaying organism is borne by the very young and the very old (e.g. MacIntire, 1977). Their physiological vulnerability often combines with other disadvantages associated with disenfranchised status such as class or race. The aged in the lowest social class and those of non-white race are shown to be the most endangered in various respects (Kosa and

Zola, 1969/75; Townsend, 1789). In a similar vein, N. Hart (1978) shows that the average physical growth of lower-class children is poorer than that of upper-class children, and more lower-class babies suffer from low and very low birth weight. As regards differential generalised health risks, adulthood defines employ- ment status and 'life chances' for social participation (Dahrendorf, 1979); future research will undoubtedly give it more attention.

Race is not always separable from culture. Zborowski (1952) and Zola (1966) emphasise cultural tendencies to perceive and react to symptoms. These certainly represent differential suscepti- bility to illness. Delay in seeking care (which exacerbates disease) is not the reverse of cultural propensity to perceive symptoms. Some racially distributed risks are genetic such as, for instance blacks' higher susceptibility to hypertension or sickle-cell anaemia. Most salient are relationships between race and poverty since ethnic origin is a powerful determining factor of social-class status and life chances. Dohrenwend and Dohrenwend (1970) phrase the disadvantage which race (and class) entails as lowered levels of material resources engendering lower levels of capacity to use available resources successfully.

Social class, in a broad range of literature, is shown to be inversely related to health. Epidemiology gives a rather daunting picture of increased morbidity as well as mortality rates for lower- class populations (particularly the lowest strata of mostly unskilled workers). Explanations range from poor environmental conditions (housing, exposure to pollution) through stressful work conditions (including low job security) to insufficient nutrition and largely unavailable or unsympathetic medical care. To these are added unsatisfactory coping mechanisms. Syme and Berkman (1976/78), in a secondary analysis of data collected by Kitagawa and Hauser (1973), attribute the very large number of disease in the lower- class population to less effective coping styles (life styles). They write:

> Generalised susceptibility to disease may be influenced . . . also by differences in the way people cope with . . . stress. Coping, in this sense, refers . . . to the more generalised ways in which people deal with problems in their everyday life. It is evident that such coping styles are likely to be products of environmental situations and not indepen- dent of such factors. Several coping responses that have a wide range of disease outcomes have been described. Cigarette smoking is one such coping response that has been associated with virtually all causes of morbidity and mortality; obesity may be another coping style associated with a high rate of many diseases and conditions; pattern A behaviour is an example of a third coping response that has been shown to have

relatively broad disease consequences. There is some evidence that persons in the lower classes experience more life changes and that they tend to be more obese and to smoke more cigarettes. (1976/78, p. 402).

Recently, unemployment has been added to the range of problems which imply higher disease risk. While, in the 1970s, the debate between Brenner (1971, 1973, 1975) and Eyer (1977) made it evident that a statistical link exists between unemployment, morbidity (hospital admission) and mortality, it left unsolved whether unemployment affects mortality, or whether business booms cause more stresses and therefore more disease. In an overview of relevant research literature, Colledge (1982) hypothesised that unemployment was associated with increased susceptibility to illness through mediation of identity loss. He wrote:

> Unemployment, or the threat of unemployment, is an assault not only on economic stability, but the deeper social roots of the individual. The total lack of control felt by the worker over the situation, their inability to sell their labour could be the largest single hazard to their health, outside physical and environmental factors. Therefore the 'dole' and the lack of dignity that surround claiming social security benefits is a powerful cause of stress for the worker facing redundancy or intermittent periods of unemployment. (1982, p. 1926)

If the question is how the loss of the roots in the identity of working men (or women) erodes the resistance of adults to disease, the answer cannot lie in how susceptibility develops because, as mentioned earlier, various authors emphasise that there is a general risk in a normal population for subpopulation but only a fraction of those at risk fall ill. Two further conditions have to be met. One is that counteracting forces which help to preserve normality (or health) do not work in a particular case, or are not strong enough. The second is that additional aggravating forces impinge which upset the balance between vulnerability and protective influences.

Resources and relations. When Cassel (1976) developed his ideas about host resistance, and Cobb (1976) in the same year put forward his conjectures on the protective effect of social support, both were concerned with the at-risk individual's avoidance of breakdown. The conception which they endorsed, and which has since become corroborated by widespread evidence from research, was that breakdown is only likely in cases of increased stress (including conditions defining both vulnerability and susceptibility) where forces establishing host resistance are too weak to mitigate the danger.

As regards the nature of these forces, two hypotheses are ventured. One is that stable social relations have a health-preserving, even life-prolonging effect. Berkman and Syme (1979) find among Alameda County respondents of nine years earlier that many with a small or unreliable network of social relations (scoring low on the Social Network Index) are not alive at follow-up. The quality of social support derived from their social networks at the time of the original interviews and in times of crises thereafter must have been lower than that of those who had more support, and survived. Elinson (1985), emphatically reporting on this research, remarks: 'From a theoretical perspective, Berkman and Syme's findings were interpreted as providing evidence linking sociology and physiology through a mechanism described as host resistance. Other investigators, notable in Sweden . . ., have shown relationships between blood chemistry and socially stressful situations and roles' (1985, p. 273).

The other hypothesis contends that the benefit derived from relations is mainly psychological. Thus, Shuval (1981) suggests to disregard physiological processes 'since resources controlling levels of resistance are largely socially and psychologically determined' (1981, p. 337). Her approach is based on that of Antonovsky (1974, 1979) who understands resistance resources as the propensity to give meaning to events even of threatening nature. Antonovsky maintains: 'If anything has been learned in the study of stressful life events, it is that what is important for their consequences is the subjective perception of the meaning of the event rather than its objective character' (1974, p. 246).

In a similar vein, Cobb (1976) defines as supportive any relationship conveying to the person information making him or her valid in partnership, or community. Conversely, H. G. Wolff (1953/68) defines as stressful (i.e., threatening) significant events with negative meaning: for instance, 'parents, power, possession, sexuality, the hours of work, or even the type of work or the amount of freedom of action' (1953/68, p. 203). These explicitly include 'seemingly benign circumstances, events or demands' (1953/68, p. 5) which nevertheless may eventually become antecedents to 'irreversible tissue damage' (1953/68, p. 134). The idea is that no objectively menacing quality of events but subjective feelings of threat are at the root of lacking resistance resources.

This has a methodological implication. Antonovsky insists on the subjective character of negative consequences of stressful life events, and Wolff points out that what matters is whether the person feels threatened rather than whether an issue 'is' threatening. Both argue in favour of methodological individualism: that is, they make each person in his or her particular life situation the measuring rod for the social-science assessment of threat. They reject the 'objective' parameters used by epidemiology. The latter are deemed incapable of accounting for vicissitudes as well as blessings of particular biographical settings and contexts.

Although seemingly contradicting such methodological individualism G. W. Brown (1974) makes the same point. He insists that resources and relations which constitute a woman's actual life situation ought to be assessed (by a research team) as a composite picture. In this, the woman's own attempt to give meaning to her situation ought not be regarded as altogether objective. Instead, the woman's account is possibly influenced by an urge to make sense of what happened, particularly if her experiences are bad. In this, the less support received through resources and relations, the more may the individual feel obliged towards an interviewer to create an impression of coping well with a highly upsetting event (such as, for instance, unemployment, divorce, or eviction). Therefore, Brown suggests, the researcher must find ways of assessing the 'objective' level of threat through taking into account the particular context of the overall life situation, and then looking at what an added loss experience means in the light of it all. The relationship of this to the subjective feelings of loss for a woman and therefore her emotional reaction to a loss (life) event or sustained difficulty is explained later as one where, in each separate case, context is all-important. So G. W. Brown and Harris say about their method: 'First we took meaning out of our measure to avoid contamination and then in order to avoid being arbitrary and facile brought it back in the various descriptive scales' (1978, p. 99).

In sum, the normality stage as pictured by the loss approach is characterised by two sets of forces which act in opposite directions: on the one hand, vulnerability and susceptibility, deriving from biographical vicissitudes and social-status participation, lead to an increased risk of falling ill. On the other hand, relations and resources counteract the possible deleterious effects of risk and provide for security and protection. The normality phase, where people stay more or less away from the doctor and regard themselves as healthy, may thus be seen as the result of risk and resource balancing. To a certain extent, the two cancel each other out. G. W. Brown, in a recent article, phrases this in terms of class position versus stratification among the less affluent. He writes:

A particular working-class woman may have greater risk of developing a psychiatric disorder because of the raised risk of experiencing adversity stemming from her class position and at the same time a reduced risk because of the stratification system to which she belongs and the support this brings at times of adversity. (1983, p. 57)

Falling ill and seeking help

Effects of loss (conflict and change). In his monograph on the psychological effects of loss and change, Marris (1974) focuses on rehousing (slum clearance schemes), bereavement, and 'tribalism' (i.e., the expression of sense of loss in the face of changing institutions). He holds that in each instance, a mourning process sets in which may not be realised by those concerned. Behind it is what he calls 'the conservative impulse': 'If . . .consistency of purpose is one means of mastering events, the power of empathy is another: if you understand enough about other people, you can foresee how they will respond, and so govern their relationship with you in their terms as well as your own' (1974, p. 15). Once this sense of mastery is broken, Seligman (1975) argues in his book on learned helplessness, a loss of controllability and calculability of others or the world in general sets in. It gives rise to deep-seated despair, leading to an utter inability to make sensible moves. Behaviour is then severed from knowledge about the environment. That stereotyped rigidly unadapted behaviour is learned is demonstrated by Seligman through experiments which systematically frustrate animals or people. He shows how depression follows learned helplessness. Marris recognises depression as the third stage of the grieving-process sequence investigated by Parkes (1972): numbness, pining, depression, reconstruction. Following loss or change, grief for some becomes permanent: that is, depression blocks their accomplishing grief work. Brown and Harris (1978) discuss this under the label of low self-esteem. Psychiatric breakdown following a loss of role (realm of self-realisation) is facilitated by lack of self-esteem which, in turn, generates a sense of hopelessness. They write:

> The more a woman has committed herself to a given identity or cluster of identities the more her 'assumptive world', in Parkes's sense, will be caught up in it and the greater the severity of a crisis that deprives her of an essential part of it . . . Learning that one's child is in trouble with the police and that another has failed an important examination may be quite unrelated in an 'external' sense but jointly have a devastating impact on a woman's notion of herself as an effective mother. It is also possible to conceive of a specific appraisal of 'one' event influencing several identities . . . In our various discussions of the 'additivity' of provoking agents we have suggested that it is hopelessness about restoring a particular source of value that is usually crucial. (G. W. Brown and Harris, pp. 236–7)

A similar hypothesis is ventured by Antonovsky (1979) on the health-preserving effect of a generalised sense of coping. Ben-Sira (1985), following Antonovsky, sees feelings of *potency* as a crucial buffer against illness-inducing effects of stress. Antonovsky (1979, Chs. 5,6) maintains that one's sense of coherence regarding the world in general and one's personally experienced world in particular is strongly related to health and its breakdown. Among other data, he uses those of Engel (1974) on the *giving-up-given-up syndrome*[39] to explain the negative effect of lacking feelings of mastery. Ben-Sira holds that 'a feeling of potency, comprising confidence both in one's own capacities and in society which is perceived as basically ordered, predictable and meaningful [is] a stress-buffering mechanism in the coping-stress-disease relationship' (1985, p. 597).

Feelings of potency and self-esteem are understood as personality dispositions, but they are also seen as learned. The other possibility is that environmental stresses impinge to activate one's coping capacities. Pearlin *et al.* (1981) relate the buffering effect of supportive network ties to a facilitating stressor such as job disruption which brings out the buffering effect (or its absence) in the first place. The dependent variable in their study is depression. They explain:

> Do coping and supports combine with the sources of stress to mediate their effects? The answer is affirmative, but it is qualified by the fact that the statistically significant interactions almost exclusively involve job disruption . . . That is, the effectiveness of the mediators in vitiating strain, in buttressing the self, and in buffering depression is greater among the job losers than those who have been stably employed. This does not mean that job losers are more likely to be active copers or to have greater access to social supports; indeed, in the case of coping it is the opposite. What the results do indicate, quite clearly, is that when job losers do possess these resources, they are more likely to be the recipients of their benefits than are those with the same resources but whose employment has not been disrupted. (1981, pp. 349–50)

Pearlin *et al.*, like many others, confine their work to depression as an investigated outcome whose antecedents are studied. In recent years, the buffering effect has also been studied for illnesses other than psychiatric ones. Following on from the earlier work, Murphy and Brown (1980) investigate untreated illness in a London suburb and find that physical disorder is usually accompanied, and often preceded, by emotional disturbance. Psychiatric symptoms, they suggest, often follow severe life events before organic illness sets in. They therefore stipulate 'a causal link between severe events and organic illness, mediated by the development of psychiatric disorder' (1980, p. 334).

The nature of this link is further explored by research where the psychological is understood as mediator. This literature is concerned with the role of distress in, for example, myocardial infarction, or the stunted discharge of hostile emotions for aetiology of cancer(s). Siegrist *et al.* (1982) show for myocardial infarction that prior to their heart attacks, patients experienced major distress as documented by an increased life-event score and lack of social support at the workplace. In an overview of the literature on socio-cultural factors in the aetiology of cancer, Cox and Mackay (1982) criticise earlier psychological approaches. They propose that recent research establishes as influential 'first, the loss of, or lack of closeness or attachment to an important relation (often a parent) early in life, and second, the inability to express hostile feelings or more generally the abnormal release of emotion' (1982, p. 381). They resort to psychophysiological mechanisms regulating the immune system to explain the disease outcome. The argument that a unitary psychiatric pattern is to be found for various illnesses is further developed by McQueen and Celentano (1982). They focus on the multiple-disease outcome of a pattern of social factors which cause stress which, in turn, causes psychological deviance (disturbance). A buffering effect is seen to originate in social relations (i.e., 'social support systems and networks': 1982, p. 398).

In this literature, the effect of loss preceding illness is seen as psychological impairment. The fragile balance between susceptibility and support characterising the social functioning of an individual in the normality stage is broken by conflict or a change of environment. This triggers off the impairment of psychological fitness, particularly loss of identity or related feelings of potency or self-esteem (often due to a lost role). This, in turn, upsets psychophysiological mechanisms which affect the body's immune system. This explanation of disease onset has much in common with Mason's (1975) critical reinterpretation of Selye's (1956) attempt to account for the spectrum of physical lesions by an interplay between the GAS and the LAS. Selye contends that both are reactions to uniformly experienced stress stemming from a variety of environmental stressors. Mason maintains that the uniformity of reaction is due to the fact that there *is* only one reaction: namely, emotional disturbance is the explanatory factor representing the common element of different answers to a variety of stressful environmental stimuli.

What Mason and other researchers seem to overlook or undervalue is the variable nature of the buffering effect. Lazarus and

Opton (1966) point at the mitigating effects of interpretations on the perceived stressfulness of stimuli. Pearlin *et al.* (1981) call attention to the interactive effects between context and coping. Brown and Harris (1978) analyse each case separately and assess the degree of severity of life events in the light of a buffering effect of environmental protective factors. More broadly speaking, it is here that *meaning construction* must be considered.

Although on a survey-data basis, Pearlin and Radabaugh (1977) argue that an 'activity' such as alcohol consumption has a stress-buffering function. Similarly, smoking is often accounted for as a means of relaxation in tension situations (Wetterer and von Troschke, 1986). Not enough is known so far on a case basis on such (themselves noxious) efforts to offset the effect of noxious circumstances by behavioural self-support. What matters about them is that they are *meant* to be ameliorative. It may be assumed that this is also a level where individuals fight back against the deleterious effect of loss (conflict and change).

The concept of countervailing forces pitching loss against support only makes sense if the idea is introduced that eventually not only the quantity but also the quality of psychological deterioration matters. Seligman's (1975) conjecture of a state of *helplessness* may be understood as an attempt to understand the altered psychological state where the means–end association is broken and controllability and calculability of the world are no longer valid. The helpless person's or animal's behaviour (including endurance of hitherto presumably intolerable pains such as, for instance, electric shocks) documents how different the state of helplessness is from that of low but intact psychological prowess. It is this altered state of negative energy, so to speak, which can be understood as the point where the immune system may fail, and neuroendocrinological mechanisms may contribute to incipient lesions of organic functioning.

This may account for the origin of major disease such as myocardial infarction or cancer. It may help to understand the difference between acute and chronic disease, minor ailments and major sickness. Unfortunately, Seligman's more recent work (Garber and Seligman, 1980) does not elucidate the difference further. Rather, more experimental evidence is given of the existence of helplessness, using more variables. But it may be worthwhile to extend Seligman's original argument in the direction of life-change research exploring further the breakdown of grief work/social support buffers.[40]

Seeking medical care.   That a person is ill does not have to mean that he or she goes to see a doctor (or does so immediately upon noticing symptoms). That someone sees a doctor does not presuppose that he or she is ill. The disjunction between illness and illness behaviour, Armstrong (1984) argues, is one of the assumptions which allows for the notion that everybody who goes about his or her daily business is also potentially or actually ill. This implies that anyone can come under the scrutiny of being screened for illness, even those who feel that they do not need a doctor. On the other hand, those who see a doctor are understood to do so for other reasons than that their health fails. Zola (1970/73), under the title *From Person to Patient*, describes five reasons why someone decides to seek medical care. They are:

> (1) the occurrence of interpersonal crisis; (2) the *perceived* interference with social or personal relations; (3) sanctioning [from significant others]; (4) the *perceived* interference with vocational or physical activity; and (5) a kind of temporalizing of symptomatology [i.e. setting a time limit until when the complaint has to be gone, otherwise help is sought]. (1970/73, p. 114; emphasis mine)

To be sure, concomitant would be the presence of symptoms, but crucial for actually seeking care are additional social reasons of the five kinds.

Regarding the types one, two and four, Zola stresses the perceived nature of what becomes the reason. This calls to mind Mechanic's finding that *distress* plays a major role in determining a person's decision to seek medical or other help. Mechanic argues that psychological disturbance is at the root of illness, on the one hand, and underlies the perception of being ill as well as the decision to use medical facilities, on the other. The two issues, (illness and illness behaviour) are both seen to depend on psychological distress while not necessarily being related to each other. Mechanic writes:

> There is considerable evidence in both animals and humans that altered psychological states as induced by 'learned helplessness', lack of predictability, hopelessness, distorted feedback, loss, and a variety of other stressors affect bodily processes and the occurrence of disease . . . Moreover, such factors condition the ways people define health and illness, respond to symptoms and incapacity, and utilize the medical care system. (1978, p. 26)

The crux is that doctor and patient harbour different definitions of what illness means. While patients, usually spurred on by psychological distress, act on 'significant departures from their usual sense of wellbeing' (Mechanic, 1978), doctors tend to define illness as an organic lesion or psychiatric malfunctioning using an explanatory model derived from natural science.

The clash between doctor's and patient's perspectives is directly or indirectly pictured in much of the literature. Armstrong notes that the elaboration of the patient perspective into a view supposedly equal to that of the doctor is a recent accomplishment, dating back no longer than 50 years, even to its first very faint beginnings. Medical sociology supposedly has helped to elevate the patient perspective to more than secondary importance by giving it the grand name of a 'lay theory'. Basically, however, it is not the patient's view which matters, if we follow Armstrong's argument; rather, the medical paradigm itself is changing towards one of biographical medicine. Within it, what matters is what the doctor *hears* (not sees, as in the traditional clinical gaze), and this includes the patient's more or less garbled story, phrased in more or less medically meaningful lay-theoretical terms.

Against this background, the underutilisation of medical services by lower-class populations becomes a matter of two social worlds clashing. Although some figures for the use of medical care by middle- and lower-class patients show no marked discrepancy, a noticeable disadvantage for the latter is diagnosed (N. Hart, 1986a). Sociological literature frequently suggests that the lower-class population receives poorer services because of elitism. For instance, Riessman (1974) charges that the layout (and staffing) of services for the poor convey the impression to clients of being unwanted. She writes: 'The poor have undergone multiple negative experiences with organizational systems, leading to avoidance behavior, lack of trust and hence a disinclination to seek care and follow medical regimens except in dire need' (1974, p. 44).

The question is raised of whether this is due to cultural divergencies (facilitating elitism as an unavoidable consequence), or to deficiencies in the organisation of services which could easily be remedied. Riessman, to be sure, opts for the latter. She maintains: 'The assumption is that "good" experiences will result in behavioral change: the lack of appropriate utilization of health care by lower socioeconomic groups is not deeply culture bound, but can be modified given changes in the professional and the organization of medical care' (1974, p. 44).

The sociological credo is that medical care should be for everybody at all times, and that doctors and patients should be interested in providing and receiving care at all costs. This is no strong argument against the sprawling growth of medical services. If spread evenly over all countries and classes, and catering to all ills, professional medicine inevitably is caught in over-medicalisation. Some recent research challenges the idea that medicine tends to incorporate more and more previously non-medical issues into its jurisdiction. The case is made for alcoholism which receives a medical label since Jellinek's typology (1942, 1960) facilitates differential diagnosis.

P. M. Strong (1980), using material from two studies of general practitioners in Scotland, shows that there is little inclination to accept responsibility for, or haste to treat, patients' alcoholism. Most respondents express either mild empathy with some clients' sad fate or stress the fact that alcohol consumption is a matter of willpower and ought not come under medical jurisdiction. All doctors, however, report that they willingly treat a patient who feels able to abstain from drinking and needs a doctor's support. Strong suggests that dealing with alcoholics is part of what constitutes 'dirty work' for a clinically trained professional. The reason is that cures, if attainable, have little to do with the GP's efforts but come through changes in family ties, or attendance of Alcoholics Anonymous.

Partly using the same data, and focusing on the issue of whether a diagnosis is made, Blaxter (1978) finds that GPs have little avowed inclination to take on alcoholics. She argues that the reason lies in the nature of diagnosis itself. It is, she says, prescriptive (which means that it is geared towards potentially effective treatment). In fact, without prospects of successful cure diagnosis is said to appear rather meaningless within the confines of clinical practice. Blaxter goes on to point out that doctors may even react unfavourably to the idea that alcoholism comes under their jurisdiction:

> Dismay at the implication for action of social diagnosis may then create a reaction against the widening of the disease concept. This has been evident in the field of mental illness generally and the field of alcoholism specifically . . . Returning to diagnosis-as-category, it can be suggested that if the categories and the process get out of step – if the classificatory system no longer matches the generally accepted concepts of disease – then the result may be arbitrary choices of label and perhaps inappropriate action. (1978, pp. 16–17)

Seeking medical help, then, may not always be encouraged by the physician even in cases where the International Classification of Diseases (ICD) provides a diagnostic category. The sociological viewpoint, however, tends to disregard doctors' lack of acceptance of more and more aspects of life style-related behaviour being incorporated under disease labels.

In this, it is not held against the patients that they seek care not solely depending on severity of symptoms, but also propelled by psychological distress. Although the latter contributes to overly frequent use of medical services, and thus represents an aspect of medicalisation of life, sociologists tend to acquit the patient from attempting to exploit the doctor or medical system. In general, the patient is regarded as the weaker partner in a potentially conflict-prone doctor–patient encounter. Here, ramifications of the under-dog philosophy are obvious.

Behind the empathy between sociologist and patient, it seems, may be the latter's presumed need for social support. Various studies show that use of medical help increases after moving house, or migration in general, and settles down after a person lives in an area for a number of years; in the same vein, divorcees and recently bereaved have a higher incidence of visits to the doctor, as do women in general (Banks *et al.*, 1975; Beresford *et al.*, 1977). These groups may all be said to be in more need of social support. They have recently lost a source of support or have not yet built a network of support or are more likely not only to give but also receive or need support in accordance with the more nurturant role associated with female sex.

Disability and support

The loss paradigm's concern with illness and disability is with the form and amount of support which the sick and disabled can muster. Two topics in particular are discussed. On the one hand, the question is posed what positive effects support has on rehabilitation and recovery. On the other hand, it becomes a matter of debate whether the negative effect of lack of support (including social isolation) on longevity can be explained further. Both aspects, the positive and the negative, are often addressed in a descriptive manner. Numerous studies measure the amount of support received or sought after, and the degree of social isolation suffered, by various categories of the chronically ill and disabled.

Regarding what can be called the positive-effect thesis, Pearlin and Aneshensel (1986) elucidate it thus:

> In effect, the illness, injury, disability, or distress is treated as the stressor, and recovery from it or adjustment to it are the desired outcomes. The outcomes, in turn, are influenced by . . . the 'varying perceptions, thoughts, feelings, and acts affecting the personal and social meanings of symptoms, illness, disabilities and their conse-quences' (Mechanic 1977). Within the context of this model, interest is in part directed to the influence of coping and social supports on actions such as symptom recognition, help seeking, health services utilization, compliance, and rehabilitative activity. (1986, p. 427)

For instance, Finlayson and McEwen (1977) show that one year after myocardial infarction, the chance of having gone back to work is significantly higher for those patients whose wives name multiple sources of social support during the crisis and after, and also themselves think their husbands' bout of illness is over.

If the question is asked what social support *does* to achieve recovery and rehabilitation, two answers are provided. Both highlight the function of support in (re-)establishing environmental control (i.e. the feeling of control over one's environment). The first answer may be exemplified by Egbert *et al.*'s finding (1964) that encouragement and instruction on the expectable course of post-operative pain given by an anaesthetist to patients prior to intra-abdominal surgery considerably help to reduce post-operative narcotics use. In a similar vein, Querido (1959) finds that pre-operative counselling has a positive effect on patients' post-operative distress as well as recovery. Egbert *et al.* explain their result through an *active placebo effect*: 'We believe that our discussions with patients have changed the meaning of the postoperative situation for these patients. By utilizing an active placebo action, we have been able to reduce their postoperative pain' (1964, p. 826).

The second answer is more tentative. Hypothesising what happens when a severe loss threatens an individual's ability to cope, an article attempting a theoretical reconstruction of life-event research suggests that the restitutive function of *talk* ought to be recognised:

> The individual's privation is incorporated into a framework of 'understandable' and 'reasonable' patterns which may furnish two explanations: namely, why did the [illness] happen to the individual (and that it could have happened to others), and how can one's social environment be rearranged to overcome the undesirable and unsettling situation. In other words, talk provides explanatory accounts which in turn give meaning. (Gerhardt, 1979b, p. 214)

Support in the face of disability, therefore, is hypothesised as *interpersonal* process heavily relying on language and emotions. To a large extent support may be a function of talk that (re)arranges one's manageable world and (re)makes it into a controllable and calculable environment.

This can tentatively elucidate the negative-effect thesis of social support. The question is how, for example, can Berkman and Syme's (1979) epidemiological finding on the lower life expectancy of persons (patients) with poor supportive networks be accounted for? What is the *action rationale* or action story (Gerhardt, 1985a)? Research results distinguish between types of support. For example, Croog, Lipson and Levine (1972) investigate the triad *financial help/emotional support* through encouragement and morale boosting/*use of institutional services*. They find that recovery and occupational rehabilitation of heart patients have more to do with the first two than the third type of support. Equally, Morgan, Patrick and Charlton (1984) find among a community sample of the disabled in the London Borough of Lambeth that community services are relatively little used while intra-familial support is remarkably high. The separate effects of primary group affiliations and welfare-state support services (secondary group resources) are demonstrated by R. T. Smith and Midanik (1980). They show that rehabilitation and recovery, if successful, have nothing to do with one's primary-group resources of support, and are negatively related to one's use of secondary resources. In particular, 'the disabled who did not utilize secondary group resources and placed less reliance on physician support during the time of claim adjudication were more likely to recover' (1980, p. 54).

Smith and Midanik are puzzled by their results because they 'do not lend support to the hypothesis of a positive relationship between social resources and recovery status' (1980, p. 57). Their results seem to show, however, that the positive-effect and negative-effect sides of the stress/support/illness link are separate phenomena, and are both stages of a *deteriorative process*.

The psychological deterioration preceding illness incumbency, it was argued above, may be divided into two phases: that of a decreasing level of sense of control, and that of a more or less complete loss of controllability altogether (helplessness). The use of secondary services as sources of help may be more related to the latter than the former. Non-use of welfare-support resources may signify a higher degree of reversibility of the loss of feelings of potency that, in turn, may occur in all illnesses to a certain extent. From this vantage point, Berkman and Syme's (1979) Alameda County residents whose premature mortality proves related to their poor received social support may fall among the category of secondary-sources users. In fact, persons scoring low on the Social Network Index are more often single and living alone, and tend to use evening classes and church services as sources of social support rather than encounters with friends and family.

Therapy and the self-care of patients

Aetiology is conceptualised as a failure of protective resources in the face of conflict, change and hardship. The turning point remains not altogether clear where coping, if unaided by social support, fails to reverse the deterioration of health-preserving abilities. The loss model's notion of treatment focuses on the patient's ability to build up resistance resources which may (re-) establish an acceptable level of psychological and/or physiological functioning. Due to an alleged lack of appropriate help-giving in medical practice, the idea is that patients' own capacities to take care of their health ought to be strengthened. This explicitly includes measures beyond doctors' efforts.

In this, therapy's task is to build up resources of emotional support which boost the patient's ability for self-care. Professional medical practice is understood as a lever to render patients capable of promoting their own health. Since emotional equilibration is the most salient source of well-being, affective therapy should be the doctor's goal. The sociologist concerned with quality of care reverses the analytical perspective. Now, the patient is the primary locus of health promotion. Levin, Katz and Holst (1977) write in their summary of the results of a conference sponsored by the WHO on the topic of 'The Individual in Primary Care' (Copenhagen, 11–15 August 1975):

> The labor-intensive character of health services, particularly in meeting the increased demands for preventive care and chronic disease management, suggests a new look at the lay resources as the *primary*, primary health care resource. This is not to argue that achieving a more individually responsible and self-active society would immediately result in cost containment or reduction. (1977, p. 25)

Medical treatment's primary focus is what ought to be primary: namely, the patient as responsible lay person. This means that medical practice must counteract the patient's susceptibility to illness, irrespective of whether this fits into the traditional organisation of medical services. Self-care and prevention make the patient and the state equal partners of the doctor in his therapeutic role. In particular, three issues are focused on:

(a) primacy of primary care over hospital, with special reference to patients' self-help;
(b) replacement of cure (or care) by prevention which calls for

state-funded prevention programmes including health education;

(c) prority of patients' rights as a political tenet of medical sociology.

Redefining primary care

From the perspective of patients as self-propelled individuals everything medical has to succumb to the lay perspective of explanation and action. What matters is that patients' propensity to sustain stress, including their coping ability as well as access to social support, is kept intact or made stronger. They are to become able to combat sickness risk inherent in their various social statuses as well as in ambiguities and privations stemming from their various biographies and life styles. This relies heavily on emotional equilibration, and coping capacities promote what social support often provides: emotional ease and equilibrium leading to happiness and/or satisfaction.[41] Research using the loss model is often concerned with the quality of intimate relationships (e.g., whether marriage partners are confidants for each other) because emotional equilibration is a source of protection against stress and subsequent disease.

Ben-Sira (1986) develops a theory delineating the function of primary care as giving emotional support. The starting-point is that the patients' aim in illness behaviour is to attain affective satisfaction. They utilise medical care because it renders them capable of alleviating their anxieties and thus able to cope responsibly with their everyday lives. If such affective needs are not met, patients are more prone to succumb to the stress–disease mechanism stemming from lack of social support. Unfortunately, Ben-Sira contends, doctors are rarely inclined to provide sufficiently the 'affective behaviour' which has the most beneficial effect on their patients' satisfaction level. The placebo function of medical care which physicians' affective behaviour entails is thus curtailed by a 'vicious circle of primary care frustration'. He writes:

> We have seen that the pressures both on patients and on doctors may lead to the development of a vicious circle of frustrations in the realm of primary care: chances are that lay-persons will be pressed toward 'medicalized somatization' of their emotional problems due to primary care practitioners' tendency to ignore the necessity for relating to the patient's emotional state throughout the medical intervention. Not getting the needed satisfaction of anxiety alleviation, will set into

motion a process of 'shopping around' for affect. Physicians, on the other hand, as a response to the pressure on them by 'shopping' patients and by bureaucratic employers, will be even less inclined to demonstrate affective behavior. The . . . conclusions . . . lead us to the hypothesis that the greater the progress in the medical profession's body of knowledge, the greater the chances for a *counter-health-promoting* effect of primary medical care, this counter-healthpromoting effect being a consequence of the . . . *primary care frustrations.* (1986, p. 150)

Such counterproductive development, in turn, could be curtailed. Robinson (1980) suggests that self-help be put into the forefront. In 1977, Robinson and Henry delineate the positive ways of handling health problems by various self-help groups such as Alcoholics Anonymous or CARE, a network of groups through which cancer victims can come to terms with their lives. In particular, such groups enable the afflicted to identify with their condition, cope with practicalities as well as stigma, and – as in the case of alcoholism – often regain control over their disease. Robinson (1980) endorses this by referring to the WHO's Alma Ata Declaration on Primary Health Care (which also formulates the goal of Health for all by the year 2000). The idea is that primary care lies with the person who is or is not a patient, and community participation is a major source of proper health care. Robinson elucidates: 'Fending for yourself means, also, that all citizens have a right and a duty to create the conditions and contribute to the measures whereby anyone can live a healthy life. Developed countries, no less than developing ones, must learn to "fend for themthelves" in this sense' (1980, p. 416).

According to Levin, Katz and Holst (1977, p. 78) this redirection of health care towards self-help must follow the *primum non nocere* principle of medical work: This ethical principle formulated by Hippocrates and valid for ancient Greece as well as modern society demands that therapy should *do no harm*. This contains a criticism of medicine insofar as many authors deplore the extent to which modern medical practice allegedly produces iatrogenic disease. Illich's (1975a, 1975b) charging medicine with three-level iatrogenesis (clinical, social and structural) is widely accepted in medical sociology as far as the lowest level is concerned (namely, the creation of illness through clinical treatment). Other authors emphasise more strongly the unfavourable relationship between the cost of medical care and the proportion of morbidity treated. For instance, Levine, Feldman and Elinson (1983), in an article entitled 'Does Medical Care do any Good?' urge medical sociology to ask the following type of questions, 'in keeping with a social rather than distinctively biological view of health':

> To what extent is medical care able to maintain sick people at home with their families and in the community as against relegation to an institution? . . . To what extent does medical care compensate for negative impacts of the larger social system, e.g. exposure to hazards of dangerous occupations, poor housing, automobile accidents, food and tobacco policies? To what extent does medical care provide useful advice to promote preventive health behavior with regard to smoking, diet, and exercise? (1983, p. 400)

As much as the answers are not in the affirmative, a change of direction of effective health care is advised. If the 'real needs' of the population are to be met, primary care ought to tackle the above issues. It is assumed that what produces patients' satisfaction is also good for their health. Their self-preservation strengthens emotional resources which enhance ability to cope with stress and offset risks of susceptibility. Coping, to be sure, interrupts the stress (susceptibility)/loss/disease cycle, preferably at an early stage. Whatever provides social support is understood as 'good for your health'. Self-help groups are seen to buttress, supplement or replace the family (as prime resource-giver) or other social relations networks where they are deficient or absent.

The new role of the welfare state

When the state became involved in issues of health care provision, in the nineteenth century, its role was that of guarantor of medical care irrespective of patients' ability to pay. Behind the German Empire's setting up of Sick Funds together with Accident and Old-Age Pension Funds in 1883–9 was the state's interest that inaccessibility of health care should not drive workers into the arms of the Socialist party (Gerhardt and Kirchgässler, 1986a, p. 50). A democratising effect also spurred the 1911 Social Insurance Act in the UK and, expecting to serve the aims of equal access and equal care even better, the 1946 National Health Service Act (Forsyth, 1973). The various revisions of the structure of the National Health Service between 1974 and 1982 were meant to improve upon the two aspects of the democracy problem under a state-funded service. These are, first, the ratio between cost and effectiveness (since taxation funds stem from every citizen, they ought to be spent in the interest of most); and, second, equal distribution of services and their use over all social classes and geographic regions (Levitt, 1976; Levitt and Wall, 1984). Equally, in the US, a health system providing equal access and clinically appropriate treatment for everybody has been a tenet of state (federal) policy since the 1930s. With the *New Deal* philosophy of state-engendered redistribution of unequal resources failing,[42] only in the 1950s were welfare programmes providing health care for the indigent population instigated by federal legislation, but they often could not win approval by individual states. To a certain extent, legislation passed in the 1960s on behalf of the elderly (Medicare) and poor (Medicaid) facilitated partial democratisation of access and distribution (Marmor, 1970).

Nevertheless, the situation is one of less than satisfactory democratisation despite the state's heavy financial involvement. Looking for reasons why policies have remained relatively ineffective, medical sociology names *professional autonomy* as the culprit. In 1972, analysing the triad colleague control/client control/state control in the National Health Service, Gill and Horobin come to the conclusion that all three types of control are relatively ineffective because they are overridden by clinical autonomy. They write:

> The National Health Service is so organized as to subject *all* doctors to some measure of colleague control (via the monitoring of prescription charges), while at the same time the tradition of clinical (functional) autonomy has operated in such a way as to reduce colleague control even where the potential for it exists. (1972, p. 507)

In a similar vein, Haywood and Alaszewski (1980) recognise a *crisis* in the health service. One point, in their opinion, is low cost-effectiveness ('based on the continuing overwhelming preoccupation with acute hospital medicine in spite of the changing nature of demand and evidence that some expensive medical practices produce at best marginal returns': 1980, p. 16). Another point is that the managerial strategies introduced through state-legislated changes in the structure of the service in the 1970s failed to produce a more equitable distribution of morbidity and mortality (1980, Ch. 3). The result is a political situation where clinicians are more important than managers on the central as well as local levels. Haywood and Alaszewski write with reference to the latter:

> Our argument . . . is that local health authorities will be influenced by *different* ideas about ways of working (structure, process) and which values should be given the highest priority. The ideas about structure, process and values that inform the formal management arrangement are only one set of influences, and others such as the different ideology and interests of clinicians, are more important. (1980, p. 129)

The solution seems to come from circumventing the medical profession altogether and establishing a direct link between government and citizen regarding health control. The doctors' reluctance to sacrifice clinical autonomy in the interest of equality of morbidity and mortality makes self-care the most promising state-funded strategy towards better health. To safeguard cost-effectiveness of treatment on a total population/total cost basis, the state makes itself an advocate of health care *beyond* the modern hospital and the clinically-minded practitioner.

The most conspicuous area where the new role of the state is put into effect is *mental health*. In Italy, Law No. 833 passed in 1978 abolished all mental hospitals for good. The model for this measure, the step by step closure of the Trieste Mental Asylum under the directorship of Franco Basaglia from 1968 onwards, was made possible by municipal legislation sponsored by the Conservatives in the Town Hall (Hartung, 1980; Simons, 1980; Ramon, 1985). Similarly, in the US, deinstitutionalisation became a widespread policy which drastically reduced the number of mental patients or favoured the closure of mental hospitals altogether (Scull, 1977; Lamb, 1979; P. Brown, 1985).

Another area where the state becomes heavily involved is *prevention*. In the mid-1970s, the British government's DHSS issued a Consultative Document entitled *Prevention and Health: Everybody's Business*. After recounting some success stories of the past (relating to the virtual extinction of such diseases as cholera and scarlet fever), the leaflet addressed the 'problems of today and tomorrow'. The message was that the incidence of chronic conditions like cancer and coronary heart disease could be drastically reduced if the public were aware of the relationship between health and such 'habits' as smoking, alcohol and drug use as well as the unwise use of leisure time such as watching television instead of exercising. A chapter on the 'sexual revolution' urges contraception and warns against unwanted teenage pregnancies.

Such direct addressing of the public by the government to promote prevention through instigating behavioural change suggests that the public must be provided with usable *health education*. In fact, the British Health Education Council, a semi-official agency, receives considerable government funds to devise advice how to stop smoking, avoid heart disease through dietary control and exercise, foster childrens' psychiatric health through better educational skills of mothers and so on. Similar initiatives have been launched in other countries. Since the mid-1970s, the WHO has adopted an active policy of promoting health education.[43]

The medical profession is more or less left out of the picture. It frequently responds to this by emulating government-sponsored health education through its own preventive advice. For instance, in the same year as the British government's *Everybody's Business* brochure (1976), the Royal College of Physicians together with the British Cardiac Society issued its own leaflet on the 'Prevention of Coronary Heart Disease'.

Ten years on, the governments' involvement with health-promoting behaviour continues unabated. As of May 1987 smoking in public buildings and subway stations was made an offence in New York City. But the state has also been confronted during the decade since the mid-1970s with citizens who fight public-health measures on the ground that they curtail individual freedom. In a comprehensive article entitled 'The Resistable Rise of Preventive Medicine', Stone (1986) documents for four areas of prevention the dilemmas which the 'new' role of the welfare state poses. For immunisation, she shows, the risk of acquiring the disease through vaccination has been accepted by the American government which has agreed to be sued for damages by injured victims. For life style issues (smoking, overeating, drinking), it has turned out that insurance companies attempt to use the epidemiological evidence (and the American Surgeon General's 1979 report, *Healthy People*) to impose higher premiums on those who indulge in unhealthy life styles. As for screening, the American government has 'stalled, delayed and constricted' its massive screening programme because of evidence that it would lead to stigmatisation of risk groups and loss of job opportunities for risk carriers. As for occupational safety and health, industry as well as unions have fought governmental control because it means hazards to jobs as well as discrimination towards the hypersusceptible worker.

In this situation, the government is caught in a dilemma. On one hand, it feels responsible for public health and is willing to stipulate coercive measures; on the other, it is the guarantor of individual freedom which is firmly anchored in the constitution and the philosophy of civil liberty. In fact, the state is forced by litigation brought against it to grant individuals the rights to self-expression to which they are politically entitled. Self-care in health matters, therefore, finds its limit in civil rights.

The welfare state in its 'new' role as agent of prevention and self-care finds itself pitched against the citizens which it attempts to serve. Stone concludes her article by taking sides with the person (patient) against the state. She writes:

> Individuals resort to the one sort of protection American society finds legitimate and acceptable – civil rights. That is the one form consistent

with individualism. Civil rights policy is based on the principle that one stands or falls on one's own merits. A person may not be treated according to, or have his life chances determined by, group characteristics that have no relation to individual achievement – race, gender, age and now physical health. With the tools of civil rights, citizens fight the harm of group classification inherent in life style, screening, and occupational safety approaches to prevention. (1986, p. 690)

The purpose of patient advocacy

Behind the sociologist's efforts is concern with the patient's undervalued interests as the weaker partner in the unequal relationship with the doctor. The issues are emotion and explanation.

As for emotion, Parsons notes how much the patient is in a state of emotional disturbance. Restriction on profit motives and competition in the physician's role act as a safeguard against exploiting the patient's weakness, emotional upset and anxiousness to agree to a medical measure as long as it promises swift pain relief or recovery. In the situation of distressing or disabling illness, Parsons argues (paraphrasing Henderson who, in turn, cites Pareto), doctor and patient both have a 'need to manifest sentiments by external acts'. Both sides (with the patient joined by his or her family) opt in favour of active, preferably surgical intervention which gives most dramatic relief to the feelings of anxiety on the patient's side, and uncertainty on the doctor's side. Parsons elucidates:

> In general it is clear that there tends to be a bias in favor of operating. After all the surgeon is trained to operate, he feels active, useful, effective when he is operating. For the patient and his family, in their state of anxiety and tension also, inactivity, just waiting to see how things develop is particularly hard to bear. A decision to operate will, in such a situation, almost certainly 'clear the air' and make everybody 'feel better'. At least 'something is being done'. (1951a, pp. 466–7)

From this it is not far to a scathing criticism of one-sided bias in medical practice. Morgan, Calnan and Manning (1985, p. 137) characterise the situation intolerable to the patient in the same way as Parsons: 'The most prevalent form of relationship is one characterized by a dominant and active doctor and a passive and dependent patient.'

It is widely accepted that *education* is a potent remedy against doctor–patient inequality. This may attempt to strengthen either of the two sides. If the *doctor* is to be trained to become more patient-oriented in terms of improved emotional empathy, this qualifies as a reform target for medical education (Engelhardt, Wirth and Kindermann, 1973). Such reform could match Armstrong's suggestion (1979, 1983, 1984) that the dominant paradigm changes towards what he terms biographical medicine. But authors like Morgan *et al.* caution: 'The image of the doctor as health educator freely giving out information is not one which appears to have a realistic basis' (1985, p. 137). The answer, then, is *deprofessionalisation*. That is, the shift of responsibility for health maintenance is from the doctor (back) to the *patient*. In this, as discussed in more detail above, the state's health education, insofar as it follows the advice of and gains the approval of sociologists, is acknowledged as a proper agent of responsible health care.

The other issue regarding patient advocacy is explanation. In a reply to Waitzkin's (1979) statement that the medical practitioner is utterly manipulative converting the consultation into a setting for micro-politics, P. M. Strong (1979b) opts for a range of illness explanations that go far beyond contemporary clinical theory. He writes:

> Since human action is embodied the care and maintenance of our body is a pre-condition for *all* human action . . . We are obliged to be doctors to ourselves and to others and as such we acquire and refine a variety of medical theories, diagnostic procedures and treatment practices. Thus . . . 'professional' medicine is only one part, and the smaller part at that, of a more general medical practice and though the similarities and differences between professional, lay and tribal medicine have yet to be properly examined, it seems likely that there are many constancies to be found. (1979b, p. 615)

In particular, lay explanations often emphasise the interpersonal or person-environment origin of illness. That is, lay theories addressed in medical anthropology's 'health-belief model' pinpoint the stress upon the individual to meet society's demands as a major source of ubiquitous illness. In an overview of medical-anthropology's views on *culture, health and illness*, Helman (1984) cites Hahn and Kleinman (1981) who identified a *nocebo* phenomenon as a negative counterpart of the placebo phenomenon. He links the stress explanations of lay persons directly to research focusing on emotional disturbance as a noxious agent:

> As Hahn and Kleinman put it 'belief kills; belief heals', and certain kinds of stress can be 'culturogenic' . . . In each society, individuals try to reach the defined goals, levels of prestige and standards of behaviour that the culture expects of its members. Failure to reach these goals

(even if these goals seem absurd to members of another society) may result in frustration, stress response, and the 'giving-up-given-up complex' . . . Some beliefs can be directly stressful, such as the belief that one has been 'cursed' or 'hexed' by a powerful person . . . Other cultural values that may induce stress are an emphasis on war-like activities, or intense competition for marriage partners, goods or prestige. The unequal distribution of wealth in a society is usually stressful to its poorer members, but economic privileges, too, can involve high levels of stress, based on competitiveness and fear of the poor. (1984, p. 173)

Effective healing, in the eye of many sociologists, should take into account the dialectics between social stress and social support. This means that theories of disease ought to be more perceptive to the patients' lay explanations of illness. Why this is important makes sense in terms of *power* relations: if the patient is an equal partner in health care, often fostering his or her own health by adopting self-care rather than professional help, that person's explanatory theories (albeit rooted in lay beliefs) have every right to be taken as seriously as medical explanations by those who decide upon health care financing and organisation.

Why should the medical profession which obviously harbours explanatory models far remote from lay theories receive more state funding and public acclaim than the self-help movement which adapts to the patients' own ideas about cause and consequence of illness? In this, Levin, Katz and Holst's insight is crucial: 'no life practices can be absolutely ruled out as healthy practices' (1977, p. 7). On one hand, this adds credence to the WHO's tenet that health is more than the absence of illness and comprises physical, psychological and social well-being; on the other hand, this brings research fully into the picture which shows how social environments lacking supportive social relations can be hazardous to health and mean danger to survival in the long run.

The purpose of patient advocacy by medical sociology clearly is that patients' well-being and satisfaction are to be maximised. They are to suffer least and benefit most from whatever medical, paramedical or lay help they require. As a general value, modern (wo)men are to enjoy as much health and as long a life span as can be achieved under modern-society conditions. Sociology is concerned that optimal chances should be opened up to everyone irrespective of gender, age, class, race or other social status.

However, it appears that such political enthusiasm in favour of a world of minimal suffering faces some dilemmas. For one, Najman casts doubt on the social susceptibility model of health and its concomitant recommendations of healthy life styles. He points out that the level of control imposed upon the individual in the name of health could be so high that its prospects appear daunting. Interventions in the economic system (particularly with regard to inequality and unemployment) may be as ethically problematic as 'interventions for those who are not married, perhaps prescribing more healthful bonding relationships' (1980, p. 236). Najman goes on to say that no easy answers are available: 'To fail to intervene, at least using pilot or experimental communities, in the face of available evidence raises a different, but no less substantial, set of ethical concerns' (1980, p. 236).

Another dilemma is that the patient envisaged by sociological research and focused upon by state-engendered or community-medicine based interventions is the *typical* (average) rather than the individual patient. For example, statistical results show that to break down with depression is much more likely subsequent to a severe life event for women who have more vulnerability factors; or, to quote another example, a low score on the Social Network Index in the Alameda County study statistically predicts a higher chance not to be alive at follow-up nine years later. Such findings may be qualified by social class and can further be refined taking into account age, race, gender and so on. However, it is always the *average* person to whom the results apply. The research identifies the individual person's or patient's problems as ones typical for the majority of the population and thus makes the individual hypothetically the same as any other member.

It may be argued that clinical medicine is different from epidemiology and social medicine with regard to precisely this point. As discussed above, Feinstein (1967) delineates clinical judgment as geared towards the particular case (with its peculiarities being understood as special forms of generally known diagnostic patterns). Keeping the difference between clinical reasoning and epidemiology in mind, Freidson (1985) suggests that the medical profession consists of two separate and far from consensual groups standing for two contradictory conceptualisations of medical concerns. On the one side, researchers and administrators' scientific or therapeutic aims are that whole populations or organisations get served. On the other side stand practitioners whose aim is clinical care for the individual on a 'micro' level. While the former advocate social medicine on a typical-patient (person) basis, the latter promulgate clinical medicine on an individual-patient (case) basis. Freidson recognises a recent shift towards the former (namely, administrators and public-health bureaucrats). He sees clinical medicine and its interest in the particular patient's unique case becoming outmanoeuvred by state-engendered health organisations whose interest is in solving generalised problems lodged with the typical patient. He elucidates:

There is . . . bound to be tension if not conflict between the practitioners of the profession and the administrators who supervise them by
employing the standards that are created by the researchers . . . Where
once all practitioners could employ their own clinical judgment to
decide how to handle their individual cases independently of whatever
medical school professors asserted in textbooks and researchers in
journal articles, now the professors and scientists who have no firsthand
knowledge of those individual cases establish guidelines that administrators who also lack such firsthand experience may attempt to enforce. Where once all practitioners were fairly free to decide how to
manage their relations with patients, now administrators attempt to
control the pacing and scheduling of work in the interest of their
organization's mission, which may regard the collective interests of all
patients (or of investors or insurance funds) to be more important than
the interests of individual practitioners and their relations with individual patients. (1985, pp. 30–1)

The conflict is similar to what Alford (1972, 1975) analyses as a
power struggle between the traditional views of 'professional
monopolisers' and the progressive views of 'bureaucratic rationa-
lisers'. Going beyond Alford's juxtaposition Freidson points out
that the paradigm shift has unanticipated consequences for the
patient's prospects of being served as an individual clinical case in
a non-perfunctory way by whoever gives the medical care. In other
words, Freidson realises that the change from clinical therapy to
self-help is not without consequences for the patient. If the medical profession is replaced by the state as guarantor of the patient's
rights and well-being, this has far-reaching – albeit widely unnoticed – consequences for what the chances of individualised treatment are for the patient.

In particular, as Stone (1986) exemplifies for prevention, the
patient's freedom as an individual citizen is in jeopardy and may
have to be fought in court when public-health issues override the
alliance between individual illness and clinical practice. Medical
sociology identifying with the state in the interest of the health of
the total population may face the unwanted fact that this curtails
rather than fosters the individual's rights and freedom.

It is at this point that the question surfaces again what the
purpose is of medical sociology's advocacy of patients' rights.
Clearly, it is in the interest of improving the patients' chances for
optimal care of their illness(es) and optimal realisation of their
personal selves that the medical sociologist engages in criticising
clinical practice.

If to loosen the relationship between doctor and patient means
harm to the patient, the sociologist may not wish to advocate

further such loosening. Sociologists' credo is that the placebo effect is positive since it means no harm to the patient while it is therapeutically powerful. But if to debunk clinical medicine means to affect the placebo effect negatively, sociologists may revoke their criticism. Levin, Katz and Holst (1977), for example, endorse the women's health movement originating in the Boston Women's Health Collective's self-care manual entitled *Our Bodies, Ourselves* (1971). Levin, Katz and Holst support the women's turning against their doctors:

> The women's movement has focused national attention on the quality of care received by women in a male-dominated medical care system. Specifically, it has been charged that women are subjected to a wide range of abuses, physical, psychological, and civil. Gynecological and obstetrical services are of particular concern. Recommendations for change center on the woman herself, in terms of increased knowledge of her anatomy, physiology, risk status for sex-related morbidities, and techniques of self-examination. (1977, p. 22)

Would Levin and other authors revoke their partisanship with the critics of medical practice if they learned that the quality of treatment is lowered if the placebo effect is thus broken? Would this particularly concern serious illness necessitating a clinician rather than self-help? Parsons, in his attempt to find a genuinely social aspect of medical care, recognises the placebo effect as the very real outcome of the sentimental order of the doctor–patient encounter. By putting emotional disturbance at the root of the social origin of sickness, the loss model's aetiology–therapy conceptualisation inadvertently emulates Parsons' ideas. This implies that if the patient is distrustful or even hostile to the doctor, an adverse effect on recovery may not be ruled out.

Not realising Parsons' conjectures about trust means that the loss model could forsake its own political aim: namely, to advocate the patient's individual rights as a person. To stipulate an independent aetiological and therapeutic salience of emotional needs means that the importance of the *placebo effect* is writ large into the conceptualisation of medical work, whether of a self-help or clinical nature.

Chapter 14
The Domination–Deprivation Model

In the early 1970s, Freidson's (1970a, 1970b) strictures against professional dominance made clear that the reality of illness is embedded in institutional conditions of its diagnosis and treatment. Both depend on the social construction of knowledge which, in turn, is lodged with a category of experts hermetically distinguished from the lay public. Freidson acknowledges an intellectual debt to Berger and Luckmann's *The Social Construction of Reality* (1966) which he quotes, declaring that

> reality is socially defined. But the definitions are always *embodied*, that is, concrete individuals and groups of individuals serve as definers of reality. To understand the state of the socially constructed universe at any given time, or its change over time, one must understand the social organization that permits the definers to do their defining. (1966, p. 107; cited by Freidson, 1970a, p. 379)

Interpreting Berger and Luckmann's propositions, and summing up his own stance as a sequel to theirs, Freidson goes on to point out how much a social construction of knowledge equals the creation of a universe of discourse. It serves the power interest of insiders vested against that of the uninitiated masses of outsiders who are also the 'object' on whom the knowledge is practised. Freidson writes:

> The consulting profession's . . . segment of the socially constructed universe . . . creates . . . relatively reliable knowledge, its sense of mission, and its practical institutions. The substance of those creations arises from the experience of the creators. The experience of the creators is a function of the perspective they have gained by virtue of being in an especially protected, autonomous position in the social structure, a position which systematically discounts the experience and evaluation of the laymen outside. (1970a, pp. 379–80).

Elaborating on the societal function of the medical profession's monopoly over illness-relevant knowledge and practice, Zola (1972, 1975) follows Freidson's (1970a) criticism of Parsons. Parsons certainly recognises medical practice as social control unfolding in the doctor–patient relationship over four successive stages of resocialisation. Freidson holds against this that it is the medical profession as a social institution in which social control is lodged; in particular, medical knowledge as a reality-defining creation of illness is where social control surfaces (1970a, pp. 205–6).

Zola takes up Freidson's ideas in two steps. In 1972, he made it clear that medicine as an institution of social control meant the extension of medical jurisdiction to: (a) an increasing number of aspects of life like diet or worries; (b) an increase in the number and scope of technical procedures to areas beyond curative purpose (e.g., plastic surgery); (c) a near-absolute control of taboo areas such as alcoholism or pregnancy; and (d) an encroachment on the idea of good practice of life stipulating 'how much' of, say, exercise or work 'is good for you' (1972, p. 496ff.) In 1975, he took up the other aspect: namely the medicalisation of deviance which, apart from Freidson, was also castigated by earlier critics like Szasz. In 'In the Name of Health and Illness', Zola suggested that modern society imposes stigmatisation upon the disabled, distasteful and disenfranchised.

The 'mechanics' of how this is done – representing a general cultural feature of American society – is discussed in Ryan's book, *Blaming the Victim* (1971). He suggests that politics as well as science (including social science) explain as a default of the 'distressed and disinherited' what, in fact, is due to their lack of money and power. That 'the poor, the black, the ill, the jobless, the slum tenants . . . think in different forms, act in different patterns, cling to different values, seek different goals, and learn different truths' (1971, p. 10) is shown 'to make it possible for us to look at society's problems and to attribute their causation to the individuals affected' (1971, p. 10). With regard to health care, Ryan contends, a two-tier system prevails along race and class lines which is wrongly attributed to health beliefs. Rather, he insists, a cleavage exists between the privileged and the underprivileged which means that the latter become victimised by the former. His evidence is mostly anecdotal but none the less compelling. He writes, for instance:

Most of the poor have to turn to tax-supported or charitable clinics and emergency rooms for their medical care, and the results are so horrifying that they scarcely need repetition. The obscenities of clinic practices and emergency room brutality are too well known to repeat in detail: the long waits, the cursory examinations, the impersonal cold world of nameless men and women in white – a cast of characters that seems to be exchanged almost daily, each set of replacements being more discourteous, prejudiced, and unsympathetic than the last. Instances of the dramatic stories are known to almost everyone – the patient bleeding to death unattended while the health professionals prolong their coffee break; the misdiagnoses; the grossly incompetent treatments; the constant, obsessive concern with paying the bill. (Ryan, 1971, p. 159)

Such cultural criticism is extended by Illich (1975a, 1975b) into a fully-fledged criticism of modern society as being colonised by medicine through a process which he calls the 'medicalization of life'. Illich identifies three layers of such colonisation, each under the term of iatrogenics which in its original meaning denotes illness as produced by medical treatment. The level of *clinical iatrogenesis* refers to the expansion of illness under the reign of an ever-expanding medicine which itself is said to become an epidemic. The level of *social iatrogenesis* refers to the medicalisation of the life span, and all other aspects of life such that the person automatically becomes a patient or pre-patient at every point in life. This, in turn, is related to 'an overindustrialized society' where the professions and other agents (including drugs, machines and so on) are introduced to solve the problems which, basically, are the domain of the person. This becomes obvious on the level of *structural iatrogenesis*. It refers to the destruction of indigenous and folk medical cultures and the alienation of the unwell from their bodies, which leads to what Illich using a Marxist term, calls the expropriation of health. He writes: 'When dependence on the professional management of pain, sickness and death grows beyond a certain point, the healing power in sickness, patience in suffering and fortitude in the face of death must decline. These three regressions are symptoms of third-level iatrogenesis: their combined outcome is Medical Nemesis' (1975a, p. 92).

Illich's cultural criticism of medicine, aiming at 'over-industrialization' of health care as well as alienation of the person from his or her body, addresses similar issues as the political economy of health (first introduced by Ginzberg, 1965, later elaborated by Kelman, 1971, among others). In 1970, Ehrenreich and Ehrenreich published their analysis of the American health-care system which attempted to show that what made it a system was that it had no structure except the logic of 'power, profits and politics'. In this, scientific knowledge served as a vehicle of the application of technology which, in turn, benefited from the 'medical-industrial complex' of big business aligning itself with the leading teaching hospitals (Ch. 7). The rationale of the medical profession's putting self-interest over collectivity-interest, in Ehrenreich's and Ehrenreich's opinion, was that 'who pays the piper, calls the tune' (Ch. 8). In other words, the financial crisis which was said to have haunted medicine since the 1930s put physicians in a bind between the federal government which instituted programmes like Medicare and Medicaid, and the private insurance companies and Blue Cross who competed with the state for power over health care. The message was that the consumer received the wrong type of care because medical knowledge (pure as well as applied) followed the wrong principle. Accordingly, Ehrenreich and Ehrenreich contended, patients were dominated by the system and could not make their needs felt: 'Patients, who want only decent, available health care, may not care about preserving Blue Cross or letting the hospital directors and doctors spend freely. But patients will have very little say about the next jury-rigged solution to the financing crisis' (1970, p. 132). The political economy of health since the Ehrenreichs' work has comprised three arguments. Although closely linked, they are here presented separately: namely, the production – consumption argument, the class-conflict argument and the ideology argument.

The *production–consumption* argument is further advanced by Krause (1971) in an article entitled 'Health and the Politics of Technology' (see also Krause 1973, 1975, 1977). He contends that technical progress in medicine follows the logic of political dynamics: that is, in the medical realm, 'corporations in the health business, medical research physicians, university medical-school teaching hospitals [and] the Federal government' (1971, p. 52) form an alliance which organises consumption according to production. In particular, whatever medical equipment as well as drugs are produced for profit have to be consumed through health care irrespective of patients' well-being. In this scenario, the state attempting to curtail the profit-orientation of medical actors since the 1960s (or 1930s) has no chance of winning. The reason is that the state is tied to industrialism in two ways.

First, Renaud (1975) argues that the state is committed to the *conditions of capital accumulation* and therefore cannot break loose into favouring a more people-prone type of health care. The only effective measure, according to Renaud, would be 'decommodification of health needs' (1975/78, p. 117). But this the state in capitalist (and most existing socialist) societies will never manage, Renaud concludes.

The other way in which the state is tied to industrialism and must therefore enforce consumption of whatever is produced by capitalist industry is through the *fiscal crisis* which is endemic. O'Connor (1973) argues that health care (among other issues), while partly coming under the jurisdiction of the state, also serves a legitimation function. Welfare-state funded health services document for the populace in capitalist societies that need and want are conquered by the modern world. On the other hand, the need for welfare services is greatest in times of economic recession when least taxation money comes into the state's coffers (the state may then attempt to boost the economy by extra expenditure). In order to counterbalance business cycles and safeguard welfare services, the state takes to borrowing and accumulates massive debts while fulfilling its legitimating function for the capitalist system, particularly in times of crisis. But in times of boom, industry profits more than the state which cannot risk citizens' loyalty through drastic taxation and cannot switch to a policy of massive savings either. The fiscal crisis of the state is permanent insofar as the state must be loyal to capitalist production but must also offset losses due to business cycles when they occur. Health care, like many other areas, is caught in this vicious circle.

The *class-conflict* argument is first raised by B. and J. Ehrenreich (1973) in an article on hospital workers. It is tightly linked with the argument about the oppression of women since most hospital and/or health workers are and have been women throughout history. The gist of the matter is that when women are patients, whatever is enforced upon them is supposedly 'for their own good': that is, expert advice to women, while it serves the logic of men who predominantly are their doctors, is *mystified* into beneficial diagnosis. For instance, under the heading *The Sexual Politics of Sickness*, Ehrenreich and English (1979) picture the no-win situation of women in the late nineteenth century, caught between the labels of being uterine as opposed to brain-dominated:

> Even the woman who opted for the sexless, mental life could not expect the brain to have an easy victory. The struggle between the brain, with its die-hard intellectual pretensions, and the primitive, but tenacious uterus could tear a woman apart – perhaps destroying both organs in the process. So in the end all that awaited the brain-oriented woman was in most cases sickness, which of course is precisely what awaited herself if she remained a 'good' uterine woman. (1979, p. 117)

The class-conflict argument is extended to the whole of health care in capitalism by two standpoints. First, Waitzkin and Waterman (1974) point out that the exploitation of illness in capitalist society happens through illness treated for profit by medicine, an institution of social control. Medical care then becomes an aspect of stratification in society because medical services are better and more easily accessible for the upper classes. Besides, the latter's morbidity and mortality rates are more favourable. But stratification also prevails in the medical system insofar as professionalism and elitism favour the physician's authority (and income) while de-valuing low-level health workers' competence (and earning capacity). The situation is one of conflict because contradictory interests of the status groups are involved. The lowest level in the stratified system are the patients who need to be awakened to political awareness. Waitzkin and Waterman are convinced that patients as well as, among others, nurses, aides, orderlies, ward clerks and medical social workers, form a category with separate latent interests, in Dahrendorf's terms. That they could organise themselves into a fully-fledged interest group is phrased in orthodox Marxian terms: 'As a politically organised interest group, patients would be an example of a class in the fourth Marxian sense . . . The revolutionary potential of such a patient class implies the reorganisation of authority relations within medicine to create a health system which no longer oppresses and exploits its consumers' (1974, p. 69).

The second version of the class-conflict argument is promoted by Navarro in numerous articles and books since the early 1970s (A first collection of his articles is entitled *Medicine Under Capitalism*, 1976; a second one *Crisis, Health, and Medicine*, 1986.) He believes that conflict between capitalists and workers, the owners of the means of production and the expropriated and therefore exploitable owners of nothing but their labour force, has two layers. On one hand, underdevelopment in Latin American, African and Asian countries is said to be a function of the hegemony of Western capitalism, establishing exploitative domination in order to colonise markets (including those for pharmaceutical and other products). On the other hand, within Western medicine's several systems (the US, Great Britain, the Soviet Union), the composition of the medical profession is seen to mirror elitism by race, sex or class origin of its members; the composition of the health services sector, *in toto*, thus mirrors the division between the privileged and underprivileged in society. The function of medicine accordingly is reproduction of the class structure in capitalist society. State interventions concerning health are said to serve only the aim of reproducing bourgeois ideology. The ultimate aim of medicine under capitalism, says Navarro, is the reproduction of alienation. He writes:

The expropriation of political power from the citizenry that takes place in the political process, and the absence of control over the product and nature of work that workers face in the process of production, are accompanied by the expropriation of control from the patient and potential patient over the nature and definition of health in the medical sector. (1976, p. 208)

The *ideology* argument has been directed, among others, against Illich who is accused to 'suggest reforms of medicine along bourgeois ideological lines' (Berliner 1977, p. 116). It may be said to have been raised as early as 1965 by Rossdale, who maintains that health in a sick society cannot but be of the wrong kind; permanent sickness masked as temporary health. This casts doubt on medicine serving the 'sick society'. The scientific nature of medicine, and its supposedly politically neutral character, are questioned. Allegedly timeless 'objective' facts and laws on which natural science-oriented medicine bases its claim to power over patients are unmasked as historically relative and socially constructed.

The process of how scientific facts wrongly come to be seen as beyond social relations is explained in an analogy to Marx's notion of *commodity fetishism*. With regard to things, Marx stipulates, we tend to forget that they were made by people and thus are products of human labour. We wrongly take them as devoid of that origin. The same holds for scientific facts, R. M. Young (1977) maintains in his lengthy essay entitled 'Science *Is* Social Relations'. Based on Young's 'proof' that scientific discoveries are but reflections of historical stages of the production process, Figlio (1977, 1978, 1982) undertakes to show that medicine is wrongly taken as a natural science and falsely considers itself politically neutral.

Figlio argues that medicine – like science – has an ideological function *because* it cannot admit its own historical relativity and social constructedness. This ideological function serves the aims of domination: that is, the capitalist mode of production – so the argument runs – is so far beyond the interest of people's health that mass illness is one of its most conspicuous corollaries. But society nevertheless avoids being taken to task for its noxious impact because medicine functions to cure the victims of capitalist exploitation, at least to the extent that they can re-enter the labour force. In this, science plays the role of a quasi-natural, but actually socially constructed, body of knowledge.

The intellectual debt to Foucault of this is considerable. Through reference to Foucault, a basically social medical perception can be proved, and a domination interest of scientific knowledge can be documented. In *The Birth of the Clinic* (1963/75), Foucault holds that seeing and knowing in medical perception (where the visible is key to the invisible, or inferred) constitutes clinical medicine since the early nineteenth century. Recognition and subsequent explanation – Foucault speaks of discourse – is a part of the general order of modern society. Medicine is but one field where 'docile bodies' are produced through strategies of discipline monitoring individual's conduct as well as misconduct (Foucault, 1963/75). In the same vein, Young (1977, p. 71) holds that medicine constitutes a hegemonic body of knowledge to interpret bodily relations as if they were things and exterior to those whom they concern, the patients. Figlio (1975, 1976) maintains that the metaphors used by late eighteenth and early nineteenth-century medical theory are but reflections of the mind –body dualism in Cartesian philosophy and woven into the social institutions of Britain in a different way from those of France, the two major countries of the then fervent dispute over explanatory models. Eventually, Figlio (1978) turns to the issue of historicity of diagnosis, using chlorosis and (1982) workers' nystagmus as examples.

Addressing the problem of whether illnesses are real when their diagnostic categories are historically relative, Figlio affiliates himself with Rossdale's (1965) *ecological definition of health*. The latter is also reintroduced by Turshen (1977) who also relies on Foucault's work. Her basic idea is that health is twofold: beyond the ideological realm of medical discourse is a realm of suffering.[44] Foucault, by insisting how malleable the human body is under the influence of power, implicitly maintains that there must be a realm of potential non-domination where no such disciplining occurs. Subscribing to this implication of Foucault's argument is easy under a Marxist perspective. The Utopian tenet saves the ideology argument from the nominalism into which some 'radical' labelling theorists fall and which often besets psychosomatic theory.

Freidson's and Zola's criticism of professional autonomy come together with the Marxist view under a *cultural*-crisis perspective where Foucault's lessons are heeded. The idea is that medicine is an institution of social control where knowledge serves the purpose of domination. Science and its application in capitalist society is given an ideological character because it follows the logic of exchange value. The economic rationale of medical knowledge, prone to class conflict and other divides, is adopted by all three Marxist arguments. Although they rely on the classic *critique of political economy* at various points, their basic understanding is

possibly not plausible in a Marxian frame alone. They owe much
to the sociology of knowledge's recent social-construction view of
science.

Similarly viewed by Marxism and this knowledge-oriented political economy of health is the *image of mankind*. It harks back to
the idea of alienation: while in a truly socialist society men would
not be alienated from their fellow men, in capitalist society men
are alienated from their species-being which, in turn, leads to their
alienation from their product (Marx, 1844/1975). Similarly, while
in a truly socialist society mankind would be healthy in a wholesale
manner which is said to even go beyond the comprehensive definition promoted by the WHO (Reverby, 1972, p. 1145), in capitalist
society ('sick society') at best the absence of illness or not undergoing repair of diseased organs or minds through professional
medicine may be called health. This denotes a double meaning of
health, an alienated and a non-alienated form.

In modern capitalist society illness is thus given a double meaning. On the one hand, it is *collective* insofar as it is produced by
capitalist production and its consequences; on the other hand, it is
individual insofar as it becomes the focus of professional medicine.
The fact that modern medicine treats individually a collective
phenomenon results in its basic incapacity to treat effectively and
efficiently. This is thought to be a valid criticism of medicine
irrespective of however much it costs and however rationally it
attempts to reorganise its services and use its technology.

The three stages of aetiology

The production of ill health

Societal origin of bodily dysfunction, as distinct from medical
explanatory theory, is *collectivist*. Figlio (1982) makes it clear that
the process of becoming ill relates not to an individual's losing his
or her level of functioning but one of 'a social "I" . . . engaged
with "otherness"' (1982, p. 176). In other words, hardship and
collectively experienced deprivation are met by a set of medical
practices which can possibly not avoid damage to the bodies and
minds of those exposed. Figlio (1978) explains that chlorosis is/was
a feminine illness mainly diagnosed for girls working long hours in
the notorious sweat shops of clothes-making. How the symptoms
are ordered along medicine's nosological categories undergoes
historical change between 1870 and 1930, but lets the symptoms
invariably be produced by the girls' working conditions. In the

1982 article, Figlio addresses illness as *faux frais* of the production process: 'From the capitalist point of view, incapacity is slippage – not a personalised notion of sluggishness, but rather the calculable unproductivity of labour in the aggregate' (1982, p. 184).

Doyal (1979) extends this collectivist origin of illness in capitalist production to include also its products. Taking into account noxious effects of relations of production in developed and developing countries, and focusing on pollution and toxic waste as well as unsafe goods and dangerous services as equally coming out of capitalist production, Doyal paints a picture of widespread negative impact. She writes:

> Clearly the imperatives of capital accumulation condition the nature of the labour process, and the need for shiftwork, de-skilling, overtime or the use of dangerous chemicals, will all be reflected in the health or ill health of workers. They may suffer directly, either through industrial injuries and diseases, or in more diffuse ways with stress-related ill health, or psychosomatic problems. Yet commodity production also has more *indirect* effects on health, and the physical effects of the production process extend beyond the workplace itself. Damage to the surrounding environment and pollution of various kinds are often the by-products of industrialised production. Finally, commodity production may damage health through the nature of the commodities themselves. Capitalist production is concerned with exchange values and, as a result, concern about the quality of a product (including its effects on health) will usually arise only in the context of an assessment of its selling potential. If it will sell, then its effects on health are likely to be of little concern to the producer, so that many health-damaging products will continue to be made simply because they are profitable. (1979, p. 25)

A third source of illness-producing forces in capitalist society concerns life styles. It also is more indirect which means that not much so far is known in detail about *how* the morbidity develops which is said to be caused by life styles (apart from illness-specific evidence, such as the statistically sound and clinically plausible link between smoking and lung cancer). One example is Eyer's work. He finds that hypertension is a disease prevalent in capitalist but not in hunter-gatherer societies. He also finds that by the latters' standards of blood pressure, 'most of the American population is hypertensive' (1975, p. 539). Universal stress from the industrial world of work and urban environment, therefore, drives blood pressure to pathological levels. This, in turn, suggests that only political changes overcoming modern technological organisation of particular environments can conquer society-produced modern levels of illness.

Eyer sees no beneficial function in medical practice's alleviating or curing social-system produced disease. In a way, disease levels seem to remain unaffected by being treated (or not treated); in fact, drug treatment of hypertension is only mentioned for producing dangerous or disabling side-effects. In a similar vein, Eyer's (1977) controversy with Brenner (1971, 1973, 1975) conspicuously fails to mention medical treatment's ` mediation between pathogenic societal forces and illness or death rates. The controversy is about whether the peak or slump in business cycles 'produces' more disease and subsequent death (to be precise, death concerns overall mortality rates as well as rates from specific causes). The idea is that more or less automatically stress on the workers translates into ill health and eventually death. Overtime during booms and underuse during unemployment are both said to damage greater numbers of population such that death rates peak.

The meaning of medical practice

Seeking care and aiming at cure, above all, means patients exposing themselves to the influence and impact of the medical profession. This is collective as well as individual.

As collective, the medical profession embodies the social function of medicine: namely, social control. Ehrenreich and Ehrenreich (1974) argue that this control is twofold. On one hand, for members of the upper classes, social control is cooptative in the sense that more and more areas of life style are incorporated into the realm of medical jurisdiction. On the other hand, for members of the lower classes as well as those of non-white races, social control is disciplinary which means that they often are excluded from effective or amenable treatment and may even be driven away from considering illness as a viable solution to problems resulting from their dismal lives. Health care is thus divided into *expansionist* and *exclusionary* sectors which, to be sure, serve the same function in different ways. Ehrenreich and Ehrenreich write:

> Expansionary sectors, which exert co-optative control, are characterised by relatively low barriers to entry and acceptable, even sympathetic, treatment of those who do enter. Such services encourage people both to enter sick roles and to seek professional help in a variety of nonsick situations (preventive care, contraceptive services, marital difficulties). In so doing they bring large numbers of people into the fold of *professional management* of various aspects of their lives . . . Exclusionary sectors of the medical system, which exert disciplinary control, are characterised by high barriers to entry (high costs, geographical inaccessibilily) and/or socially repellent treatment of those who do

enter (discourtesy, extreme impersonality, racism, fragmentation of care, long waits). The impact of exclusionary sectors on the populations they are supposed to serve is to discourage entry into sick roles, either because of the visible barriers to entry or because of public knowledge of the treatment experienced by those who do enter, or in some cases *both*. Such services exert disciplinary social control in that they *encourage* people to maintain work or family responsibilities no matter what subjective discomfort they may be experiencing. (1974, p. 29)

When it comes to elucidating further why the poor are not treated by medicine even when sick, and the rich are treated even when not sick, Ehrenreich and Ehrenreich make a most noteworthy distinction between being sick in the *sociological* as opposed to the *medical* sense (Ehrenreich and Ehrenreich, 1974). Those on whom disciplinary control is practised, they suggest, are those who are 'not "sick" in the sociological sense' (Ehrenreich and Ehrenreich, 1974) which can only mean, by implication, that the upper classes and the owners of the means of production are deemed sick 'in the sociological sense'. Those among the lower classes who are sick (in the medical sense) are subject to massive disciplinary (repressive, intimidating) action. Ehrenreich and Ehrenreich cite Foucault as a witness:

At times [disciplinary control] has been used quite consciously to maintain industrial discipline in the work force. Foucault describes the combined poorhouses/insane asylums of eighteenth- and nineteenth-century Paris and London, which were maintained as *public spectacles* to remind the populace of what awaited them if they opted to 'drop out' into pauperism or madness. In much the same way today, exposés of conditions in state mental hospitals serve to discourage 'madness' as an out, and public knowledge of the indignities inflicted on welfare recipients serves to discourage willful unemployment. (Ehrenreich and Ehrenreich, 1974)

Domination exerted by the ruling over the powerless manifests itself in conscious oppressive strategies. These are presumably so intimidating that the powerless abandon all self-preserving opposition. Public exposure of the unfortunate who dare(d) to oppose the system serves to make their subjugation complete. Illness, in this, is a condition which the frightened oppressed often renounce.

The doctor–patient relationship is more or less a farce. Being exposed to the doctor as an individual, Waitzkin (1979, 1983; Waitzkin and Stoeckle, 1976) suggests, means micro-politics becoming enacted which always works against the patient. Analysing dialogue from consultations, Waitzkin (1983, pp. 137–83) shows that the patients' questions are not answered. Instead of giving information, doctors mystify their patients regarding causes of illness and most effective treatment. The latter, says Waitzkin, would often mean joining a trade union rather than taking medication. The message is that the doctor encroaches on the patient's privacy and frequently talks about subjects having nothing to do with the illness or its treatment, and the patient complies with whatever the doctor wants in a docile, laconical and courteous way.

Individual care is thus ideological. Clinical medicine pinpoints the person as locus of illness while, in fact, it is society where illness is generated. From this vantage point, medicine is accused of participating in the 'blaming the victim' strategy endemic of upper-class domination. Turshen (1977) juxtaposes implications of the functional (presently prevailing) as opposed to the experiential (Utopian) concept of health on the basis of Rossdale's (1965) ecological definition, she castigates individualism as the main default of clinical thinking: 'The overwhelming concern with the individual is a major limitation of the paradigm of clinical medicine' (Turshen, 1977, p. 49).

The perspective taken by Waitzkin on the consultation implies that it is no wonder that manipulative and distasteful encroachments on the patient's person occur: they only document that the whole individualistic approach of clinical work goes in the wrong direction. This, however, is not to be remedied by incorporating aspects of behaviour into the confines of medicine. In an article mocking medical care in its title, 'You are Dangerous to Your Health', Crawford (1977) holds that the recent discovery of life style as relevant to health worsens the individual's situation. The stakes are still against the 'real' causes of illness because, he says: 'The victim blaming ideology . . . instructs people to be individually responsible at a time when they are becoming less capable as individuals of controlling their health environment. Although environmental dangers are often recognised, the implication is the little can be done about the ineluctable, modern, technological, and industrial society' (1977, p. 671). The message is, of course, that health care as such is a part of domination and intimidation. As long as it identifies individualised origins of disease (if only because individuals are treated) and wishes to change individuals' behaviour rather than society's structure, medical care is said to be counterproductive.

The sickness of society

The literature maintains that not only is individual health and illness separated from societal health and pathology, but giving priority to the former is ideological while focusing on the latter is in the 'real' interest of 'the' people.

The notions of sickness are used, and the traditional individualistic one is to be replaced by a new collectivist one. Kelman (1975) distinguishes between *health in inverted commas* (achievable in capitalism), defined as 'functional' conformity and capacity in one's roles in repressive organizations, and *health without inverted commas*, denoting self-realisation, 'experiential' health in a to-be-realised society. It may be noted that the individualistic clinical notion of health is linked to the idea that individuals' sickness is socially determined, while the new collectivist notion of health is linked to the idea of inner-directed, self-propelled, mind–body unity. Kelman clarifies: 'Stated another way, experiential health refers to *intrinsically* defined organismic integrity, whereas functional health refers to *extrinsically* defined organismic integrity' (1975, p. 630).

Among others, Schatzkin (1978) extends Kelman's notion of experiential health such that already in the present capitalist society it has a role. Namely, it is what the capitalist class as well as the working class strive at although the former stands a better chance of realising it for themselves. The reason is that they have better access to a style of living which includes 'fine foods, housing, cars, clothes, vacations, . . . but also living as long and as comfortably as their wealth can make possible' (1978, p. 216). From this vantage point, sickness in capitalist society equals loss of labour and earning power (making for a loss of living power, so to speak). Accordingly, health equals the capacity to maximise the exploitation of others. Schatzkin contends:

> It is the conception of health as labor-power that leads us to what primarily determines the level of health and medical care in a capitalist society: the tendency towards maximization of the rate of exploitation. It is, after all, the exploitation of labor which lies at the heart of the capital accumulation process. (1978, p. 217; emphasis omitted).

Similarly, Waitzkin (1983) attempts to make it clear that where the sickness *really* lies is not with the person but with the system. He calls his book *The Second Sickness* in order to separate the societal level of causation of rates of sickness where mechanisms of capitalism are at work from the (hitherto falsely stressed) level of individual misbehaviour or lesion. The 'second sickness' denotes a structural pathology rooted in capitalist production as well as ruling-class domination. Both levels of sickness have to be overcome. Waitzkin implies through the motto for his book which quotes a 'surgeon to the liberation forces of China, 1939' as saying that the 'second sickness' means for political activists that they fail to recognise the 'first sickness' (namely, individual illness) as being 'not merely a disease of the body but a social crime' (1983, p. x). In other words: that the society is sick and promotes the wrong kind of health (i.e., the one in inverted commas) may be seen as a corollary of a more general tendency of modern society, which is its propensity to overemphasise personal freedom and self-interest. The latter includes freedom to exploit others as well as that to fall ill.

There seems to be a contradiction between Waitzkin's view that an ideal society means more collectivism, and Kelman's idea that the liberated society allows for full self-realisation. Both authors claim to derive their perspectives from Marx (1844/1975). He argues that socialist society is the negation of class society (which, since the working class is the negation of the bourgeois class, means negation of the negation of class power). Waitzkin sees non-alienation in negating individualism, Kelman in superseding role diversity. Waitzkin and Kelman both insist that they envisage a non-pathological society.

Therapy and the change of society

Since aetiology is conceived on an aggregate level, involving categories of 'social "I"'(Figlio, 1982), therapy must avoid the level of individuals' treatment. When personal or bodily illness and its cure or care are conceptualised as a matter of individuals, 'victim blaming' is suspected. Since problems of society surface as rates of morbidity and (premature) mortality, it is social change which deals responsibly with the modern evil of ubiquitous disease.

As for sources of illness, deprivation must be separated from domination. Inequality in society regarding occupation, education, income, housing and nutrition, between social classes, races or ethnic groups (more so than sex or age) result in deprivation being a major antecedent to morbidity and (premature) mortality. Statistical associations between status incumbency and health risk (or life expectancy) render uncontroversial the negative impact of deprivation. On the other hand, an unknown but suspectedly large amount of illness is said to be due to the vicissitudes of medicine. In particular, iatrogenic disease – originating in medical practice – is placated following the widely accepted critique by Illich (1975a, 1975b; Illich, et al,. 1977) and Carlson (1975). Other authors stress the ideological nature of medical science: that is, medical theory's being far from socially neutral. Armstrong, relying extensively on Foucault's understanding of the medical perspective speaks of the 'invention' of infant mortality (Armstrong, 1986) and 'creation' of neurosis (1983).[45] Strategies connected with this are often addressed as 'politics' (e.g., Armstrong, 1986, cites a book by J. Lewis, 1980, entitled *The Politics of Motherhood*). The role of medicine in this context is understood as domination. Individualising a collective phenomenon, and submitting the person to the rigours of patienthood (despite the fact that illness 'is' not individualistic), medicine is seen to exert power. This reveals its focus on treatment (using the 'wrong' individualising knowledge) as an additional – that is, iatrogenic – 'creation' of illness.

The notion of therapy must go beyond the level of clinical treatment (which denotes domination) and social inequality (which signifies deprivation). If therapy as suggested by the sociological analysis using the deprivation–domination model is not to fall under the verdict of 'blaming the victim' and adding to rather than relieving deprivation and domination in society, only a notion of therapy which is inclusive enough on a societal level can meet the target of helping towards better health. Thus social change is advocated which transcends modern medicine as well as capitalist (or, at least, exploitative) society.

Three issues raised under the domination–deprivation perspective are noteworthy.

1. To conquer domination means to overcome clinical medicine. The general idea is that clinical medicine ought to be replaced by support networks created through policies of 'demedicalisation', 'deprofessionalisation', and/or 'decommodification' of health care.
2. Deprivation can be tackled through the welfare state. The latter ought to become more active than hitherto, either abolishing capitalist forms of production and/or appropriation, or deliberately enforcing protective measures benefiting the poor and the disadvantaged. The aim is to promote affluence for everybody through social policies which redistribute wealth. This, in turn, is deemed the best way to promote health for all.
3. Although modern medicine as well as modern society – under the aegis of democracy – are required to change in the interest of the needs and welfare of the individual, the notion of the individual which is used by the literature promoting the deprivation–domination approach is curiously close to an 'oversocialised conception of man'.

Replacing clinical practice by ecological medicine

The hypothesis is widely accepted that clinical medicine which evolved between the mid-eighteenth and late nineteenth centuries, has little chance of surviving. Three reasons are presented: Dubos (1959, 1965) or McKeown (1965, 1975, 1979) argue that natural science-based and bacterial agent-oriented disease theory was adequate as long as infectious diseases were most prevalent. But since chronic diseases have become the most frequent cause of death, and more prevalent among the living in modern society, environment-oriented disease theory is imperative. Furthermore, the point of cost is raised. Even substantive increases in expenditure for modern clinical practice are said to improve the overall health status of the population only marginally. Finally, a new self-awareness of patients challenges clinical practice. The patient develops into a partner in a 'mutuality' dyad rather than a passive recipient of responsible care. In this Szasz and Hollender's (1956) distinction between three types of doctor–patient relationship is taken as evidence that the history of medical care 'moves' from activity–passivity to mutual responsibility (Szasz, Knoff and Hollender, 1958).

According to Armstrong (1979, 1983, 1984), that the patient becomes important as a person, not just a body displaying lesions, is due to a change in the medical paradigm. The same point is made by Arney and Bergen (1983, 1984), whose book *Medicine and the Management of Living* carries the subtitle *Taming the Last Great Beast*. They allude to the patient's life style as the new target of medical surveillance. So far, they contend, the manifestations of everyday life have escaped the 'prepared gaze' (Armstrong, 1986, p. 230) of the doctor. But now problems of living have come to be incorporated into the realm of medical management. The 'new' medical knowledge (also addressed by Wright and Treacher's (1982) collection of Foucault-informed approaches) is said to focus on the involvement of patterns of living in the definition of disease. Arney and Bergen do not hesitate to call the change revolutionary; they write:

> How are we to understand this new medical revolution? We believe we are witnessing a great reversal in medicine. Once, as Ariés has shown, considerable work was devoted to the task of taming death. Death was the great beast that stalked in the darkness and threatened to attack unannounced at any moment. Now, in a Frankensteinian reversal, the great beast is no longer death but life. Life and living threaten, not death and dying. It is the lives of patients that present the most difficult medical issues today; their deaths are just special management problems. (1984, p. 97)

The argument is that in medical cosmology (to use Jewson's 1976 term) 'sick man' re-enters the scene of relevance after the Second World War (especially since 1970). To be sure, 'sick man' is said to have disappeared from the array of what is clinically important since natural science-based modern reasoning became imperative. But now the patient comes to matter as one who feels pain, or experiences satisfaction: that is, as the person in his or her entirety of previously clinically irrelevant identity. Through this incorporation of person-related aspects, mirrored in how medical care is received and experienced, the realm of what comes under medical control is broadened considerably.

At this point of the argument, Arney and Bergen introduce a crisis hypothesis which differs from the views of Armstrong (1983) and the authors in Wright and Treacher (1982). The logical consequence of the change of paradigm, say Arney and Bergen, should be that the doctor as primary care-giver steps back into the ranks of multiple care-givers assembled in the health-care team which acts as support group. Physicians themselves as individual people thus become subject to a critical evaluation by their patients as well as their co-workers in the team. Their being scrutinised by others concerns less their technical competence than what hitherto was kept separate from the doctor–patient encounter: namely, their qualities as individuals. Arney and Bergen elucidate:

> The systems-theoretic-ecological-problem-oriented approach to medicine reorganises medical care. One theoretical article went so far as to say that under the new approach 'the physician . . . would cease to exist as such'. Under the new medical logic, 'the physician would be a systems manager' who, like the factory manager, would ensure that data are collected and pertinent parts of a person's life are monitored, and who would send out information (via the medical record) that certain adjustments in the patients' holon hierarchy of systems need to be made. The new logic causes the physician to become a person. The physician as a person is subject to all the human problems faced by the patient-person and others. (1984, p. 90)[46]

In this situation, Arney and Bergen contend, the medical profession fights back. It is unwilling to let go of the power which the established clinical attitude gave it over its patients as well as its conditions of work. The result is that two new elements are introduced into the clinical perspective which serve the purpose of preserving medical power by stalling unimpeded change to the new ecological paradigm. One is the strategy of 'victim blaming'. Taking up Ryan's (1971) idea that the powerless are charged with causing their affliction (and the sick supposedly are but a category of the powerless), Arney and Bergen maintain that 'victim-blaming [became] diffused throughout the medical policy-making apparatus in the 1970s' (1984, p. 124). The other aspect is surveillance. Total control over the patient's medically relevant features is not relinquished while more and more sides of the person/patient's life come under medical jurisdiction. The idea of order is upheld while its realm broadens considerably. The newly developing medical perspective unites two seemingly contradictory elements under the auspices of unrelenting professional dominance. The latter pervades the image of the support group. Arney and Bergen write: 'It is by resolving this incompatibility between the problem of order and the emergence of the individual that the sociological beauty and the full power of the support group become fully evident' (Arney and Bergen, 1984, p. 113).

The solution of the incompatibility problem, Arney and Bergen argue, lies in submitting both the medical need for order and the emergent idea of individuality to a 'higher' sense of control. The person *in his or her individuality* is thus the 'real' issue of medical surveillance. Rather than withdrawing its claim to be fully responsible for everybody's health (the definition of which has become extensively broadened), Arney and Bergen maintain, the medical profession now reaches out into the community. It sees all manifestations of life in the 'natural' social habitat as potentially subject to medical control.

To be sure, Arney and Bergen understand the 'blaming the victim' ideology as well as the 'new vision of order' as a reaction of the medical world to the threat to its established power. Threatened by an imminent new paradigm of support medicine where the doctor is but one among many care-givers, and support groups become the real source of care, the medical mind allegedly strikes back. The modern rise of 'sociobiology', therefore, is recognised as the medical profession's defence against the danger of being lowered to the level of one among a multitude of care-givers (where the patient – *horribile dictu* – would be on an equal footing with the doctor).

From this vantage point, sociology's attacks against professional dominance clarify an untenable situation. Zola (1972) and the Ehrenreichs (1974) reveal that medicine becomes an institution of all-pervasive social control; Conrad and Schneider (1980a, 1980b) see medicalisation of life; and Illich (1975a, 1975b) discovers clinical (together with social and structural) iatrogenesis. These sociological warnings disclose the dangers of a situation where the medical profession refuses to let go of its unlimited control. In the crisis, sociology has a function. It may pave the way for medicine's giving up its unrelenting domination. How can the 'cutting back to size', so to speak, of medicine occur? What changes are needed such that the switch to the *ecological* model of health care can take place? The sociological literature advocates three processes, under the labels 'demedicalisation', 'deprofessionalisation', and 'decommodification'. All are depicted as more or less revolutionary. This either suggests radical changes of medical thinking, taking into account 'historical necessity' as, for instance, Arney and Bergen suggest (1984, p. 97); or a political and economic revolution is envisaged along the lines of Marx's prophecy of a socialist (Communist) society, now based on a health-oriented rationale.

The demedicalisation argument.   In the version proposed by Conrad and Schneider (1980b) and Zola (1972, 1975) the demedicalisation argument is based on two assumptions. A moral dimension is said to have been given to the state of sickness which aids it being applicable to the powerless, suggesting their 'treatment'. Furthermore, the realm of medical work is said to have been extended to such non-medical areas as pregnancy, alcoholism, and death.

With regard to the latter, demedicalisation means reversal of the trend: that is, childbirth ought to take place in the home rather than the hospital; alcoholism ought to be regarded as an educational rather than treatment problem; death ought to be brought back to 'tame' coming-to-terms, to use Ariès' words (1974). He suggests that what prevailed until the Enlightenment ought to be reintroduced: death should take place publicly with no paraphernalia of intensive care but in the midst of kin and friends whom the dying person knew and loved in his or her lifetime.

In a more radical version, Illich (1975a) suggests that the 'expropriation of health' and the alienation of people from their bodies, ought to be overcome. He claims that suffering should be 'given back' to people who should be allowed to sense vicissitudes of their bodily existence rather than delegating their care to the expert: namely, the physician. Illich argues that demedicalisation should be achieved by more or less abolishing the medical profession, which means deprofessionalisation demedicalising large parts of what hitherto defines clinical work. It is somewhat unclear, however, whether self-help groups are meant to take over the function of doctors, or whether individuals then have to fend for themselves.

The other side of the argument concerns stigmatisation. To combat it, only an onslaught on medical knowledge's objectivity appears effective. The critical attitude which, for example, R. M. Young (1977) and Figlio (1978, 1982) take against scientific medicine derives from their interest in destigmatisation. They emphasise that scientific medicine is but a socially organised body of knowledge, and they advocate neutralising the moral dimension of the sickness label. Bury (1986) holds against such 'constructionism' that reducing medicine to a societally relative taxonomy of diseases, and a historically transient array of treatments, opens the door to untenable relativism. Bury thus implies that evaluation should not be separated from medical cognition.

The deprofessionalisation argument.   In a way, the deprofessionalisation argument is but an aspect of the demedicalisation argument (such that the two are difficult to separate). It is taken here that deprofessionalisation is favoured particularly by those authors who, instead of advocating the abolition of medicine altogether propose to make it into a 'benign' special support service.

As a step in the right direction, opening up the concept of treatment to any help benefiting the patient is envisaged. Freidson, (1970a, 1970b) but also – using a Marxist framework – Larson (1977), suggest doing away with licensing, autonomy of control over conditions of work and other features characteristic of professional dominance. In this connection, Salmon and Berliner (1980) suggest a change of paradigm from that of clinical medicine to that of *holistic* medicine. The latter takes into account what, say, Eastern cultures contain, 'which tend to understand human development as a journey toward becoming conscious of the integration of the internal self' (1980, p. 543). If this is made fundamental to diagnosis and treatment (which, in turn, presupposes a changed conception of health), no limit to expertise curtails administration of care. What are now alternative healers or non-professions (e.g., homeopathy, herbalism, naturopathy and also chiropractice and osteopathy) then become fully-fledged specialities on an equal footing with medical practice. The reason why the change is necessary and unproblematic, say Salmon and Berliner, is the *placebo effect* (1980, p. 544). They hold 'the existence [of] the placebo effect' against 'the paradigm of clinical medicine'. The former, they say, suggests the latter's limitations 'despite all the latest technical advances'. Consequently, clinical practice ought to be overcome by the wider 'holistic health movement'.

If the question is asked what the doctor would be like who practices under the auspices of the placebo effect made deliberate, Waitzkin (1983) suggests a 'pastoral role' for the physician (Waitzkin refers to McKeown, 1979, for details). The doctor is envisaged as a source of social support and as an agent of emotional encouragement. Here the deprofessionalisation argument merges with ideas suggested by Ben-Sira (1986)[47]. He thinks primary care predominantly should give support to distressed persons/patients who then become able to solve their life-problems themselves. Such support-giving would spare them unduly 'somatising' their problems, he says. This, in turn, could possibly help avoid iatrogenic disease from unwarranted drug treatment or unnecessary surgery.

The decommodification argument. For Marxists, the culprit is the capitalist economy. Its being based on the principle of exchange value, not use value, means that truly socialist health care must reverse the picture. Kelman (1975, p. 630) suggests that health in capitalism 'is subordinate to production rather than an end in itself', Waitzkin and Waterman (1974, p. 86ff.) see 'medical imperialism' as the reason for the high level of untreated morbidity among non-insured poor (to recall Lenin's dictum: imperialism is the last developmental stage of capitalism). Reverby (1972) says that treatment of illness as a commodity is the 'root cause' of the widespread non-use of services (which, in turn, aggravates the deterioration of health 'produced' by exploitative waste conditions under the capitalist mode of production).

Decommodification, therefore, lets health be valued, 'as an end in itself', to quote Kelman, rather than as a target of paid medical services. As such, it is all-pervasive. Everything that is related to feeling well can, under this definition, become recognised as having health-producing use value. In similar vein, Carpenter (1979) demands that it is not only 'that the "whole person" rather than the "symptoms" should be treated. It is the notion of "treatment" that we must attack which implies that the sick person is someone "to be dealt with" whether whole or fragmented' (1979, p. 9). The decommodification argument, therefore, holds that sickness and health *per se* should no longer be distinguished. Supportive help in a socialist society should be such that it benefits everybody all the time, with the proviso that no one gets more than others.

Redirecting social policy

When, in 1970, the Ehrenreichs maintained that the American system of health care was held together by 'power, profit and politics', their aim was not to instigate a socialist revolution. Rather, they wished to argue in favour of health care which should be more accountable to the public as regards its cost-effectiveness as well as its adhering to Hippocrates' principle of *doing no harm*. Therefore they diagnosed a *cultural crisis of medicine*, not a crisis of capitalist society. Likewise, when Navarro (1976, 1978a, 1986) demanded more democracy within the health services as well as more equally distributed 'health of the public' (1974), he did not expect everything from an imperative socialist revolution. Instead, he realistically admitted that changes within contemporary society could improve the population's health status. In this he saw a vital role for epidemiology as practised by the new specialty of community medicine and taught at the *Schools of Public Health*.

Short of the all-pervasive cure of all ills in society by a revolution (negation of everything presently dominant), many authors make workable suggestions as to what ought to change. In this, the dividing line is blurred between Marxist or socialist solutions, and what may qualify as social-democrat or even Fabian views.[48] It is usually the state which is endowed with measures bringing about more equality in society (which, in turn, mean better health and less suffering). The realm where the state serves this function is more often beyond than within current medical practice: that is, *prevention* is writ large. This means *welfare policy*, which preempts the origin of disease, is to abolish pathogenic conditions such as low standards of nutrition, bad housing, poor working conditions and unemployment, to name but a few.

The relevant literature makes two arguments which will be mentioned briefly. N. Hart (1982), in her review of Doyal's *The Political Economy of Health* (1979), suggests that the poor overall health status of the population, particularly at the bottom of the socio-economic scale, should not make us blind to the fact that life expectancy in modern society is vastly better than it ever was in pre-capitalist societies. Therefore not the abolition of capitalism but rather the enlightened use of welfare politics within the confines of capitalist society may further help to improve the situation. In a recent article on various explanations of inequalities in health, she maintains that it is wrong to make the individual responsible for his or her poor physical or mental condition. She emphasises the fact that in most of the diseases which shorten the lives of working class people, it is environmental factors and not innate predispositions which have been shown to be of primary causal significance' (N. Hart, 1986b, p. 236). Consequently, the class gradient of morbidity and mortality can be overcome through anti-poverty policies deliberately protecting the poor from the hardships of 'grimy inner city neighbourhoods, dilapidated schools and housing, poor employment opportunities, low income and material insecurities and shortages of every kind' (1986b, p. 238). This entails a lesson which many governments in the 1970s and 1980s seem not to have heeded. She writes:

Reflecting now with hindsight on the lessons of what happened to health in Britain in the first three decades of this century, we may guess that the cost of policies designed to stimulate the economy by abolishing legislation to protect the poor from market forces e.g. wage councils and state underwritten pension schemes, are likely to be counted in widening differentials in health and survival. (N. Hart, 1986b, p. 239)

The other argument relates to whether or not the state should take over health care from the medical profession. Various authors advocate or endorse a *nationalised health service* (or at least national health insurance, as far as the USA is concerned). However, the proviso is that it is unable to tackle the allegedly dismal health situation when the power of the medical profession is left intact. Salaried positions are all that doctors ought to be able to attain; in this way, health is to be exempted from 'production for profit'. The reason why the National Health Service in Britain has been unable to do away with inequality, Navarro (1978b) maintains, is that health services in the UK are still a part of class society sustained by capitalist economy (although partially masterminded by the state). This means, says Navarro, that the profession's power has become stronger rather than weaker which, in turn, neutralises the beneficial effect of state administration on services.

Individualism versus collectivism

The deprivation–domination model is critical of the prevailing health situation and clinical medicine for the benefit of the suffering patient, or individual. The question may be asked whether individuality is truly endorsed.

That social influences on individuals' lives and health are discussed from a collectivist standpoint raises the caveat whether individuals are seen as anything but docile members of a pervasive social order. According to the deprivation–domination view, only wholesale societal changes (and anti-inequality policies) combat the aetiology of disease on the level of the 'social "I"' (Figlio, 1982). Most authors are convinced that only drastic political involvement of the welfare state or even a socialist revolution can achieve the aim of *health for all*. In the light of this, it may not be too far-fetched that many authors put little trust in responsible *individual* citizens' *collectivity orientation*.

There are three reasons why individualism appears *not* to be highly valued although collective action is suggested in the interest of the individual. First of all, health care in modern society is haphazard and even harmful, says Illich (1975a, 1975b) but patients claim to be satisfied and reassure their doctors that they do competent work. In his rebuttal of sociology's attacks against 'medical imperialism', Strong (1979b) states that Illich (explains) this situation by a 'delusion argument': namely, 'that clients have become addicted to the products which professionals have to sell and in the throes of their delirium now demand that the professional empire be expanded . . . Thus, Illich represents the British National Health Service as a product not just of ambitious doctors but of deluded patients also' (P. M. Strong, 1979b, p. 200).

Indeed, patients who are seen as dependent on their doctors as if they were addicts and deluding themselves with fetish-like help-seeking cannot, at the same time, be responsible persons who could easily take their lives into their own hands. Behind the idea of 'delusion' seems to stand an image of mankind which does not think highly of individuality and personal freedom but expects everything from a 'new', all-powerful collective which 'educates' the patient/person as to his or her 'real' interests.[49]

Second, if society may be called sick, as Rossdale puts it (1965) – and these views are endorsed by many others – the question arises how health is possible at all. A possible answer is that two kinds of health exist. One is the absence of illness which the individual experiences in modern society. However, this is a minor form, 'health', at best allowing the individual to function in society's repressive roles. The other form, called 'experiential' by Kelman (1975), is the only way to self-realisation. But its feasibility presupposes the advent of a future liberated society.

In other words, the individual in present-day as well as historical societies supposedly more or less equals a cogwheel in a machine-like social system that grinds almost everybody to the size of a victim. In an article devoted to the topic of medical and psychological problems of torture in modern Latin-American dictatorships, Bendfeldt-Zachrisson (1985) argues that both the tortured and the torturer are victims. Ryan (1971) sees 'blaming the victim' as an all-pervasive ideology sustaining inequality in modern society. Regarding medical practice, authors advocating the political economy of health (such as Ehrenreich and Ehrenreich, 1974) or a Foucault-inspired approach (such as that of Arney and Bergen, 1984) equally state that clinical medicine becomes entangled in 'victim blaming'. This may be said to make the individual medical practitioner – as well as the patient – a victim of the social system. While the doctor allegedly functions as the oppressor of his or her patients (exposed by the doctor to diagnostic labelling) the doctor is also a victim of the system whose ideology he or she practices.

The conclusion may be drawn that the potential of the individual to fend for him- or herself (i.e., the individual's freedom and/or health) is not deemed promising for those on the prongs of the 'sick society'.

Third, Foucault maintains that the clinical gaze of modern medicine has established 'docile bodies'. They are open to inspection regarding every aspect of their physiological functioning as well as psychological make-up. However, clinical medicine's diagnostic–therapeutic perspective is said not to be interested in the person of the patient but only in his or her 'caseness' as specimen. Armstrong (1976, 1979, 1983) argues that this perspective has recently broadened to include the person/patient's biography. But the latter does not denote an individual's personal life-history but rather the realm of life style factors whose changeability through manipulative management masked as treatment allegedly becomes imperative. Arney and Bergen (1984) make it clear that this enhances rather than relinquishes professional power which takes on an aura of unlimitedness. In consequence, O'Neill (1986) pictures modern medicine as the backbone of an all-powerful 'therapeutic state' which suppresses its citizens' unwieldiness in the name of health and illness.

It might be ventured that such conjectures leave little room for what the individual is: namely, the everyday person trying as hard as possible to lead his or her life, have a family and hold down a job as well as look after his or her health seems to be much too adaptive, if not subservient to the ideological system which regulates each person's whole being (according to social constructionism). Moreover, curiously little of the patient's privacy (or its recognition through stressing the normative limits to its breach built into the physician-patient role system) appears to be honoured in the depicted image of medicine. This raises the question of whether the authors of these approaches are so fascinated by their vision of total control that they clandestinely or implicitly decide not to want to know about whatever liberal 'checks and balances' of freedoms and obligations prevail in modern medicine and democratic society.

These apparently anti-individualistic views draw their fervour from a strong belief in the undeniably fundamental value of individualism. What hinders them from expressing this in less collectivist terms? They promote a curiously hermetic notion of society. In their understanding, modern society belies the tenets of equality and liberty (let alone fraternity) and imposes upon its members a relentlessly forceful undemocratic social order. Between the social order and the individual is a very wide gap due to a very unequal distribution of power. While 'the' society and its ruling classes (including dominant professions) are granted near-absolute control, 'the' individual is viewed as 'docile body'. To make it worse, such a body is even understood to be disjoined from its mind, the split allegedly being the *raison d'être* of 'modern bio-medicine'. According to Comaroff (1982, p. 60), 'modern bio-medicine' uses 'unifactorial models'; their prevailing dominance 'assures that the healing process lays stress on an opposition between man and nature, a discontinuity between the individual and the social, and an opposition *within* the individual of body and mind'.

What kind of individual is envisaged against such all-encompassing medicine and society? What can the person – whether patient or not – be like who stands against such an overpowering medical world perceived as the nucleus of the modern repressive social order? Can the limited freedom of the person in liberal democracy, pitched against that of fellow-citizens, be enough? Constitutional rights are granted by governments and, in actual political practice, may often be withheld, watered down or have to be fought for (and can be denied) in the courts of law. Can this be enough to satisfy the ideals of equality and liberty?

The answer for most literature using the deprivation–domination view appears to be 'No'. These authors advocate more than the present-day scope of individual freedom (and health). It seems to them that an individual sphere is not sufficient which is legitimated by the 'formally democratic' bureaucratic state and backed up by class society. The latter incorporates capitalist production depending on the exploitation and discrimination of workers, if not the powerless in general. How can this be satisfactory under an emphatic image of mankind? The magnitude of the perceived irreconcilability between the imperative social order and the mystified helpless individual is enormous. It seems to necessitate that medical sociology goes *beyond* present-day society when a suitable environment for truly individual-prone conditions is envisaged.

Chapter 15
Conflict Theory and the Two Models of Illness

As a breakdown of supports that hold at bay pathogenic risks of susceptibility and life-change, and as a breakdown of health of social groups under the onslaught of external forces originating in pathogenic environments, illness takes on two different forms in the loss and deprivation-domination models. Both may be traced to conflict theory's making sense of the diversity and contradictions of modern society.

The two approaches remain in relative isolation from each other. The loss model emerges from discussions on stress and its impact which, since the mid-1950s and particularly in the 1970s, take place not only in books and articles but also through a large number of conferences worldwide. In fact, it may be said that conferences mark the history and development of the loss approach. Particularly influential are that convened by Barbara and Bruce Dohrenwend on 'Stressful Life Events' in Norway in June 1973, and that organised by Lowell Levin, assisted by Erik Holst and Marsden Wagner, under the sponsorship of the WHO in Denmark in August 1975. The problems discussed on such occasions are overwhelmingly research-based. They generate more research which is then published in journals such as the *Journal of Health and Social Behavior, Psychosomatic Medicine,* the *Journal of Psychosomatic Research*, and *Social Science and Medicine*. In contrast, authors proposing deprivation–domination explanations hardly take part in such activity, using research evidence often selectively or in an assertive manner where it fits into their *wider* ideas of pathological society. The contexts of their discussions are not so much topic-specific international meetings but *ad-hoc* groups set up at Annual Conferences of the American or British Sociological Associations. Frequently, small conferences or evening seminars organised by political groups or at universities discuss issues of deprivation–domination. The somewhat exclusive, albeit internationally attended, gatherings around the *International Journal of Health Services* have also contributed (since 1976). While lively exchange occurs between authors *within* each of the two approaches, apparently 'traditions' develop somewhat separately, at least in terms of journals and conferences.

This chapter attempts three things. It goes back to the two explanatory models, pointing out similarities between their views of pathogenic process, particularly with regard to how conflict relates to social order, and then the contribution of the idea of conflict-generated illness for general sociological theory is discussed. What the social order entails for the individual is the central point of discussion. The loss model focuses on the individual person's suffering generated by ambiguities, changes, and losses afforded by the modern unsettled world. The domination–deprivation model focuses on rigours which the social order in its more or less hermetic grip on the individuals' environment entails for individualism in general. Both perceive *incommensurability* between 'the' healthy individual and 'the' power-monopolising society. Such dichotomous conceptualisation brings back the issues connected with the problem of anti-Semitism. As in previous parts of this book, the literature on Fascism will again be mentioned. In particular, the recent book on *Nazi Doctors* (Lifton, 1986) will be related to the sociological idea of 'sick society'.

The final part of the chapter is devoted to the problem of what medical sociology can aspire to be. In the wake of 'sociological imperialism', sociology, on the one hand, deems itself competent to criticise clinical practice as alleged 'medical imperialism', and even proposes to replace, partly or wholly, contemporary medicine. On the other hand, such self-assertiveness is warned against by some of sociology's more self-conscious representatives. By attempting a sociological explanation of the rise of medical sociology, they relativise "new" medicine but also partly endorse it by arguing that it is historically inescapable.

Indeed, this brings the discussion back to the point concerning what sociology is and can be, whether *in*, *of*, or *with* medicine. It will be argued that what needs clarifying is predominantly the scope of medicine, as opposed to that of sociology, and the role of both *vis-à-vis* society. Such clarification brings to the fore their alignment with different types of praxis. This makes clinical practice the apex of medical reasoning, but sociological analysis the apex of the sociologist's work. Sociology, contrary to Comte's classic triad, appears treacherously ambitious if it maintains that *savoir* means *prévoir*, and *prévoir* means *règler*.

The two models revisited

The loss approach states that the aetiology of illness is due to a breakdown or lack of social support. Losses occur through life changes (life events) which, in turn, exacerbate the risk of illness incumbency incorporated in social statuses as well as biographical or psychological vulnerability (conceptualised as vulnerability factors). In case of breakdown, coping efforts usually have failed which otherwise would have offset the noxious effects from the three sources: namely, social status, vulnerability and loss (change). Accordingly, the task of therapy is to rebuild the person's coping. This can be done by enhancing his or her personal capabilities, or by improving upon his or her more general chances. The therapeutic process is conceptualised from the two perspectives of the individual as well as the environment. On the one hand, this focuses on self-care, denoting social support which can improve a person's ability to cope with actual illness or the risk of potential illness. On the other hand, this brings the state and wider society into the picture. Through the sort of prevention that fights sickness before it occurs, the state can help to safeguard public health.

The deprivation–domination model also states that the breakdown of health is due to environmental deficiencies. However, it is not the social context of personal relationships which is deemed responsible for illness incumbency. The 'wider' environment of pollution, poor working conditions, or low educational or housing standards, together with definitional segregation between sick and working through the medical profession's 'clinical gaze' all combine to confirm the reality of illness. Incumbency of illness is thus partly a product of definition based on medical knowledge which is ideological. Its being historically relative means that it is socially constructed.In the light of this, therapy can only aim at curing the ills of a 'sick society' (which, to be sure, 'produces' illness since it embraces exploitative capitalism and, on this basis, is deemed 'sick' in its own right). The strategies to achieve the aim of better health for all are openly political. In order to combat domination of the medical profession, demedicalisation, deprofessionalisation, and/or decommodification of health care appear appropriate. To do away with or mitigate deprivation, either a revolution of society in the Marxist sense, or far-reaching redistributive welfare politics are frequently suggested.

The ideas on the aetiology–therapy process endorsed by both models can be brought into parallel pictures combining an 'outer' collective (societal) level and an 'inner' individual level, as shown

Table 15.1　Aetiology and therapy according to loss and deprivation/domination models

	Aetiology		Therapy	
	Collective level	*Individual level*	*Individual level*	*Collective level*
Loss	Susceptibility due to social status, etc.	Loss	Self-care	Prevention due to public-health measures
Deprivation/ denomination	Pathogenic environments	Seeking professional care	Deprofession- alisation, etc., of care	Political change of environments

in Table 15.1. The two models have in common that they conceptualise illness risk, in the first instance, through *social-environmental influences* (be they social status, which is a collective feature, or unhealthy conditions of life to which either segments of the population or the whole populace are exposed). Actual breakdown of an individual's health, however, is due to individual factors. That not everybody becomes ill can be traced to support received after an experienced life-change, or to decisions of those not feeling well nevertheless not to seek medical care. The move from the collective to the individual levels in the aetiological process is mirrored in an individual and a collective stage in therapy. Adequate (i.e., not simply sickness-reproducing) therapy, for both models, suggests innovative changes on the individual as well as community levels. These are meant to transform the health care system but also involve redirection of the modern welfare state in its 'legitimating' function (all the more since the latter, according to Habermas (1971/73), is undergoing a crisis).

While both paradigms embrace an individual as well as a collective side of the aetiology and the therapy process, they differ with regard to how they bring *conflict* into the picture.

Conflict, in the loss approach, is entailed by the circumstances which are illness-provoking: that is, the individual would stay healthy were it not for life changes bringing him or her into conflict with the environment. (One could also say people are protected from the risk engendered by their susceptibility as long as they receive sufficient support from their social environment.) When the support diminishes due to events or changes (which may heighten previously neutralised susceptibility), individuals are at odds with or pitched against their current environment. In this situation of momentarily produced or exacerbated *conflict between individual and social context*, illness may strike (or, rather illness may ensue because of minimised host resistance). In due course, the sources of conflict that facilitate the aetiology of illness must be overcome through therapy. The movement advocating self-care (self-help) avowedly aims to decrease conflict between an individual's inner and external social world. Self-help is meant to overcome the impact of life-changes such as migration, divorce or job loss, or the incapacitation due to continued difficulties inherent in, say, being a single parent, having an alcoholic spouse, having a relative in prison, or raising an unusually gifted child (Robinson and Henry, 1977, p. 47).

Conflict, in the deprivation–domination view, is *contradiction between the ruling classes and the powerless* or working classes in modern society. In the light of this, the juxtaposition between doctor and patient apparently is but a replica of that between capitalist and worker. For many authors, doctors are quasi-capitalists, not individuals but , to quote Marx, 'personifications of economic categories, embodiments of particular class-relations and class-interests' (1867/1906, p. 15). To be sure, Marx-oriented authors put deprivation in the forefront emphasising how blunt they think the class or professional domination is. In contrast, the Foucault-oriented authors focus more on domination as a modern form of social power, and they introduce deprivation as domination's underside. Both groups of authors draw the connection between medicine and ideology. Whether ideology is understood as necessarily false consciousness in the context of class contradiction, or a hegemonic knowledge system domesticating the bodies and minds of society's ruled masses, both conceptualisations imagine a structural dichotomy between power and powerlessness. Medicine, in this view, is but a representation of structural societal conflict.

Conflict between individual and society, therefore, is at the root of illness incumbency for the loss *and* the deprivation–domination views. Type and extension of the conflict, however, seem different. The loss model conceives of temporary conflict between the individual and the social order or social environment, created through changes in the individual's situational back-up of protective resources. The deprivation–domination model proposes permanent conflict between above and below in society, due to the nature of the social order where power resources are most unequally distributed.

Both approaches, on close scrutiny, are convinced that inequality is the main feature of the modern social structure. They also surmise that this entails unnecessary and potentially avoidable consequences for the individual. In other words, both views see a contrast between the individual and society. One may say that the conflict between the health-interested, well-being oriented nature of the individual and the illness-producing, hardship-prone nature of the social order is obvious. While the latter is recognised as a source of suffering and repression (including repression of one's inner self), the former is explicitly or implicitly hailed as the epitome of a better state of mind, self and society.[50]

Such views blend in with the idea that structure and power are intimately intertwined. Does this *necessarily* entail an image of mankind whereby the individual is reduced to subservient obedience to external constraints? Giddens (1984) points out that limited realms of subordinate freedoms appear to be granted to members by the social order. This principle of structuration ascertains their voluntary incorporation into the system. The result is that autonomy is less an indicator of individualism than of the sophistication of social control. A truncated reciprocity which leads to a more or less camouflaged reality of social power renders the fundamental schism between high and low tolerable. Giddens writes:

> We can express the duality of structure in power relations in the following way. Resources (focused via signification and legitimation) are structured properties of social systems, drawn upon and reproduced by knowledgeable agents in the course of interaction. Power is not intrinsically connected to the achievement of sectional interests. In this conception the use of power characterises not specific types of conduct but all action, and power is not itself a resource. Resources are media through which power is exercised, as a routine element of the instantiation of conduct in social reproduction. We should not conceive of the structures of domination built into social institutions as in some way grinding out 'docile bodies' who behave like the automata suggested by objectivist social science. Power within social systems which enjoy some continuity over time and space presumes regularised relations of autonomy and dependence between actors or collectivities in contexts of social interaction. But all forms of dependence offer some resources whereby those who are subordinate can influence the activities of their superiors. This is what I call the *dialectics of social control* in social systems. (Giddens, 1984, pp. 15–16)

The contribution to general sociological theory

When Giddens calls society a social system, he means something different from Parsons. The latter's notion excludes conflict as well as deviance. Both for Parsons remain outside the system boundaries, being subject to social control which either neutralises their impact or relinquishes their existence. The world is here pictured as containing continuous conflict not within the system but *between* the (inherently harmonious) social/cultural/psychological system(s), on the one side, and the extra- or anti-social forces of inhumane technological revolutions or irresponsible pleasure-seeking on the other. In contrast, when Giddens speaks of the social system he envisages conflict *within* it. For him, there is nothing outside this system of any relevance for the sociologist: everything societally salient must be found within the system's confines. This does away with the distinction between the analytical and empirical level which Parsons uses to introduce his abstract propositions of the social system where he nevertheless maintains that a realm of historical–political life remains beyond sociological explanation. Giddens sees the social system as also endowed with everything which Parsons manages to keep outside the sociologist's gaze. Thus, Giddens' analysis (or Collins', for that matter) includes the ugly face of repression in society more than Parsons', and sociology must now take account of the struggle between high and low. It can no longer exempt itself from political responsibility or, at least, accountability under the excuse that the sociologist must observe analytical neutrality.

This, however, raises the question of sociology's value commitment. When individuals and their total lives are included in the conflict-prone society one has to ask from whence derives the sociologist's standpoint? If there is no moral or systematic stance beyond the confined realms of conflict-riddled society, what allows the sociologist to say that there is no escape from the social system? How can he suggest that the individual's autonomy is but the realisation of a 'dialectics of control' if that, in itself, could be but an expression of the 'dialectics of control' ? It may be argued that conflict theory *presupposes* a *dichotomy* between the individual and society. Although this dichotomy allegedly is neutralised by basing the notion of system on that of conflict, and although a trickle of autonomy for the individual in society is perceived under the notion 'instantiation of conduct in social reproduction' (Giddens, 1984, p. 16), it may be argued that nevertheless a cleavage between the individual and the social order is assumed.

The problem can be highlighted by two dilemmas which are faced by Giddens' position as well as by most conflict-theory oriented literature on illness. One concerns the issue of *relativism*. Bury (1986), in his critique of constructionism, argues that if rationality is relativised as a principle of natural science in medicine, nothing is left except a basically arbitrary array of practices. He writes:

In offering an account of modes of knowledge, especially medical knowledge and the part they play in modern social relations, social constructionism implicitly raises the issue of its own knowledge base . . . The issue which arises can be simply put: if all forms of knowledge are part of 'discourses' where does that leave constructionism? . . . This places us in a circle from which there appears to be no escape. (1986, pp. 152–3)

However, Bury's strictures face the same dilemma with which he charges constructionism. In order to refute the latter's alleged conjecture of unanalysable practices in medicine, Bury has to presuppose an equally unanalysable, all-pervasive quality of what is human (otherwise he could not charge his opponents with anti-humanism). The same may be said, for instance, about Collins' (1975) endeavour to establish conflict as the basic category for sociological analysis. Charging other theories with manipulative tendencies, Collins sums up his efforts as follows:

The task of creating a social science has been much more difficult for the conceptual side than in the natural sciences . . . This is because the material with which we deal consists of our constructed realities: the organization of our collective behavior, and the labels we ordinarily place upon it. The necessary detachment does not come easily here. In fact, most 'practical' sociology has consisted of efforts to construct a particular type of reality through the categories and focus of descriptive studies, and of efforts to manipulate other people's political belief and behavior. (1975, p. 524)

The question, however, remains open as to where the detachment which Collins does not find easy comes from, and on what grounds it rests. The hypothesis may be ventured that the implicit standpoint which his orientation sets, and from which it draws its justification, is a notion of the individual which envisages, so to speak, a trans-socially pure human of idealised, if not Utopian, dimensions.

A similar argument may be made regarding the line of thought proposed by what has been called the loss approach. That social stress leads to illness, if unhindered by countervailing supportive resources, can only be maintained if the nature of society is conceptualised as basically opposed to the nature of the individual. If society were conceptualised as a system of checks and balances, allowing for negotiations which achieve purposeful rearrangements of parts of one's world, it would make little sense to make the suffering individual a victim of tensions (stresses) originating in an overwhelming social pathology.

The second dilemma concerns the relationship between *society and the state*. On the one hand, societal conflict is shown to permeate all manifestations of social life. This includes the fact that the state is often conceptualised, akin to a Marxist view, as some kind of 'agent' of the capitalist class; in Foucault's terms, the same is expressed by saying that the state is an instrument of domination of the ruling circles, and in Althusser's terms (1984) it is called an 'ideological apparatus' (which is also said about medicine). On the other hand, deliberately redistributive welfare politics are believed capable of counteracting societal ills. Emanating from the state, supplemented by public-health measures, wealth-sharing political changes are believed possible. They are to do more than combat the *faux frais* of economic exploitation. Their purpose is to go beyond curtailing the greediness of dominating institutions including the medical profession. They are to bring about controlled change in the guise of a definite democratisation of society.

On the one hand, then, the state is envisaged as a huge machinery of social control acting 'in the name of health and illness' (Zola, 1975), even raising the spectre of the all-pervasive 'therapeutic state' (O'Neill, 1986) where society comes under totalitarian rule. On the other hand, the state is cast in the role of saviour from the dangers which seem to come from society, and the state is recognised as powerful and beneficial enough to rescue society from the unanticipated consequences of production and consumption within it. To be sure, it is this latter vision of the state which Virchow (1848/1968) has in mind when he surmises that 'politics is nothing but medicine on a grand scale' (see Taylor and Rieger, 1984). In contrast, O'Neill's (1986) or Frankenberg's (1986) warnings against a 'therapeutic state' in which medical sociology plays the role of a power servant refers to a different kind of state. In it, not politics is curative of social (and physical) illness with the benevolent ways of medicine. But medicine is an instrument of repressive political manipulation which uses selective labelling and rigorous domination over 'docile bodies'.

In both versions conflict is suggested between the individual and the state or society. The state, in this, acquires two meanings. First, it represents an executor of anti-human interests of the ruling classes in society; second, it is pitched against such society as a refuge for the beleaguered individual's chances for satisfactory survival. If this argument holds, the basic conflict is not between state and society, or state and individual, but individual and society. The state is given a double function, either as an agent of welfare politics against society's dominating forces, or as an agent of the latter's powerful totalitarian world.

In both versions, it seems, the sociologist takes sides with the *individual*. This means that either society represents the 'sick' principle of class, status and power (particularly in its repressive and exploitative aspects), and it is agreed that the state acts more in the interest of the individual, particularly with regard to publicly monitored health preservation; or the sociologist feels obliged to oppose both the state *and* society in order not to abandon the beleaguered individual. In this case, the all-powerful 'therapeutic state' (which supposedly imposes a dominating order of knowledge and practice) is rejected from the standpoint of a not-at-present-realised, possibly Utopian image of autonomous and responsible (wo)man.

One might argue that such partisanship for the oppressed individual is based on an unrealistically hermetic notion of social control. It seems likely that the idea of social order which stands behind the analysis of clinical/social/structural iatrogenesis is far too deterministic to be sociologically satisfactory. Is it really true, one might ask, that modern society is so 'sick' that is 'makes' its members sick (which is what psychosomatic as well as sociosomatic research proposes)? Can it really be said that the modern state is all-powerful like a totalitarian regime which reaches into the bodily spheres of its citizens by measures controlling life style and health behaviour? Is there a union between medicine and the state? Is it realistic that an ideology of domination over individuals' bodies and minds unites with an all-dominating social order? It seems strange to think that such 'oversocialized conception of society', an image of an apparently totalitarian social order, should be adequate. One cannot accept that this pictures satisfactorily the relationship between clinical practice and modern liberal democracies.

The only way in which the obviously overdrawn notion of the state and medicine seems to make sense is to relate it neither to the contemporary liberal-democratic state nor case-based patient-concerned medical practice. The stark conflict between the individual and the social order in a presumed 'sick' society only seems to have prevailed in the Fascist society of yesteryear. Before 1945, under National Socialism, individuals were relinquished to become either docile party members or join another Fascist association, if they did not wish to withdraw into the precarious existence at the time called *inner emigration*. The only other possibilities were emigration, joining the highly endangered underground resistance, or (following often shockingly minor infractions of rules) being incarcerated by the Gestapo who mishandled and tortured many hundreds of thousands of people.

There seems to have prevailed an intricate connection between medical ideology and the National-Socialist state. In a recent book, Lifton (1986) undertakes to argue that the principle of National Socialism itself was professedly medical (i.e., therapeutic). In an intriguing analysis of documents as well as interviews, Lifton reveals the 'euthanasia program' instituting the killing of 'life unworthy of life' as a 'genetic cure' meant to improve the purity of the Aryan race. Likewise, Auschwitz and the programme of concentration camps are understood as a 'racial cure'. Selections on the ramps and in the camps (weeding out the non-able bodied) followed the principle of eliminating poor biological stock, Lifton argues.

Lifton's main point is that medicine was not peripheral to the National Socialist doctrine that demanded mass murder. Rather, the biological principle of racial purification as political aim made it necessary that the regime used doctors. They were needed as willing hands to supervise the killings and as researchers who helped to formulate ideological targets of experimental investigation. In all, it was not medicine as clinical practice but medical doctors as agents of biological knowledge of which the regime made use. It put its political practice under a leading perspective of biological upgrading. This more than anything else gave the most atrocious systematic killing the dignity of a seemingly impersonal motive. As Lifton phrases it, the state became a *biocracy* where an avowedly therapeutic mission became associated with the most terrible killing in history. Lifton writes:

> One can speak of the Nazi state as a 'biocracy' . . . In the case of the Nazi biocracy, the divine prerogative was that of cure through purification and revitalization of the Aryan race . . . Among the biological authorities called forth to articulate and implement 'scientific racism' – including physical anthropologists, geneticists, and racial theorists of every variety – doctors inevitably found a unique place. It is they who work at the border of life and death . . . In Auschwitz, Nazi doctors presided over the murder of most of the one million victims of the camp. Doctors performed selections – both on the ramp among arriving transports of prisoners and later in the camps and on the medical blocks. Doctors supervised the killing in the gas chambers and decided when the victims were dead . . . In connection with all these killings, doctors kept up a pretense of medical legitimacy for deaths of Auschwitz prisoners and of outsiders brought there to be killed, they signed false death certificates listing spurious illnesses. Doctors consulted actively on how . . . to burn the enormous numbers of bodies that strained the facilities of the crematoria. (1986, pp. 17–18)

As an addendum to Lifton's analysis, it may be mentioned that Foucault relates the Nazi biological ideology to the nineteenth century precursors of racism. In the first volume of *Histoire de la sexualité* (1976), Foucault argues that since the eighteenth century the body has become an object of power. The political merges with the biological, he contends, and this explicitly also includes sexual drives, activities and relations. The latter are put under the surveillance of authorities which safeguard the distinction between normal and pathological (perverse) in the interest of the continuation and purity of the Victorian family structure. The latter, in turn, is based on a biologically grounded ideology of racial prowess. Foucault implies that what comes to the fore in Nazi racism has its roots in the biological foundations of power established decades earlier.

If related to Fascism, the hermetic notion of social control does not appear overdrawn. The idea does not appear too far-fetched that the individual is reduced to a limited scope of autonomy carefully controlled within the 'dialectics of social control'. The statement rings true that individualism may be altogether impossible since the social grid of ideological categories forms 'docile bodies' during socialisation. Last but not least, that medicine has a menacing quality is only too understandable if looked at in the context of German Fascism. If endowed with the task of genetically and physically improving the racial quality of mankind through such means as sterilisation and killings, a medical establishment backed up by a Fascist state is justly valued as an all-powerful arbitrator over life and death.

It seems that much of the literature proposing the deprivation–domination view directly or indirectly implies that our society resembles a Fascist one. Only from this vantage point are the drastic reforms and political measures not overdrawn which are suggested to improve the general health situation. Demedicalisation, deprofessionalisation and decommodification propose drastic changes because these appear as the only effective solution under an assumed quasi-Fascist social order in modern industrial society.

Equally, the loss approach distrusts professional medical care, and it takes refuge in self-care and state-sponsored prevention. With regard to illness avoidance, these authors favour the forces of the private sphere (support networks), and they accuse the stresses of the work world and modern urban life (style) in general. The latter seem to refer to secondary groups or larger impersonal social milieux as pathological (Tönnies' idea of *Gesellschaft*) whereas the former represent primary groups and small communities which foster healthy and normal lives (Tönnies' *Gemeinschaft*). It is well known that Fascism represents more secondary than primary group relations. While National Socialism managed to penetrate the whole of political and occupational-economic as well as educational realms, it found it difficult to invade people's private spheres to the same extent. At least, the family and other sources of social support are described also as 'counterstructure' within the Fascist state and society (Rosenbaum, 1978). In this connection – that the loss model identifies sources of illness in the *social* ('Gesellschaft') and sources of protection in the *private* ('Gemeinschaft') spheres – may point to the same basic hypothesis of inherent social pathology as raised by the deprivation–domination view. The implication that the social may be associated with totalitarian rule is not ruled out for present-day social order.

The message is that totalitarianism, if not prevailing, is at least a possibility in the modern world. The contribution which the loss as well as the deprivation–domination views make to general sociological theory lies along these lines. The liberal-democratic society with its tolerant citizens and apparently humane institutions is revealed as a somewhat treacherous façade for a deeper structure. Underneath the surface of affluence and harmony, it is surmised or implied, one has to sense the essence of expropriation and conflict. That the latter is not obvious is itself an aspect of domination: the powerless, turned into docile bodies by powerful 'biocracy', cannot even articulate their emotions and interests. Their domination must be envisaged as so complete that any emotions and interests of their own – whatever they may be – have not had a chance even to develop. It is here that Collins' idea of 'emotional production' (1975, p. 58) may merge with Foucault's conjecture of 'docile bodies'.

Implied in this postulate of potentially omnipresent Fascism is a hypothesis about the extension of its realm of power. Traditional sociological theory, as was argued above at the outset of this book, stops where individual personal integrity begins. In other words, the smallest unit of social-action theory and classical theory of social structure (social order) is the member. He or she forms a unity of body and mind that represents, in turn, the person with full social competence. But the new sociological theory developing also through medical sociology and finding a resource in Foucault's work goes further than the traditional view. Now the individual is no longer the smallest unit, and health and illness are no longer beyond the sociological gaze. On the contrary, the body is now revealed as a major target of social formation. The social order is now demonstrated in its effect of how docile bodies may become.

In this vein, the contribution to general sociological theory of the conflict-theory oriented approaches in medical sociology is also that health and illness are very much *within* the realm of society. This finally brings to the fore how crucial the bodily issues are for what general sociological theory is concerned about: namely, actors' behaviour and society's rules (and constraints) are now opened up for a theoretical enquiry about illness – on both levels – as a central topic.

The place of sociology

This book argues that one of the main theoretical questions of sociology emerging after the Second World War is whether whole societies may be regarded as pathological. Now one has to ask: if it can be taken for granted that a Fascist society is *sick* (and that all societies can potentially turn Fascist), what does this entail for sociology? In his then well-received article 'Society as the Patient' (1936), Frank argues that the sociologist must become an activist. He writes:

> The disintegration of our traditional culture, with the decay of those ideas, conceptions, and beliefs upon which our social and individual lives were organized, brings us face to face with the problem of treating society, since individual treatment or punishment no longer has any value beyond mere alleviation of symptoms . . . The concept of a sick society in need of treatment has many advantages for diagnosis of our individual and social difficulties and for constructive therapy, although we may find it necessary to prescribe a long period of preparation before the patient will be ready for the remedies indicated. (1936, pp. 335–6)

As regards the solution which could help society and direct the efforts of sociologists, Frank becomes quite enthusiastic about what at the time can only have been authoritarian regimes. It is unclear whether he refers to Fascist Germany, Italy, Spain, or to Communism in Russia. The former belonged to the period when it was neither already discredited by the bombardment of Guernica nor had the positive echo of the 1936 Berlin Olympics subsided (although emigrés must have reported that concentration camps existed since March 1933). Russia, at the time, was in her period of show trials and purges but many found it difficult to stop admiring its revolution. Frank writes:

> The process of remaking our culture is under way. The new social orders abroad have initiated the program, each with different goals and

values, but agreeing in their repudiation of many of the older social theories and myths that forbade social change and in their relinquishment of the idea of human volition and an individualistic freedom with little or no responsibility. Their specific aims and the frequently ruthless execution of these programs affront our sensibilities, but we must acknowledge that they are experimenting with cultural reorganization – the task we must also undertake, peacefully and more humanly, we hope, and with real respect for individual differences. (1936, p. 344)

Frank's position highlights the dilemma in which the sociologists turned activists find themselves. As soon as they leave the detached stance of clearly delineated analytical concepts, they cannot maintain value-free neutrality. They must enter a realm where identification with contemporary or historical (or future) model societies is imperative for their value commitments. This brings with it that theory and praxis can no longer be separated from each other.

As regards medical sociology, Freidson (1983b) highlights the pitfalls of a political position which takes for granted that to criticise medical practice 'is truly helpful to actually improving the character of human life' (1983b, p. 215). To be sure, in Freidson's view it is not wrong to abstain from identifying with the tenets of medical practice in our society; but it is problematic to put another seemingly strong and valid identification in its place (for instance, with neighbourhood health centres in Nicaragua today, or Chile under Allende, or with barefoot-doctor medicine in China). Freidson insists on deliberate non-identification with the medical scene, but also deliberate non-identification with any available alternative. He writes:

> Part of the value of such a discipline is the very fact of its being outside – congenitally and deliberately outside – the routines of health service and health administration, capable of questioning their settled assumptions and pointing to their deeper roots in the political economy and culture of which they are a part. Another part of its value lies in its disciplined character – its systematic and self-conscious methods of data-collection and its theoretically organized methods of analysis. (1983b, p. 219)

Does Freidson's warning and advice go far enough? The question arises as to whether sociology is adequately pictured if its presumed knowledge interest is the political economy and culture of health service and health administration. To be sure, Freidson's idea contradicts both alternatives for sociology's stance towards medicine which R. Straus (1957) envisages. He delineates a sociology *in* medicine which he contrasts with a sociology *of* medicine.

While the latter attempts a more or less structural-functionalist analysis, the former lends itself to a not-altogether-clear 'integration of concepts, techniques and personnel'. Straus states that there are no easy answers: 'These two types of medical sociology tend to be incompatible with each other; that the sociologist of medicine may lose objectivity if he identifies too closely with medical teaching or clinical research while the sociologist in medicine risks a good relationship if he tries to study his colleagues' (1957, p. 203).

One way out is suggested by Horobin (1985), who advocates that sociology be *with* medicine. This means, given 'the profoundly social nature of illness and health, thanks in no small measure to sociology' (1985, p. 105) that cooperation with no encroachments is suggested. Horobin's insight that medical sociologists do not like the outside stance which their discipline requires them to have is valid. He writes: 'Medical sociologists are doubly alienated, for not only do they share this unease about the validity of experience, but they inhabit the interstices between the citadel of medicine and the suburb of sociology' (1985, p. 95).

All these authors appear to warn that in a situation such as that of medical sociology it is all too easy to leap into initiatives concerning 'how to subvert, change and remodel the social world' (Horobin, 1985, p. 104). In the same vein, Strong (1979a) warns that Illich's (1975b) and Waitzkin and Waterman's (1974) idea of 'medical imperialism' is but a derivative of a 'sociological imperialism'. This criticism can also be directed against Conrad and Schneider's (1980a) conjectures that a 'medicalization of society' is imminent, itself based on Zola's (1972) and the Ehrenreichs' (1974) notion that medicine is but an institution of social control.

If medical sociology's overly self-centred image is refuted, the crucial issue is that medicine's task be adequately recognised. In 1975, Conrad writes about the medicalisation of deviant behaviour as if it were a fact, using as an example the 'discovery of hyperkinesis'. In a careful criticism of his standpoint, Whalen and Henker (1977) highlight what they term 'the pitfalls of politicization'. Namely, individual cases are taken as but a specimen of societal processes, and the individual in his or her unique physical or psychological suffering is not acknowledged as the focus of the doctor's wish to help. Thus, write Whalen and Henker:

> Conrad asserts that medicalization and individualization of hyperkinetic behavior serve to depoliticize deviance *in the same manner* as that used in the Soviet Union when political dissenters are declared mentally ill and hospitalized . . . Less dramatically, Conrad is arguing, directly

or by implication, that we should stop focusing on troubled children and begin dissecting social systems. It is certainly likely that changes in society's expectations about child behavior, and alterations of the physical, temporal, and social structures of learning environments, might reduce the problems encountered by these youngsters. Eliminating malnutrition, reducing prenatal and perinatal complications, and lowering environmental lead levels would also help. We are concerned that the replacement of medicalization by politicization of deviant behavior may increase the distance between problem and solution and, if available intervention procedures are denied while necessary social changes are sought, will exclude the children themselves from consideration. (1977, p. 593)

Thus the message is that clinical practice and sociological thinking are two *different* realms. The former is concerned with how children's illness and treatment are best approached in each individual case, whereas the latter, to be sure, is concerned with what it *means* that illness in modern clinical practice takes the form not so much of a natural process as of a socially caused incapacitation.

In other words, the distinction between theory and praxis is crucial for sociology. If it does not wish to overstep its boundaries and end up in untenably imperialist contentions, sociology must realise this distinction. As Feinstein (1967) and Wieland (1975) argue, clinical work is *practical* and therefore case-bound, concrete and always situationally specific. As practical action, it avails itself of theory which fosters explanatory models which help to make sense of what comes under the practitioner's gaze. Sociology, insofar as a 'profoundly social nature of illness and health' may be assumed (Horobin, 1985, p. 105), is or might become one of the theoretical disciplines of which clinical practice makes use.

Thus sociology is an *analytical* science while medicine is a *practical* endeavour. The latter may avail itself of various insights of the former, if they are carefully researched. But never should sociology which, within the confines of medicine, is at best one of its theoretical disciplines attempt to overcome or replace medicine. The danger hidden in such an undertaking is that sociology itself forgoes its roots and abandons its tenable aims. Its roots are in the theoretical reflection of societal goings-on. Its tenable aims are the systematic description and methical explanation of social life and social structures.

Epilogue: The Future of Medical Sociology

In the four parts of this book, theoretical paradigms used in conceptualising aetiology and treatment have been outlined. The structural-functionalist approach proposes a capacity model which phrases aetiology as a loss of role capacity, and treatment as its restoration through sick-role incumbency. The deviance model conceptualises aetiology as a breakthrough of dependency needs, and therapy as social control re-repressing them. The interactionist paradigm suggests a crisis model where aetiology equals acquiring a stigmatising label (role), and treatment accomplishes its internalisation. The negotiation model which is further ventured sees aetiology as bargaining connected with diagnosis, and therapy as work in organisations conceived as negotiated order. The phenomenological paradigm's trouble model may be divided into a clinical reasoning and a micro-politics view; its idea of aetiology is that the trouble–trust cycles of taken-for-granted everyday life are broken by an instance of trouble which necessitates restitutive or punitive restoration of trust by a professional agency (e.g., therapy). The conflict-theory paradigm establishes a loss model where aetiology means a loss of illness-buffering protective support, and therapy (preferably self-help and public-health preventive measures) restores or reinforces support sources. The deprivation–domination model characterises aetiology as succumbing to the ill-effects of pathological social structures, and therapy as the latter's reformist or revolutionary change.

Each of the four paradigms is said to contribute to general sociological theory an important idea. The structural-functionalist paradigm ventures that health is a matter of the individual while medical practice is crucial as the institution of social order. Health, to be sure, means psychological well-being further explained by psychoanalytic thinking. For the interactionist paradigm, the contribution to general sociological theory is that society rather than the individual harbours forces determining the individuals' illness and health. Such societal forces can leave more or less room for

individuals' self-determination incorporated into imposed or negotiated rules of conduct and work. Health here means culturally
relative issues of interpersonal judgment. The phenomenological
paradigm establishes a model of trouble–trust dialectics as its
contribution to sociological theory. It explains how institutional
settings function by remedying physical, psychological and role
incompetence and incapacities through practices defining trouble
(e.g., illness), and re-establishing trust, medical treatment itself
being based on this. Health here is social proficiency of the indisputably competent member, as attributed by others. The conflict-
theory's paradigm's contribution to sociological theory reveals the
covert underground of conflict that looms under the surface of taken-
for-granted order which the phenomenologists disclose. Health
here is a more or less idealised state of physical, psychological and
social well-being of the person while illness, induced through
discrepancies and deficiencies of society's realities, signifies an
unsatisfactory prevalence of political and economic inequity.

It has also been argued that these contributions to sociological
theory may be seen as four attempts to characterise the problem
level of social order and sick society. The latter emerges as a
problem of *society,* not sociology, following the era of European
Fascism, particularly after the Second World War. To face the
horrifying facts of totalitarian society in terms of general sociological theory means to address the problem of social order from the
vantage point of sick society as a potentially viable analytical
standpoint. Obviously, due to the Fascist declaration as sick of
so-called inferior races, this option met with justified theoretical
caution. On the other hand, defining a relativist notion of health
and illness as a basis for conceptualising societal influences on
disease definition and treatment could not satisfactorily solve the
theoretical question. In steps of implicit progression this book
contends that the problem of sick society has come to the forefront
of theoretical interest in medical sociology over the last 40 years.

The hidden agenda of such development, however, also curtails
medical sociology's scope and interest. The last parts of Chapters
4, 8, 11 and 15 raise criticisms against the four paradigms' sociological ventures. One is that the focus on psychological, mainly
psychiatric aspects of health during much of the first 20 years of
medical sociology appears astonishing. Another is that to tear
down the divide between normal and pathological appears treacherously conducive to 'sociological imperialism'. The same holds
for extending illness categorisations or their perception into realms
of crime, or diagnosing such alleged extension, when this combines with generalised criticism of clinical medicine's professional

power. Last but not least, sociology is urged to realise that its territory is the *theoretical* understanding of social goings-on while medicine means *practical* participation in specific social tasks: namely, diagnosis-related therapy.

In all this, it is presumed, medical sociology is not a subdiscipline unconnected with general theory's problems. In particular, that the issue of social order looms large in matters of deviance seems to put medical sociology more in the front line of general sociological reasoning than has hitherto been widely recognised. The political driving force behind its intellectual history is what ties medical sociology to, and makes it an important part of, mainstream sociological thought.

The thoughts expressed here about medical sociology's *ideas about illness* face an academic public. It is intended that they clarify how intricately sociology's and society' problems and development were connected over the last 40 years or so. Sociology's understanding of its own history appears to be easier if it aims at general theory embedded in a particular empirical realm such as, for example, that concerned with illness.

If it comes to the future of medical sociology, this book may contain something like a lesson from the past. It is that *society* rather than sociology, to a considerable extent, appears to direct the interests of those who look at illness sociologically. Therefore, the imminent world-wide epidemic of behaviour-induced incurable disease – that is, AIDS (Acquired Immune Deficiency Syndrome) – may drastically change the scene and scenario of medical sociology within the next few years or decades.

Notes

If reference is to a chapter in a book containing contributions from several authors, any letter after the date in brackets at the end of the entry refers to the chapter cited rather than the book entry.

1. Wolff, in his introduction to an edited selection of Simmel's work, *The Sociology of Georg Simmel* (1964), calls them 'notes' (p. xiii).

2. The theory of vital energy, relating to physical as well as mental illness, became widespread in the late eighteenth century, promulgated by the then famous Edinburgh School of medicine, and its eminent *Roger Brown*.

3. In 1939, Horkheimer was in Switzerland after having fled his native Germany where, in 1930, he had become director of the Institute of Social Research in Frankfurt. Its heritage and journal (*Zeitschrift für Sozialforschung* or *Studies in Philosophy and Social Science*), around which gathered Herbert Marcuse, Franz Neumann and Leo Lowenthal, to name but a few, Horkheimer managed to bring to the New School of Social Research, New York, in 1940.

4. This view, and the citation of Rank to endorse it, was first introduced by Lawrence K. Frank (1936, p. 341). But the last sentence of the quotation seems to represent Lemert's own view.

5. This book is quoted by C. W. Mills as having been highly influential. Mills neither spells the full name, nor does he name the publisher or place of publication. Although I take it that the book exists, I was unable to locate it in London (including Interlibrary Loans), at Harvard or Wisconsin or, in fact, in Germany (again using Interlibrary Services).

6. To my knowledge, Scambler's (ed.) recent *Sociological Theory and Medical Sociology* (1987) is the first book to make a serious attempt in this direction. It is interesting that only Goffman and Parsons are there dealt with as theoretical approaches relevant for medical sociology while other theories (e.g. Foucault) are not sociological, or have not led to explicitly medical-sociological work but are only shown to be relevant indirectly and through interpretation (e.g., Durkheim, Offe).

7. Biographically, it may be of interest that Parsons read biology at Amherst before he turned to economics and later, as a graduate student, studied anthropology and sociology in England and Germany (Maus, 1962, p. 154ff.).

8. Waitzkin, it may be remembered, was a student of Parsons, and his

1971 article is very much in this tradition, adding to Parsons' view the critical stance which is meant not to contradict but to clarify. Parsons' influence on Waitzkin can indirectly still be felt in his 1974 *The Exploitation of Illness in Capitalist Society* (with B. Waterman) which contains a knowledgable (albeit critical) chapter on Parsons. But the book's explicit aim is to show that Parsons' categories are not realistic; that is, where he thinks that the physician-role sick-role system is a safeguard against exploitation of the patient, Waitzkin and Waterman show that the safeguard is practically ineffective.

9. 'Attachment to common values means, motivationally considered, that the actors have common "sentiments"* in support of the value patterns, which may be defined as meaning that conformity with the relevant expectations is treated as a "good thing" relatively independently of any specific instrumental "advantage" to be gained from such conformity, e.g., in the avoidance of negative sanctions. Furthermore, this attachment to common values, while it may fit the immediate gratificational needs of the actor, always has also a "moral" aspect in that to some degree this conformity defines the "responsibilities" of the actor in the wider social action system in which he participates.'
* 'The term "sentiments" is here used to denote culturally organized cathectic and/or evaluative modes or patterns of orientation toward particular objects or classes of objects. A sentiment thus involves the internalization of cultural patterns.'
(Parsons, 1951a, p. 41, incl. footnote.)

10. Translation mine.

11. See also above, p. 21.

12. It may be noted that Parsons quotes Freud's interpretation of melancholia as depicting the penetration of the social structure into the ego but fails to take into account that he might wrongly have criticised Freud for an allegedly too rigid notion of superego (see Parsons, 1960/64a, p. 108).

13. Translation mine.

14. Parsons refers to illness as a special form of deviance under the assumption that all deviance results from reactions to role strain (1951a, p. 477; 1960/64a, p. 123, etc.). As a corollary of the disequilibrium between obligations and gratification which results from role strain, the individual suffers a deterioration of being wanted. This, in turn, has adverse affects on interpersonal exchanges in a 'vicious circle' fashion until the point of breakdown is reached (1951b, p. 453ff.). If we ask how the original role strain comes about, this might well lead to the discovery of heightened demands on one's role conformity. These may be due to previous loss of a source of gratification or, alternatively, an increase in level of responsibility without a parallel increase in others' nurturant responses. Parsons refers to Freud to explain that loss of a social object (sexual object), and introjection into the ego by the child in the oral phase of development or by the adult who regresses to this stage, are intricately related: 'It may even be that this identification is the sole condition under which the id can give up its objects' (1960/64a, p. 108). Life-event research has shown that depression in women may result from losing a

loved person (or place to live, job, companion, etc.). The depression is depicted as withdrawal reaction to loss of role *vis-à-vis* persons or an environment which – at least temporarily – leaves a void in an afflicted woman's life (Brown and Harris, 1978).

15. It is interesting to note that this tendency towards 'doctor bashing' often claims Parsons not as its proponent, but opponent. Gold (1977) analyses articles from over a decade of the *Journal of Health and Social (Human) Behavior*, taking a positive stance towards Parsons as indicating a sociology-averse, medicine-prone standpoint, and O'Neill (1986) and Frankenberg (1986) also think, on different grounds, that to endorse Parsons' teachings means to lose medical sociology's identity.

16. Offe's book was originally written in the 1960s (it is based on his PhD dissertation at the University of Frankfurt, 1968, with Habermas as supervisor). Therefore, Offe's work (published 1970), and D. Atkinson's (published 1971), both were conceptualised in, and carry the 'spirit' of, the 1960s in Europe (Germany and England).

17. It might be worth a separate investigation into what the relationship is between Merton's categories of anomie – as potential moulds of an analysis of Fascism – and Parsons'. In his article on fascist movements (1942b), Parsons relies heavily on Merton's distinctions (first introduced 1936), and in his *Social System*, the idea of compulsive conformity plays a major role in various ways.

18. Sigerist's 'The Place of the Sick' was first published in 1929 in a German journal, and then incorporated as Chapter 2 into his *Einführung in die moderne Medizin* (1931), translated into English in 1932 (*Man and Medicine*) in an extended version. The original version did not appear in English until 1960 when it was incorporated into Milton Roemer's edited volume of H. E. Sigerist's writings on medical sociology.

19. I am tempted to take the word 'prevert' – although only occasionally in inverted commas in the original – as a spelling mistake, but other authors quote it as if it were a word existing in the English language. The author himself claims that it was phrased by a former colleague of his at Quinnipiag College.

20. See M. Roth's (1976) remarks on Szasz' dichotomies.

21. This article of Garfinkel's is used here (although, strictly speaking, it belongs to the phenomenological paradigm) because it is reprinted in many readers on the 'symbolic interactionist' perspective on deviance as one of its influential contributions (see Rubington and Weinberg, 1968/73/78; Manis and Meltzer, 1967/72; Farrell and Swigert, 1975).

22. The idea is that sociology here uses historical data – namely, life-histories and biographical data – and may therefore take advantage of Weber's ideas on how to analyse historical data sociologically. This also throws a new light on the notorious validity problem in qualitative research (Gerhardt and Kirchgässler, 1986b, 1987).

23. For instance, the well-known psychologist Charles E. Osgood who, in 1957, first introduced the method of semantic profiles, contributes an article on *How I Became A Peacenik* to a reader on *Taboo Topics* edited by N. L. Farberow (1963).

24. It ought to be remembered, however, that the translation into

English of Schütz's *The Phenomenology of the Social World* did not appear until 1967, and that crucial articles of Schütz's frequently cited by Garfinkel (1967a, *passim*) were only published in 1953 and 1954, respectively; Garfinkel was, however, familiar with Schütz's articles on *The Problem of Rationality in the Social World* (1943) and *On Multiple Realities* (1945a) as documented by their frequent citation with mostly original bibliographical references rather than reference to the *Collected Works* (1967, pp. 55, 68, 111, 114, 263, 272).

25. Wilhelm Dilthey (1833–1911) undertook a *critique of historical reason* by basing philosophical thinking on psychological method in his *Introduction into Hermeneutic Sciences* (*Einleitung in die Geisteswissenschaften*); he discussed the accomplishment and danger of historical *Weltanschauung* (Dilthey was the first to use the term). Ernst Troeltsch (1865–1923) undertook to show that the problems of historicism can be solved by introducing social sciences which – as historical sciences – elucidate psychologically plausible causal relationships.

26. Sacks' dissertation was, however, submitted to Goffman at the University of California at Berkeley (1966).

27. It may be remembered that Garfinkel's first publication in 1949 focuses on inter- and intra-racial homicides.

28. I owe this insight to a medical colleague of mine.

29. One example of this would be Gouldner's *Patterns of Industrial Bureaucracy* (New York: Free Press, 1954).

30. Wieland (1975) refers to action sciences as a third category of sciences into which clinical medicine belongs.

31. It may briefly be mentioned here that this, of course, contradicts Parsons' basic thesis that clinical medicine is characterised by affective neutrality (in the interest of dealing with all patients alike), and not affectivity (which is said to invite an expression of sympathy and antipathy into the picture).

32. But it can also happen that either is missed which may end up in further trouble-'troubleshooting' cycles.

33. This was said by Gerald Holton, Professor of physics and history of science at Boston University when commenting on Garfinkel, Lynch and Livingston's analysis (1981) of work by three scientists done with a photomultiplier to discover an optical pulsar (Holton, 1981, p. 161).

34. Schütz (1932/67), it may be added, follows this up and wishes to overcome some of Weber's debated limitations.

35. The latter is often called the *Frankfurt School* after the location of its first (1921–33), and second (refounded 1951) *Institute of Social Research* (Jay, 1973). Its mentor from the 1920s to the early 1960s is Max Horkheimer whose enlightened Marxism combines a criticism of economic determinism with the idea that cultural realms within the social world have a dynamism in their own right (Horkheimer and Adorno, 1956).

36. The phrase was used by Lord Moran, Chairman of the Royal College of Physicians, who negotiated with Aneurin Bevan the terms on which hospital doctors joined the National Health Service in 1946.

37. Robert Musil, in his novel *Der Mann ohne Eigenschaften* (originally 1952) has this to say, quoted here from Dahrendorf (1958/68, p. 56):

The inhabitant of a country has at least nine characters: an occupational character, a national character, a civic character, a class character, a geographical character, a sex character, a conscious character, and an unconscious character, and perhaps a private character as well. He combines them all in himself, but they dissolve him, and he is really nothing but a small channel washed out by these trickling streams, which they flow into and leave again to join other little streams and fill another channel. This is why every inhabitant of the earth has a tenth character as well, which is nothing more or less than the passive fantasy of unfilled spaces. It permits man everything except one thing: to take seriously what his nine or more characters do and what happens to them. In other words, then, it forbids him precisely that which would fulfil him.

Further on, after having quoted Kant (*Critique of Pure Reason*) as a key witness to his distinction between the sociological and the 'real' (image of) man, Dahrendorf continues:

Musil dissolves Kant's empirical character into a series of characters; but Kant's intelligible character is precisely Musil's 'tenth character', a unit of an utterly different kind from the others. As a phenomenon, i.e., in his observable behavior, man is a role-playing, determinate creature. But he has in addition a character of freedom and integrity, which is completely unaffected by his phenomenal character and its laws. 'Thus freedom and nature, each in its complete meaning, would in the same actions, depending on whether one considers their intelligible or their sensible cause, be encountered simultaneously and without any contradiction'. (1958/68, p. 62, the last quote being from Kant)

38. The Cornell Laboratory's director, and mentor of, among others, Lawrence K. Hinkle and Thomas H. Holmes, has been Harold G. Wolff since the 1940s.

39. The *giving-up-given-up syndrome* was conceptualised at Rochester Medical School by Georg H. Engel and his collaborators in the 1960s. It is based on psychoanalytic ideas of regression and neurosis. For instance, Schmale and Iker's work on the prognostic value of periods of helplessness for cervical dysplasia's becoming malignant growth is based on the work of Engel.

40. See also Gerhardt and Brieskorn-Zinke (1986) for another, again different, use of Seligman's work (as a theoretical background for interpreting normalisation in home-dialysis patients).

41. On the topic of happiness in sociology, cf. Michalos, 1986.

42. This, of course, may only be said with regard to health-care related services. One might remember Parsons' difficulties to find his pro-

insurance view accepted by AMA in 1932. The Wilbur Committee's report on financial aspects of health care to which Parsons contributed with the criticism of being pro-Communist (see above, p. 71).

43. This relates particularly to the 33 countries which are served by the European Office at Copenhagen. In 1980, an executive officer for health education was oppointed there. The post is held by a sociologist.

44. Kelman (1975), with Marxist but not Foucaultian leanings, makes a somewhat different distinction focusing on a functional as opposed to an experiential definition of health.

45. The term 'creation' is already extensively used by Freidson (1970a).

46. The concept of holon refers here to the social habitat of a person (patient) incorporating all aspects of life style and social environment combining to make up the 'hierarchy of natural systems' which 'constitute "Man" and also make for what "humane" health care should take into account' (Arney and Bergen, 1984, Ch. 5).

47. See above, p. 296–7.

48. It appears to me that the label of 'Fabianism' is shunned even by authors whose viewpoints I would be inclined to find kindred to the Fabians' circumspect reformism, suitably modernised.

49. It may be added that the 'delusion argument' can also be found in a less rigorous version in Freidson's understanding of the 'placebo effect'; see above, p. 118–9.

50. Mead's terms are here only used for the sake of convenience, not because I want here to endorse interactionism instead.

References

T. W. Adorno, E. Frenkel-Brunswick, D. J. Levinson and R. Nevitt Sanford, *The Authoritarian Personality* (New York: Harper, 1950).

T. W. Adorno, 'Sociology and Psychology', *The New Left Review*, 46 (1967), 68–80, and 47 (1968), 79–97.

L. H. Aiken and D. Mechanic (eds), *Application of Social Science to Clinical Medicine and Health Policy* (New Brunswick: Rutgers University Press, 1986).

R. L. Akers, 'Problems in the Sociology of Deviance: Social Definitions and Behavior', *Social Forces*, 46 (1968), 455–65.

R. L. Akers, 'Comment on Gove's Evaluation of Societal Reaction as an Explanation of Mental Illness', *American Sociological Review*, 37 (1972), 487–8.

G. L. Albrecht, 'The Negotiated Diagnosis and Treatment of Occlusal Problems', *Social Science and Medicine*, 11 (1977), 277–83 (repr. in G. L. Albrecht and P. C. Higgins (eds), *Health, Illness, and Medicine*, Chicago: Rand McNally, 1979).

F. Alexander, *The Medical Value of Psychoanalysis* (London: George Allen & Unwin, 1932).

F. Alexander, *Fundamentals of Psychoanalysis* (London: George Allen & Unwin, 1949).

F. Alexander, *Psychosomatic Medicine: Its Principles and Applications* (New York: W. W. Norton, 1950).

F. Alexander and W. Healy, *Roots of Crime*, Psychoanalytic Studies (London/New York: Knopf, 1935).

R. Alford, 'The Political Economy of Health Care: Dynamics Without Change', *Politics and Society*, 2 (1972), 127–64.

R. Alford, *Health Care Politics* (Chicago: University of Chicago Press, 1975).

L. Althusser, *Essays on Ideology* (London: Verso, 1984).

R. Andersen, J. Lion and O. Anderson, *Two Decades of Health Services: Social Survey Trends in Use and Expenditure* (Cambridge, MA: Ballinger, 1976).

O. W. Anderson, *Health Care: Can There be Equity?. The US, England and Sweden* (New York: Wiley, 1972).

O. W. Anderson, *Health Services in the United States: A Growth Enterprise since 1975* (Ann Arbor, MI: Health Administration Press, 1985).

W. T. Anderson and D. T. Helm, 'The Physician–Patient Encounter: A Process of Reality Negotiation', in E. G. Jaco (ed.), *Patients, Physicians and Illness*, 3rd edn (New York: Free Press, 1979).

A. Antonovsky, 'Conceptual and Methodological Problems in the Study of Resistance Resources and Stressful Life Events', in B. S. Dohrenwend and B. P. Dohrenwend (eds), *Stressful Life Events* (New York: Wiley, 1974).

A. Antonovsky, *Health, Stress and Coping* (San Francisco, CA: Jossey Bass, 1979).

D. Apple, 'How Laymen Define Illness', *Journal of Health and Human Behavior*, 1 (1960) 219–25.

C. d'Arcy, 'The Contingencies and Mental Illness in Societal Reaction Theory: A Critique', *Canadian Review of Sociology and Anthropology*, 13 (1976), 43–54.

H. Arendt, *Between Past and Future* (New York: Viking Press, 1968).

H. Arendt, *On Violence* (London: Allen Lane, 1970).

P. Ariès, *Western Attitudes Toward Death* (Baltimore, MD: Johns Hopkins University Press, 1974).

A. Arluke, 'Social Control Rituals in Medicine', in Dingwall *et al.* (1977).

A. Arluke, L. Kennedy and R. C. Kessler, 'Reexaming the Sick-Role Concept: An Empirical Assessment', *Journal of Health and Social Behavior*, 20 (1979), 30–6.

D. Armstrong, 'The Decline of Medical Hegemony: A Review of Government Reports during the NHS', *Social Science and Medicine*, 10 (1976), 157–63.

D. Armstrong, 'The Emancipation of Biographical Medicine', *Social Science and Medicine*, 13A, 1 (1979), 9–12.

D. Armstrong, *Political Anatomy of the Body – Medical Knowledge in Britain in the Twentieth Century* (Cambridge University Press, 1983).

D. Armstrong, 'The Patient's View', *Social Science and Medicine*, 18 (1984), 737–44.

D. Armstrong, 'The Invention of Infant Mortality', *Sociology of Health and Illness*, 8 (1986), 211–32.

W. R. Arney and B. J. Bergen, 'The Anomaly, the Chronic Patient and the Play of Medical Power', *Sociology of Health and Illness*, 5 (1983), 3–24.

W. R. Arney and B. J. Bergen, *Medicine and the Management of Living: Taming the Last Great Beast* (Chicago/London: University of Chicago Press, 1984).

A. B. Atkinson, *Unequal Shares*, rev. edn (Harmondsworth: Penguin, 1972).

D. Atkinson, *Orthodox Consensus and Radical Alternative: A Study in Social Theory* (London: Heinemann, 1971).

J. M. Atkinson, 'On the Sociology of Suicide', *Sociological Review*, 16 (1968), 83–92.

J. M. Atkinson, 'Versions of Deviance', *Sociological Review*, 22 (1974), 616–25.

J. M. Atkinson, *Discovering Suicide: Studies in the Social Organization of Sudden Death* (London: Macmillan, 1978).

P. Atkinson, 'The Reproduction of Medical Knowledge', in Dingwall *et al.* (1977).

P. Atkinson, *The Clinical Experience: The Construction and Recon-struction of Medical Reality* (London: Gower, 1981a).

P. Atkinson, 'Time and Cool Patients', in P. Atkinson and Heath (1981b).

P. Atkinson and C. Heath (eds), *Medical Work: Realities and Routines* (Aldershot: Gower, 1981).

P. Atkinson, M. Reid and P. Sheldrake, 'Medical Mystique', *Sociology of Work and Occupations*, 4 (1977), 243–80.

P. Attewell, 'Ethnomethodology since Garfinkel', *Theory and Society*, 1 (1974), 179–210.

V. Aubert and S. Messinger, 'The Criminal and the Sick', *Inquiry*, 3 (1958), 137–60 (repr. E. Freidson and J. Lorber (eds), *Medical Men and Their Work*, Chicago: Aldine, 1972).

S. Avineri, *The Social and Political Thought of Karl Marx* (Cambridge University Press, 1968).

M. Balint, *The Doctor, his Patient, and the Illness* (London: Pitman Medical, 1957).

M. H. Banks, S. A. A. Beresford, D. C. Morrell, J. J. Waller and C. J. Watkins, 'Factors Influencing Demand for Primary Medical Care in Women', *International Journal of Epidemiology*, 4 (1975), 189–95.

R. Barton, *Institutional Neurosis* (Bristol: Wright, 1959).

G. Baruch, 'Moral Tales: Parents' Stories of Encounters with the Health Professions', *Sociology of Health and Illness*, 3 (1981), 275–95.

P. Bebbington, C. Tennant and J. Hurry, 'Adversity, Labelling, and the Disease Theory of Depression', in U. Gerhardt and M. E. J. Wadsworth (eds), *Stress and Stigma: Explanation and Evidence in the Sociology of Crime and Illness* (Frankfurt: Campus; London: Macmillan; New York: St Martin's Press, 1985).

H. Becker, 'Becoming a Marihuana User', *American Journal of Sociology*, 59 (1953), 235–42.

H. Becker, *Outsiders: Studies in the Sociology of Deviance* (New York: Free Press, 1963).

H. Becker (ed), *The Other Side: Perspectives on Deviance* (New York: Collier Macmillan, 1964).

H. Becker, 'Whose Side Are We On?', *Social Problems*, 14 (1967), 239–47.

H. Becker, 'History, Culture and Subjective Experience: An Exploration of the Social Bases of Drug-Induced Experiences', *Journal of Health and Social Behavior*, 9 (1968), 961–8.

H. Becker, 'Labelling Theory Reconsidered': paper presented to the annual meetings of the British Sociological Association (1971).

H. Becker, 'Labelling Theory Re-Considered', in P. Rock and M. McIntosh (eds), *Deviance and Social Control* (London: Tavistock, 1974).

H. Becker, B. Geer, D. Riesman and R. S. Weiss (eds), *Institution and the Person: papers presented to E. C. Hughes* (Chicago: Aldine, 1968).

H. K. Beecher, *Measurement of Subjective Responses* (New York: Oxford University Press, 1959).

D. A. Begelman, 'Misnaming, Metaphors, the Medical Model, and Some Muddles', *Psychiatry*, 34 (1971), 38–58.

F. Bendfeldt-Zachrisson, 'State (Political) Torture: Some General, Psychological, and Particular Aspects', *International Journal of Health Services*, 15 (1985), 339–49.

Z. Ben-Sira, 'Potency: A Stress-Buffering Link in the Coping-Stress-Disease Relationship', *Social Science and Medicine*, 21 (1985), 397–406.

Z. Ben-Sira, *Stress, Stigma and Primary Medical Care* (Aldershot: Gower, 1986).

D. Benson and J. A. Hughes, *The Perspective of Ethnomethodology* (London: Longman, 1983).

S. A. A. Beresford, J. J. Waller, M. H. Banks and C. J. Wale, 'Why Do Women Consult Doctors? Social Factors and the Use of the General Practitioner', *British Journal of Preventive and Social Medicine*, 31 (1977), 220–6.

P. Berger and T. Luckmann, *The Social Construction of Reality: A Treatise in the Sociology of Knowledge* (New York: Doubleday, 1966).

L. F. Berkmann and L. S. Syme, 'Social Network, Host Resistence and Mortality: A Nine-Year Follow-up Study of Alameda County Residents', *American Journal of Epidemiology*, 190 (1979), 186–204.

H. S. Berliner, 'Emerging Ideologies in Medicine', *Review of Radical Political Economics*, 9 (1977), 116–24.

D. Bertaux (ed), *Biography and Society* (Beverly Hills, CA: Sage, 1981).

M. Betz and L. O'Connell, 'Changing Doctor–Patient Relationships and the Rise in Concern for Accountability', *Social Problems*, 31 (1983), 84–95.

R. Bierstedt, 'Nominal and Real Definitions', in L. Gross (ed.), *Symposium on Sociological Theory* (New York: Harper & Row, 1959).

E. Bittner, 'The Concept of Organization', *Social Research*, 32 (1965), 239–55.

E. Bittner, 'Police Discretion in Emergency Apprehension of Mentally Ill Persons', *Social Problems*, 14 (1976), 278–92.

M. Black (ed), *The Social Theories of Talcott Parsons* (Carbondale and Edwardsville, IL: Southern Illinois University Press, 1961).

D. Blane, 'Inequality and Social Class', in Patrick and Scambler (1982).

P. Blau, *Power and Exchange in Social Life* (New York: Wiley, 1964).

M. Blaxter, 'Diagnosis as Category and Process: The Case of Alcoholism', *Social Science and Medicine*, 12 (1978), 9–17.

M. Blaxter and R. Cyster, 'Compliance and Risk-taking: The Case of Alcoholic Liver Disease', *Sociology of Health and Illness*, 6 (1984), 290–310.

S. W. Bloom, 'Rehabilitation as an Interpersonal Process', in M. Sussman (ed.), *Sociology and Rehabilitation* (Washington, DC: American Sociological Association, 1966).

M. Bloor, 'Professional Autonomy and Client Exclusion: A Study of ENT Clinics', in Wadsworth and Robinson (1976a).

M. Bloor, 'Bishop Berkeley and the Adenotonsillectomy Enigma: An Exploration of Variation in the Social Construction of Medical Disposals', *Sociology*, 10 (1976b), 43–61.

M. Bloor, 'Social Control in the Therapeutic Community: Re-Examination of a Critical Case', *Sociology of Health and Illness*, 8 (1986), 305–24.

M. J. Bloor and J. D. Fonkert, 'Reality Construction, Reality Exploration and Treatment in Two Therapeutic Communities', *Sociology of Health and Illness*, 4 (1982), 125–40.

M. Bloor and N. McKeganey, 'Review Article: The Social Context of Psychiatric Care', *Sociology of Health and Illness*, 2 (1980), 223–7.

A. Blum, 'The Sociology of Mental Illness', in J. Douglas (ed.), *Deviance and Respectability* (New York: Basic Books, 1970).

A. Blum and P. McHugh, 'The Social Ascription of Motives', *American Sociological Review*, 36 (1971), 98–109.

H. Blumer, 'Collective Behavior', in Park (1939).

H. Blumer, 'What is Wrong with Social Theory?', *American Sociological Review*, 19 (1954), 3–10 (repr. Blumer, 1969).

H. Blumer, 'Attitudes and the Social Act', *Social Problems*, 3 (1955), 59–65 (repr. Blumer, 1969).

H. Blumer, 'Sociological Analysis and the "Variable"', (1956), 683–90 (repr. Blumer, 1969).

H. Blumer, 'Society as Symbolic Interaction', in A. M. Rose (ed.), *Human Behavior and Social Processes* (Boston, MA: Houghton Mifflin, 1962).

H. Blumer, 'Sociological Implications of the Thought of George Herbert Mead', *American Journal of Sociology*, 71 (1966), 535–47.

H. S. Blumer, 'The Methodological Position of Symbolic Interactionism' (1969a), in H. S. Blumer, (1969b).

H. S. Blumer, *Symbolic Interactionism: Perspective and Method* (Englewood Cliffs, NJ: Prentice-Hall, 1969b).

D. Bordua, 'Recent Trends: Deviant Behavior and Social Control', *Annals of the American Academy for Political and Social Sciences*, 57 (1967), 149–63.

Boston Women's Health Collective, *Our Bodies, Ourselves: A Book by and for Women* (New York: Simon & Schuster, 1971).

M. Boulton, D. Tuckett, C. Olson and A. Williams, 'Social Class and the General Practice Consultation', *Sociology of Health and Illness*, 8 (1986), 325–50.

J. Bowlby, *Separation: Anxiety and Anger* (New York: Basic Books, 1973).

B. M. Braginski and D. D. Braginski, 'Schizophrenic Patients in the Psychiatric Interview: An Experimental Study of their Effectiveness at Manipulation', in R. R. Price and B. Denner (eds), *The Making of a Mental Patient* (New York: Holt, Rinehart & Winston, 1973).

B. M. Braginski, M. Grosse and K. Ring, 'Controlling Outcomes Through Impression-Management: An Experimental Study of the Manipulative Tactics of Mental Patients', *Journal of Consulting Psychology*, 30 (1966), 95–100 (repr. R. R. Price and B. Denner (eds), *The Making of a*

Mental Patient, New York: Holt, Rinehart & Winston, 1973).

H. Bravermann, *Labor and Monopoly Capital* (New York: Monthly Review Press, 1974).

M. H. Brenner, 'Economic Changes and Heart Disease Mortality', *American Journal of Public Health*, 61 (1971), 606–11.

M. H. Brenner, *Mental Illness and the Economy* (Cambridge, MA: Harvard University Press, 1973).

M. H. Brenner, 'Trends in Alcohol Consumption and Associated Illnesses', *American Journal of Public Health*, 65 (1975), 1279–92.

U. Bronfenbrenner, 'Parsons' Theory of Identification', in Black (1961).

G. W. Brown, 'Meaning, Measurement, and Stress of Life Events', in B. S. Dohrenwend and B. P. Dohrenwend (eds), *Stressful Life Events: Their Nature and Effects* (New York: Wiley, 1974).

G. W. Brown, 'Accounts, Meaning and Causality', in G. Nigel and P. Abell (eds), *Accounts and Action*: Surrey Conferences on Sociological Theory and Method (Aldershot: Gower, 1983).

G. W. Brown, M. N. Bhrolcháin and T. O. Harris, 'Social Class and Psychiatric Disturbance among Women in an Urban Population', *Sociology*, 9 (1975), 225–54.

G. W. Brown, J. L. T. Birley and J. K. Wing, 'Influence of Family Life on the Course of Schizophrenic Disorders', *British Journal of Psychiatry*, 121 (1972), 241–58.

G. W. Brown and T. Harris, *Social Origins of Depression* (London: Tavistock, 1978).

L. G. Brown, *Social Pathology: Personal and Social Disorganization* (New York: Crofts, 1942).

P. Brown (ed.), *Mental Health Care and Social Policy* (Boston, MA: Routledge & Kegan Paul, 1985).

V. A. Brown, 'From Sickness to Health: An Altered Focus for Health-Care Research', *Social Science and Medicine*, 15A (1980), 195–201.

M. Bulmer, *The Chicago School of Sociology: Institutionalization, Diversity, and the Rise of Sociological Research* (Chicago/London: University of Chicago Press, 1984).

M. Bury, 'Chronic Illness as Biographical Disruption', *Sociology of Health and Illness*, 4 (1982), 167–82.

M. R. Bury, 'Social Constructionism and the Development of Medical Sociology', *Sociology of Health and Illness*, 8 (1986), 137–69.

M. R. Bury, 'Social Constructionism and Medical Sociology: A Rejoinder to Nicholson and McLaughlin', *Sociology of Health and Illness*, 9 (1987), 439–41.

M. Calnan, 'Managing "Minor" Disorders: Pathways to a Hospital Accident and Emergency Department', *Sociology of Health and Illness*, 5 (1983), 149–67.

M. Calnan, 'Clinical Uncertainty: Is it a Problem in the Doctor–Patient Relationship?', *Sociology of Health and Illness*, 6 (1984), 74–85.

W. B. Cannon, *The Wisdom of the Body* (New York: Norton, 1932).

R. Carlson, *The End of Medicine* (New York: Wiley-Interscience, 1975).

M. Carpenter, 'Discussion Paper: Left Orthodoxy and the Politics of Health', mimeo (1979).

A. Cartwright and M. O'Brien, 'Social Class Variations in Health Care and the Nature of General Practitioner Consultations', in M. Stacey (ed.), *The Sociology of the NHS* (Keele: Sociological Review Monographs, 22, 1976).

J. Cassel, 'Psychosocial Processes and "Stress": Theoretical Formulation', *International Journal of Health Services*, 5 (1975), 471–82.

J. Cassel, 'The Contribution of the Social Environment to Host Resistance', *American Journal of Epidemiology*, 104 (1976), 107–23.

K. Charmaz, 'The Social Construction of Self-Pity in the Chronically Ill', in N. K. Denzin (ed.), *Studies in Symbolic Interactionism*, Vol. 3 (Greenwich, CT: JAI Press, 1980).

K. Charmaz, 'Loss of Self: A Fundamental Form of Suffering in the Chronically Ill', *Sociology of Health and Illness*, 5 (1983), 168–95.

S. Chorover, *From Genesis to Genocide: The Meaning of Human Nature and the Power of Behavior Control* (Cambridge, MA: MIT Press, 1979).

L. Churchill, 'Ethnomethodology and Measurement', *Social Forces*, 50 (1971), 182–91.

A. V. Cicourel, *Method and Measurement in Sociology* (New York: Free Press of Glencoe, 1964).

A. V. Cicourel, *The Social Organization of Juvenile Justice* (New York: Wiley, 1968).

A. V. Cicourel, 'Language as a Variable in Social Research', *Sociological Focus*, 3 (1970), 43–52.

A. Cicourel, 'Delinquency and the Attribution of Responsibility', in Scott and Douglas (1972).

A. Cicourel, *Cognitive Sociology* (Harmondsworth: Penguin, 1973a).

A. V. Cicourel, 'Interviewing and Memory', manuscript (San Diego: mimeo, 1973b); published in C. Cherry (ed.), *Pragmatic Aspects of Human Communication* (Dordrecht: Reidel, 1974).

A. Cicourel, *Theory and Method of Argentine Fertility* (New York: Wiley, 1974).

A. V. Cicourel, 'Discourse and Text: Cognitive and Linguistic Processes in Studies of Social Structure', in *Versus: Quaderni de Studi Semiotici* (1975).

A. V. Cicourel, 'Discourse, Autonomous Grammars, and Contextualized Processing of Information', mimeo (paper presented at Conference on Gesprächsanalyse, Institut für Kommunikationsforschung und Phonetik, University of Bonn, West Germany, 1976).

A. V. Cicourel, 'Notes on the Integration of Micro- and Macro-Levels of Analysis', in K. Knorr-Cetina and A. Cicourel (eds), *Advances in Social Theory and Methodology* (Boston, MA: Routledge & Kegan Paul, 1981a).

A. V. Cicourel, 'Language and Medicine', in C. A. Ferguson and S. B. Heath (eds), *Language in the USA* (Cambridge University Press, 1981b).

A. V. Cicourel, 'Language and Belief in a Medical Setting', in H.

Byrnes (ed.), *Contemporary Perceptions of Language: Interdisciplinary Dimensions* (Washington, DC: Georgetown University Press, 1982).

A. V. Cicourel, 'Language and the Structure of Belief in Medical Communication', in Fisher and Todd (1983a).

A. Cicourel, 'Social Measurement as the Creation of Expert Systems': paper presented at Conference on 'Potentialities for Knowledge and Social Science', University of Chicago (1983b).

A. V. Cicourel, 'Diagnostic Reasoning in Medicine: The Role of Clinical Discourse and Comprehension': paper presented at Conference on the Philosophy of Human Studies sponsored by Bryn Mawr College, Temple University, University of Pennsylvania and Villanova (1984).

A. V. Cicourel and J. I. Kitsuse, *The Educational Decision Makers* (Indianapolis: Bobbs-Merrill, 1963).

A. Clare, *Psychiatry in Dissent* (London: Methuen, 1975; 2nd edn, 1980).

R. E. Clark and E. E. LaBeff, 'Death Telling: Managing the Delivery of Bad News', *Journal of Health and Social Behavior*, 23 (1982), 366–80.

J. A. Clausen and M. R. Yarrow, 'Paths to the Mental Hospital', *Journal of Social Issues*, 11 (1955), 25–32.

C. von Clausewitz, *Vom Kriege* (originally Berlin, 1832); *On War* (transl. Colonel J. J. Graham), 2nd impression (London: K. Paul, Trench, Trübner, 1911).

S. Cobb, 'Social Support as a Moderator in Life Stress', *Psychosomatic Medicine*, 38 (1976), 300–14.

A. Cochrane, *Effectiveness and Efficiency* (London: Nuffield Hospital Trust, 1972).

R. Cochrane, *The Social Creation of Mental Illness* (London/New York: Longman, 1983).

E. A. Cohen, *Human Behaviour in the Concentration Camp* (transl. from the Dutch by M. H. Braalsma) (New York: Norton, 1953).

J. D. Colfax and J. L. Roach (eds), *Radical Sociology* (New York: Basic Books, 1971).

M. Colledge, 'Economic Cycles and Health: Towards a Sociological Understanding of the Impact of the Recession on Health and Illness', *Social Science and Medicine*, 16 (1982), 1919–27.

R. Collins, *Conflict Sociology: Toward an Explanatory Science* (New York: Academic Press, 1975).

J. Comaroff, 'Conflicting Paradigms of Pregnancy: Managing Ambiguity in Ante-natal Encounters' in A. Davis and Horobin (1977).

J. Comaroff, 'Medicine: Symbol and Ideology', in Wright and Treacher (1982).

Commission on Chronic Illness, *Chronic Illness in the United States*, Vol. 4: *Chronic Illness in a Large City* (1957); Vol. 3: *Chronic Illness in a Rural Area* (1959) (Cambridge, MA: Harvard University Press, 1957/59).

P. Conrad, 'The Discovery of Hyperkinesis: Notes on the Medicalization of Deviant Behavior', *Social Problems*, 23 (1975), 12–21.

P. Conrad, 'Types of Medical Social Control', *Sociology of Health and Illness*, 1 (1979), 1–11.

P. Conrad, 'The Experience of Illness: Recent and New Directions', in

J. A. Roth and P. Conrad (eds), *The Experience and Management of Chronic Illness: Research in the Sociology of Health Care*, Vol. 6 (Greenwich, CT: JAI Press, 1987).

P. Conrad and R. Kern (eds), *The Sociology of Health and Illness: Critical Perspectives*, 2nd edn (New York: St Martins Press, 1980).

P. Conrad and J. Schneider, 'Looking at Levels of Medicalization: A Comment on Strong's Critique of the Thesis of Medical Imperialism', *Social Science and Medicine*, 14A (1980a), 75–9.

P. Conrad and W. Schneider, *Deviance and Medicalization: From Badness to Sickness* (St Louis, MO: Mosby, 1980b).

C. H. Cooley, *Human Nature and the Social Order* (New York: Scribner's, 1902).

C. H. Cooley, *Social Organization: A Study of the Larger Mind* (New York: Scribner's, 1909).

C. H. Cooley, *Social Process* (New York: Scribner's, 1918).

D. Cooper, *The Death of the Family* (New York: Pantheon, 1971).

J. M. Corbin and A. L. Strauss, 'Issues Concerning Regimen Management in the Home', *Ageing and Society*, 5 (1985), 249–65.

L. Coser, *The Functions of Social Conflict* (New York: Free Press of Glencoe, 1956).

J. Coulter, *Approaches to Insanity* (Oxford: Martin Robertson, 1973).

J. Coulter, 'Perceptual Accounts and Interpretive Asymmetries', *Sociology*, 10 (1976a), 385–96.

J. Coulter, 'Harvey Sacks: A Preliminary Appreciation', *Sociology*, 10 (1976b), 507–12.

B. Cowie, 'The Cardiac Patient's Perception of His Heart Attack', *Social Science and Medicine*, 10 (1976), 87–96.

C. Cox and A. Mead (eds), *A Sociology of Medical Practice* (London: Macmillan, 1975).

T. Cox and C. Mackay, 'Psychosocial Factors and Psychophysiological Mechanisms in the Etiology and Development of Cancers', *Social Science and Medicine*, 16 (1982), 381–96.

R. Crawford, 'You are Dangerous to Your Health: The Ideology and Politics of Victim Blaming', *International Journal of Health Services*, 7 (1977), 663–80.

S. H. Croog, A. Lipson and S. Levine, 'Help Patterns in Severe Illness: The Role of Kin, Network, and Non-family Resources', *Journal of Marriage and the Family*, 34 (1972), 32–41.

R. Dahrendorf, 'Out of Utopia', *American Journal of Sociology*, 64 (1958a), 115–27.

R. Dahrendorf, 'Homo Sociologicus', *Kölner Zeitschrift für Soziologie und Sozialpsychologie*, 10, 2–3 (1958b); (transl. *Homo Sociologicus* (London: Routledge and Kegan Paul, 1968).

R. Dahrendorf, *Class and Class Conflict in Industrial Society* (Stanford University Press, 1959; first published in shorter version in German, 1957).

R. Dahrendorf, *Life Chances: Approaches to Social and Political Theory* (London: Weidenfeld & Nicolson, 1979).

A. K. Daniels, 'Normal Mental Illness and Understandable Excuses',

The Philosophy of Combat Psychiatry, *American Behavioral Scientist*, 14 (1970a), 167–84.

A. K. Daniels, 'The Social Construction of Military Psychiatric Diagnoses', in H. P. Dreitzel (ed.), *Recent Sociology No. 2* (London: Macmillan, 1970b).

A. Davis (ed.), *Relationships Between Doctors and Patients* (Farnborough: Westmead, 1979).

A. Davis and G. Horobin, *Medical Encounters* (London: Croom Helm, 1977).

A. Davis and P. M. Strong, 'Aren't Children Wonderful? – A Study of the Allocation of Identity in Development Assessment', in M. Stacey (ed.), *The Sociology of the NHS*, Sociological Review Monograph 22 (Keele: University of Keele, 1976a).

A. Davis and P. M. Strong, 'The Management of a Therapeutic Encounter', in Wadsworth and Robinson (1976b).

F. Davis, 'Uncertainty in Medical Prognosis, Clinical and Functional', *American Journal of Sociology*, 66 (1960), 41–7.

F. Davis, 'Deviance Disavowal: The Management of Strained Interaction by the Visibly Handicapped', *Social Problems*, 9 (1961), 120–32.

F. Davis, *Passage Through Crisis* (Indianapolis: Bobbs-Merrill, 1963).

M. Davis, *Living With Multiple Sclerosis* (Springfield, IL: Thomas, 1973).

M. Z. Davis, 'The Organizational, Interactional, and Care-Orientated Conditions for Patient Participation in Continuity of Care: A Framework for Staff Interaction', *Social Science and Medicine*, 14 (1980), 39–47.

N. J. Davis, 'Labelling Theory in Deviance Research: A Critique and Reconsideration', *Sociological Quarterly*, 13 (1972), 447–74.

A. Dawe, 'The Two Sociologies', *British Journal of Sociology*, 21 (1970), 207–18.

B. Deacon, 'Medical Care and Health Under State Socialism', *International Journal of Health Services*, 14 (1984), 453–80.

N. K. Denzin, 'The Self-Fulfilling Prophecy and Patient-Therapist Interaction', in S. P. Spitzer and N. K. Denzin (eds), *The Mental Patient: Studies in the Sociology of Deviance* (New York: McGraw-Hill, 1968).

N. K. Denzin, 'Symbolic Interactionism and Ethnomethodology: A Proposed Synthesis', *American Sociological Review*, 34 (1969), 922–34.

N. K. Denzin, 'Symbolic Interactionism and Ethnomethodology', in Douglas (1970).

DHSS, *Prevention and Health: Everybody's Business: A Reassessment of Public and Personal Health* (London: Her Majesty's Stationery Office, 1976).

R. Dewey, 'The Jury Law for Commitment of the Insane in Illinois', *American Journal of Insanity*, 69 (1913), 579–84.

L. A. Dexter, 'On the Politics and Sociology of Stupidity in our Society', in Becker (1964).

R. Dingwall, 'Conceptions of Illness', mimeo: paper presented to British Sociological Association Medical Sociology Conference, York (1974).

R. Dingwall, *Aspects of Illness* (Oxford: Martin Robertson, 1976).

R. Dingwall, C. Heath, M. Reid and M. Stacey (eds), *Health Care and Health Knowledge* (London: Croom Helm; New York: Prodist, 1977).

R. Dingwall and P. Lewis (eds), *The Sociology of the Professions: Lawyers, Doctors and Others* (London: Macmillan, 1983).

R. Dingwall and T. Murray, 'Categorization in Accident Departments: "Good" Patients, "Bad" Patients and "Children"', *Sociology of Health and Illness*, 5 (1983), 127–48.

S. Dinitz, R. R. Dynes and A. C. Clarke (eds), *Deviance: Studies in the Process of Stigmatization and Societal Reaction* (New York: Oxford University Press, 1979).

B. P. and B. S. Dohrenwend, *Social Status and Psychological Disorder: A Causal Inquiry* (New York: Wiley, 1969).

B. S. and B. P. Dohrenwend, 'Class and Race as Status-Related Sources of Stress', in Levine and Scotch (1970).

B. S. and B. P. Dohrenwend (eds), *Stressful Life Events: Their Nature and Effects* (New York: Wiley, 1974).

J. D. Douglas, *The Social Meaning of Suicide* (Princeton, NJ: Princeton University Press, 1967).

J. D. Douglas (ed.), *Understanding Everyday Life: Toward a Reconstruction of Sociological Knowledge* (Chicago: Aldine, 1970).

D. Downes and P. Rock (eds), *Deviant Interpretations* (New York: Barnes & Noble, 1979).

D. Downes and P. Rock, *Understanding Deviance: A Guide to the Sociology of Crime and Rule-Breaking* (Oxford: Clarendon Press; New York: Oxford University Press, 1982).

L. Doyal with I. Pennell, *The Political Economy of Health* (London: Pluto, 1979).

K. A. Drass, 'Negotiation and the Structure of Discourse in Medical Consultation', *Social Health and Illness*, 4 (1982), 320–41.

R. Dubos, *Mirage of Health* (New York: Harper & Row, 1959).

R. Dubos, *Man Adapting* (New Haven, CT: Yale University Press, 1965).

H. W. Dunham, 'The Schizophrene and Criminal Behavior', *American Sociological Review*, 4 (1939), 352–61.

W. Dunham, 'Who Loads the Dice?' (Comment on Mohavedi), *Journal of Health and Social Behavior*, 17 (1976), 311–12.

K. Dunnell and A. Cartwright, *Medicine-Takers, Prescribers and Hoarders* (London: Routledge & Kegan Paul, 1972).

E. Durkheim, *De la Division du Travail Social* (1895). *On the Division of Labour in Society*, being a translation with an estimate of his work by George Simpson (New York: Macmillan, 1933).

E. Durkheim, *Le Suicide* (1897). *Suicide: A Study in Sociology*, Transl. A. Spaulding and George Simpson, ed. with an introduction by George Simpson (London: Routledge & Kegan Paul, 1952).

T. Duster, *The Legislation of Morality: Law, Drugs and Moral Judgement* (New York: Free Press, 1970).

R. B. Edgerton, *The Cloack of Competence: Stigma in the Lives of the*

Mentally Retarded (Berkeley, CA: University of California Press, 1967).

R. C. Edwards, M. Reich and T. E. Weisskopf (eds), *The Capitalist System* (Englewood Cliffs, NJ: Prentice-Hall, 1972).

L. D. Egbert, G. E. Battit, C. E. Welsh and M. K. Bartlett, 'Reduction of Postoperative Pain by Encouragement and Instruction of Patients', *New England Journal of Medicine*, 270 (1964), 825–7.

B. and J. Ehrenreich, *The American Health Empire: Power, Profits and Politics* (New York: Random House, 1970).

B. and J. Ehrenreich, 'Hospital Workers: A Case Study of the New Working Class', *Monthly Review*, 24 (1973), 12–27.

B. and J. Ehrenreich, 'Health Care and Social Control', *Social Policy*, 5 (1974), 26–40.

B. Ehrenreich and D. English, *For Her Own Good: 150 Years of Experts' Advice to Women* (London: Pluto, 1979).

J. Ehrenreich (ed.), *The Cultural Crisis of Modern Medicine* (New York/London: Monthly Review Press, 1978).

N. Elias, *Der Prozess der Zivilisation*, first published Zurich 1939: Vol. 1: *The History of Manners*; Vol. 2: *Power and Civility* (transl. Edmond Jephcott) (New York: Pantheon, 1982).

J. Elinson, 'The End of Medicine and the End of Medical Sociology?', *Journal of Health and Social Behavior*, 26 (1985), 268–75.

J. P. Emerson, 'Nothing Unusual is Happening': paper presented to American Sociological Association meetings, San Francisco, mimeo 1969b; published in Tamotsu Shibutani (ed.), *Human Nature and Collective Behavior: Papers in Honor of Herbert Blumer* (Englewood Cliffs, NJ: Prentice-Hall, 1970).

J. Emerson, 'Behavior in Private Places: Sustaining Definitions of Reality in Gynecological Examinations', in H. P. Dreitzel (ed.), *Recent Sociology, No. 2: Patterns of Communicative Behavior* (New York: Macmillan, 1970).

R. M. Emerson, 'Some Problematics of Rule Violation', mimeo, 1973; published in J. Kitsuse and P. Rains (eds), *The Labeling and Social Differentiation of Deviants* (New York: Basic Books, 1974).

R. M. Emerson and S. L. Messinger, 'The Micro-Politics of Trouble', *Social Problems*, 25 (1977), 121–34.

R. M. Emerson and M. Pollner, 'Dirty Work Designations: Their Features and Consequences in a Psychiatric Setting', *Social Problems*, 23 (1976), 243–54.

R. M. Emerson and M. Pollner, 'Policies and Practices of Psychiatric Case Selection', *Sociology of Work and Occupations*, 5 (1978), 75–96.

G. L. Engel, 'The Psychosomatic Approach to Individual Susceptibility to Disease', *Gastroenterology*, 67 (1974), 1085–93.

K. Engelhardt, A. Wirth and L. Kindermann, *Kranke im Krankenhaus. Grenzen und Ergänzungsbedürftigkeit naturwissenschaftlich-technischer Medizin* (Stuttgart: Enke, 1973).

F. Engels, 'The Condition of the Working-Class in England from Personal Observation and Authentic Sources' (originally 1847); in Karl Marx and Frederick Engels, *On Britain* (Moscow: Foreign Languages Publishing House, 1953).

K. T. Erikson, 'Patient Role and Social Uncertainty', *Psychiatry*: 20 (1957), 263–74.

K. T. Erikson, 'Notes on the Sociology of Deviance', 1962 (repr. Becker 1964).

S. E. Estroff, *Making it Crazy: An Ethnography of Psychiatric Clients in an American Community* (Berkeley, CA: University of California Press, 1981).

J. Eyer, 'Hypertension as a Disease of Modern Society', *International Journal of Health Services*, 5 (1975), 539–57.

J. Eyer, 'Does Unemployment Cause the Death Rate Peak in Each Business Cycle? A Multifactor Model of Death Rate Change'. *International Journal of Health Services*, 7 (1977), 625–62.

S. Y. Fagerhaugh and A. Strauss, *Politics of Pain Management: Staff–Patient Interaction* (Menlo Park, CA: Addison-Wesley, 1977).

E. Fairhurst, 'On Being a Patient in an Orthopaedic Ward: Some Thoughts on the Definition of the Situation', in A. Davis and Horobin (1977).

N. L. Farberow and E. S. Shneidman, *The Cry For Help* (New York: McGraw-Hill, 1961).

N. L. Farberow (ed.), *Taboo Topics* (New York: Atherton, 1963).

N. L. Farberow (ed.), *Proceedings of the Fourth International Conference for Suicide Protection* (Los Angeles, CA: Delmar, 1967).

N. L. Farberow, *Bibliography on Suicide and Suicide Prevention 1897–1957, 1958–1967* (Washington, DC: Government Printing Office, 1969).

R. A. Farrell and V. L. Swigert (eds), *Social Deviance* (Philadelphia: Lippincott, 1975).

M. Fears, 'Therapeutic Optimism and the Treatment of the Insane: Some Comments on the Integration of Psychiatric Reform at the End of the Eighteenth Century', in Dingwall *et al.* (1977).

A. R. Feinstein, *Clinical Judgment* (Malabar, FL: Krieger, 1967).

C. and T. Fengler, *Alltag in der Anstalt* (Wunstorf: Psychiatrie Verlag, 1983).

M. G. Field, *Doctor and Patient in Soviet Russia* (Cambridge, MA: Harvard University Press, 1957).

K. M. Figlio, 'Theories of Perception and the Physiology of Mind in the Late Eighteenth Century', *History of Science*, 12 (1975), 177–212.

K. M. Figlio, 'The Metaphor of Organization: An Historiographical Perspective on the Bio-Medical Sciences of the Early Nineteenth Century', *History of Science*, 14 (1976), 17–53.

K. M. Figlio, 'The Historiography of Scientific Medicine: An Invitation to the Human Sciences', *Contemporary Studies in Society and History*, 19 (1977), 262–86.

K. M. Figlio, 'Chlorosis and Chronic Disease in Nineteenth-Century Britain: The Social Constitution of Somatic Illness in a Capitalist Society', *Social History*, 3 (1978), 167–97.

K. M. Figlio, 'How does Illness Mediate Social Relations? Workmen's Compensation and Medico-Legal Practices, 1890–1940', in Wright and Treacher (1982).

P. Filmer, M. Phillipson, D. Silverman and D. Walsh, *New Directions in Sociological Theory* (London: Collier Macmillan, 1972).

A. Finlayson and J. McEwen, *Coronary Heart Disease and Patterns of Living* (London: Croom Helm, 1977).

S. Fisher, 'Doctor Talk/Patient Talk: How Treatment Decisions are Negotiated in Doctor–Patient Communication', in Fisher and Todd (1983).

S. Fisher, 'Institutional Authority and the Structure of Discourse', *Discourse Processes*, 7 (1984), 201–24.

S. Fisher and A. Todd (eds), *The Social Organization of Doctor–Patient Communication* (Washington, DC: Center for Applied Linguistics 1983).

R. Fitzpatrick, 'Social Concepts of Disease and Illness'; 'Society and Changing Patterns of Disease'; 'Social Causes of Disease'; in Patrick and Scambler (1982).

R. Fitzpatrick, J. Hinton, S. Newman, G. Scambler and J. Thompson (eds), *The Experience of Illness* (New York: Tavistock, 1984).

J. Floud, 'Sociology and the Theory of Responsibility: Social Background as an Excuse for Crime', *Psychological Medicine*, 5 (1975), 227–38.

N. M. Foote, 'Identification as a Basis for a Theory of Motivation', *American Sociological Review*, 16 (1951), 14–21.

G. Forsyth, *Doctors and State Medicine*, 2nd edn (London: Pitman Medical, 1973).

M. Foucault, *The Birth of the Clinic* (originally 1963) (New York: Vintage, 1975).

M. Foucault, *Histoire de la Sexualité: La Volonté de Savoir* (Paris: Éditions Gallimard, 1976).

M. Foucault, *Discipline and Punish* (originally 1975) (New York: Vintage, 1979).

L. K. Frank, 'Society as the Patient', *American Journal of Sociology*, 42 (1936), 335–44.

R. M. Frankel, 'The Laying on of Hands: Aspects of the Organization of Gaze, Touch, and Talk in a Medical Encounter', in Fisher and Todd (1983).

R. M. Frankel, 'From Sentence to Sentence: Understanding the Medical Encounter through Micro-Interactional Analysis', *Discourse Processes* 7 (1984), 135–70.

R. Frankenberg, 'Functionalism and After? Theory and Developments In Social Science Applied to the Health Field', *International Journal of Health Services*, 4 (1974), 411–27.

R. Frankenberg, 'Sickness as Cultural Performance? Drama, Trajectory, and Pilgrimage Root Metaphors and the Making Social of Disease', *International Journal of Health Services*, 16 (1986), 603–26.

H. E. Freeman, S. Levine and L. G. Reeder (eds), *Handbook of Medical Sociology* (Englewood Cliffs, NJ: Prentice-Hall, 1963, 1972).

E. Freidson, *Patients' View of Medical Practice* (Chicago: University of Chicago Press, 1961).

E. Freidson, 'Disability as Social Deviance', in M. Sussman (ed), *Sociology and Rehabilitation* (Washington: American Sociological Association, 1966).

E. Freidson, 'The Impurity of Professional Authority', in H. Becker *et al.* (1968).

E. Freidson, *Profession of Medicine* (New York: Dodd, Mead, 1970a).

E. Freidson, *Professional Dominance: The Social Structure of Medical Care* (Chicago: Aldine, 1970b).

E. Freidson, 'Professionalism: The Doctor's Dilemma', *Social Policy*, 2 (1971), 35–40.

E. Freidson, *Doctoring Together: A Study of Professional Social Control* (New York: Elsevier, 1976).

E. Freidson, 'The Theory of Professions: State of the Art', in Dingwall and Lewis (1983a).

E. Freidson, 'Viewpoint: Sociology and Medicine: A Polemic', *Sociology of Health and Illness*, 5 (1983b), 208–19.

E. Freidson, 'The Reorganization of the Medical Profession', *Medical Care Review*, 42 (1985), 11–35.

E. Freidson, 'The Medical Profession in Transition', in Aiken and Mechanic (1986).

A. Freud, *The Ego and the Mechanisms of Defence* (London: Hogarth Press and Institute of Psycho-Analysis, 1937).

S. Freud, 'The Ego and the Id', in *The Standard Edition of the Complete Psychological Works of Sigmund Freud*, Vol. 19 (1923–1925) (London: Hogarth Press and Institute of Psycho-Analysis, 1961) (originally published Vienna: International Psycho-Analytical Press, 1922).

S. Freud, *Civilization, War and Death: Selections from Three Works by Sigmund Freud*, ed. John Rickman (London: Hogarth Press and Institute of Psycho-Analysis, 1939).

S. Freud, 'An Outline of Psychoanalysis' (1938); first published in German in *Internationale Zeitschrift für Psychoanalyse und Imago* (1940); in *The Standard Edition of the Complete Psychological Works of Sigmund Freud*, Vol. 23 (London: Hogarth Press and Institute of Psycho-Analysis, 1964).

K. Friedlander, *The Psycho-Analytical Approach to Juvenile Delinquency* (New York: International Universities Press, 1960).

M. Friedman and R. H. Rosenman, 'Type A Behavior Pattern: Its Association with Coronary Heart Disease', *Annals of Clinical Research*, 3 (1971), 300–12.

E. Gallagher, 'Lines of Reconstruction and Extension in the Parsonian Sociology of Illness', *Social Science and Medicine*, 10 (1976), 207–18.

J. Garber and M. E. P. Seligman (eds), *Human Helplessness: Theory and Applications* (New York: Academic Press, 1980).

H. Garfinkel, 'Research Note on Inter- and Intra-Racial Homicides', *Social Forces*, 27 (1949), 370–81.

H. Garfinkel, 'Perception of the Other: A Study of Social Order', PhD Dissertation (Harvard University, unpublished, 1952).

H. Garfinkel, 'Conditions of Successful Degradation Ceremonies',

American Journal of Sociology, 61 (1956a), 420–4.

H. Garfinkel, 'Some Sociological Concepts for Psychiatrists', *Psychiatric Research Reports*, 6 (1956b), 181–95.

H. Garfinkel, 'Aspects of the Problem of Commonsense Knowledge of Social Structures', *Proceedings of the 4th World Congress of Sociology* (Milan: Stressa, 1959).

H. Garfinkel, 'The Rational Properties of Scientific and Common-Sense Activities', *Behavioral Science*, 5 (1960), 72–83.

H. Garfinkel, 'Common-Sense Knowledge of Social Structure: The Documentary Method of Interpretation', in J. M. Scher (ed.), *Theories of the Mind* (New York: Free Press, 1962).

H. Garfinkel, 'A Conception of, and Experiments With, "Trust" as a Condition of Stable Concerted Actions', in E. J. Harvey (ed.), *Motivation and Social Interaction* (New York: Ronald Press, 1963).

H. Garfinkel, *Studies in Ethnomethodology* (Englewood Cliffs, NJ: Prentice-Hall, 1967a).

H. Garfinkel, 'Practical Sociological Reasoning', in E. S. Shneidman (ed.), *Essays in Self Destruction* (New York: International Science Press, 1967b).

H. Garfinkel, 'On the Origins of the Term "Ethnomethodology"', in R. Turner (ed.), *Ethnomethodology* (Harmondsworth: Penguin, 1974).

H. Garfinkel, M. Lynch and E. Livingston, 'The Work of a Discovery Science Construed with Materials from the Optically Discovered Pulsar', *Philosophy of the Social Sciences*, 11 (1981), 131–58.

H. Garfinkel, M. Lynch and E. Livingston, 'Temporal Order in Laboratory Work', in Knorr-Cetina and Mulkay (1983).

H. Garfinkel and H. Sacks, 'On Formal Structures of Practical Actions', in J. C. McKinney and E. A. Tiryakian (eds), *Theoretical Sociology* (New York: Appleton-Century-Crofts, 1970).

U. Gerhardt, *Rollenanalyse als kritische Soziologie* (Neuwied: Luchterhand, 1971).

U. Gerhardt, 'Krankenkarriere und Existenzbelastung' (Illness Career and Economic Risk), *Zeitschrift für Soziologie*, 5 (1976a), 215–36.

U. Gerhardt, 'Careers and Coping': paper presented to British Sociological Association Medical Sociology Conference, York (1976b).

U. Gerhardt, 'The Sociological Relevance of the Work of Ronald Laing': paper presented to British Sociological Association Medical Sociology Conference, York (1978).

U. Gerhardt, 'The Parsonian Paradigm and the Identity of Medical Sociology', *Sociological Review*, 27 (1979a), 229–51.

U. Gerhardt, 'Coping and Social Action: Theoretical Reconstruction of the Life-Event Approach', *Sociology of Health and Illness*, 1 (1979b), 195–225.

U. Gerhardt, 'Introduction: Stress and Stigma – The Dilemma of Explanation', in U. Gerhardt and M. E. J. Wadsworth (eds), *Stress and Stigma* (Frankfurt: Campus; London: Macmillan; New York: St Martin's Press, 1985a).

U. Gerhardt, 'Stress and Stigma Explanations of Illness', in U. Gerhardt and M. E. J. Wadsworth (eds), *Stress and Stigma* (Frankfurt: Campus; London: Macmillan; New York: St Martin's Press, 1985b).

U. Gerhardt, *Patientenkarrieren* (Frankfurt: Suhrkamp, 1986).

U. Gerhardt, 'Parsons, Role Theory and Health Interaction' in G. Scambler (ed.), *Sociological Theory and Medical Sociology* (London: Tavistock, 1987).

. U. Gerhardt and M. Brieskorn-Zinke, 'The Normalization of Hemodialysis at Home', in J. Roth and S. Ruzek (eds), *The Adoption and Social Consequences of Medical Technologies: Research in the Sociology of Health Care*, Vol. 4 (Greenwich, CT: JAI Press, 1986).

U. Gerhardt and K. U. Kirchgässler, 'The Federal Republic of Germany', in R. Illsley and P. G. Svensson (eds), *The Health Burden of Social Inequities* (Copenhagen: WHO Regional Office for Europe, 1986a).

U. Gerhardt and K. U. Kirchgässler, 'Levels of Validity in Qualitative Research': paper presented to 11th World Congress of Sociology, New Delhi (1986b).

U. Gerhardt and K. Kirchgässler, 'Analyse idéaltypique de carrières de patients', *Science Sociales et Santé*, 5 (1987), 41–91.

E. Gerson, 'Social Character of Illness: Deviance or Politics?', *Social Science and Medicine*, 10 (1976a), 219–24.

E. Gerson, 'On the Quality of Life', *American Sociological Review*, 41 (1976b), 793–806.

J. Gibbs, 'Conceptions of Deviant Behavior: The Old and the New', *Pacific Sociological Review*, 9 (1966), 9–14.

J. Gibbs, 'Issues in Defining Deviant Behavior', in Scott and Douglas (1972).

A. Giddens, *Capitalism and Social Theory* (Cambridge University Press, 1971).

A. Giddens, *Central Problems in Social Theory: Action, Structure and Contradiction in Social Analysis* (Berkeley, CA: University of California Press, 1979).

A. Giddens, *The Constitution of Society: Outline of the Theory of Structuration* (Berkeley/Los Angeles, CA: University of California Press, 1984).

D. S. Gill and G. W. Horobin, 'Doctors, Patients and the State: Relationships and Decision-Making', *The Sociological Review*, 20 (1972), 505–20.

J. L. Gillin, *Social Pathology* (New York: Century, 1933; rev. edn 1939, rev. 3rd edn: Appleton-Century, 1946).

E. Ginzberg, 'The Political Economy of Health', *Bulletin of The New York Academy of Medicine*, 41 (1965), 1015–36.

B. G. Glaser, 'The Constant Comparative Method of Qualitative Analysis', *Social Problems*, 12 (1965), 436–45.

B. G. Glaser, 'Disclosure of Terminal Illness', in Jaco (1958/79), 83–91.

B. G. Glaser and A. L. Strauss, 'The Social Loss of Dying Patients', *American Journal of Nursing*, 64 (1964a), 119–21.

B. G. Glaser and A. L. Strauss, 'Awareness Contexts and Social Interaction', *American Sociological Review*, 29 (1964b), 669–79.

B. G. Glaser and A. L. Strauss, 'Temporal Aspects of Dying as a Non-Scheduled Status Passage', *American Journal of Sociology*, 71 (1965a), 48–59.

B. G. Glaser and A. L. Strauss, 'Discovery of Substantive Theory: A Basic Strategy Underlying Qualitative Research', *American Behavioral Scientist*, 8 (1965b), 5–12.

B. G. Glaser and A. L. Strauss, *Awareness of Dying* (Chicago: Aldine, 1965c).

B. G. Glaser and A. L. Strauss, *The Discovery of Grounded Theory* (Chicago: Aldine, 1967).

B. G. Glaser and A. L. Strauss, *Time for Dying* (Chicago: Aldine, 1968).

E. Goffman, 'On Cooling the Mark out: Some Aspects of Adaptation to Failure', *Psychiatry*, 15 (1952), 451–63.

E. Goffman, 'Communication Conduct in an Island Community', PhD Dissertation (Chicago University: unpublished, 1953).

E. Goffman, 'The Nature of Deference and Demeanor', *American Anthropologist*, 58 (1956a), 473–502.

E. Goffman, *The Presentation of Self in Everyday Life* (Edinburgh: University of Edinburgh Social Sciences Research Centre, 1956b).

E. Goffman, 'Normal Deviants', in M. Greenblatt *et al.* (eds), *The Patient and the Mental Hospital* (New York: Free Press, 1957).

E. Goffman, *The Presentation of Self in Everyday Life* (New York: Doubleday, 1959).

E. Goffman, 'The Moral Career of the Mental Patient', *Psychiatry*, 22 (1959), 123–42 (repr. *Asylums*).

E. Goffman, *Asylums: Essays on the Social Situation of Mental Patients and Other Inmates* (New York: Anchor (Doubleday), 1961).

E. Goffman, *Stigma: Notes on the Management of Spoiled Identity* (Englewood Cliffs, NJ: Prentice-Hall, 1963).

E. Goffman, *Strategic Interaction* (Oxford: Blackwell, 1969a).

E. Goffman, 'The Insanity of Place', *Psychiatry*, 32 (1969b) 357–88.

M. Gold, 'A Crisis of Identity: The Case of Medical Sociology', *Journal of Health and Social Behavior*, 18 (1977), 160–8.

N. Goldie, 'The Division of Labour among the Mental Health Professionals – A Negotiated or an Imposed Order? in Stacey *et al.* (1977).

M. S. Goldstein, 'The Politics of Thomas Szasz: A Sociological View', *Social Problems* 27 (1980), 570–83.

J. H. Goldthorpe, 'A Revolution in Sociology?', *Sociology*, 7 (1973), 449–62.

J. H. Goldthorpe, in Collaboration with C. Llewellyn and C. Payne, *Social Mobility and Class Structure in Britain* (Oxford: Clarendon Press, 1980).

G. Gordon, *Role Theory and Illness: A Sociological Perspective* (New Haven, CT: College and University Press, 1966).

A. Gouldner, 'The Sociologist as Partisan: Sociology and the Welfare State', *American Sociologist*, 3 (1968), 103–16.

A. Gouldner, *The Coming Crisis of Western Sociology* (London: Heinemann, 1970).

W. R. Gove, 'Societal Reaction as an Explanation of Mental Illness: An Evaluation', *American Sociological Review*, 35 (1970a), 873–84.

W. R. Gove, 'Who is Hospitalized: A Critical Review of Some Sociological Studies of Mental Illness', *Journal of Health and Social Behaviour*, 11 (1970b), 294–304.

W. R. Gove, 'Reply To Akers', *American Sociological Review*, 36 (1972), 488–90.

W. R. Gove, 'Sex, Marital Status and Mortality', *American Journal of Sociology*, 79 (1973a), 45–67.

W. R. Gove, 'The Stigma of Mental Hospitalization', *Archives of General Psychiatry*, 28 (1973b), 494–500.

W. R. Gove, 'Individual Resources and Mental Hospitalization: A Comparison and Evaluation of the Societal Reaction and Psychiatric Perspectives', *American Sociological Review*, 39 (1974), 86–100.

W. R. Gove, 'The Labelling Theory of Mental Illness: A Reply to Scheff', *American Sociological Review*, 40 (1975), 242–8.

W. R. Gove (ed.), *The Labelling of Deviance: Evaluation a Perspective* (New York: Halsted, 1975; 2nd edn, 1980).

W. R. Gove (ed.), *Deviance and Mental Illness* (Beverly Hills, CA: Sage, 1982a).

W. R. Gove (ed.), 'The Current Status of the Labelling Theory of Mental Illness', in Gove (1982b).

W. R. Gove and M. Hughes, 'Possible Causes of the Apparent Sex Differences in Physical Health: An Empirical Investigation', *American Sociological Review*, 44 (1979), 126–46.

M. Granovetter, 'The Strength of Weak Ties', *American Journal of Sociology*, 78 (1973), 1360–80.

R. Grathoff, *The Theory of Social Action: The Correspondence of Alfred Schütz and Talcott Parsons* (Bloomington: Indiana University Press, 1978).

J. R. Greenley, 'The Psychiatric Patient's Family and Length of Hospitalization', *Journal of Health and Social Behavior*, 13 (1972), 25–37.

J. R. Greenley, 'Familial Expectations, Posthospital Adjustment, and the Societal Reaction Perspective on Mental Illness', *Journal of Health and Social Behavior*, 20 (1979), 217–27.

J. R. Greenley, 'Family Symptom Tolerance and Rehospitalization Experiences of Psychiatric Patients', in R. G. Simmons (ed.), *Research in Community Mental Health* (Greenwich, CT: JAI Press, 1980).

O. Grusky and M. Pollner, 'Preface', in O. Grusky and M. Pollner (eds), *The Sociology of Mental Illness: Basic Studies* (New York: Holt, Rinehart & Winston, 1981).

J. Gück, E. Matt and E. Weingarten, 'Zur interaktiven Ausgestaltung der Arzt-Patient-Beziehung in der Visite', in H. U. Deppe, U. Gerhardt and P. Novak (eds), *Medizinische Soziologie*, Jahrbuch 3 (Frankfurt: Campus, 1983).

J. R. Gusfield, *Symbolic Crusade: Status Politics and the American Temperance Movement* (Urbana, IL: University of Urbana Press, 1963).

L. D. Haber and R. T. Smith, 'Disability and Deviance: Normative Adaptation of Role Behavior,' *American Sociological Review*, 36 (1971) 87–97.

J. Habermas, 'Kritische und konservative Aufgaben der Soziologie', in *Theorie und Praxis* (Frankfurt 1971; originally Neuwied 1963).

J. Habermas, 'Technology and Science as "Ideology"', in *Toward A Rational Society* (London: Heinemann Educational, 1971; originally in German, 1968).

J. Habermas, *Legitimation Crisis of the State* (Boston, MA: Beacon Press, 1973; originally in German, 1971).

R. A. Hahn and A. Kleinman, 'Belief as Pathogen, Belief as Medicine: "Voodoo Death" and the "Placebo Phenomenon" in Anthropological Perspective': paper presented at Society for Anthropology Annual Meeting, Edinburgh (1981).

D. Hall, R. Pill and F. Clough, 'Notes For a Conceptual Model of Hospital Experiences as an Interaction Process', in M. Stacey (ed.), *The Sociology of the NHS*. Sociological Review Monographs, 22 (Keele: University of Keele, 1976).

P. M. Hall and D. A. Spencer Hall, 'The Social Conditions of the Negotiated Order', *Urban Life*, 11 (1982), 328–49.

A. H. Halsey, A. F. Heath and J. M. Ridge, *Origins and Destinations: Family, Class and Education in Modern Britain* (Oxford: Clarendon, 1980).

D. R. Hannay, *The Symptom Iceberg: A Study of Community Health* (London/Boston: Routledge & Kegan Paul, 1979).

M. Harrison, *The Other America: Poverty in the United States* (New York: Macmillan, 1962; rev. edn, 1971).

J. T. Hart, 'The Inverse Care Law', *Lancet*, 27 February 1971, i, 405–12.

N. Hart, 'Health and Inequality' (University of Essex: mimeo, 1978).

N. Hart, 'Is Capitalism Bad For Your Health?', *British Journal of Sociology*, 33 (1982), 435–43.

N. Hart, *The Sociology of Health and Medicine* (Ormskirk: Causeway, 1986a).

N. Hart, 'Inequalities in Health: The Individual versus the Environment', *Journal of the Royal Statistical Society*, Series A (General), 149 (1986b), 228–46.

K. Hartung, *Die neuen Kleider der Psychiatrie: Vom antiinstitutionellen Kampf zum Kleinkrieg gegen die Misere* (Berlin: Rotbuch, 1980).

S. Haywood and A. Alaszewski, *Crisis in the Health Service: The Politics of Management* (London: Croom Helm, 1980).

J. L. Heap and P. A. Roth, 'On Phenomenological Sociology', *American Sociological Review*, 38 (1981), 354–67.

C. Heath, 'The Opening Sequence in Doctor–Patient Interaction', in Atkinson and Heath (1981).

C. Heath, 'Preserving the Consultation: Medical Record Cards and Professional Conduct', *Sociology of Health and Illness*, 4 (1982), 56–74.

C. Heath, 'Talk and Recipiency: Sequential Organization in Speech and Body Movement', in M. Atkinson and J. Heritage (eds), *Structures of Social Action* (Cambridge University Press, 1984).

C. Helman, *Culture, Health and Illness: An Introduction for Health Professionals* (Bristol: Wright, 1984).

C. R. Henderson, *Introduction to the Study of the Dependent, Defective and Delinquent Classes and of Their Social Treatment*, 2nd edn (Boston, MA: D. C. Heath, 1901).

L. J. Henderson, *Pareto's General Sociology: A Physiologist's Interpretation* (Cambridge, MA: Harvard University Press, 1935a).

L. J. Henderson, 'Physician and Patient as a Social System', *New England Journal of Medicine*, 212 (1935b), 819–23.

L. J. Henderson, *On the Social System*, ed. B. Barber (Chicago/London: University of Chicago Press, 1970).

J. P. Henry, 'The Relation of Social and Biological Processes of Disease', *Social Science and Medicine*, 16 (1982), 369–80.

J. P. Henry and P. M. Stevens, *Stress, Health and the Social Environment* (Berlin: Springer, 1977).

J. Heritage, *Garfinkel and Ethnomethodology* (Cambridge: Polity Press, 1984).

B. Heyl, 'The Harvard "Pareto Circle"', *Journal of the History of the Behavioural Sciences*, 4 (1968), 316–34.

R. Hilberg, *The Destruction of the European Jews* (Chicago: Quadrangle Books, 1961).

R. Hilberg, 'The Destruction of the European Jews', in Rosenberg, Gerver and Horton (1964).

C. R. Hill and K. S. Crittenden (eds), *The Purdue Symposion on Ethnomethodology* (Purdue University, Institute for the Study of Social Change, 1968).

R. Hilliard, 'Categorizing Children in the Clinic', *Sociology of Health and Illness*, 3 (1981), 317–36.

R. Hingson, N. A. Scotch, J. Sorensen and J. P. Swazey, *In Sickness and in Health* (St Louis, MO: Mosby, 1981).

L. E. Hinkle, 'The Effect of Exposure to Culture Change, Social Change, and Changes in Interpersonal Relationships on Health', in Dohrenwend and Dohrenwend (1974).

L. E. Hinkle, R. H. Pinsky, I. D. J. Bross and N. Plummer, 'The Distribution of Sickness Disability in a Homogenous Groups of "Healthy Adult Men"', *American Journal of Hygiene*, 64 (1956), 220–42.

A. B. Hollingshead and F. C. Redlich, *Social Class and Mental Illness* (New York: Wiley, 1958).

G. Holton, 'Comment on Professor Harold Garfinkel's Paper', *Philosophy of the Social Sciences*, 11 (1981), 159–61.

G. Homans, *Social Behavior: Its Elementary Forms* (New York: Harcourt, Brace & World, 1961).

G. Homans, 'Bringing Men Back In', *American Sociological Review*, 25 (1964), 809–18.

M. Horkheimer (ed.), *Studien über Autorität und Familie* (Paris: Librairie Felix Alcan, 1936).

M. Horkheimer, 'Die Juden und Europa', *Zeitschrift für Sozialforschung*, 8 (1939; repr. Munich: Kösel, 1970), 115–37.

M. Horkheimer and T. Adorno, *Aspects of Sociology* (London: Heinemann, 1974; originally in German, 1956).

J. S. Horn, *Away With All Pests* (New York/London: Monthly Review Press, 1969).

G. Horobin, 'Professional Mystery: The Maintenance of Charisma in General Medical Practice', in Dingwall and Lewis (1983).

G. Horobin, 'Review Essay: Medical Sociology in Britain: True Confessions of An Empiricist', *Sociology of Health and Illness*, 7 (1985), 94–107.

P. B. Horton and G. R. Leslie, *The Sociology of Social Problems* (New York: Appleton-Century-Crofts, 1955; 4th edn, 1970).

A. Horwitz, 'Models, Muddles, and Mental Illness Labelling', *Journal of Health and Social Behavior*, 20 (1979), 296–300.

D. Hughes, 'Everyday and Medical Knowledge in Categorizing Patients', in Dingwall *et al.* (1977).

D. Hughes, 'The Ambulance Journey as an Information Generating Process', *Sociology of Health and Illness*, 2 (1980), 115–32.

D. Hughes, 'Control in the Medical Consultation: Organizing Talk in a Situation Where Co-Participants have Differential Competence', *Sociology*, 16 (1982), 359–76.

E. C. Hughes, 'Institutions', in Park (1939).

E. C. Hughes, 'Dilemmas and Contradictions of Status', *American Journal of Sociology*, 50 (1945), 353–9.

E. C. Hughes, *Men and Their Work* (Glencoe: Free Press, 1958).

E. C. Hughes, 'Good People and Dirty Work', *Social Problems*, 10 (1962), repr. Becker (1964).

E. C. Hughes, *The Sociological Eye*: Selected Papers (Chicago: Aldine Atherton, 1971).

L. Humphreys, *Tearoom Trade* (Chicago: Aldine, 1970).

I. Illich, *Medical Nemesis* (London: Calder & Boyars, 1975a).

I. Illich, *Limits to Medicine: The Expropriation of Health* (London: Calder & Boyars, 1975b).

I. Illich, I. K. Zola, J. McKnight, J. Caplan and H. Shaiken, *Disabling Professions* (London: Marion Boyars, 1977).

E. G. Jaco (ed.), *Patients, Physicians, and Illness* (New York: Free Press, 1958; 2nd edn, 1972; 3rd edn, 1979).

M. Jay, *The Dialectical Imagination* (Boston: Little, Brown, 1973).

G. Jefferson, 'On Stepwise Transition from Talk about a Trouble to Inappropriately Next-Positioned Matters', in M. Atkinson and J. Heritage (eds), *Structures of Social Action* (Cambridge University, 1984).

G. Jefferson, 'On the Organization of Laughter in Talk about Troubles', in M. Atkinson and J. Heritage (eds), *Structures of Social Action* Cambridge University Press, 1984).

R. Jeffrey, 'Normal Rubbish: Deviant Patients in Casualty Departments', *Sociology of Health and Illness*, 1 (1979), 90–107.

M. Jellinek, *Alcohol Consumption and Chronic Alcoholism* (New Haven, CT: Yale University Press, 1942).

M. Jellinek, *The Disease Concept of Alcoholism* (New Haven, CT: Yale University Press, 1960).

N. D. Jewson, 'The Disappearance of the Sick Man From Medical Cosmology, 1770–1870', *Sociology*, 10 (1976), 225–44.

R. Jobling, 'Learning to Live with it: An Account of a Career of Chronic Dermatological Illness and Patienthood', in Davis and Horobin (1977).

Journal of the Royal College of Physicians, 10 (1976), 3, Prevention of Coronary Heart Disease: Report of a Joint Working Party of the Royal College of Physicians of London and the British Cardiac Society.

H. B. Kaplan, S. S. Martin and C. Robbins, 'Application of a General Theory of Deviant Behavior: Self-Derogation and Adolescent Drug Use', *Journal of Health and Social Behavior*, 23 (1982), 274–94.

S. V. Kasl and S. Cobb, 'Health Behavior, Illness Behavior, and Sick Role Behavior', *Archives of Environmental Health*, 12 (1966).

G. G. Kassebaum and B. O Baumann, 'Dimensions of the Sick Role in Chronic Illness', *Journal of Health and Human Behavior*, 6 (1965), 16–27.

S. Kelman, 'Toward the Political Economy of Medical Care', *Inquiry*, 8 (1971), 30–8.

S. Kelman, 'The Social Nature of the Definition Problem in Health', *International Journal of Health Services*, 5 (1975), 625–42.

E. M. Kitagawa and P. M. Hauser, *Differential Mortality in the United States* (Cambridge, MA.: Harvard University Press, 1973).

J. I. Kitsuse, 'Societal Reactions to Deviant Behavior: Problems of Theory and Method', *Social Problems*, 9 (1962), repr. Becker (1964).

J. I. Kitsuse, 'Deviance, Deviant Behavior, and Deviants: Some Conceptual Problems', in W. J. Filstead (ed.), *An Introduction to Deviance* (Chicago: Markham, 1972).

J. I. Kitsuse and A. V. Cicourel, 'A Note on the Use of Official Statistics', *Social Problems*, 11 (1963), 131–9.

B. Klapp, *Psychosoziale Intensivmedizin* (Berlin: Springer, 1985).

S. Kleinman, '"Actors'" Conflicting Theories of Negotiation', *Urban Life*, 11 (1982), 312–27.

K. D. Knorr-Cetina, 'Introduction: The Micro-Sociological Challenge of Macro-Sociology: Towards a Reconstruction of Social Theory and Methodology', in K. Knorr-Cetina and A. V. Cicourel (eds), *Advances in Social Theory and Methodology* (Boston, MA: Routledge & Kegan Paul, 1981).

K. Knorr-Cetina and M. Mulkay (eds), *Science Observed* (London: Sage, 1983).

E. Kogon, *The Theory and Practice of Hell: The German Concentration Camps and the System Behind Them* (transl. H. Norden) (New York:

Farrar, Straus, 1950; originally *Der SS-Staat*, 1946).

Kölner Zeitschrift für Soziologie, 25 (1973), 2, Special Issue on Ethnomethodological Research in Psychiatric Sociology.

E. Koos, *The Health of Regionville* (New York/London: Hafner, 1954).

J. Kosa, 'Entrepreneurship and Charisma in the Medical Profession', *Social Science and Medicine*, 4 (1970), 25–45.

J. Kosa and I. Zola (eds), *Poverty and Health*, 2nd rev. edn (Cambridge, MA: Harvard University Press, 1975; 1st edn, 1969).

E. Krause, 'Health and the Politics of Technology', *Inquiry*, 8 (1971), 51–9.

E. Krause, 'Health Planning as a Managerial Ideology', *International Journal of Health Services*, 3 (1973), 445–63.

E. Krause, 'The Political Context of Health Service Regulation', *International Journal of Health Services*, 5 (1975), 593–607.

E. Krause, *Power and Illness* (New York: Elsevier, 1977).

L. Kriesberg, 'Internal Differentiation and the Establishment of Organizations', in Becker *et al.* (1968).

R. D. Laing, *The Divided Self* (London: Tavistock, 1959; 2nd edn Penguin, 1965).

R. D. Laing, *The Politics of Experience* (New York: Pantheon, 1967).

R. D. Laing, *The Politics of the Family and Other Essays* (New York: Vintage, 1969).

R. D. Laing and D. G. Cooper, *Reason and Violence* (London: Tavistock, 1964).

R. D. Laing and A. Esterton, *Sanity, Madness and the Family* (London: Tavistock, 1964).

H. R. Lamb, 'The New Asylums in the Community', *Archives of General Psychiatry*, 36 (1979), 129–34.

R. E. Lamy, 'Social Consequences of Mental Illness', in R. H. Price and B. Denner (eds), *The Making of a Mental Patient* (New York: Holt, Rinehart & Winston, 1973).

M. S. Larson, *The Rise of Professionalism* (Berkeley, CA: University of California Press, 1977).

R. S. Lazarus and E. M. Opton, 'A Study of Psychological Stress: A Summary of Theoretical Formulations and Experimental Findings, in C. D. Spielberger (ed.), *Anxiety and Behavior* (New York: Academic Press, 1966).

D. C. Leighton, J. S. Harding, D. B. Macklin, A. M. Macmillan and A. H. Leighton, *The Character of Danger* (London/New York: Basic Books, 1963).

E. Lemert, *Social Pathology* (New York: McGraw-Hill, 1951).

E. M. Lemert, 'Paranoia and the Dynamics of Exclusion', *Sociometry*, 25 (1962), 2–20; repr. *Human Deviance, Social Problems and Social Control* (Englewood Cliffs, NJ: Prentice-Hall, 1967a).

E. M. Lemert, 'Alcohol, Values, and Social Control' (1962), in *Human Deviance, Social Problems and Social Control* (Englewood Cliffs, NJ: Prentice- Hall, 1967b).

E. M. Lemert, 'The Concept of Secondary Deviation', in *Human*

Deviance, Social Problems and Social Control (Englewood Cliffs: Prentice-Hall, 1967c).

E. M. Lemert, *Human Deviance, Social Problems and Social Control*, 2nd edn (Englewood Cliffs, NJ: Prentice-Hall, 1972).

E. M. Lemert, 'Beyond Mead: The Societal Reaction to Deviance', *Social Problems*, 21 (1974), 457–67.

E. M. Lemert, 'Response to Critics: Feedback and Choice', in L. Coser and D. Larson (eds), *The Uses of Controversy in Sociology* (New York: Macmillan, 1976).

V. I. Lenin, *Imperialism: The Highest State of Capitalism* (New York: International Publishers, 1939).

R. Lettau, *Täglicher Faschismus: Amerikanische Evidenz aus 6 Monaten* (Munich: Hanser, 1971).

L. S. Levin, A. H. Katz and E. Holst, *Self-Care: Lay Initiatives in Health* (London: Croom Helm, 1977).

S. Levine and N. A. Scotch (eds), *Social Stress* (Chicago: Aldine, 1970).

S. Levine and M. A. Kozloff, 'The Sick Role: Assessment and Overview', *Annual Review of Sociology*, 4 (1978), 317–43.

S. Levine, J. J. Feldman and J. Elinson, 'Does Medical Care Do Any Good?' in D. Mechanic (ed.), *Handbook of Health, Health Care and the Health Professions* (New York: Free Press, 1983).

R. Levitt, *The Reorganized National Health Service* (London: Croom Helm, 1976).

R. Levitt and A. Wall, *The Reorganized National Health Service*, 3rd edn (London: Croom Helm, 1984).

A. Liazos, 'The Poverty of the Sociology of Deviance: Nuts, Sluts, and "Preverts"', *Social Problems*, 20 (1972), 103–20; repr. S. H. Traub and C. B. Little (eds) *Theories of Deviance* (Itasca, IL: Peacock, 1975).

C. W. Lidz and A. L. Walker, *Heroin, Deviance and Morality* (Beverly Hills, CA: Sage, 1980).

R. J. Lifton, *The Nazi Doctors: Medical Killing and the Psychology of Genocide* (New York: Basic Books, 1986).

A. R. Lindesmith and A. Strauss, *Social Psychology* (Hinsdale, IL: Dryden Press, 1949; 3rd edn New York: Holt, Rinehart & Winston, 1968; 4th edn with N. Denzin, Hinsdale, IL: Dryden Press, 1975).

R. Linton, *The Structure of Society* (New York: Appleton-Century, 1936).

D. Locker, *Symptoms and Illness: The Cognitive Organization of Disorder* (London: Tavistock, 1981).

D. Locker, *Disability and Disadvantage* (London: Tavistock, 1983).

J. Lorber, 'Deviance and Performance: The Case of Illness', *Social Problems*, 14 (1967), 302–10.

J. Lorber, 'Good Patients and Problem Patients: Conformity and Deviance in a General Hospital', *Journal of Health and Social Behavior*, 16 (1975), 213–25.

D. R. Loseke and S. E. Cahill, 'The Social Construction of Deviance: Experts on Battered Women', *Social Problems*, 31 (1984), 296–310.

S. M. Lyman and M. B. Scott, *A Sociology of the Absurd* (New York: Appleton-Century-Crofts, 1970).

M. Lynch, 'Accommodation Practices: Vernacular Treatments of Madness', *Social Problems*, 31 (1983), 152–64.

S. MacIntire, 'Old Age as a Social Problem', in Dingwall *et al.* (1977).

S. MacIntire and D. Oldman, 'Coping With Migraine', in A. Davis and Horobin (1977).

B. Malinowski, *Argonauts of the Western Pacific* (London: Routledge, 1922).

B. Malinowski, *Crime and Custom in Savage Society* (London: K. Paul, Trench, Trubner, 1926).

G. B. Mangold, *Social Pathology* (New York: Macmillan, 1932).

J. G. Manis and B. N. Meltzer (eds), *Symbolic Interaction* (Boston, MA: Allyn & Bacon, 1967; 2nd edn, 1972).

K. Mannheim, 'On the Interpretation of Weltanschauung' in *Essays on the Sociology of Knowledge by Karl Mannheim*, ed. P. Kekskemeti (London: Routledge & Kegan Paul, 1952; originally *Jahrbuch für Kunstgeschichte*, 1 (1921/22), Vienna, 1923).

P. K. Manning, 'The Decline of Civility: A Comment on Erving Goffman's Sociology', *Canadian Review of Anthropology and Sociology*, 13 (1976), 13–25.

T. R. Marmor, *The Politics of Medicare* (Chicago: Aldine, 1970).

P. Marris, *Loss and Change* (New York: Pantheon, 1974).

K. Marx, 'Economic and Philosophical Manuscripts', in *Early Writings*, intr. L. Colletti (trans. R. Livingstone and G. Benton) (Harmondsworth: Penguin, 1975; originally written 1844, first published 1932).

K. Marx, *Capital*, Vol. 1 (London: Swan Sonnenschein, 1906; originally published 1867).

W. Mason, 'A Historical View of the Stress Field', *Journal of Human Stress*, 1 (1975), 6–12, 22–36.

D. Matza, *Becoming Deviant* (Englewood Cliffs, NJ: Prentice-Hall, 1969).

H. Maus, *A Short History of Sociology* (London: Routledge & Kegan Paul, 1962).

R. Mayntz, 'The Nature of Genesis of Impersonality: Some Results of a Study on the Doctor–Patient Relationship', *Social Research*, 37 (1970), 428–46.

R. McCleary, 'How Parole Officers use Records', *Social Problems*, 24 (1977), 576–89.

J. McCord, 'A Longitudinal Perspective on Patterns of Crime', *Criminology*, 19 (1981), 211–18.

P. McHugh, *Defining the Situation: The Organization of Meaning in Social Interaction* (Indianapolis: Bobbs-Merrill, 1968).

P. McHugh, 'A Common-Sense Perception of Deviance', in H. P. Dreitzel (ed.), *Recent Sociology No. 2: Patterns of Communicative Behavior* (New York: Macmillan, 1970a).

P. McHugh, 'A Common-Sense Conception of Deviance', in J. Douglas (ed.), *Deviance and Respectability* (New York: Basic Books, 1970b).

T. McKeown, *Medicine in Modern Society* (London: George Allen & Unwin, 1965).

T. McKeown, *The Modern Rise of Population* (London: Edward Arnold, 1975).

T. McKeown, *The Role of Medicine: Dream, Mirage, or Nemesis?* (Oxford: Blackwell, 1979).

D. V. McQueen and D. D. Celentano, 'Social Factors in the Etiology of Multiple Outcomes: The Case of Blood Pressure and Alcohol Consumption Patterns', *Social Science and Medicine*, 16 (1982), 397–418.

D. V. McQueen and J. Siegrist, 'Social Factors in the Etiology of Chronic Disease: An Overview', *Social Science and Medicine*, 16 (1982), 353–67.

G. H. Mead, 'The Working Hypothesis of Social Reform', *American Journal of Sociology*, 5 (1899), 367–71.

G. H. Mead, 'The Psychology of Punitive Justice', *American Journal of Sociology*, 23 (1918), 577–602.

G. H. Mead, 'The Genesis of the Self and Social Control', *International Journal of Ethics*, 35 (1924/5), 251–77; repr. *Selected Writings*, ed. A. J. Peck (Indianapolis: Bobbs-Merrill, 1964).

G. H. Mead, *Mind, Self and Society from the Standpoint of a Social Behaviorist*, ed. and with intro. by C. W. Morris (University of Chicago Press, 1934).

G. H. Mead, *The Philosophy of the Act*, ed. and with intro. by C. W. Morris in collab. with J. M. Brewster, A. M. Dunham and D. L. Miller (Chicago University Press, 1938).

G. H. Mead, *Selected Writings*, ed. and with intro. by A. J. Peck (Indianapolis: Bobbs-Merrill, 1964).

D. Mechanic, 'Illness and Social Disability: Some Problems of Analysis', *Pacific Sociological Review*, 2 (1959), 37–41.

D. Mechanic, 'Some Problems in Developing a Social Psychology of Adaptation to Stress', in J. E. McGrath (ed.), *Social and Psychological Factors in Stress* (New York: Holt, Rinehart & Winston, 1970).

D. Mechanic, 'Sex, Illness, Illness Behavior, and the Use of Health Services', *Journal of Human Stress*, 2 (1976), 29–40.

D. Mechanic, 'Illness Behavior, Social Adaptation, and the Management of Illness: A Comparison of Educational and Medical Models', *Journal of Nervous and Mental Disease*, 165 (1977), 79–87.

D. Mechanic, *Medical Sociology: A Selective View* (New York: Free Press, 1968); 2nd edn: *A Comprehensive Text* (New York: Free Press, 1978).

D. Mechanic, 'Effects of Psychological Distress on Perception of Physical Health and Use of Medical and Psychiatric Facilities', *Journal of Human Stress*, 4 (1978), 26–32.

D. Mechanic, 'Comment on Gove and Hughes', *American Sociological Review*, 45 (1980), 513–14.

D. Mechanic and E. H. Volkart, 'Illness Behavior and Medical Diagnoses' *Journal of Health and Human Behavior*, 1 (1960), 86–94.

H. Mehan and H. Wood, *The Reality of Ethnomethodology* (New York: Wiley, 1975).

B. N. Meltzer, J. W. Petras and L. T. Reynolds, *Symbolic Interactionism* (London/Boston: Routledge & Kegan Paul, 1975).

J. R. Mercer, 'Social System Perspective and Clinical Perspective: Frame of Reference for Understanding Career Patterns of Persons Labelled as Mentally Retarded', *Social Problems*, 13 (1965), 18–34.

R. K. Merton, 'Social Structure and Anomie', in R. N. Anshen (ed.), *The Family: Its Function and Destiny* (New York: Harper, 1949).

R. J. Meyer and R. J. Haggerty, 'Streptococcal Infections in Families', *Pediatrics*, 29 (1962), 539–49.

A. C. Michalos, 'Satisfaction and Happiness with Life as a Whole: Survey Results from 23 Countries': paper presented at 11th World Congress of Sociology, New Delhi (1986).

D. Miller and D. H. Dawson, 'Effects of Stigma on Re-employment of Ex-Mental Patients', in R. H. Price and B. Denner (eds), *The Making of a Mental Patient* (New York: Holt, Rinehart & Winston, 1973).

R. S. Miller, 'The Social Construction and Reconstruction of Physiological Events: Acquiring the Pregnancy Identity', in N. K. Denzin (ed.), *Studies in Symbolic Interaction*, Vol. 1 (Greenwich, CT: JAI Press, 1978).

M. Millman, *The Unkindest Cut: Life in the Backrooms of Medicine* (New York: William Morrow, 1977).

C. W. Mills, 'The Professional Ideology of Social Pathologists', *American Journal of Sociology*, 49 (1943), 165–80.

E. G. Mishler, 'The Social Construction of Illness', in E. G. Mishler, L. R. Amarasigham, S. D. Osherson, S. T. Hauser, N. E. Waxler and R. Liem, *Social Contexts of Health, Illness, and Patient Care* (Cambridge University Press, 1981).

E. G. Mishler, *The Discourse of Medicine: Dialectics of Medical Interviews* (Norwood, NJ: Apex, 1984).

W. C. Mitchell, *Sociological Analysis and Politics: The Theories of Talcott Parsons* (Englewood Cliffs, NJ: Prentice-Hall, 1967).

S. F. Miyamoto, 'The Social Act: Re-examination of a Concept', *Pacific Sociological Review*, 2 (1959), 51–5.

S. Mohavedi, 'Loading the Dice in Favor of Madness', *Journal of Health and Social Behavior*, 16 (1975), 192–7.

S. Mohavedi, 'How Should one Load the Dice?', *Journal of Health and Social Behavior*, 17 (1976), 312–14.

H. Molotch and M. Lester, 'Accidents, Scandals, and Routines: Resources for Insurgent Methodology', *The Insurgent Sociologist*, 3 (1973), 1–11.

H. Molotch and M. Lester, 'News as Purposive Behavior: On the Strategic Use of Routine Events, Accidents, and Scandals', *American Sociological Review*, 39 (1974), 101–12.

M. Morgan, M. Calnan and N. Manning, *Sociological Approaches to Health and Medicine* (London: Croom Helm, 1985).

M. Morgan, D. L. Patrick and J. R. Charlton, 'Social Networks and Psychosocial Support among Disabled People', *Social Science and Medicine*, 19 (1984), 489–97.

J. P. Morrissey, 'Deinstitutionalizing the Mentally Ill', in Gove (1982).

C. Morse, 'The Functional Imperatives', in Black (1961).

O. H. Mowrer, *Identification: A Link Between Learning Theory and Personality Dynamics* (New York: Ronald Press, 1950).

P. Moynihan, *Maximum Feasible Misunderstanding: Community Action in the War on Poverty* (New York: Free Press, 1970).

A. Murcott, 'On the Typification of "Bad" Patients', in P. Atkinson Heath (1981).

E. Murphy and G. Brown, 'Life Events, Psychiatric Disturbance and Physical Illness', *British Journal of Psychiatry*, 136 (1980), 326–38.

J. M. Najman, 'Theories of Disease Causation and the Concept of General Susceptibility', *Social Science and Medicine*, 14A (1980), 231–7.

C. A. Nathanson, 'Illness and the Feminine Role: A Theoretical Review', *Social Science and Medicine*, 9 (1975), 57–62.

V. Navarro, 'From Public Health to Health of the Public: The Redefinition of our Task', *American Journal of Public Health*, 64 (1974), 538–42.

V. Navarro, 'Social Policy Issues: An Explanation of the Composition, Nature and Functions of the Present Health Sector of the U. S.', *Bulletin of the New York Academy of Medicine*, 51 (1975), 199–234.

V. Navarro, *Medicine under Capitalism* (New York: Prodist, 1976).

V. Navarro, *Social Security and Medicine in the U. S. S. R.: A Marxist Critique* (Lexington, MA: Heath, 1977).

V. Navarro, 'The Crisis of the Western System of Medicine in Contemporary Capitalism', *International Journal of Health Services*, 8 (1978a), 179–211.

V. Navarro, *Class Struggle, the State, and Medicine* (Oxford: Martin Robertson, 1978b).

V. Navarro, *Crisis, Health and Medicine: A Social Critique* (New York/London: Tavistock, 1986).

F. L. Neumann, *Behemoth: The Structure and Practice of National Socialism* (London: Victor Gollancz, 1942; 2nd edn New York: Oxford University Press, 1944; repr. New York and Evanston, IL: Harper & Row, 1966).

M. Nicholson, *Conflict Analysis* (London: English Universities Press, 1970).

J. O'Connor, *The Fiscal Crisis of the State* (New York: St Martin's Press, 1973).

C. Offe, *Industry and Equality: The Achievement Principle in Work and Social Status* (transl. J. Wickham) (London, 1976; originally *Leistungsprinzip und industrielle Arbeit*, Frankfurt: Europäische Verlagsanstalt, 1970).

J. Olds, *The Growth and Structure of Motives* (Glencoe, IL: Free Press, 1955).

J. O'Neill, 'The Medicalization of Social Control', *The Canadian Review of Sociology and Anthropology*, 23 (1986), 350–64.

H. Orlans, 'An American Death Camp', *Politics* (1948), 162–7, 205; repr. Rosenberg, Gerver and Horton (1964).

W. Outhwaite, *Understanding Social Life* (London: George Allen & Unwin, 1976).

M. A. Paget, 'On the Work of Talk: Studies in Misunderstandings', in Fisher and Todd (1983).

R. E. Park, 'Social Planning and Human Nature', in E. C. Hughes, C.

S. Johnson, J. Masuoka, R. Redfield and L. Wirth (eds), *The Collected Papers of Robert Ezra Park*, Vol. 3: *Society* (Glencoe, IL: Free Press, 1955; originally 1935).

R. E. Park (ed.), *An Outline of the Principles of Sociology* (New York: Barnes & Noble, 1939).

C. Murray Parkes, *Bereavement: Studies of Grief in Adult Life* (New York: International Universities Press, 1972).

P. A. Parsons, *Responsibility for Crime: An Investigation of the Nature and Causes of Crime and a Means of its Prevention. Studies in History, Economics, and Public Law*, 34 (1909), 3 (whole No. 91).

T. Parsons, *The Structure of Social Action*, 2 vols (New York: McGraw-Hill, 1937; 2nd edn Glencoe, IL: Free Press, 1949).

T. Parsons, 'The Professions and Social Structure', *Social Forces*, 17 (1939), 457–67.

T. Parsons, 'The Motivation of Economic Activities', *Canadian Journal of Economics and Political Science*, 6 (1940), 187–203.

T. Parsons, 'The Sociology of Modern Anti-Semitism', in I. Graeber and S. H. Britt (eds), *Jews in a Gentile World* (New York: Macmillan, 1942a).

T. Parsons, 'Some Sociological Aspects of Fascist Movements', *Social Forces*, 21 (1942b), 138–47.

T. Parsons 'Democracy and the Social Structure in Pre-Nazi Germany', *Journal of Legal and Political Sociology*, 1 (1942c), 96–114.

T. Parsons, 'Age and Sex in the Social Structure of the United States', *American Sociological Review*, 7 (1942d), 604–16.

T. Parsons, 'The Problem of Controlled Institutional Change: An Essay on Applied Social Science', *Psychiatry*, 8 (1945), 79–101.

T. Parsons, 'Weber's Methodology of Social Science', in *Max Weber: The Theory of Social and Economic Organization* (transl. by A. M. Henderson and T. Parsons) (New York: Free Press, 1947a).

T. Parsons, 'Certain Primary Sources and Patterns of Aggression in the Social Structure of the Western World', *Psychiatry*, 10 (1947b), 167–81.

T. Parsons, *The Social System* (Glencoe, IL: Free Press, 1951a).

T. Parsons, 'Illness and the Role of the Physician', *American Journal of Orthopsychiatry*, 21 (1951b), 452–60.

T. Parsons, 'The Superego and the Theory of Social Systems', *Psychiatry*, 15 (1952), repr. *Social Structure and Personality* (London: Free Press, 1964).

T. Parsons, 'Family Structure and the Socialization of the Child', in T. Parsons and R. Bales (eds), *Family, Socialization and Interaction Process* (Glencoe, IL: Free Press, 1955a).

T. Parsons, 'The Organization of Personality as a System of Action', in T. Parsons and R. Bales (eds), *Family, Socialization and Interaction Process* (Glencoe, IL: Free Press, 1955b).

T. Parsons, 'Definitions of Health and Illness in the Light of the American Values and Social Structure', in Jaco (1958), repr. Parsons, *Social Structure and Personality* (London: Free Press, 1964a).

T. Parsons, 'Social Structure and the Development of Personality:

Freud's Contribution to the Integration of Psychology and Sociology', *Psychiatry*, 21 (1958), 321–40, repr. Parsons, *Social Structure and Personality* (London: Free Press, 1964b).

T. Parsons, 'A Short Account of My Intellectual Development', *Alpha Kappa Deltan*, 29 (1959), 3–12.

T. Parsons, 'Some Reflections on the Problems of Psychosomatic Relationships in Health and Illness', in Parsons, *Social Structure and Personality* (London: Free Press, 1964a; originally 1960).

T. Parsons, 'Mental Illness and "Spiritual Malaise"', in Parsons, *Social Structure and Personality* (London: Free Press, 1964b; originally 1960).

T. Parsons, 'Toward a Healthy Maturity', *Journal of Health and Human Behavior*, 1 (1960c), 163–73.

T. Parsons, 'Death in American Society – A Brief Working Paper', *American Behavioral Scientist*, 6 (1963a), 61–5.

T. Parsons, 'Social Change and Medical Organization in the U. S.: A Sociological Perspective', *Annals of the American Academy of Political and Social Science*, 396 (1963b), 21–33.

T. Parsons, 'Some Theoretical Considerations Bearing on the Field of Medical Sociology', in Parsons, *Social Structure and Personality* (London: Free Press, 1964).

T. Parsons, *Societies: Evolutionary and Comparative Perspectives* (Englewood Cliffs, NJ: Prentice-Hall, 1966).

T. Parsons, *Politics and Social Structure* (New York: Free Press, 1969).

T. Parsons, 'Research With Human Subjects and the "Professional Complex"', *Daedalus*, 98 (1969); repr. *Action Theory and the Human Condition* (New York: Free Press, 1978).

T. Parsons, 'Some Trends of Change in American Society: Their Bearing on Medical Education', in *Structure and Process in Modern Societies* (New York: Free Press, 1970a).

T. Parsons, 'On Building Social Systems Theory: A Personal History' *Daedalus*, 99 (1970b), 826–81.

T. Parsons, 'The Interpretation of Dreams by Sigmund Freud', in *Action Theory and the Human Condition* (New York: Free Press, 1978; originally 1974).

T. Parsons, 'The Sick Role and the Role of the Physician Reconsidered', *Milbank Memorial Fund, Health and Society*, 53 (1975), 257–78.

T. Parsons, 'Health and Disease: A Sociological and Action Perspective', in *Action Theory and the Human Condition* (New York: Free Press, 1978a).

T. Parsons, 'Death in the Western World', in *Action Theory and the Human Condition* (New York: Free Press, 1978b).

T. Parsons and R. Fox, 'Introduction', *Journal of Social Issues*, 8 (1952a), 2–3.

T. Parsons and R. Fox, 'Illness, Therapy and the Modern Urban Family', *Journal of Social Issues*, 8 (1952b), 31–44.

T. Parsons, E. A. Shils, G. W. Allport, C. Kluckhohn, H. A. Murray, R. R. Sears, R. C. Sheldon, S. A. Stouffer and E. C. Tolman, 'Some Fundamental Categories of the Theory of Action: A General Statement', in T. Parsons and E. A. Shils (eds), *Toward a General Theory of Action* (Cambridge, MA: Harvard University Press, 1951; repr. New York: Harper & Row, 1962).

T. Parsons, E. A. Shils and R. Bales, *Working Papers in the Theory of Action* (Glencoe, IL: Free Press, 1953).

T. Parsons, E. Shils and J. Olds, 'Values, Motives, and Systems of Action', in T. Parsons and E. A. Shils (eds), *Toward a General Theory of Action* (New York: Harper & Row, 1962; originally 1951).

T. Parsons and N. Smelser, *Economy and Society* (London: Routledge & Kegan Paul, 1956).

D. Patrick and H. Peach, *Disablement in the Community* (Oxford University Press, 1985).

D. Patrick and G. Scambler (eds), *Sociology as Applied to Medicine* (London: Billière Tindall, 1982).

L. I. Pearlin and C. S. Aneshensel, 'Coping and Social Supports: Their Functions and Applications', in Aiken and Mechanic (1986).

L. I. Pearlin, E. G. Menaghan, M. A. Lieberman and J. T. Mullan, 'The Stress Process', *Journal of Health and Social Behavior*, 22 (1981), 337–56.

L. I. Pearlin and C. W. Radabough, 'Economic Strains and the Coping Functions of Alcohol', *American Journal of Sociology*, 82 (1977), 652–63.

G. Pearson, *The Deviant Imagination: Psychiatry, Social Work and Social Change* (London: Macmillan, 1975).

M. Pflanz and J. J. Rohde, 'Illness: Deviant Behavior or Conformity?' *Social Science and Medicine*, 4 (1970), 645–53.

R. Pies, 'On Myths and Countermyths', *Archives of General Psychiatry*, 36 (1979), 139–44.

M. Pollner, 'Sociological and Common-Sense Models of the Labelling Process', in R. Turner (ed.), *Ethnomethodology* (Harmondsworth: Penguin, 1974).

A. Pomerantz, 'Attributions of Responsibility: Blamings', *Sociology*, 12 (1978), 115–21.

T. Posner, 'Magical Elements in Orthodox Medicine', in Dingwall *et al.* (1977).

R. H. Price, 'The Case for Impression Management in Schizophrenia: Another Look', in R. H. Price and B. Denner (eds), *The Making of a Mental Patient* (New York: Holt, Rinehart & Winston, 1973).

I. Procter, 'Parsons' Voluntarism and his Analysis of "the Case of Modern Medical Practice"', *Sociology of Health and Illness*, 4 (1982), 40–55.

G. Psathas (ed.), *Phenomenological Sociology* (New York: Wiley, 1979).

S. A. Queen and D. M. Mann, *Social Pathology* (New York: Thomas Y. Crowell, 1925).

S. A. Queen and J. R. Gruener, *Social Pathology: Obstacles to Social Participation* (New York: Thomas Y. Crowell, 1940).

A. Querido, 'Forecasted Follow-Up: An Investigation into the Clinical, Social and Mental Factors Determining the Results of Hospital Treatment', *British Journal of Preventive and Social Medicine*, 13 (1959), 33–49.

R. Quinney, 'From Repression to Liberation: Social Theory in a Radical Age', in Scott and Douglas (1972).

J. C. Quint and A. Strauss, 'Nursing Students, Assignments and Dying Patients', *Nursing Outlook*, 12 (1964), 24–7.

A. R. Radcliffe-Brown, 'On the Concept of Function in Social Science,' in *Structure and Function in Primitive Society* (London: Cohen & West, 1952; originally 1935).

S. Ramon, 'The Italian Psychiatric Reform', in S. P. Mangen (ed.), *Mental Health in the European Community* (London: Croom Helm, 1985).

M. B. Ray, 'The Cycle of Abstinence and Relapse among Heroin Addicts', in Becker (1964).

G. Rayner, 'Medical Errors and the "Sick Role": A Speculative Enquiry', *Sociology of Health and Illness*, 3 (1981), 296–316.

C. Rees, 'Records and Hospital Routine', in P. Atkinson and Heath (1981).

L. Reif, 'Ulcerative Colitis: Strategies for Managing Life', *American Journal of Nursing*, 73 (1973), 261–4; repr. A. L. Strauss and B. G. Glaser (eds), *Chronic Illness and the Quality of Life* (St Louis MO: Mosby, 1975).

A. J. Reiss, Jr, 'The Social Integration of Queers and Peers', in Becker (1964).

I. L. Reiss, 'Premarital Sex as Deviant Behavior: An Application of Current Approaches to Deviance', *American Sociological Review*, 35 (1970), 78–87.

M. Renaud, 'On the Structural Constraints to State Intervention in Health', *International Journal of Health Services*, 4 (1975), 559–72.

S. Reverby, 'A Perspective on the Root Causes of Illness', *American Journal of Public Health*, 62 (1972), 1140–2.

C. K. Riessman, 'The Use of Health Services by the Poor', *Social Policy*, 5 (1974), May/June, 41–9.

C. K. Riessman and C. A. Nathanson, 'The Management of Reproduction', in Aiken and Mechanic (1986).

V. Riley, 'Psychoneuroendocrine Influences on Immunocompetence and Neoplasia', *Science*, 212 (1981), 1100–9.

D. Robinson, *The Process of Becoming Ill* (London: Routledge & Kegan Paul, 1971).

D. Robinson, 'Please See and Advise: Handling Referrals to a Psychiatric Hospital', in Wadsworth and Robinson (1976).

D. Robinson, '*Talking Out of Alcoholism: The Self-Help Process of Alcoholics Anonymous* (Baltimore, MD: University Park Press, 1979).

D. Robinson, 'The Self-Help Component of Primary Health Care', *Social Science and Medicine*, 14A (1980), 415–21.

D. Robinson and S. Henry, *Self-Help and Health: Mutual Aid for Modern Problems* (Oxford: Martin Robertson, 1977).

P. Rock, *Deviant Behaviour* (London: Hutchinson, 1973).

P. Rock, *The Making of Symbolic Interactionism* (London: Macmillan, 1979).

J. W. Rogers and M. D. Buffalo, 'Fighting Back: Nine Modes of Adaptation to a Deviant Label', *Social Problems*, 20 (1971), 101–18.

A. M. Rose, 'A Systematic Summary of Symbolic Interaction Theory', in A. Rose (ed.), *Human Behavior and Social Processes* (Boston, MA: Houghton Mifflin, 1962).

H. Rosenbaum, *Familie als Gegenstruktur zur Gesellschaft* (Stuttgart: Enke, 1978).

R. Rosenberg, I. Gerver and W. Horton (eds), *Mass Society in Crisis: Social Probléms and Social Pathology* (New York: Macmillan, 1964; 2nd edn, 1971).

D. L. Rosenhan, 'On Being Sane in Insane Places', *Science*, 179 (1973), 250–8.

R. H. Rosenman, 'The Interview Method of Assessment of the Coronary-Prone Behavior Pattern', in T. M. Dembrowski, S. M. Weiss, S. G. Haynes and M. Feinleib (eds), *Coronary-Prone Behavior* (New York: Springer, 1978).

M. Rossdale, 'Health in a Sick Society', *New Left Review*, 34 (1965), 82–90.

J. A. Roth, 'The Treatment of Tuberculosis as a Bargaining Process', in A. M. Rose (ed.), *Human Behavior and Social Processes* (Boston, MA: Houghton Mifflin, 1962).

J. A. Roth, *Timetables: Structuring the Passage of Time in Hospital Treatment and Other Careers* (Indianapolis: Bobbs-Merrill, 1963a).

J. A. Roth, 'Information and the Control of Treatment in a Tuberculosis Hospital', in E. Freidson (ed.), *The Hospital in Modern Society* (Glencoe, IL: Free Press, 1963b).

J. A. Roth, 'Staff-Inmate Bargaining Tactics in Long-Term Treatment Institutions', *Sociology of Health and Illness*, 6 (1984), 111–31.

M. Roth, 'Schizophrenia and the Theories of Thomas Szasz', *British Journal of Psychiatry*, 129 (1976), 317–26.

E. Rubington and M. S. Weinberg (eds), *Deviance: The Interactionist Perspective* (New York: Macmillan, 1968; 2nd edn, 1973; 3rd edn, 1978).

J. Ryan, 'The Production and Management of Stupidity: The Involvement of Medicine and Psychology', in Wadsworth and Robinson (1976).

W. Ryan, *Blaming the Victim* (London: Orbach & Chambers, 1971).

H. Sacks, 'Sociological Description', *Berkeley Journal of Sociology*, 8 (1963), 1–7.

H. Sacks, 'The Search for Help: No One to Turn to', PhD Dissertation (University of California, Berkeley: unpublished, 1966).

H. Sacks, 'The Search for Help: No One to Turn to', in Shneidman (1967).

H. Sacks, 'On Doing "Being Ordinary"' (compiled from 1970/71 lecture notes by G. Jefferson), in M. Atkinson and J. Heritage (eds), *Structures of Social Action* (Cambridge University Press, 1984).

H. Sacks, 'Notes on Police Assessment of Moral Character', in D. Sudnow (ed.), *Studies in Interaction* (New York: Free Press, 1972a).

H. Sacks, 'An Initial Investigation of the Usability of Conversational Data for Doing Sociology', in D. Sudnow (ed.), *Studies in Social Interaction* (New York: Free Press, 1972b).

H. Sacks, 'Facets Of the Organization of Story-Telling in Conversation', unpublished paper, 1973.

H. Sacks, E. A. Schegloff and G. Jefferson, 'A Simplest Systematics for the Organization of Turn-Taking in Conversation', *Language*, 50 (1974), 696–735.

J. W. Salmon and H. S. Berliner, 'Health Policy Implications of the Holistic Health Movement', *Journal of Health Politics, Policy and Law*, 5 (1980), 535–53.

H. Sampson, S. L. Messinger and R. L. Towne, 'The Mental Hospital and Marital Family Ties', (originally 1961) repr. in Becker (1964).

H. Sampson, S. L. Messinger and R. Towne, 'Family Processes and Becoming a Mental Patient', *American Journal of Sociology*, 68 (1962), 88–96.

H. Sampson, S. L. Messinger, R. L. Towne, *Schizophrenic Women: Studies in Marital Crisis* (New York: Pantheon, 1964).

G. Scambler (ed.), *Sociological Theory and Medical Sociology* (London: Tavistock, 1987).

G. Scambler and A. Hopkins, 'Being Epileptic: Coming to Terms With Stigma', *Sociology of Health and Illness*, 8 (1986), 26–43.

B. Schaffner, *Fatherland*: A Study of Authoritarianism in the German Family (New York: Columbia Univ. Press, 1948).

A. Schatzkin, 'Health and Labor-Power: A Theoretical Investigation', *International Journal of Health Services*, 8 (1978), 213–34.

L. Schatzman and A. L. Strauss, *Field Research: Strategies of Natural Research* (Englewood Cliffs, NJ: Prentice-Hall, 1973).

T. J. Scheff, 'Legitimate, Transitional, and Illegitimate Mental Patients in a Midwestern State', *American Journal of Psychiatry*, 120 (1963), 267–9.

T. J. Scheff, 'The Societal Reaction to Deviance: Ascriptive Elements in the Psychiatric Screening of Mental Patients in a Midwestern State', *Social Problems*, 11 (1964a), 401–13.

T. J. Scheff, 'Social Conditions for Rationality: How Urban and Rural Courts Deal with the Mentally Ill', *American Behavioral Scientist*, 7 (1964b), 21–4.

T. Scheff, *Being Mentally Ill: A Sociological Theory* (Chicago: Aldine, 1966a).

T. G. Scheff, 'Typification in the Diagnostic Practices of Rehabilitation Agencies', in M. B. Sussman (ed.), *Sociology and Rehabilitation* (Washington: American Sociological Association, 1966b).

T. J. Scheff (ed.), *Mental Illness and Social Processes* (New York: Harper & Row, 1967).

T. Scheff, 'Negotiating Reality: Notes on Power in the Assessment of Responsibility', *Social Problems*, 16 (1968), 3–17.

T. J. Scheff, 'The Labelling Theory of Mental Illness', *American Sociological Review*, 39 (1974), 444–52.

T. J. Scheff, 'On Reason and Sanity: Some Political Implications of Psychiatric Thought', in T. J. Scheff (ed.), *Labeling Madness* (Englewood Cliffs, NJ: Prentice-Hall, 1975a).

T. J. Scheff, 'Schizophrenia as Ideology', in T. J. Scheff (ed.), *Labeling Madness* (Englewood Cliffs, NJ: Prentice-Hall, 1975b).

E. A. Schegloff, 'Sequencing in Conversational Openings', *American Anthropologist*, 70 (1968), 1075–95.

E. A. Schegloff, 'The Routine as Achievement', *Human Studies*, 9 (1986), 111–51.

E. A. Schegloff and H. Sacks, 'Opening Up Closings', *Semiotica*, 8 (1973), 289–327.

T. C. Schelling, 'An Essay on Bargaining', *American Economic Review*, 46 (1956), repr. *The Strategy of Conflict* (Oxford University Press, 1960).

P. G. Schervish, 'The Labelling Perspective: Its Bias and Potential in the Study of Political Science', *The American Sociologist*, 8 (1973), 47–57.

A. H. Schmale and H. Iker, 'Hopelessness as a Predictor of Cervical Cancer', *Social Science and Medicine*, 5 (1971), 95–100.

J. Schneider, *Stress, Loss, and Grief* (Baltimore, MD: University Park Press, 1984).

J. W. Schneider and P. Conrad, *Having Epilepsy: The Experience and Control of Illness* (Philadelphia: Temple University Press, 1983).

E. M. Schur, 'Drug Addiction under British Policy', in Becker (1964).

E. M. Schur, 'Reactions to Deviance: A Critical Assessment', *American Journal of Sociology*, 75 (1969), 309–22.

E. M. Schur, *Labeling Deviant Behavior* (New York: Harper & Row, 1971).

E. M. Schur, *The Politics of Deviance: Stigma Contests and Uses of Power* (Englewood Cliffs, NJ: Prentice-Hall, 1980).

A. Schutz, *Der sinnhafte Aufbau der sozialen Welt* (Vienna: Julius Springer, 1932), trans. *The Phenomenology of the Social World* (Evanston, IL: Northwestern University Press, 1967).

A. Schütz, 'The Problem of Rationality in the Social World', *Economica*, 10 (1943), 130–49.

A. Schütz, 'On Multiple Realities', *Philosophy and Phenomenological Research*, 5 (1945a), 533–75.

A. Schütz, 'Some Leading Concepts of Phenomenology', *Social Research*, 12 (1945b), 77–97.

A. Schütz, 'Common-Sense and Scientific Interpretation of Human Action', *Philosophy and Phenomenological Research*, 14 (1953), 1–38.

A. Schütz, 'Concept and Theory Formation in the Social Sciences', *Journal of Philosophy*, 51 (1954).

A. Schütz, 'Husserl's Importance for the Social Sciences', in *Edmund Husserl 1859–1959* (The Hague: Nijhoff, 1959).

E. Schwanenberg, *Soziales Handeln – Die Theorie und ihr Problem* (Berne: Hans Huber, 1970).

C. G. Schwartz, 'The Stigma of Mental Illness', *Journal of Rehabilitation*, 22 (1956), 6–25.

C. G. Schwartz, 'Perspectives on Deviance – Wives' Definition of their Husbands' Mental Illness', *Psychiatry*, 20 (1957), 275–91.

H. Schwartz, 'Mental Disorder and the Study of Subjective Experience: Some Uses of Each to Elucidate the Other', PhD Dissertation (University of California, Los Angeles: unpublished, 1971).

M. Schwartz, G. F. N. Fearn and S. Shryker, 'A Note on Self-Conception and the Emotionally Disturbed Role', *Sociometry*, 29 (1966), 300–5, repr. Manis and Meltzer, 2nd edn, 1972.

J. F. Scott, 'The Changing Foundations of the Parsonian Action Scheme', *American Sociological Review*, 28 (1963), 715–36.

M. B. Scott and S. M. Lyman, 'Accounts', *American Sociological Review*, 33 (1968), 46–62.

R. A. Scott, *The Making of Blind Men* (New York: Russell Sage, 1969).

R. A. Scott, 'The Construction of Conceptions of Stigma by Professional Experts', in J. D. Douglas (ed.), *Deviance and Respectability* (New York: Basic Books, 1970).

R. A. Scott and J. D. Douglas (eds), *Theoretical Perspectives on Deviance* (New York: Basic Books, 1972).

A. Scull, 'Social Control and the Amplification of Deviance', in Scott and Douglas (1972).

A. T. Scull, *Decarceration: Community Treatment and the Deviant: A Radical View* (Englewood Cliffs, NJ: Prentice-Hall, 1977).

P. Sedgwick, 'Mental Illness *Is* Illness', *Salmagundi*, 20 (1972), 196–224.

P. Sedgwick, 'Goffman's Anti-Psychiatry', *Salmagundi*, 26 (1974), 26–51.

P. Sedgwick, *Psycho-Politics: Laing, Foucault, Goffman, Szasz and the Future of Mass Psychiatry* (New York: Harper & Row, 1982a).

P. Sedgwick, 'Anti-Psychiatry from the Sixties to the Eighties', in W. R. Gove (ed.), *Deviance and Mental Illness* (Beverly Hills, CA: Sage, 1982b).

A. Segall, 'The Sick Role Concept: Understanding Illness Behavior', *Journal of Health and Social Behavior*, 17 (1976), 163–70.

M. E. P. Seligman, *Helplessness: On Depression, Development, and Death* (New York: Freeman, 1975).

H. Selye, 'The General Adaptation Syndrome and the Diseases of Adaptation', *The Journal of Clinical Endocrinology*, 6 (1946), 117–96.

H. Selye, *The Stress of Life* (New York: McGraw-Hill, 1956).

A. K. Shapiro, 'A Contribution to the History of the Placebo Effect', *Behavioral Science*, 5 (1960), 109–35.

A. K. Shapiro, 'Factors Contributing to the Placebo Effect', *American Journal of Psychotherapy*, 43 (1961), 73–88.

E. S. Shneidman (ed.), *Essays in Self-Destruction* (New York: International Science Press, 1967).

E. S. Shneidman and N. L. Farberow (eds), *Clues to Suicide* (New York: McGraw-Hill, 1957).

S. Shryker, *Symbolic Interactionism: A Social Structural Version*

(Menlo Park, CA: Benjamin/Cummings, 1980).

J. T. Shuval, 'A Contribution of Psychological and Social Phenomena to an Understanding of the Aetiology of Disease and Illness', *Social Science and Medicine*, 15A (1981), 337–42.

R. W. Shuy, 'The Medical Interview. Problems in Communication', *Primary Care*, 3 (1976), 365–86.

M. Siegler and H. Osmond, 'Models of Madness', *British Journal of Psychiatry*, 112 (1966), 1193–1203.

S. Siegler and H. Osmond, 'Models of Drug Addiction', *International Journal of the Addictions*, 3 (1968), 3–24.

M. Siegler, H. Osmond and H. Mann, 'Laing's Models of Madness', *British Journal of Psychiatry*, 115 (1969), 947–58.

J. Siegrist, *Lehrbuch der medizinischen Soziologie* (Munich: Urban & Schwarzenberg, 1974; 3rd edn, 1977).

J. Siegrist, K. Dittmann, K. Rittner and I. Weber, 'The Social Context of Active Distress in Patients with Early Myocardial Infarction', *Social Science and Medicine*, 16 (1982), 443–53.

H. E. Sigerist, 'The Special Position of the Sick', in M. Roemer (ed.), *Henry E. Sigerist on Sociology of Medicine* (New York: MD Publications, 1960; originally in German, *Kyklos*, 1929).

H. E. Sigerist, *Einführung in die moderne Medizin* (1931), transl. *Man and Medicine: An Introduction to Medical Knowledge* (London: George Allen & Unwin, 1932; New York: W. W. Norton, 1932).

H. Sigerist, 'The Medical Student and the Social Problems Confronting Medicine Today', *Bulletin of the Institute of the History of Medicine*, 4 (1936), 411–22; repr. M. Roemer (ed.), *H. E. Sigerist on Sociology of Medicine* (New York: MD Publications, 1960).

H. E. Sigerist, 'The Place of the Physician in Modern Society', *Proceedings of the American Philosophical Society*, 90 (1946), 275–9; repr. M. Roemer (ed.), *H. E. Sigerist on Sociology of Medicine* (New York: MD Publications, 1960).

D. Silverman, *The Theory of Organizations* (London: Heinemann, 1970).

D. Silverman, 'The Child as a Social Object: Down's Syndrome Children in a Pediatric Cardiology Clinic', *Sociology of Health and Illness*, 3 (1981), 254–74.

E. Simmel (ed.), *Anti-Semitism: A Social Disease* (New York: International Universities Press, 1946).

G. Simmel, *Über sociale Differenzierung* (Leipzig: Duncker & Humblot, 1890).

G. Simmel, *Soziologie: Untersuchungen über die Formen der Vergesellschaftung* (Leipzig: Duncker & Humblot, 1908).

G. Simmel, *Georg Simmel on Individuality and Social Forms*, ed. D. N. Levine (Chicago: Chicago University Press, 1971).

G. Simmel, *The Sociology of Georg Simmel*, transl., ed. and with an intro. by K. H. Wolff (New York: Free Press of Glencoe, 1964).

T. Simons, 'Psychiatrie im Übergang: Von der Verwaltung der sozialen Ausgrenzung zum sozialen Dienst', in T. Simons (ed.), *Absage an die*

Anstalt: *Programm und Realität der demokratischen Psychiatrie in Italien* (Frankfurt/New York: Campus, 1980)

D. Smith, 'K is Mentally Ill: The Anatomy of a Factual Account', *Sociology*, 10 (1976), 23–53.

D. E. Smith, 'No One Commits Suicide. Textual Analysis of Ideological Practices', *Human Studies*, 6 (1983), 309–59.

R. T. Smith and L. Midanik, 'The Effects of Social Resources on Recovery and Perceived Sense of Control Among the Disabled', *Sociology of Health and Illness*, 2 (1980), 48–63.

S. Sontag, *Illness as Metaphor* (New York: Farrar, Strauss & Giroux, 1978).

A. B. Sorensen, 'Processes of Allocation to Open and Closed Positions in Social Structure', *Zeitschrift für Soziologie*, 12 (1983), 203–24.

M. Speier, *How to Observe Face-To-Face Communication: A Sociological Introduction* (Pacific Palisades, CA: Goodyear, 1973).

H. Spencer, *The Principles of Sociology*, 3 vol (London: William & Norgate, 1876–96).

R. Spitz, '*La première année de la vie de l'enfant: Genèse des premières relations objectales* (Paris: Presses Universitaires de France, 1958).

R. L. Spitzer, 'More On Pseudoscience and the Case of Psychiatric Diagnosis', *Archives of General Psychiatry*, 33 (1976), 459–70.

S. P. Spitzer and N. K. Denzin (eds), *The Mental Patient: Studies in the Sociology of Deviance* (New York: McGraw-Hill, 1968).

L. Srole, T. S. Michael, M. K. Opler and A. C. Rennie, *Mental Illness in the Metropolis: The Midtown Manhattan Study* (New York: McGraw-Hill, 1962).

M. Stacey with H. Homans, 'The Sociology of Health and Illness: Its Present State, Future Prospects and Potential for Health Research', *Sociology*, 12 (1978), 281–307.

M. Stacey, M. Reid, C. Heath and R. Dingwall (eds), *Health and the Division of Labour* (London: Croom Helm, 1977).

G. Stimson and B. Webb, *Going to See the Doctor* (London: Routledge & Kegan Paul, 1975).

R. J. Stoller, H. Garfinkel and A. C. Rosen, 'Passing and the Maintenance of Sexual Identification in an Intersexed Patient', *Archives of General Psychiatry*, 17 (1960), 379–84.

R. J. Stoller, H. Garfinkel and A. C. Rosen, 'Psychiatric Management of Intersexed Patients', *California Journal of Medicine*, 96 (1962), 30–4.

D. A. Stone, 'The Resistable Rise of Preventive Medicine', *Journal of Health Politics, Policy and Law*, 11 (1986), 671–96.

R. Straus, 'The Nature and Status of Medical Sociology', *American Sociological Review*, 22 (1957), 200–04.

A. Strauss, *Mirrors and Masks: The Problem of Identity* (Chicago: Aldine, 1959).

A. Strauss, 'Transformations of Identity', in A. M. Rose (ed.), *Human Behavior and Social Processes* (Boston, MA: Houghton-Mifflin, 1962).

A. Strauss, *Negotiations: Varieties, Contexts, Processes and Social Order* (San Francisco, CA: Jossey-Bass, 1978a).

A. Strauss, 'Social World Perspective', in N. K. Denzin (ed.), *Studies in Symbolic Interaction*, Vol. 1 (Greenwich, CT: JAI Press, 1978b).

A. Strauss, 'Chronic Illness', *Social Science and Medicine, Medical Geography*, 14D (1980), 351–3.

A. Strauss, 'Interorganization Negotiation', *Urban Life*, 11 (1982a), 293–311.

A. Strauss, 'Social Worlds and Legitimation Processes', in N. K. Denzin (ed.), *Studies in Symbolic Interaction*, Vol. 4 (Greenwich, CT: JAI Press, 1982b).

A. Strauss, 'Social Worlds and their Segmentation', in N. K. Denzin (ed.), *Studies in Symbolic Interaction*, Vol. 5 (Greenwich, CT: JAI Press, 1984).

A. Strauss, S. Fagerhaugh, B. Suczek and C. Wiener, 'Patients' Work in the Technological Hospital', *Nursing Outlook*, 29 (1981), 404–12.

A. Strauss, S. Fagerhaugh, B. Suczek and C. Wiener, 'Sentimental Work in the Technological Hospital', *Sociology of Health and Illness*, 4 (1982a), 254–78.

A. Strauss, S. Fagerhaugh, B. Suczek and C. Wiener, 'The Work of Hospitalized Patients', *Social Science and Medicine*, 16 (1982b), 977–86.

A. Strauss, S. Fagerhaugh, B. Suczek and C. Wiener, *Social Organization of Medical Work* (Chicago/London: University of Chicago Press, 1985).

A. Strauss and B. Glaser, *Anguish: Case History of a Dying Woman* (San Francisco, CA: Sociology Press, 1970).

A. Strauss and B. Glaser, *Chronic Illness and the Quality of Life* (St Louis, MO: Mosby, 1975).

A. Strauss, B. Glaser and J. Quint, 'The Non-Accountability of Terminal Care', *Hospitals*, 36 (1964), 73–87.

A. Strauss, L. Schatzman, R. Bucher, D. Ehrlich and M. Sabshin, *Psychiatric Ideologies and Institutions* (New York: Free Press, 1964).

A. Strauss, L. Schatzman, D. Ehrlich, R. Bucher and M. Sabshin, 'The Hospital and its Negotiated Order', in E. Freidson (ed.), *The Hospital in Modern Society* (London: Free Press, 1963).

P. M. Strong, 'Medical Errands: A Discussion of Routine Patient Work', in Davis and Horobin (1977).

P. M. Strong, 'Sociological Imperialism and the Profession of Medicine' *Social Science and Medicine*, 13A (1979a), 199–215.

P. M. Strong, 'Materialism and Medical Interaction – A Critique of "Medicine, Super-Structure and Micropolitics"', *Social Science and Medicine*, 13A (1979b), 601–9.

P. M. Strong, *The Ceremonial Order of the Clinic: Parents, Doctors and Medical Bureaucracies* (London: Routledge & Kegan Paul, 1979c).

P. M. Strong, 'Doctors and Dirty Work', *Sociology of Health and Illness*, 2 (1980), 24–47.

P. M. Strong, 'Review Essay. The Importance of Being Erving: Erving Goffman, 1922–1982', *Sociology of Health and Illness*, 5 (1983), 345–55.

P. M. Strong and A. Davis, 'Who's Who in Paediatric Encounters: Morality, Expertise and the Generation of Identity and Action in Medical Settings', in A. Davis (1979).

B. Suczek, 'Chronic Renal Failure and the Problem of Funding', in A. Strauss and B. Glaser, *Chronic Illness and the Quality of Life* (St Louis, MO: Mosby, 1975).

D. Sudnow, 'Normal Crimes: Sociological Features of the Penal Code in a Public Defender Office', *Social Problems*, 12 (1965), 255–76.

D. Sudnow, *Passing On*: *The Social Organization of Dying* (Englewood Cliffs, NJ: Prentice-Hall, 1967).

D. Sudnow (ed.), *Studies in Social Interaction* (New York: Free Press, 1972).

N. M. Sugrue, 'Emotions As Property and Context for Negotiation', *Urban Life*, 11 (1982), 280–92.

M. W. Susser and W. Watson, *Sociology in Medicine*, 2nd edn, (Oxford University Press, 1971; 1st edn, 1962).

G. M. Sykes and D. Matza, 'Techniques of Neutralization: A Theory of Delinquency', *American Sociological Review*, 22 (1957), 664–70.

S. L. Syme and L. F. Berkman, 'Social Class, Susceptibility, and Sickness', *American Journal of Epidemiology*, 104 (1976), 1–8, repr. H. D. Schwartz and C. S. Kart (eds), *Dominant Issues in Medical Sociology* (Reading, MA: Addison-Wesley, 1978).

T. S. Szasz, 'Some Observations on the Relationship Between Psychiatry and the Law', *AMA Archives of Neurology and Psychiatry*, 75 (1956), 297–315.

T. S. Szasz, *Pain and Pleasure: A Study of Bodily Feelings* (New York: Basic Books, 1957a).

T. S. Szasz, 'The Problem of Psychiatric Nosology', *American Journal of Psychiatry*, 114 (1957b), 405–15.

T. S. Szasz, 'Men and Machines', *British Journal of Philosophy of Science*, 8 (1958a), 310–17.

T. S. Szasz, 'Politics and Mental Health. Some Remarks Apropos of the Case of Mr. Ezra Pound', *American Journal of Psychiatry*, 115 (1958b), 508–11.

T. S. Szasz, 'Scientific Method and Social Role in Medicine and Psychiatry' *A. M. A. Archives of Internal Medicine*, 101 (1959), 232–3.

T. Szasz, 'The Myth of Mental Illness', *American Psychologist*, 15 (1960), 113–18.

T. S. Szasz, *The Myth of Mental Illness: Foundations of a Theory of Personal Conduct* (New York: Hoeber-Harper, 1961).

T. S. Szasz, *Law, Liberty, and Psychiatry: An Inquiry into the Uses of Mental Health Practices* (New York: Macmillan, 1963).

T. S. Szasz, *Psychiatric Justice* (New York: Macmillan, 1965).

T. S. Szasz, 'The Psychiatrist as Double Agent', *Trans-Action*, 4 (1967), 16–24.

T. Szasz, *The Manufacture of Madness*: *A Comparative Study of the Inquisition and the Mental Health Movement* (New York: Dell, 1970a).

T. Szasz, *Ideology and Insanity*: *Essays on the Psychiatric Dehumanization of Man* (New York: Anchor, 1970b).

T. S. Szasz, 'The Ethics of Addiction', *International Journal of Psychiatry*, 10 (1972), 51–61.

T. S. Szasz, 'Schizophrenia: The Sacred Symbol of Psychiatry', *British Journal of Psychiatry*, 129 (1976), 308–16.

T. Szasz, *The Theology of Medicine: The Political–Philosophical Foundations of Medical Ethics* (New York: Harper & Row, 1977).

T. Szasz, *The Myth of Psychotherapy: Mental Healing as Religion, Rhetoric and Repression* (Garden City: Anchor Press, 1978).

T. S. Szasz, *The Therapeutic State: Psychiatry in the Mirror of Current Events* (Buffalo N. Y.: Prometheus Books, 1984).

T. S. Szasz and M. H. Hollender, 'A Contribution to the Philosophy of Medicine: The Basic Model of the Doctor–Patient Relationship', *Archives of Internal Medicine*, 97 (1956), 585–92.

T. S. Szasz, W. F. Knoff and M. H. Hollender, 'The Doctor–Patient Relationship and its Historical Context', *American Journal of Psychiatry*, 115 (1958), 522–7.

L. Taylor, *Deviance and Society* (London: Michael Joseph, 1971).

R. Taylor and A. Rieger, 'Rudolf Virchow and the Typhus Epidemic in Upper Silesia: An Introduction and Translation', *Sociology of Health and Illness*, 6 (1984), 201–17; repr. 'Medicine as Social Science: Rudolf Virchow on the Typhus Epidemic in Upper Silesia', *International Journal of Health Services*, 15 (1985), 547–59.

J. W. Thibaut and H. H. Kelley, *The Social Psychology of Groups* (New York: Wiley, 1959).

A. Thio, 'Class Bias in the Sociology of Deviance', *The American Sociologist*, 8 (1973), 1–12.

W. I. Thomas, *The Unadjusted Girl* (Boston: Little, Brown, 1925).

A. Todd, 'A Diagnosis of Doctor–Patient Discourse in the Prescription of Contraception', in Fisher and Todd (1983).

A. Todd, 'The Prescription of Contraception: Negotiations Between Doctors and Patients', *Discourse Processes*, 7 (1984), 171–200.

F. Tönnies, *Gemeinschaft und Gesellschaft: Abhandlung des Communismus und des Socialismus als empirischer Culturformen* (Leipzig: Fues's Verlag (R. Reisland), 1887); *Community and Society* (transl. and ed. C. P. Looms) (Michigan State University Press, 1957).

P. Townsend, 'Inequality and the Health Service', *Lancet*, 15 June 1974, 1179–89.

P. Townsend, *Poverty in the United Kingdom* (Harmondsworth: Penguin, 1979).

P. Townsend and N. Davidson, *Inequalities in Health: The Black Report* (Harmondsworth: Penguin, 1982).

H. M. Trice and P. M. Roman, 'Delabeling, Relabeling and Alcoholics Anonymous', *Social Problems*, 17 (1970), 536–48.

D. Tuckett, *Introduction to Medical Sociology* (London: Tavistock, 1976).

Ralph Turner, 'Role-Taking: Process vs. Conformity', in A. Rose (ed.), *Human Behavior and Social Processes* (Boston, MA: Houghton Mifflin, 1962).

Roy Turner, 'Deviance Avowal as Neutralization of Commitment', *Social Problems*, 19 (1972a), 307–21.

Roy Turner, 'Some Formal Properties of Therapy Talk', in Sudnow (1972b).

M. Turshen, 'The Political Ecology of Disease', *Review of Radical Political Economy*, 9 (1977), 45–60.

A. Twaddle, 'Health Decisions and Sick Role Variations: An Exploration', *Journal of Health and Social Behavior*, 10 (1969), 105–15.

A. C. Twaddle and R. M. Hessler, *A Sociology of Health* (St Louis, MO: Mosby, 1977).

D. R. Unruh, 'The Social Organization of Older People: A Social World Perspective', in N. K. Denzin (ed.), *Studies in Social Interaction*, Vol. 3 (Greenwich, CT: JAI Press, 1980).

L. M. Verbrugge, 'Multiple Roles and Physical Health of Women and Men', *Journal of Health and Social Behavior*, 24 (1983), 16–30.

R. Virchow, *Die Not im Spessart: Mitteilungen über die in Oberschlesien herrschende Typhus-Epidemie* (1848; reprinted Hildesheim: Georg Olms, 1968).

M. Voysey, 'Official Agents and the Legitimation of Suffering', *Sociological Review*, 20 (1972a), 533–52.

M. Voysey, 'Impression Management by Parents with Disabled Children: The Reconstruction of Good Parents', *Journal of Health and Social Behavior*, 13 (1972b).

M. Voysey, *A Constant Burden: The Reconstitution of Family Life* (London: Routledge & Kegan Paul, 1975).

C. Waddell, 'The Process of Neutralization and the Uncertainties of Cystic Fibrosis', *Sociology of Health and Illness*, 4 (1982), 210–20.

M. E. J. Wadsworth, W. J. H. Butterfield and R. Blaney, *Health and Sickness: The Choice of Treatment* (London: Tavistock, 1971).

M. Wadsworth and D. Robinson (eds), *Studies in Everyday Medical Life* (Oxford: Martin Robertson, 1976).

H. Waitzkin, 'Latent Functions of the Sick Role in Various Institutional Settings', *Social Science and Medicine*, 5 (1971), 45–75.

H. Waitzkin, 'How Capitalism Cares for our Coronaries', in E. B. Gallagher (ed.), *The Doctor-Patient Relationship in the Changing Health Scene* (Washington, DC: Government Printing Office, 1978).

H. Waitzkin, 'Medicine, Superstructure and Micropolitics', *Social Science and Medicine*, 13 (1979), 601–9.

H. Waitzkin, 'The Social Origins of Illness: A Neglected History', *International Journal of Health Services*, 11 (1981), 77–103.

H. Waitzkin, *The Second Sickness: Contradictions of Capitalist Health Care* (New York: Free Press, 1983).

H. Waitzkin and J. Stoeckle, 'Information Control and the Micropolitics of Health Care: Summary of an Ongoing Project', *Social Science and Medicine*, 10 (1976), 263–76.

H. B. Waitzkin and B. Waterman, *The Exploitation of Illness in Capitalist Society* (Indianapolis: Bobbs-Merrill, 1974).

D. R. Watson, 'Calls for Help: A Sociological Analysis of Telephoned Calls to a "Crisis Intervention Centre"', PhD Dissertation (University of Warwick: unpublished, 1975).

D. R. Watson, 'Categorization, Authorization, and Blame Negotiation in Conversation', *Sociology*, 12 (1978), 105–13.

D. R. Watson, 'Conversational and Organisational Uses of Proper Names: An Aspect of Counsellor–Client Interaction', in P. Atkinson and Heath (1981).

B. Webb, 'Trauma and Tedium: An Account of Living in on a Children's Ward', in A. Davis and Horobin (1977).

B. Webb, and G. Stimson, 'People's Accounts of Medical Encounters', in Wadsworth and Robinson (1976).

M. Weber, '"Objectivity" in Social Science and Social Policy', in *The Methodology of the Social Sciences Max Weber* (transl. and ed. E. A. Shils and H. A. Finch) (New York: Free Press, 1949; originally in German, 1904).

M. Weber, *Economy and Society*, 2 vol (transl. G. Roth and C. Wittich) (New York: Bedminster Press, 1968; originally in German, 1922).

H. Weiner, M. Thaler, M. F. Reiser and I. A. Mirsky, 'Etiology of Duodenal Ulcer. I. Relation of Specific Psychological Characteristics to Rate of Gastric Secretion (Serum Pepsinogen)', *Psychosomatic Medicine*, 19 (1957), 1–10.

E. Weingarten, F. Sack and J. Schenkein (eds), *Ethnomethodologie: Beiträge zu einer Theorie des Alltagshandelns* (Frankfurt: Suhrkamp, 1976).

E. A. Weinstein and P. Deutschberger, 'Tasks, Bargains, and Identities in Social Interaction', *Social Forces*, 42 (1964), 451–6.

F. Weinstein, *The Dynamics of Nazism: Leadership, Ideology, and the Holocaust* (New York: Academic Press, 1980).

R. M. Weinstein, Labeling Theory and Attitudes of Mental Patients: A Review', *Journal of Health and Social Behavior*, 24 (1983), 70–84.

D. Weir, 'The Moral Career of the Day Patient', in A. Davis and Horobin (1977).

R. Weiss, 'The Fund of Sociability', *Transaction*, 7 (1969), 36–43.

R. Weiss, *Loneliness: The Experience of Emotional and Social Isolation* (Cambridge, MA: MIT Press, 1973).

C. West, '"Ask Me No Questions . . .". An Analysis of Queries and Replies in Physician–Patient Dialogues', in Fisher and Todd (1983).

C. West, 'Medical Misfires: Mishearings, Misgivings, and Misunderstandings in Physician–Patient Dialogue', *Discourse Processes*, 7 (1984a), 107–34.

C. West, *Routine Complications: Trouble with Talk between Doctors and Patients* (Bloomington, IN: University of Indiana Press, 1984b).

P. West, 'The Physician and the Management of Childhood Epilepsy', in Wadsworth and Robinson (1976).

P. West, 'Becoming Disabled: Perspectives on the Labelling Approach', in U. E. Gerhardt and M. E. J. Wadsworth (eds), *Stress and Stigma* (Frankfurt: Campus; London: Macmillan; New York: St James' Press, 1985).

A. Wetterer and J. B. von Troschke, *Smoker Motivation: A Review of Contemporary Literature* (Berlin: Springer, 1986).

C. K. Whalen and B. Henker, 'The Pitfalls of Politicization: A Response to Conrad's "The Discovery of Hyperkinesis: Notes on the Medicalization of Deviant Behavior"', *Social Problems*, 24 (1977), 590–8.

S. Wheeler (ed.), *On Record: Files and Dossiers in American Life* (New York: Basic Books, 1969).

D. L. Wieder, 'On Meaning By Rule', in J. Douglas (ed.), *Understanding Everyday Life* (Chicago: Aldine, 1970).

W. Wieland, *Diagnose* (Berlin: de Gruyter, 1975).

C. L. Wiener, 'The Burden of Rheumatoid Arthritis', in A. Strauss and B. Glaser, *Chronic Illness and the Quality of Life* (St Louis, MO: Mosby, 1975).

C. Wiener, *The Politics of Alcoholism* (New Brunswick, NJ: Transaction Books, 1980).

C. Wiener, S. Fagerhaugh, A. Strauss and B. Suczek, 'Patient Power: Complex Issues need Complex Answers', *Social Policy*, 11 (1980), 31–8.

C. Wiener, A. Strauss, S. Fagerhaugh and B. Suczek, 'Trajectories, Biographies, and the Evolving Medical Scene: Labor and Delivery in the Intensive Care Nursery', *Sociology of Health and Illness*, 1 (1979), 261–83.

G. Williams, 'The Genesis of Chronic Illness: Narrative Reconstruction', *Sociology of Health and Illness*, 6 (1984), 175–200.

R. Williams, 'Concepts of Health: An Analysis of Lay Logic', *Sociology*, 17 (1983), 185–205.

T. P. Wilson, 'Conceptions of Interaction and Forms of Sociological Explanation', *American Sociological Review*, 35 (1970), 697–709.

J. K. Wing, 'A Review of Sanity, Madness, and the Family', *New Society*, 7 May, 1964, 23–4.

J. K. Wing, *Reasoning about Madness* (Oxford University Press, 1978).

J. Wing and G. Brown, *Institutionalism and Schizoprenia: A Comparative Study of Three Mental Hospitals* (Cambridge University Press, 1970).

C. Winick, 'The Image of Mental Illness in the Mass Media', in W. R. Gove (ed.), *Deviance and Mental Illness* (Beverly Hills, CA: Sage, 1982).

H. G. Wolff, *Stress and Disease* (Springfield, IL: Thomas, 1953; 2nd edn, rev. and ed. S. Wolf and H. Goodell, 1968).

H. G. Wolff, S. G. Wolf and C. C. Hare, *Life Stress and Bodily Disease* (Baltimore, MD: Williams & Wilkins, 1950).

K. Wolff, 'Notes Toward a Sociocultural Interpretation of American Sociology', *American Sociological Review*, 11 (1946), 545–53.

P. Wright, 'Some Recent Developments in Social Studies of Science and their Relevance to the Sociology of Medicine': paper presented to British Sociological Association Medical Sociology Conference, Warwick (1977).

P. Wright and A. Treacher (eds), *The Problem of Medical Knowledge: Examining the Social Construction of Medicine* (Edinburgh University Press, 1982).

D. Wrong, 'The Oversocialized Conception of Man in Modern Sociology', *American Sociological Review*, 26 (1961), 183–93.

M. R. Yarrow, C. G. Schwartz, H. S. Murphy and L. C. Deasy, 'The Psychological Meaning of Mental Illness in the Family', *Journal of Social Issues*, 11 (1955), 12–24.

J. Young, *The Drugtakers* (London: McGibbon & Kee, 1970).

R. M. Young, 'Science *Is* Social Relations', *Radical Science Journal*, 5 (1977), 65–129.

M. Zborowski, 'Cultural Components in Response to Pain', *Journal of Social Issues*, 8 (1952), 16–30.

D. H. Zimmerman, 'Record-Keeping and the Intake Process in a Public Welfare Agency', in Wheeler (1969a).

D. H. Zimmerman, 'Tasks and Troubles', in D. A. Hansen (ed.), *Explorations in Sociology and Counselling* (Boston, MA: Houghton Mifflin, 1969).

D. Zimmerman and M. Pollner, 'The Everyday World as a Phenomenon', in Douglas (1970).

I. K. Zola, 'Culture and Symptoms – An Analysis of Patients Presenting Complaints', *American Sociological Review*, 31 (1966), 615–30.

I. K. Zola, 'Pathways to the Doctor – From Person to Patient': paper presented at 3rd Social Science and Medicine Conference, 1970; published *Social Science and Medicine*, 7 (1973), 677–87; repr. *Socio-Medical Inquiries* (Philadelphia: Temple University Press, 1983).

I. K. Zola, 'Medicine As an Institution of Social Control', *Sociological Review*, 20 (1972), 487–503.

I. K. Zola, *De Medische Macht: De Invloed van de Gesondheitszwong op de Maatschappij* (transl. M. Veelema) (Amsterdam: Boom Meppel, 1973).

I. K. Zola, 'In the Name of Health and Illness: On some Socio-Political Consequences of Medical Influence', *Social Science and Medicine*, 9 (1975), 83–7.

I. K. Zola, *Socio-Medical Inquiries: Recollections, Reflections, and Reconsiderations* (Philadelphia: Temple University Press, 1983).

Name Index

Subject Index